1985

FROGS AND SCORPIONS

FROGS AND SCORPIONS

Egypt, Sadat and the Media

Doreen Kays

Frederick Muller Limited
London

First published in Great Britain in 1984 by
Frederick Muller Limited, Dataday House,
8 Alexandra Road, London SW19 7JZ.

British Library Cataloguing in Publication Data

Kays, Doreen
    Frogs and Scorpions, Egypt, Sadat and the media.
    1. Sadat, Anwar el-   2. Egypt—Politics and government—1970–
    I. Title
    962′.054′0924   DT107.85
    ISBN 0–584–11057–X

Phototypeset by Input Typesetting Ltd., London
Printed in Great Britain by
Billing and Sons Ltd., Worcester

Contents

In loving memory
of
my father
Saied Nicholas Kays

Acknowledgements

I AM indebted to the cast of thousands – now spread around the globe – who played a part in the story upon which this book is based, and I apologize for not being able to thank everyone individually.

Special thanks go to some former ABC News colleagues with whom I share fond memories. And my deepest gratitude to Egypt and her warm and wonderful people who shall forever remain in my heart, especially many friends who continue to enrich my life with their love and generosity. Meet alf shuk' ran ou el salaam aleykum . . . Inshallah.

As for the book itself, my sincerest thanks to all who made it possible. They are too numerous to mention but some rather special individuals – some of whom were perfectly sane before I dragged them into my world of Middle East tales – merit attention.

I am deeply grateful to: Janet Thorpe whose friendship and editorial prodding helped transform my thoughts into a book proposal and whose subsequent readings of the manuscript in progress encouraged me through to the end; Helen Brann, my literary agent, whose enthusiasm and optimism carried me through from book proposal to manuscript and beyond; Katie Cohen, my editor, who latched onto the book before one word ever materialized on paper; Peter Daniel whose enduring friendship, comforting counsel and regular vigilance rarely permitted the author to despair or stray from her typewriter and its self-imposed deadlines; Nathaniel and Margaret Harrison who lived the Egypt 'story' with me and who relived it through their meticulous readings of the manuscript in progress, for their chapter by chapter questions, notes, corrections and critiques on all personal, professional and political elements. Their friendship and unwavering faith and trust in the author and the book are beyond thanks; Arnie Collins, for helping jog my memory in the early anecdotal portions of the book; Ann Hallerman, Rosemary Arthy and Martha Zuber for their constant practical and moral support and affectionate vigilance; Judith Melby for her comments on early chapters of the manuscript; Nabila Megalli who while she will disagree with much of the book's political content, never flinched in her friendship, integrity and moral support.

Finally, I thank my family; my mother Esma Kays, sister Diane Kays and the Woodleys: Hazel, James and Susan, whose love and understanding have sustained me and the Canadian and international telephone companies through six years of "frogs and scorpions".

Bless you all.

Introduction

ONCE UPON A TIME a scorpion came to the banks of the Jordan River. Wanting to cross, he realized he couldn't swim. But there was a frog sitting on the nearby shore.

"Salaam Alak, dear frog. Greetings. Would you be so kind as to take me across the river?"

"Good heavens," exclaimed the frog. "I wouldn't dream of it. I know you. You might sting me."

"Oh no, no, have no fear," replied the scorpion. "Why, if I did that we would both perish, wouldn't we?"

"You're right," said the frog. "Okay, hop on my back and I will give you a ride across."

Midway the scorpion stung the frog. As the two started sinking, the frog shouted: "Scorpion, why did you do that? Now we shall both die."

And the scorpion replied: "Well, that's the Middle East."

I first heard that old Middle Eastern tale from a Lebanese emigré. And I remember on that Sunday afternoon, long ago and far away from the Jordan, saying to my storyteller: "Thank God you had the sense to stay away from those treacherous little rivers and crossed the Atlantic instead." My father did not reply. Nor, with the exception of a brief interlude when he returned to meet and marry my mother, did he ever go back to his beloved Middle East. For Saied Nicholas el-Ghouz (Kays is a compromise, produced because the Canadian immigration officers could not pronounce his name) there were ample opportunities through the decades to remember that tale. Indeed, as he lay dying, Lebanon was being devoured by the frog and the scorpion.

By then it was 1977 and I was in Europe facing choices: end a sabbatical year by returning to Montreal to resume a career with CBC Television News; remain in Brussels and watch NATO and the European Community go by; or volunteer for a Middle East assignment with an American network that had expressed interest in my journalistic and Arab credentials. Having successfully avoided four Arab-Israeli wars, a Jordanian-Palestinian war, an Egyptian-Israeli war of attrition, a Syrian-

Israeli war of attrition, a Lebanese civil war, countless Israeli-Palestinian battles, assorted clashes, skirmishes, attacks and counter-attacks, it was time to tackle the frog and the scorpion. I resigned from CBC and sat by the phone in Brussels. It rang two weeks later on an October night:

"How would you like to be Cairo bureau chief?" asked a voice in Paris.

"Cairo? You must be kidding," I laughed. "I had Beirut more in mind." But since the Paris of the Middle East that I knew and loved was now the ash-heap of the Arab world, I accepted on the spot. Two weeks later I was in New York negotiating a contract with ABC News. There was a slight problem over who would pay my Cairo rent, given the salary I had accepted, and I left them to mull it over while I flew to Canada to visit my mother. It was nothing, I felt, that a hot story could not resolve. Ten days later, Stan Opotowsky, chief of daily news operations in New York, was urgently demanding: "How soon can you get to Cairo?" In the time it takes to sign a contract and fly to the pyramids, I was there.

Egypt's President Anwar Sadat, deciding he had had enough of war, announced he was flying to the "ends of the earth" in search of peace. The Arab leader's flight – a half hour's journey away – would change the course of Middle Eastern history and nothing ever would be quite the same again. Except, of course, the Middle East. A peace treaty would be signed, peace prizes bestowed, and life would go on much as it always had in the land of the frog and the scorpion. The injustice, hatred and mistrust would continue along with the bombs, bullets and death. In fact, four years after his "sacred mission", Anwar Sadat the peacemaker would himself lie dead in a pool of blood. It was the classic Middle East story, and much more. It was Greek tragedy and American soap opera. And midway through it, I unashamedly longed for a good old-fashioned war; anything to end the agony of peace, and the media hysteria that seemed to have taken over everyone involved in this phenomenal piece of political theatre. The peace story whose beginning and end shook the world was also one – in this satellite age – which began and ended on America's nightly news. It was a prime time "made for TV" drama, written and directed by its star performer and produced and sponsored by CBS, NBC and ABC. That we frequently exchanged roles, merely reinforced the symbiotic relationship that ultimately contributed to the star's demise. This drama had it all: war and peace; Arabs and Israelis; heroes and villains; power and politics; struggle and sacrifice; courage and cowardice; hope and despair; death and destruction. The audience, unfortunately, never got to see the whole show. It never does, given the nature of television news. Regular TV programming was interrupted four times during the story's four-year run: Sadat's peace mission to Israel in November, 1977; the Camp David peace accords in September, 1978; the signing of the peace treaty in March, 1979; and the assassination and burial of President Sadat in October, 1981. In between these historic events, the audience made do with dribs and drabs; highlights conveyed in one-minute, thirty-second spurts; "spots" or "pieces" as they're so aptly called in the TV trade.

From the feedback I was able to accumulate from both sides of the screen, on both sides of the Atlantic, ABC's news coverage of the peace story was exemplary, which translated means ABC acquitted itself rather well by more often than not cleanly beating its two chief competitors, CBS and NBC. Having been intimately involved with the story, I never had any doubt that what we did we did respectably well, by TV standards. It's what we did *not* do that disturbed me then, disturbs me now and should disturb the majority of Americans who, according to polls of the past decade, get most if not all their news from television. This frightening statistic says as much about the power of television news in today's America as it does about the under-informed and/or uninterested masses. Also, the fact that TV news managers and producers traditionally complain about the difficulty of selling foreign news to the viewing public helps explain why so often it is sold in drag; dressed up in show-biz razzmatazz, sometimes beyond recognition or meaning.

The Sadat peace story, like so many events of international impact and consequence, fell victim to the paradox of TV news: media overkill on the one hand; one-dimensional images on the other.

In the version that ran for four years on American TV, the protagonist was Anwar Sadat, Egypt's magnanimous president for eleven years: a leader who did what no other Arab dared; a brave, courageous, charismatic, charming, handsome hero who won the Nobel Peace Prize and the love and attention of much of the world; a maverick who preached "no more war", single-handedly demolished the stereotype of the Arab bad guy, and helped crack the psychological barriers between Arab and Jew. The man Henry Kissinger called the "greatest statesman since Bismarck", was assassinated by four young Egyptian Moslem fanatics. Millions mourned his death.

In the version never shown on American TV, the story's protagonist was also Anwar Sadat, Egypt's autocratic president for eleven years: an opportunist who signed a peace treaty with Israel in return for his beloved Sinai; a traitor who failed to end the Arab-Israeli conflict and did not bring peace to the Middle East; a megalomaniac who in his desire to forge a favourable imprint on history silenced his opponents and critics at home, alienated his country's finest intellects, isolated himself from his fellow Arabs and neglected the economic and social welfare of his poverty-stricken people. A latter-day pharaoh in the mould of Ramses II, he sought peace at any price, and died in a hail of bullets fired by four religious zealots from his own army. Few Egyptians and fewer Arabs wept at his death, for Sadat did not inspire the same love at home as he did abroad.

Both versions are accurate. Anwar Sadat was both a hero and a villain, a man of two worlds, frog and scorpion.

That, then, is the story I spent four years covering. It's not the one you got on "World News Tonight", "Good Morning America" or any other network news show in Britain or America, partly because of the medium's limitations, constraints and superficiality and partly because, as journalists are fond of reminding one another, the best stories are the ones that never get told; the stories behind the story; the ones that get away only to resurface between deadlines and satellite transmissions, or in some foreign correspondent's memoirs years later. In short, the very stories that might have helped the viewer or reader better understand the news.

Peace, Sadat, the Middle East and US interests in this strategic region would have been better served had the American TV public been provided with a more balanced, in-depth look at the complexities of the Sadat peace story. Indeed had TV news managed the story differently, its pathetic ending might have been less inevitable.

A number of books have been written on the power of the media and television, one of the best being David Halberstam's *The Powers That Be*, and there are scores of books dealing with the complexities of the Middle East. This book reflects both worlds, both problems, through a series of vignettes and anecdotes pegged to the highlights of the media event which I reported in front of the cameras between November 1977 and December 1981. Many of these stories were conveyed to my former producers and colleagues, but not to the audience; some were not adaptable to television and/or were not considered relevant at the time. This personalized background account aims to give the reader some insight and a sharper perspective of one of the past decade's historic stories; one which continues to affect us all, and helps explain Arab-Israeli relationships in the post-Sadat era. Since American television news played such a major role in not only reporting but also shaping this story; since TV news today is more than ever in the business of high stakes diplomacy, it is vital that there be no illusions. When you tune into the news this evening, keep in mind that what you're seeing and hearing is a slickly-produced package, roughly twenty minutes in length, born of the daily battle of the ratings; one which a handful of men and women deem worthy of your attention; a programme to inform and entertain you. If it resembles your favourite soap opera, quiz show or commercial, that's because the days of unadulterated TV journalism are long over. Welcome, then, to the world of show business. And a drama of frogs and scorpions.

1. To the ends of the earth

A RABIC – A RICH, lyrical, theatrical language – lends itself especially well to hyperbole. And of all Arab leaders, Anwar Sadat was a pastmaster of powerful and overblown rhetoric. It's not surprising then, that the Egyptian President's speech to mark the annual opening of Parliament on November 9, 1977, was received with the usual loyal applause and scattered yawns. Even given Sadat's mercurial, unpredictable nature, it was pretty routine stuff: a three-hour-long rambling, largely ad-libbed progress report on the state of affairs in Egypt, the Middle East and the world. He spoke at length about preparations for reconvening the dead-locked Geneva Peace Conference, stressing the endless procedural problems and the sticky issue of Palestinian representation. He made it clear he was rather bored with all the non-substantive wrangling, that he preferred really to just get on with it, to go straight to the heart of the problem. He praised the Americans and President Jimmy Carter for infusing new life into the Conference and deliberately ignored the Soviets who, with the US, had only weeks earlier jointly and publicly endorsed the Geneva road to peace. Sadat was approaching what appeared to be the end of his address when he seemed to fumble with his notes. According to one Egyptian journalist who was watching the speech live on television: "there was a great fluttering of papers, giving the impression he had lost his place although he was not exactly following a prepared text." In any event, after much umming and ahhing and sorting of papers, Sadat told his audience he was ready, "to go to the ends of the earth if this will prevent one soldier, one officer, among my sons from being wounded – not being killed, just wounded; I say now that I am ready to go to the ends of the earth, Israel will be astonished when it hears me saying now, before you, that I am ready to go to their house, to the Knesset itself, to talk to them." (Egyptian State Information Service)

Well, no one, it seems, least of all the Israelis, was astonished. That night Israeli Defence Minister Ezer Weizman went to bed without bothering to be briefed on Sadat's speech. He was told it contained nothing new. The following morning Israeli press and radio briefly reported the speech, but according to Weizman: "Sadat's strange remark about coming to the Knesset in Jerusalem received little serious attention . . . my first response was characteristic of the effect of thirty years of enmity and war: I didn't believe a word of it." (Weizman, *The Battle for Peace*, Bantam, March 1981)

Even Sadat's tightly controlled press interpreted the remarks as nothing more than Arab rhetoric. The fact that Cairo's three major dailies had not been briefed or prepared for such an astonishing matter was apparent in next day's main headlines: *Al Ahram*: "We Are Ready to Go to Geneva Regardless of Procedural Problems." Sadat's offer to go to the Knesset was relegated to a sub-headline. The more colourful *Al Akhbar* saw it as "Sadat Challenges Israel" and quotes Sadat as saying, "We are not afraid of confrontation with Israel now that we have reduced her to size, with The October War." An eight-column headline then acknowledged that Sadat was . . . "Ready to go to the Knesset and face the Israeli leaders." Just ordinary, everyday fare. PLO Leader Yasser Arafat who heard the speech from his seat of honour in the Assembly's front row, stopped applauding following which Egypt's Foreign Minister Ismail Fahmy – seated next to him – assured him that Sadat was not serious. Egypt's leading government officials dismissed the "ends of the earth" as a figure of speech. Prime Minister Mumduh Salem, National Assembly Speaker Sayed Marei and the Chairman of the Foreign Relations Committee, Dr Leila Takla, left the Assembly for the Prime Minister's office across the street talking about committee work. Takla says: "We did not consider Sadat's remarks important enough to even discuss." Neither the American Ambassador, Herman Eilts, who heard the speech from the Assembly's visitors' gallery, nor US officials in Washington heard anything to get excited about. As for the Arab world, the peace offering constituted nothing more than good, old-fashioned Arab propaganda, Sadat-style.

When Israeli Prime Minister Menachem Begin first heard of Sadat's offer the following morning, he dismissed reporters' questions with a stock response, affirming that he was ready to meet Sadat anywhere to talk peace. He mentioned Geneva specifically, since that's where everyone involved in the Arab-Israeli conflict was gearing to go. Later that day of November 10, Begin, when cornered by a group of visiting American congressmen, said that if Sadat really intended to come to Jerusalem, he would be welcomed with "all the honour befitting a President". Now realizing he could no longer ignore Sadat's offer, Begin went on Israeli television the following night. He addressed the Egyptian people directly: "Citizens of Egypt . . . Let us say to each other, and let this be the silent vow between our two nations; no more wars, no more bloodshed, no more threats." In the international media Begin's speech got much bigger play than Sadat's. But the Egyptian press, at least, was not impressed. The weekly *Akhbar Al Yom* suggested Begin talk to his own people since he and the Israelis, it claimed, were guilty of intransigence, expansionism and the denial of Palestinian rights. It also reminded Begin of Israel's "crazy action" in South Lebanon where hundreds of women and children were killed in raids. (Only four days earlier, Israel had conducted anti-PLO raids in Lebanon.)

By November 12, the visiting American congressmen had caught up with Sadat. The Egyptian leader repeated his offer for those who seemed to miss it the first time around: "We are ready to go even if we have to spend two or three consecutive days in the Knesset. I am ready to have a discussion with all of them." (*Al Akhbar*, November 13, 1977). But he saw no sign of a welcome, he told the congressmen, and no official invitation. No sooner said than done. That evening Begin issued an invitation through the media: "In the name of the government of Israel, I officially invite the President of Egypt to come to Jerusalem. . . Ahlan Wa Sahlan," he said in Arabic. Welcome.

By the time Cairo's frustrated foreign correspondents had been able to sort the rhetoric from the reality, they found themselves upstaged by a super-star member of their own ranks: CBS News' Walter Cronkite. In separate pre-taped interviews conducted via satellite between New York, Cairo and Tel Aviv, he took the bull(s) by the horns. Starting with Sadat:

> CRONKITE: When will you go to Israel?
> SADAT: I'm just waiting for the proper invitation.
> CRONKITE: You must get something direct from Mr Begin, not through the press?
> SADAT: Right, right.
> CRONKITE: And how would that be transmitted, sir, since you do not have diplomatic relations with Israel?
> SADAT: Why not through our mutual friend, the Americans?

Cronkite then shifted to Begin in Tel Aviv, asking him when might the invitation be forthcoming.?

> BEGIN: I will, during the week, ask my friend, the American Ambassador to Israel, to find out in Cairo from his colleague, the American Ambassador to Egypt, whether he will be prepared to give us his good offices and transmit a letter from me to President Sadat inviting him formally and cordially through the good offices of the United States to come to Jerusalem.

Cronkite asked Sadat whether there were any preconditions to his trip.

> SADAT: The only condition is that I want to discuss the whole situation with the 120 members of the Knesset and put the full picture and detail the situation from our point of view.
> CRONKITE: If you get that formal invitation, how soon are you prepared to go?
> SADAT: Really, I'm looking forward to fulfil this visit in the earliest time possible.

CRONKITE: Would that be, say, a week?

SADAT: You can say that, yes.

CRONKITE: You said you wished to address the Knesset, the Parliament in Israel, would you also. . . .

SADAT: That's right.

CRONKITE: Would you also engage in substantive discussions?

SADAT: I may exchange our views or so with Begin, yes.

CRONKITE: What about the opposition from some of your fellow leaders in the Arab world to this visit? They have expressed this to you, I gather?

SADAT: I didn't tell any one of my colleagues and I didn't ask them to agree or disagree upon this. I felt that my responsibility and my responsibility as President of Egypt also is to try all means to reach peace. And I took this decision. For sure there are those who are against it. But as much as I am convinced that this is the right way and my people back me, I shall be fulfilling the whole thing.

CRONKITE: Has the PLO leader, Yasser Arafat, expressed any opinion on this visit to Premier Begin?

SADAT: Not at all. Not at all because as I told you, Walter, this is my initiative.

CRONKITE: What is the ultimate that could result from such a meeting; what's the best you could hope for?

SADAT: We are in a crucial moment. There has never been a suitable moment in the Arab world to reach genuine peace like we are now, so I want to put the facts before them and in the same time, we want to discuss what will be the other alternative if we can't achieve peace. It would be horrible. Believe me, horrible. . . .

Cronkite then asked Begin when he would take the necessary steps to move this new peace initiative from long-distance dialogue to a person-to-person meeting.

BEGIN: Tomorrow I will make a statement in our Parliament in the afternoon and I think that immediately after this statement I will get in touch with Mr Lewis, my good friend the American Ambassador, and so find out. But I can assure you, Mr Cronkite, as we really want peace, to establish permanent peace, I will not hesitate to send such a letter.

CRONKITE: Are there any preconditions? Are there any conditions under which you will be inviting him?

BEGIN: No preconditions, and I understand that also President Sadat doesn't put forward any preconditions. He has got his position, we have our position, let us sit together around the table and talk peace, and everybody will bring his position.

CRONKITE: He hinted to me this morning that he thought it

might be possible that he would be going to Israel, if the invitation was forthcoming, within a week or so. Do you think that's realistic?

BEGIN: Very good news. Well, if President Sadat is ready to come next week, if he tells me that he will come next week, I will have to postpone my trip to Britain because I am supposed to go next Sunday to London at the invitation of Prime Minister Callaghan, but I suppose that Prime Minister Callaghan will also be agreeable rather to postpone that meeting for a week and rather have President Sadat in Jerusalem, because it gives hope to have peace in the Middle East. But if President Sadat would come after my return from Europe, I will come back home next Friday after my visit to London and Geneva, and then he may come the other Monday. But anyhow, anytime, any day he is prepared to come, I will receive him cordially at the airport, go together with him to Jerusalem, also present him to the Knesset, and let him make a speech to our Parliament. I will follow him to the platform, greet him, receive him. I think it is now up to President Sadat to carry his, let me say, promise, or bring into fruition his readiness to come to Jerusalem.

And so, on November 14, 1977 – with America as witness – the CBS Evening News and the Cronkite school of TV diplomacy delivered Sadat's peace baby ... five days after it was, apparently, so casually conceived.

ABC and NBC had little time for recriminations. The following day President Sadat got his official invitation. The visit would take place that weekend and the world media, led by American television, were scrambling. Hundreds of troops had to be mobilized and deployed to do battle for history and audience ratings. ABC News, under new president Roone Arledge, was facing its first serious challenge as a competitor of CBS and NBC. The perennial poor cousin – long the butt of network news jokes – had been given a new mandate that summer when Arledge, the boy wonder who had made ABC Sports coverage an unparalleled TV success story, was hired to do the same for News. That mandate meant more money, more talent (on-air personnel), more equipment and technology, more access to the corporate brass, and by extension more air time for news and news specials. Armed with millions of dollars, Arledge had raided the competition for talent. It took one million alone to lure Barbara Walters from NBC, generating considerable controversy and publicity over the value of journalists. Other stars and personalities switched for less. Arledge also picked and plucked from local stations, their affiliates and the papers, his reach extending as far as Canada which, in the minds of many Americans and Canadians alike, constitutes America's largest television affiliate. It was not as though ABC News did not have a base on which to build reportorial excellence; it already possessed a stable of top-calibre veterans. But now, by strengthening its ranks with dozens of one-time competitors, both in front of and behind the cameras; by outfitting itself with all the financial, human and technical resources necessary to compete, third-placed ABC was ready to meet the two established giants – CBS and NBC – head on. By November, 1977, Arledge had assembled a more than respectable news team and placed it in the hands of Av Westin, one of television's most talented, ablest newsmen.

I was delighted to have Westin for my immediate boss, not least because he had picked me to be part of the new ABC News organization. I was not scheduled to take over as Cairo bureau chief until January, but on November 16, I was shipped off to Egypt to link up with the flying media circus that would cover this unprecedented peace story. During the long flight to Cairo, I thought less of Sadat's fate than my own.

The story that had landed in my lap was not exactly the one for which I had been hired two weeks earlier. In so far as one can plan a news assignment, the plan called for me to churn out "soft" news features rather than "hard" daily news, based on the assumption that a fifth Arab-Israeli war, while always threatening, was not imminent. A hard story – on-going or breaking – demands to be told. A soft story hopes to be discovered. It is the difference between a scream and a whisper.

Some reporters prefer the creativity and flexibility of soft news; others thrive on the immediacy and mechanics of hard news. I felt equally at home with both, but after a decade spent largely covering hard news, I had come to the conclusion that appearing nightly on TV does wonders for one's ego and precious little for the rest of the mind and body. So, the Cairo assignment, while it promised less excitement, drama and on-air exposure, was appealing and timely; a nice respite from the breathless pressures of daily deadlines; an opportunity to explore and develop my own stories in a region of the world that had always held a special fascination. Because these stories would not scream to be told, they would be shipped, not satellited, to New York, and aired not necessarily on arrival but when time permitted.

I should have known better. I should have figured on Anwar Sadat plotting my next story. This was an Arab leader with a history for surprises. I had no files, briefs or notes with me on the Cairo flight but I recalled certain highlights. Sadat made his first peace offering to Israel in 1971. In 1972 he threw out twenty thousand Soviet advisors and technicians. In 1973 he launched the October War against Israel, vindicating Arab honour after the humiliating defeat of the June '67 War. In 1974 he signed the First Sinai Disengagement Agreement with Israel; and he played host to the first US President – Richard Nixon – to visit Egypt. In 1975 he signed the Second Sinai Disengagement Agreement and reopened the Suez Canal as a goodwill gesture.

By 1977, then, the pattern had become clear. The Egyptian President, realizing that he and the Arabs could never win a war against Israel, set out to make peace on his own. And the road to peace, Sadat calculated, went through America, Israel's closest ally and protector. So he had befriended the powerful friend of his enemy, and he impressed the Americans with his good deeds and intentions. Now, apparently, it was time for the next step and another surprise, more dramatic than all the others combined. He would fly to "the ends of the earth" and deal with the enemy directly, unequivocally, and alone.

By the time my plane landed in Cairo the night of November 17, I thought the man was either a genius or a crackpot! All I knew for certain was that I had a breathless story on my hands.

"Welcome to Egypt," said Hassan Bahgat, ABC's resident magician. It was almost midnight but his cheery smile, courtesy, and deft movements through the steamy, stifling chaos of Cairo International Airport belied the fact that he had been on the job since early morning. My efficient Egyptian expeditor confidently pushed and pulled me through the mobs of arriving passengers, waiting relatives, under-employed airport workers and officious non-officials. Hassan's flashing ID card in one hand, my passport and visa in the other, had swept us all the way past the immigration checkpoint so swiftly, I saw neither the officer's face nor the *baksheesh* that probably greased our way into the baggage section. I left Hassan to retrieve the bags any way he could and opened the white envelope he had handed me on arrival. It was a letter from the current Cairo bureau chief. Bill Brannigan, at that moment satelliting a story, had taken the time during what must have been a particularly hectic day and night to welcome me to Cairo and to offer his assistance should it be required. It was a thoughtful gesture, and I was touched.

By now, Hassan was leading me and bags into customs, much in the manner of a fearless officer ready for hand-to-hand combat as he heads into the battle zone. His boldness appeared to increase in direct relation to proximity to the exit and now that it was in sight, he brandished our credentials with all the authority of a field marshal, declaring to two slightly overwhelmed and highly impressionable plain-clothes customs officers that I was: "Madame Doreen Kays. She's an ABC television news correspondent," he continued in Arabic. "And we have nothing to declare. Absolutely nothing." I could still hear their "Welcome, welcome!" (in English) as we cleared the airless airport for the airless parking lot. But there was little to complain about as we roared out for the journey to the hotel. I felt a slight twinge of guilt at the thought of my less privileged fellow passengers, still working their way through the labyrinth. But I recovered quickly, preferring to reflect on this Egyptian phenomenon sitting behind the wheel of his Fiat station-wagon.

Admittedly, the Egyptian authorities had ordered out the welcome mat for the American media, especially the TV networks. But no directive could possibly have cleared me in what, I calculated, was one tenth of the time it took to get a dial tone in Egypt. Hassan Bahgat, I concluded, was

Superman. He certainly drove his car as though he thought he were. And that was good enough for me. I was grateful for his Formula One speed, and the darkness. Cairo is not one of the world's most beautiful cities. But at night as one approaches the Nile, along the Corniche, it is easy to visualize what it must have been once, and what it could have been with one-quarter of the population, instead of becoming, alas, the Calcutta of the Middle East. I kept my thoughts to myself, chatting instead about the day's news and tomorrow's schedule. Hassan seemed as proud of his English as I was of my Lebanese Arabic, and by the time we screeched to a halt in front of the Nile Hilton, he had discreetly chosen English as our working language. Every foreign news bureau needs a "Bahgat," but as we parted that night I could only hope that the competition did not possess such a formidable weapon. Thanks to him, I unpacked my bags fully confident in maintaining the art of the possible in the land of the impossible. Westerners do not call Egypt the IBM country for nothing: *Inshallah* (God Willing), *Boukrah* (Tomorrow), *Malesh* (Never Mind).

Even though I had not slept in thirty-six hours, I knew I could not do so without pausing before the ancient river Nile. From my balcony, the Corniche el-Nil was blissfully deserted, as it always is between the hours of two and six in the morning. And there she was, across the boulevard: Egypt's only survivor, calmly flowing upstream, oblivious to pharaohs, wars, peace missions, poverty, and foreign correspondents with never enough time to appreciate her eternal beauty. I decided if the Nile had survived five thousand years, I could survive my new assignment for the next three. And with that reassuring thought I went to bed.

Twenty minutes later the phone rang: "Welcome to Cairo," said a familiar voice, the same one which but a month ago had asked: "How would you like to be Cairo bureau chief?" ABC's Paris producer Arnie Collins, an old Cairo hand, and Mike Dunk, a freelance British editor out of London, urged me to go to my door and open it. I was too groggy to do otherwise. As I flung the door open, my scream could be heard by more than just my colleagues, hiding behind their own doors down the corridor. I had been knocked to the floor by an eight-foot tall, four-foot wide obstruction. Collins and Dunk had, obviously stolen a floral wreath from that night's hotel wedding reception (both wreath and reception being essential to the rising class of Arab nouveau-riche). I recovered, struggled with the remains, erecting them where they would pose the least threat, and promptly dialled the practical jokers. By now all three of us thought it was a pretty good effort. And I have not liked Egyptian weddings since.

The following morning, November 17, I walked to the nearby ABC Bureau on Ramses Street, where the mounds of sand greeting me at the building's entrance were part of the decor, not a practical joke. Once inside, I found the three-room bureau equally oppressive. But, refusing to become depressed on my first working day, I concentrated on the five-man team that made up ABC's Cairo presence: bureau chief/correspondent Bill Brannigan, cameraman Rupen Vosgimourakian, soundman Peter Lousarian, secretary Magda and Superman Hassan. A coffee boy and driver popped in and out as did Collins and Dunk, who were *en forme* following the previous night's caper. In addition, Peter Jennings, ABC's London-based senior foreign correspondent was in town and an extra camera crew was due any moment from London. Everything considered, we were such an oasis of tranquillity that it was hard to believe a major story was pending. In fact, the majority of television troops had been sent to Tel Aviv and Jerusalem in preparation for President Sadat's November 19th trip, and to Damascus, where Sadat had flown for a quick visit to get Syrian President Assad's approval. Assad made it clear he did not approve. Of all the Arabs, Assad was the most vehemently opposed to the peace mission, and none of us knew then how close Sadat had come to not making it back to Cairo, let alone Israel. A couple of months after Sadat was killed, a former Syrian government minister confessed to me: "We were planning to arrest Sadat that day in Damascus. We considered detaining him then and there. President Assad," he said, "finally ruled against the action, on the grounds that it was simply not feasible."

That same day Sadat lost his own foreign minister, Ismail Fahmy. According to Leila Takla, then chairman of the Egyptian Parliament's foreign relations committee, who was on a private visit to Damascus during the Sadat-Assad meeting and tried to contact Fahmy at his Meredien Hotel suite: "I rang several times throughout the day and each time there was no response, which I found rather peculiar." So, I went down to the lobby and inquired after Fahmy. A hotel employee confirmed that Fahmy's bag had indeed arrived, but Mr Fahmy had not. Fahmy had quit, and would not go to Israel. As for his bags in Damascus, all luggage for official government trips is packed and picked up the night before a journey, indicating that the foreign minister did not believe his President was serious about actually going to Jerusalem right up to the eve of the Damascus trip. Fahmy felt Sadat was putting all his cards on the table by going to Israel; that he was recognizing the state of Israel, with Israeli-occupied Arab East Jerusalem as its de facto capital.

Later, when the ex-foreign minister resurfaced and became accessible for private chats with foreign correspondents, he told me: "I urged the President not to go to Israel, certainly not to Jerusalem. I told him, 'If you want to meet Menachem Begin, that's not a problem. I'll arrange a meeting anywhere in the world. But don't go to Israel.' By seeking no quid pro quo," said Fahmy, "Sadat was demanding nothing in return for his magnanimous gesture. Absolutely nothing. From a negotiating point of view, he was in the weakest possible position." So, Egypt's highly regarded foreign minister resigned on his principles, although on reading his statement of resignation in the Cairo press that day, I tended to view his move as a classic, historic, Arab position arguing traditional diplomacy. I thought Fahmy was suffering from a case of sour grapes; that he was upset at his boss upstaging him in a most undiplomatic, unorthodox fashion. Months later I would change my mind.

In any event, on November 17 and 18, the media focus was not on naysayers, sceptics or cynics. It was on Anwar Sadat and logistics – ensuring that enough ABC people were in the right place at the right time to cover his peace mission to Jerusalem; the most dramatic Middle East story since the creation of modern Israel. We in the Cairo bureau were the supporting cast and extras, waiting in the wings. The superstars would have to come first. And they were coming from New York. In fact, CBS' Cronkite was already in Cairo where – as Sadat's midwife – he had secured himself a seat on Sadat's plane. NBC's Chancellor who was in Tel Aviv was quick to follow which left a frantic ABC and Barbara Walters – also in Tel Aviv – scrambling to catch up. Determined not to be outdone on this critical test story in which ABC had to prove it could not only meet the competition but beat it, Walters ended up making her own history: an ABC-chartered Lear Jet flew her from Tel Aviv to Cairo – the first civilian flight between the two countries. Sadat made sure that American television's million-dollar-baby got her seat. The media-wise Egyptian president needed this powerful woman and her audience. He and his peace mission had to play to the American people. Otherwise the trip and the effort would not be worth the political and physical risks. Even if Walters had not represented ABC News, Sadat had a soft spot for the third-place network and another of its superstars, Peter Jennings. When Sadat was less of a star himself, Jennings and a film crew had spent a month filming and interviewing the Egyptian leader for a one-hour documentary entitled: "Sadat: a Biography". It provided Americans with their first and only TV portrait of the Egyptian president. The programme elevated Sadat's image and no doubt helped prepare him for the role he was about to perform live for millions of Americans.

2. Weekend in Jerusalem

I CAN ONLY HOPE the world got a better glimpse of history than I did that Saturday night of November 19, 1977. The glamour of reporting President Sadat's flight to the "ends of the earth" found me, cameraman Rupen Vosgimourakian, soundman Peter Lousarian and producer Arnie Collins aboard a dusty, nearly new, black Mercedes, headed on a supersonic journey through the bowels of Cairo. We were going to the ubiquitous coffee house, exact location unknown. Our driver Mustapha, like most Cairenes, seemed to be on intimate terms with his car, his city and all ten million of its inhabitants. And no man, he made it clear, knew his coffee houses better. Except perhaps the Armenian-Lebanese Rupen. After two years on assignment in Cairo, Rupen knew what we were looking for and where to find it. Between these two street-smart easterners, we found coffee house after coffee house after coffee house, none of them suitable. Some were too empty; some too full; some had no television set; others were too far away from the ABC bureau. Finally, when dusk had turned to dark and the clock ticked perilously close to the historic moment, we found a coffee house in the working-class district of Babalouk, which, if not ideal was at least adequate for our purposes; it had customers, a TV, space for our five-member crew and camera gear; a close proximity to the bureau, which might make the difference between meeting or missing a deadline, and an open-air entrance onto the sidewalk to help diminish any threat of claustrophobia. We explained who we were, why we were invading this sanctuary, and how everyone involved should please, simply, pretend we didn't exist. I've always enjoyed the last part of this on location ritual; the let's-all-act-normal admonishment which in my experience is always ignored by the admonished for the two simple reasons that they are not trained actors and the situation is anything but normal – which is why it is news and why we're reporting it. Rupen had a reputation as one of the finest cameramen in the business, that much I knew. But as I watched him warm up our coffee-drinking extras, on this our first assignment together, I realized he was also a born director. What a pity I thought: here was Fellini shooting the man-in-the-street/coffee-house reaction to a performance rather than the performance itself. In any event, it was too late to worry about whether our main prop – the coffee house TV set with its snowy, black and white reception – would improve sufficiently or quickly enough to allow anyone to see, let alone react to Sadat setting foot on Israeli soil; too late to worry about a back-up should our camera go on the fritz; too late to worry about whether the extras in this drama would react to us instead of Sadat; too late to worry about the competition and what it was up to (had CBS and NBC found a better coffee-house?); in short, too late to worry about all the human and technical imponderables inherent in as-it-happens television repor-ting. The show was about to go on.

We were too busy trying to record history to note the precise moment it happened. As for the other two thousand journalists covering the story, apparently they failed to synchronize their two thousand watches. The historic moment, then, was 7:58 p.m.; 7:59 p.m.; 8: p.m. (as scheduled) *or* 8:01 p.m. (local Israeli time). All I saw and heard was a colourless assortment of blurred TV images and sounds that elicited first a stunned silence, then a spontaneous clapping cheer from our packed Cairo coffee house. Rupen and his hand-held camera focused alternately on the tele-vision set then on the all-male chorus reacting to it and however it chose to interpret the unfolding drama. Through no fault of the Egyptian commentator, or the state-run TV system, or the live satellite transmission facilities, it proved a challenge to distinguish Sadat from his Boeing 707, Prime Minister Begin from former Prime Minister Golda Meir, the Israeli national anthem from the Egyptian national anthem, the Star of David from the Egyptian Eagle, the security men from the media types, let alone the art from the reality. It was comforting to note, though, that if history was indeed being made at this hour, I was not the only one it was passing by: a couple of elderly Egyptians wearing the traditional *galabayia* (long cotton robe), and hiding out in the rear of the café, looked utterly bored or dazed or both. All they seemed to want to do was go back to their hashish, their card game and their peaceful life, which had been so rudely interrupted by this spectacle of peace. It was a great shot. Unfortunately we didn't get it. The moment the camera approached, our two gems decided to come to life. By reacting to us rather than for us, we lost one of the best pictures of the story; one that would have helped us better portray the mixed mood of the crowd; the diverse reactions to the Egyptian leader's extraordinary embrace of the enemy. It was not the first or the last foiled attempt at reality in an evening that was taking on surrealistic tones. Not only were our extras hamming it up for television – some in the mistaken belief they would see themselves on Egyptian TV the next day – but by now we had attracted several dozen extra extras of all ages. At one point when Rupen had all the close-ups he and his lens could bear, and push had turned to shove, he let loose with a couple of well-chosen, least offensive expletives apparently holding in reserve the stronger stuff in his repertoire should the situation deteriorate. I was equally exasperated, but could hardly blame our coffee drinkers for being curious, excited and somewhat unsophisticated in the ways of the foreign media.

At least they were polite, pleasant and gentle, which is more than one might say about their western counterparts who, in a similar situation, could have been, if not thoroughly blasé or jaded, then downright nasty. Once order had been quickly restored, Rupen went about calmly and smoothly getting the necessary footage under the pretence that his lens was capturing one scene, while in reality it was zeroing in on another. The subterfuge was the only way to counter the crowd's excessive consciousness of the camera. Otherwise we'd wind up with a blatant distortion of reality. For the fact was that in spite of the abysmal reception of the TV set, the majority of spectators in our randomly chosen coffee house were genuinely enthusiastic about their President's arrival in Israel. This was reinforced in the brief interviews I did with several Egyptians. How typical or representative they were of Egypt's forty million citizens, is something else. Since Egypt is not a western-style democracy, since the country's media is largely government controlled and since there were no scientific polls conducted, there was little choice but to assume that Sadat's people supported his peace mission.

Outside the café, as we were attempting to film my on-camera close, a mob materialized, seemingly out of nowhere. A grinning, non-malevolent group of children, teenagers and adults closed in, threatening to smother us in their "Sadat good, America good," intentions. I had written and memorized my fifteen-second summation (the top and body of the script would be written later back at the bureau) and wanted to dispatch it in a couple of quick takes so we could head back to Ramses Street and report to New York. Each time we started a take, each time Rupen shouted "Roll," our young and not so young fans would go into action behind, in front and on both sides of Rupen, the camera and me. Even had he had the freedom to move his body in order to focus properly or zoom in on me about ten feet away, all Rupen would have got was a lens full of the Egyptian "Greek chorus". In utter frustration, we were on the verge of calling it quits and going with what we had: "Cairenes ham it up for history." Unfortunately, neither the American TV audience nor the New York show producers would have found this conclusion terribly informative or relevant. So, we lost our tempers instead: "God damn it, get away. Go. Move. Scat. Do you understand? Scram. *Imsha* (Move on)," I screamed, in an attempt to rid myself of the clinging humanity. Then I heard what sounded like a volcano erupting. Removing the mobile monopod he favoured to steady his camera, Rupen flung around and, camera in one hand, swinging monopod in the other, the Arab Fellini threw his menacingly sturdy physique in the direction of the already-fleeing culprits, following which he restrained himself from exhausting his repertoire of expletives. Instead, "you bunch of clowns," he roared. "You all think you're actors. Well, you're not. Get out of our way. Leave us to work in peace!" That seemed to do it. A dozen takes and thirty minutes later, we thanked everyone involved and fought our way the few yards to Mustapha's Mercedes. Once inside, with windows rolled up, the final battle was waged. As the Mercedes tried to move forward and as the mob tried to say hello and goodbye again, the intrepid Mustapha, deciding that the hour was late and our urgency great, stepped on the accelerator and none of us looked back. Mustapha later assured us that the thud we heard and felt against the car chrome was just a friendly farewell.

It was close to 10:00 p.m. by the time we got back to the bureau and sent the film to be processed at Egypt TV labs. It would be another hour or so before we could view the footage, and since the pictures would tell this story better than words, the script would be built around the images, not vice versa. During the long wait, we discussed the story's prospects with New York, lamenting the lack of ENG equipment (Electronic News Gathering Camera, Recorder and editing machines) that would have given us instantaneous screening and editing capability. The sympathetic foreign desk explained that all the overseas ENG equipment was covering Sadat in Israel, and that once Sadat returned in a couple of days, the mini-cams would follow.

In the meantime, we would have to make do with one ENG camera – its cameraman struck down with Pharaoh's Revenge (diarrhoea), rendering both inoperative – and Rupen, who had yet to put his eye to the ENG viewfinder. Our film eventually made it through Egypt TV's traditionally uncertain lab and chemicals, virtually unscratched, a bonus for which we were grateful. Rupen had captured some extraordinary faces and reactions; a good cross-section of emotions. One close-up of a soldier, on the verge of tears as he watched Sadat, was alone worth all the frustrations. It was still late afternoon in New York, where after the live coverage of Sadat's arrival in Israel, ABC was back on the air with the Ohio State versus University of Michigan football game. The game was of life or death interest to most Americans, and ABC was almost sued for interrupting it, for something so unimportant! The producers preparing a one-hour news special on the peace mission for transmission later that night wanted a one-minute, fifteen-second Egyptian reaction piece out of Cairo with which to follow reports from Barbara Walters and Tel Aviv bureau chief Bill Seamans. They got the following one-minute, fifteen-second report, cued to Rupen's dramatic pictures:

> Some were simply stunned. Others, moved to tears. It was an emotional night for millions of Egyptians as they watched their leader step onto Israeli territory right before their eyes – live on television. Many witnessed this historic event from the comfort of their homes.
>
> Others gathered at their favourite café. Some were too young to understand what was happening. Others, too old, perhaps, to care. But most seemed not to believe what they were seeing. This was not a movie. This was for real: Sadat smiling at and talking to ... their long-time enemy. It gripped the Egyptian viewer; this event that had their leader shaking hands with the

likes of Golda Meir, Moshe Dayan and other well-known Israeli political figures. One man summed up the views of most in this Cairo café tonight. He said: "The Arabs have tried everything from terrorism to wars. Nothing has achieved peace. This sort of thing," he said, "has not been tried before. If Sadat's trip proves fruitful – a true step towards peace – how wonderful. If not," he said, "at least we've tried this too. . . ." I signed off this first of so many reports with my call-sign: Doreen Kays, ABC News, Cairo.

I went to bed that night not knowing if the report was used, or what the competition had offered up. I was also in the dark about what really happened at Ben Gurion Airport and later in Jerusalem. Unlike the TV viewers back home, I would have to wait for accounts of President Sadat's debut in Israel. Apparently, the bugles sounded and the tension mounted as the crowd of thousands at Ben Gurion Airport waited for the door of the Arab Republic of Egypt Boeing 707 to open. When the media celebrities were safe on the ground, finally, after what seemed like hours rather than minutes, the trumpets blared again and there at the top of the El Al ramp, clearly illuminated by television's powerful kleig lights, stood the man of the hour. His poker face relaxed into a warm smile as he waved to the cheering, applauding crowd. At the foot of the ramp he found a warm greeting from Israeli President Ephraim Katzir and Premier Menachem Begin. It was much like two feuding next-door neighbours making up thirty years after they stopped talking to each other over a disputed piece of communal property. That the dispute in question was slightly more serious – involving the stateless Palestinians, four bitter Arab-Israeli wars and countless thousands of dead and wounded – made the TV images all the more unbelievable. The first Arab leader ever to visit the Jewish state stood solemnly at attention as a military band – without much rehearsal – played the Egyptian national anthem, accompanied in the background by a twenty-one-gun salute. Then there was silence – some tears – and the solemn Israeli anthem, the Hatikvah. There was no letting up of emotions. The Egyptian President proceeded to inspect the guard of honour of the Israeli Defence Forces – seventy-two pilots, soldiers and sailors. Suddenly, with formality out of the way, Sadat got down to the fun of meeting the official members of the Israeli family. The atmosphere became animated, even jovial, as Sadat moved through the receiving line of Israeli government members, past and present. Spotting Moshe Dayan, the hero of the 1956 Sinai Campaign and the 1967 Six-Day War, Sadat grinned broadly as he clasped his hand in a gesture that said what's past is past. He asked after Ariel Sharon and sure enough there he was, the former Israeli general who crossed the Suez Canal, turning the tide against the Egyptians in the 1973 war. As Sadat shook hands with him, he joked, "I tried to meet you before, but I couldn't catch you."

Sharon threw his head back laughing: "I'm glad to greet you as a guest in our country." Then Sadat came across Golda Meir, whom he used to call the "Old Lady".

"Madame," he said, "I have waited a long time to meet you. The seventy-nine-year-old former Prime Minister – the woman who had once made his life so difficult – beamed back saying how long she too had been waiting to meet him.

The glorious promise of peace continued to engulf Sadat as enthusiastic crowds tried to break through the security belt for a glimpse or a touch while the Egyptian and Israeli presidents made their way to the black bullet-proof limousine (on loan from the American embassy) for the thirty-mile ride to Jerusalem. It was a chilly night and many Israelis figured they were better off watching the spectacle on television. But thousands more lined the winding streets of the hill-top city, cheering on the motorcade, some waving a recently-manufactured batch of Egyptian flags. Even by Israeli standards, security measures were unprecedented, and thousands of extra soldiers and police competed with the curious for space, especially as the motorcade approached the King David Hotel, where Sadat would spend his two nights. This was the hotel which Begin, then leader of the Irgun organization, had bombed in 1946 as part of his campaign to rid Palestine of the British. When Sadat entered the lobby of the King David he was greeted with another cheering crowd chanting: "Sa-dat, Sa-dat." In a brief ceremony, the hotel manager handed Sadat certificates for 180 trees that had been planted in his name in the Jerusalem Peace Forest. Though the security net kept most of the gathered tourists from seeing Sadat, some said they saw him wave to them. Others seemed to be in a state of shock as tears streamed down their faces. The Egyptian leader, accompanied by a copy of the *Jerusalem Post* with a red-ink banner headline in both Arabic and English that said "Welcome President Sadat", went to Suite 622 with Premier Begin, where both men consulted briefly. When Begin returned to the lobby, reporters found him short and sweet: "We liked each other," he smiled as he departed.

The one Israeli official missing from the welcoming party that night was the one who would become President Sadat's favourite over the next months and years. Defence Minister Ezer Weizman – every bit as flamboyant as Sadat – was lying in a hospital bed, in great pain from injuries suffered in a car accident earlier in the week. He was finding the frustration of being left out of history considerably greater than the agonies of cracked ribs and a fractured leg. And when his morale was at rock bottom, Weizman summoned his doctors:

> Gentlemen, I'm going to the Knesset on Sunday – and I don't give a damn what you say! "... Listen," I said, "You're going to take your instrument cases, fill them up with heroin, cocaine, hashish, or anything else you like, then you'll come along with me and make sure I can stay on my feet for at least twenty-four hours." (Weizman, *The Battle for Peace*)

One of the reasons that Sadat chose to be in Jerusalem for Sunday, November 20, was to celebrate the Moslem feast of *Id al-adha* (the Feast of the Sacrifice), which commemorates the prophet Abraham, revered by Christians, Moslems and Jews, offering up his son as a sign of his obedience to God. So, the Egyptian President, conscious of the symbolism, started his day with the 6:45 a.m. Bairam prayers at Al Aqsa Mosque in Old Jerusalem which, after Mecca and Medina, is the third holiest shrine in the Islamic world. The hundreds of Egyptian and Israeli security men who accompanied him were a reminder to Sadat that what happened here to the Jordanian King Abdullah, twenty-six years earlier, could happen to him. Abdullah was assassinated by a Palestinian because of his secret meetings with Israeli leaders. The twenty-minute sermon carried another reminder of the dangers facing the leader of the largest Arab country. The Imam demanded justice for the Palestinians to whom, he said, occupied Palestine and Jerusalem belong. Sadat's fellow Moslem worshippers were carefully chosen by security people who in any case seemed to outnumber them. Having left Al Aqsa, Sadat walked across the square to the Dome of the Rock, the mosque with the golden cupola where, it is said, Abraham prepared to sacrifice his son, and where the prophet Mohammed ascended to heaven. On leaving the Temple Mount area, he avoided the Western Wall, sacred to Jews, and moved on by car to the Church of the Holy Sepulchre. Sadat's gesture was seen as a nod to Egypt's estimated seven million Coptic Christians. As he left the church, a group of Palestinian demonstrators denounced him as a traitor, echoing much of the Arab world's reaction to his trip. Israeli soldiers pursued them down alleyways, but not before they shouted at Sadat to "go back to Egypt with your dogs," and other Arabic curses. It hardly deterred Sadat from moving on to Yad Vashem, Israel's memorial to the Holocaust and its six million victims. He declined to wear the traditional *yarmulke* but he wrote in the guest book as he departed: "May God guide our steps toward peace. Let us end all suffering for mankind." There was a ninety-minute working lunch with Premier Begin, Foreign Minister Dayan and Deputy Premier Yigael Yadin before Sadat drove to the Israeli parliament building, to lay a wreath at the war memorial, and to deliver himself of his message.

Back at the ABC Bureau in Cairo, the television set with live coverage of Sadat's day was on but it served merely as a backdrop to our last-minute panic in the search for a typical Egyptian family to react to Sadat's address to the Knesset. In desperation, Tarek, a young Egyptian we had hired as temporary help, offered up his family. We accepted and minutes later found ourselves across the Nile, inside an elegant high-rise apartment in Zamalak directly overlooking the river. Youssef Kamal Abdel Rehim, a construction company executive (and ex-army colonel), his wife, and daughter Hoda (Tarek's ABC status exempted him from family membership that night) were typical upper-class Egyptians. The TV set was in a spacious, uncluttered salon, allowing us the necessary manoeuvrability to focus the camera alternately on the images of Sadat being transmitted live, and on the family watching and listening to Sadat. That the Abdel Rehim family was articulate and English-speaking was ideal for television; there would be no loss of dramatic impact through cumbersome translations. Our ENG cameraman Jim Godfrey had, fortunately, overcome the Revenge of the Pharaohs and set about positioning his camera on a tripod. The lighting was tested, adjusted and fixed. And so was the family. We waited expectantly, and at 4:00 p.m., the Egyptian President entered the Israeli Knesset to a standing ovation. (The Parliament's anti-applause rule was waived for this momentous occasion.)

Among those applauding was the wounded but determined Defence Minister. With the aid of a helicopter, a wheelchair and a walking stick, Ezer Weizman felt he was seeing a dream come true! Sadat, impeccably dressed in a dark striped suit, stood at the rostrum looking no different from when he addressed the Egyptian Parliament eleven days earlier. As usual, he was already perspiring, but probably less from the inner stress of the moment than from the kleig lights and his natural biological makeup. He was outwardly calm and self confident as he began his hour-long message in Arabic.

In the name of God Almighty and peace, Sadat first absolved from blame all those who were violently surprised or amazed at his decision (an allusion to his Arab critics) and those who saw it as a political manoeuvre or tactic camouflaging his intentions to launch a new war (an allusion to several Israeli officials). Continuing on this non-partisan theme, he declared that: "Any life lost in war is a human life, be it that of an Arab or an Israeli. A wife who becomes a widow is a human being entitled to a happy family life, whether she be an Arab or an Israeli ... for the generations to come, for the smile on the face of every child born in our land." That, Sadat explained emotionally, is why, despite all the hazards, he was doing what he was doing. Just as he was in danger of mesmerizing his adversaries with open-ended compassion, Sadat got to the point. While he had come in search of peace, "I have not come here for a separate agreement between Egypt and Israel ... I have not come to you to seek a partial peace ... I have not come to you for a third disengagement agreement in Sinai or in Golan or in the West Bank." No, said Sadat, he had come to break down the "psychological barriers of suspicion, fear, betrayal, misinterpretation and bad intentions," which, he said, was "seventy per cent of the whole problem". And to prove that he was playing a magnanimous leading role in demolishing the ugly past, he acknowledged Israel's right to exist, unequivocally: "You want to live with us in this part of the world. In all sincerity I tell you we welcome you among us with full security and peace." The Arabs, he admitted, had rejected Israel in the past, "we refused to meet with you anywhere, yes," but, "I have announced on more than one occasion that Israel has become an established fact." So Sadat promised, "we will accept all the international guarantees you envisage and accept ... all the guarantees you want from the two superpowers or from either of them or from the Big Five or from some of them."

Then came what the Israelis were waiting for; the conditions through which Israel could live in peace with justice and security. "Let me tell you without the slightest hesitation that I have not come to you under this roof to make a request that your troops evacuate the occupied territories. Complete withdrawal from the Arab territories occupied after 1967 is a logical and undisputed fact. Nobody should plead for that!" Genuine peace, said Sadat, can't be built on the occupation of the land of others, including Old Jerusalem.

At this point, Ezer Weizman's dream turned into a nightmare: "We must prepare for war," he scribbled in a note to Begin and Dayan who read it and nodded.

But the Egyptian President wasn't finished. As for the Palestinian cause, what he called the "crux of the problem. . . . In all sincerity I tell you there can be no peace without the Palestinians. It is a grave error of unpredictable consequences to overlook or brush aside this cause." In calling for a national homeland for the Palestinian people – their right to statehood – Sadat insisted that it wasn't fair of the Israelis to ask for themselves what they deny to others. "Even the United States," he said, "your first ally . . . has opted to face up to reality, to admit that the Palestinian people are entitled to their legitimate rights."

In what sounded like a final plea, the Arab leader urged the Israelis to face reality bravely, "as I have done". His mission, he said, "could be a radical turning point in the history of this part of the world, if not in the history of the world as a whole". Now, he implored, it was up to the Israelis. Sadat ended his passionate, rhetorical, often eloquent speech the way he began it: on a religious note, and finally with the words, "*Salaam Aleykum*" (Peace be upon you).

The former Israeli Foreign Minister Abba Eban, an Arabic linguist who did not have to rely on the faulty Hebrew translation, found the speech predictable. "I could have written it myself," he said, "but the Middle East will never be the same again." Sadat's speech got no applause at all from Premier Begin, General Sharon or Chief of Staff Mordechai Gur. As for the Defence Minister, Weizman felt Sadat, "in view of the whole world", had forced Israel into a corner. He had "sprung the surprise of a political Yom Kippur upon us", said Weizman, referring to the October '73 war.

ABC News' Egyptian family, the Abdel Rehims, thrilled with what their leader had to say, then anxiously awaited the Israeli Premier's reply, in their Cairo living room.

Menachem Begin, like Anwar Sadat, is a man of oratorical and rhetorical persuasion. But Begin, who had not seen Sadat's text in advance, delivered an impromptu response in Hebrew which fell short of his own standards and proved no match for Sadat's centre-stage performance. The Egyptian leader was a hard act to follow and Begin realized it from the start. Predictably, he recounted for the benefit of Sadat and his fellow Arabs the long, suffering history of the Jewish people, and strongly disagreed with Sadat on the conditions for peace, especially the status of East Jerusalem.

Nonetheless, he praised Sadat's courage in crossing the "almost infinite distance between Cairo and Jerusalem", and spoke of Israel's peaceful intentions: "This is a very special day in our lives," Begin acknowledged. "Let us continue the dialogue and grasp one another's hands. Israel does not wish to rule, disturb or divide," he insisted. Trying to equal Sadat's magnanimity, Begin declared that, "our country is open to all citizens of Egypt without any conditions, and may the visitors be many". The Israeli leader optimistically looked to the future, to the day when Israel and Egypt would exchange ambassadors and discuss their disagreements like cultured nations. More immediately, he expressed a hope to visit Cairo and called on the other Arab confrontation states – Syria, Jordan and Lebanon – to "come and talk to us". Begin, a devout Jew, concluded his speech much in the manner of Sadat: by calling upon the faithful to raise their voices "in prayer that we may have the strength and wisdom to reach a just peace". He never mentioned the Palestinians.

And so, both sides had put forward their familiar, seemingly inflexible positions. But for the first time an Arab leader had taken the initiative and called Israel's bluff. Now there was "someone to talk to", something Israelis had long complained was lacking when questioned on their sincerity about peace. While Sadat expected something in return, he did not expect to get it during this trip. He had only "come to deliver a message". And he delivered it, thanks, ironically enough, to a biblically-inspired super-hawk, the old independence fighter and current caretaker of Eretz Israel: Menachem Begin.

While Egyptian officials had no illusions about Begin, they found his speech, nonetheless, disappointing. The Egyptian family, whose reactions we were taping in Cairo felt much the same way. The Abdel Rehims gave high marks to their President for an altogether impressive performance, but Begin's response seemed to temper their enthusiasm.

That night I sent back to ABC News in New York via satellite transmission a report conveying their guarded optimism. As is customary with ABC television correspondents, I was required to file three thirty-five-second spots for ABC Radio as well as feed the strongest sound bites from the interviews. This was followed by a question and answer session, with the New York editor recording my material and asking questions to which I supplied ad-libbed answers. Since there was no special radio recording equipment installed in the bureau on Ramses Street, and since our one telephone line – assuming we could get a dial tone – was not always radio quality, New York advised via telex earlier in the day, "Don't call us. We'll call you," which it did frequently. So, by the end of the evening of November 20, New York Radio and TV had been fed their Cairo contributions to peace. They were covered and content.

With the historic speeches out of the way, the most interesting part of the drama was now being played out backstage, at the King David Hotel, where the Egyptians and Israelis were trying to get acquainted over dinner. At an official banquet, in honour of the Egyptian President, the atmosphere was tense, awkward and embarrassing, punctuated with long silences. Both sides tried to find something to talk about now that they had the opportunity for the first time in thirty years. Following the strained formalities of the banquet, Egypt's Mustapha Khalil and Butros Ghali and Israel's Ezer Weizman and Yigael Yadin decided to meet informally in an effort to break the ice. Ghali, a bespectacled academic and Coptic Christian, was acting Foreign Minister, freshly appointed by Sadat to succeed the two foreign ministers he had lost in as many days as a result of the peace mission. Khalil, the distinguished, silver-haired director of the ruling Socialist Union Party, was also head of the Arab World Bank and a respected Sadat aide. According to the best detailed account of the talks, as provided in Weizman's book, *The Battle for Peace*, the four men chatted amiably and frankly about such things as atom bombs, security, and the mutual desire for peace. The next day, Sadat invited Weizman for a private talk in his hotel suite in an effort to further sound out the hawkish Defence Minister on Israel's obsession with security. The emotive issue of Jerusalem came up and as they looked out the window at the Old City stretched out before them, Weizman insisted that the clock could not be turned back, while Sadat insisted that Arab soil was sacred and that if Israel stayed in the occupied Arab lands, he would not be able to face a single Egyptian. Sadat also insisted he was finished with war, wanted peace, wasn't playing games, and could be trusted. Weizman, realizing that Sadat . . . "had taken a historic step with no way back – and he knew it", was impressed but still sceptical.

President Sadat was scheduled to leave Jerusalem that afternoon. But not before he and Premier Begin performed their finale for the world media. In what was to be the first of their many joint news conferences, the two men smiled for the cameras because neither could afford, politically, to do otherwise. Peace or no peace, there was no turning back. And, we were assured in a mutual pledge – that between Egypt and Israel, at least, there would be "no more war, no more bloodshed". The other result of this historic and precipitous mission was an understanding – a commitment documented in the official joint communique – that the dialogue would continue for a comprehensive peace to be worked out in Geneva. As far as the Egyptian President was concerned, he had already done his bit, and the ball was now in the Israeli court.

President Carter had telephoned Sadat before the trip, telling him "the eyes of the world are on you" and so Sadat, aware that Washington and America were watching him live on television, said: "Let us hope, all of us, that we can keep the momentum in Geneva and may God guide the steps of Premier Begin and the Knesset because there is a great need for hard and drastic decisions. I have already, I mean, I took my share in my decision to come here and I shall be really looking forward for those decisions from Premier Begin and the Knesset."

Defence Minister Weizman, the only Israeli cabinet member other than Premier Begin to have met privately with Sadat, was by now too involved in the historic drama to be left out of the departure scene. His wheelchair got him as far as the hotel entrance where Sadat, Israeli President Katzir and Premier Begin were heading for the airport. On spotting Weizman moving out of his wheelchair, Sadat got out of his car, demanding to know where Weizman was going? "I'm going to see you off at the airport." "You go straight to the hospital," Sadat ordered. Weizman then bestowed a traditional Arabic blessing on him: "*Allah Ma'ak*" (God be with you). It was a touching moment. And according to Weizman, Sadat seized him: "He gave me a resounding kiss – at the same moment whispering in my ear: Our contacts will be kept up by way of Romanian President Ceausescu."

It was the Romanian leader from whom Sadat initially sought counsel on Begin's true intentions towards peace, and his response helped trigger Sadat's peace initiative.

Forty-four hours after he arrived, Sadat departed for Cairo, thanking the Israelis and the TV crews. And, symbolically at least, he left with more than he came: an escort of four Israeli-made Kfeir fighters that accompanied him to the Egyptian border; gifts that included an autographed copy of Begin's autobiography, a portrait of a dove, three urns of ancient patriarchs and a gift for a grandchild born while he prayed at Al Aqsa Mosque the day before and presented to him by Golda Meir "as a grandmother to a grandfather", as well as letters from schoolchildren including one asking him to "make peace so we can play with your children".

If Sadat was disappointed, neither his words nor his behaviour betrayed him. He pronounced himself "a hundred per cent satisfied" as he puffed on his pipe on the way home. Just look at what has happened in only forty hours," he exclaimed. "Did you ever dream that Anwar Sadat would be received as a hero in Israel?"

And a hero in his own country. By the time he landed in Cairo, a cacophonous audio-visual symphony of joy coloured the twelve-mile route from the airport to the presidential compound in the city's central Giza district. Tens of thousands of Egyptians welcomed him with a panoply of cheers, chants, whistles, ululations, tambourines, flutes, flying doves, olive branches, and fluttering white flower petals, as a proud and radiant Sadat nodded and waved regally from his black, open Mercedes limousine. Flanked by a motorcycle police escort and his personal bodyguards, Sadat and his motorcade crawled through downtown Cairo as police tried, vainly at times, to carve a path through the jostling crowds. Night had already fallen by the time the hero of peace arrived at Tahrir (Liberation) Square – a short distance from Sadat's home. After a shouting match with a group of nervous, bewildered security men – new to peace and American TV crews – Hassan, an ENG camera crew and I, had secured a perch on one of the pedestrian overpasses circling the square which serves as a main thoroughfare and bus terminal. Thanks to the tight security in force, pedestrians were prohibited from entering the overpass, leaving only a swell of TV crews, still photographers and reporters to manoeuvre and angle for the best vantage points. In addition to our media oasis, there was good shooting light available to record the tumultuous welcome building up. But by the time Sadat finally crept towards us, only the flickering lights of the motorcade and our two hand-held frezzo lights illuminated the actual arrival of – in the estimation of one welcome banner – the Saviour of the Masses. As for the adoring masses themselves – many of them bussed in from the countryside – they shouted: "In blood and in spirit, we sacrifice ourselves for you, O Sadat!" Their enthusiasm was part spontaneous and part orchestrated by the state, with a little help from the pervasive presence of the world media. As a member of the media, all I managed to see at that hour was a dark man, in a dark suit, in a dark car, waving through the dark while, in the background, jubilant thousands roared. Life imitating art, I thought. Slow-motion, freeze-frame television. Global theatre. A weekend of cinéma vérité.

Television's street reporters did not have the luxury of pondering the peace plot. As a member of the video screen's urban guerrilla squad, I had deadlines to meet and traffic to fight. It was night-time when the media-conscious Egyptian President landed in Jerusalem so as not to violate the Jewish Sabbath, which ends at sunset. His return to Cairo, then, had been carefully planned to occur in daylight for the benefit of his countrymen and the US evening news shows. But the boundless welcome Sadat had received left us yet again with a night-time story, ensuring a last-minute scramble to make the six o'clock Monday evening news in New York.

Even though all of Cairo's ten million inhabitants were not out in the streets that night – nor even five million of them as Sadat repeatedly claimed – those who were helped to form a solid wall between the ABC Tahrir team and the bureau, threatening more than a missed satellite transmission. At the best of times, Cairo traffic is an epileptic fit which no attending traffic cop or traffic light can control, and for which there is no known cure except death or elimination of half the population. At the worst of times, it is a struggle between life and death, between man and destiny that is better left in the hands of God. It does no good to worry, scream, plead, curse or rationalize. But one does anyway. And we did the night of November 21, 1977, because that's what TV correspondents, cameramen, sound recordists, producers and the chauffeurs hired by us, are paid to do: get the story and get it on the air; any means short of murder or other illegal acts being acceptable. In the midst of Cairo traffic, though, it is a perfectly acceptable, even daily, practice to contemplate murder on the grounds that it is preferable to suicide and also passes the time.

One mile and one hour later, then, Cairo traffic dumped us at the bureau. We had moved from one frenzy to another. Fortunately, no one was depending solely on the pictures shot from the pitch-black Tahrir Square vantage point. Other crews, brought in from the US and Europe, and positioned at several points along the motorcade route, were back with their tapes, now being screened and assessed by producers also flown in from the US and Europe. In addition, crews were out earlier in the day getting material to supplement the pictures of Sadat's homecoming.

London-based producer Pete Simmons and I discussed the pictures and story line with our show producers in New York. Together with a newly-arrived ENG tape editor from London, we added the various elements to a recorded track of my script, satelliting this report to New York at midnight Cairo time; 5:00 p.m. Eastern Standard Time N.Y.; and one hour to air:

> This is Doreen Kays in Cairo.
> The day began for most Egyptians with a close look at newspapers headlining the Sadat-Begin speeches . . . setting the mood early for President Sadat's return home. And Egyptian television was on the air live by early afternoon, keeping viewers abreast of the events – leading to the President's arrival back home. By mid-afternoon – truckloads of children, some with welcome banners, others with olive branches – were getting ready for the big moment. . . .
> (PAUSE. UP SOUND ON TAPE (SOT). Cut to CHILDREN SHOUTING "SA-DAT, SA-DAT" FOR 3 or 4 SECONDS.)
> And the police and security troops – thousands of them – were also getting ready. Hours before Sadat was due to arrive, people started to gather along the welcome route through the heart of the city. And it was difficult to find anyone who doesn't approve of Sadat or his peace mission. One Cairo university student seemed to sum up the feelings of the majority of Egyptians, be they poor or rich, educated or uneducated. . . .
> (UP SOT Cut to MAN-IN-STREET FOR 23 SECONDS.)
> The crowds waited into the night to see President Sadat. It was a tumultuous welcome. As one man put it: "We never dreamed that our President would one day go to Jerusalem."

My story merited ninety seconds on the air.

And so, the first episode of "Peace: Weekend in Jerusalem", starring Anwar Sadat, had captured the imagination of the world, i.e. the hearts and minds of Americans, the Egyptian star's new, vital constituents. And since ABC, CBS and NBC – not the State Department or the White House – had helped stage the drama, it was imperative that we sustain it to the glorious or bitter end. In the time it takes to charter a plane, and the TV networks would charter many of them in the months ahead, we, like Sadat, had embarked on a flight of no return. "Weekend in Jerusalem" could not simply fade-out like an old B-movie, only to resurface years later on the "Late Show". On TV's evening news it would "fade to black" just long enough to sell another product during the commercial break, and gear up production for the next day's episode.

Sadat, interestingly enough, wanted to be a professional actor and once played comedy and tragedy on the Cairo stage. That was before he helped overthrow King Farouk and the British and entered the real world of political drama and intrigue. As an actor he said he preferred comedy to tragedy. It would be necessary to see the rest of the peace play before determining whether Sadat's latest role would fit the comic or tragic mould. I suspected that his innate talent for both genres would produce a comi-tragic performance. In any event, being an addict of American westerns and war films, and a former newspaper editor, he knew a good story when he saw one. Now he was playing in his own diplomatic *coup de théâtre*, or, to use one of his own definitions, performing "electric-shock" diplomacy. And since the powerful medium of television was chosen to convey his message, a cast of hundreds was on location in Cairo and Tel Aviv, in addition to the supporting players permanently based in Washington, and in New York – the major production centre and clearing house. Sadat had all the qualities of a leading man and a phenomenal pitch: peace. We in TV news found him as irresistible as he found us, and before the year was out, the infatuation would turn to love and a relationship of mutual manipulation. For now, "Weekend in Jerusalem" – with all its passion, romance and forbidden pleasures – was being viewed by most members of Sadat's Arab family as a lost weekend. To them it appeared that by simply going to Jerusalem and thereby recognizing the existence of the State of Israel, with no guarantee of substantial gains in return, Sadat had betrayed them and the Arab cause: the evacuation of all Israeli-occupied Arab territory and the establishment of a national homeland or entity for the homeless Palestinians. The result, then, was shock, silence, anger and violence within the family – which Sadat, as leader of the most populous and powerful Arab state, nominally headed. As far as they were concerned, Egypt had committed adultery and treachery.

Palestinians in Lebanon and Syria set off bombs, burned tyres and photographs of Sadat in the streets, hung posters of the traitor wearing an Uncle Sam hat and a Moshe Dayan eye-patch. Libyans burned the flag of the Egyptian-Libyan Federation and the Office of Egyptian Relations in Tripoli. Libya also severed diplomatic relations the moment Sadat's plane landed in Israel. In Damascus, at that same moment, the muezzin's call to prayer rang out in mournful anger from the mosques. And in an official day of mourning, Syria lowered flags to half-mast. The Iraqis, like the Libyans and Syrians, transmitted their furore in daily radio broadcasts announcing that Sadat's days were numbered. (Egypt finally jammed Radio Baghdad.) And angry young Arabs stormed Egyptian embassies in four capitals. And in Tripoli, they burned the embassy to the ground. As for PLO chief Yasser Arafat (Sadat's honoured guest only two weeks previously) he and Sadat would never speak to each other or see each other again. Sadat, who was ambivalent about his "dear friend" Arafat and the PLO, did not mention either in his speech, reportedly at the urging of the Israelis, although he anticipated the furore and ignored it. He did care, though, about what the more influential and significant Saudis thought about his pilgrimage, but he didn't bother contacting them in advance. As Egypt's bankroller and historic guardian of Islam's sacred shrines, Saudi Arabia didn't think much of his peace mission, publicly, claiming it had put the Arab world in a precarious position. But privately, it approved and that's all that mattered to Sadat. He would have preferred the Saudis to show more courage, but appreciated their own delicate position with the PLO and the Palestinians as well as the Islamic holy places, including Arab East Jerusalem. As for Jordan's King Hussein, he neither denounced nor applauded, adopting instead a pragmatic "wait and see" approach.

The fear in the Arab family, of course, was that Sadat would end up making a separate deal with Begin, selling out the rest of the Arabs and the Palestinians in the process. Their fear was understandable, for in spite of Sadat's claim that Jerusalem was only a warm-up (albeit an earth-shattering one) for Geneva, he had no more desire than Begin to reconvene the 1973 Geneva Peace Conference. To Sadat, Geneva meant procedural obstacles, haggling over who would represent the Palestinians at the talks, and, worse, a Soviet say in the outcome. The Egyptian President, who loathed the Soviet Union, had cut it out of the post-1973 Sinai Disengagement Agreements, and clearly did not want the Soviets involved in formulating any comprehensive Middle East peace. As for his fellow Arabs, who were split into moderate and hard-line camps, Sadat was convinced that their divisiveness – exacerbated by Soviet manipulation of the Syrians and Palestinians – would drag out the peace process interminably. (Equally, Prime Minister Begin feared Israel would be cornered by the hard-line element in Geneva and forced to accept an imposed solution; one that would regard the Palestinians as something more than refugees.) Sadat would not wait that long. He needed peace now. And Egypt with debts of almost fifteen billion dollars, needed peace now if Sadat was to remain in power. Too proud to admit it publicly, privately, the Egyptian President and his aides conceded that the country's devastating poverty, and its one million new mouths to feed every year, propelled him to Jerusalem and back. The two-day January food-price riots that year, which he called an "uprising of thieves" instigated by the Soviets, were in fact a popular uprising by frustrated Cairenes and Alexandrians over the most burning issue to Egyptians. The government was about to remove subsidies on food and other staple items which would have sent prices soaring. The violent riots in which hundreds died made Sadat fear for his regime. A five-and-a-half-billion-dollar Saudi-American band-aid was quickly applied, but the wound would fester until radical surgery was carried out on an Egyptian economy that spent billions to subsidize food staples. Time was running out. Concluding that the Arabs could never defeat the Israelis militarily, and that defence outlays during the state of no war – no peace, in effect since 1973, were still eating up thirty per cent of Egypt's national budget, Sadat felt he was left with little choice. And so, at great political and physical risk, he chose an alternative to Geneva. He gambled on Jerusalem. And the moment he did, he became a marked man, an assassin's target in the larger Arab world if not yet in Egypt itself. But Sadat, like most Arab leaders, had always lived under the threat of assassination. As a devout Moslem, he was a fatalist. If anyone wanted to kill him, "No one," he said, "not the Palestinians, not Ghaddafi can deprive me of one hour of life, if God doesn't want it." Nonetheless, the security net around him increased noticeably on his return from Jerusalem, and eventually the Americans would spend twenty-five million dollars to help guard his life. The United States, as taken aback as anyone by Sadat's peace mission, had no choice but to support it, especially as Sadat had always maintained that the US "holds ninety-nine per cent of the cards in the Middle East" poker game. But because the Americans did not want a separate peace any more than the Arabs, they worried privately that Sadat's volatile mix of statesmanship and showmanship might prove to be sheer brinkmanship, hurtling everyone involved deeper into the Middle East abyss. "Weekend in Jerusalem", then, while it inspired genuine euphoria at the grassroots level in Egypt, Israel and America, and a somewhat more cosmetic euphoria at the official level, did not mean peace was at hand. Perhaps it simply meant, as Israel's *grande dame*, Golda Meir suggested, that "both Sadat and Begin deserve Oscars" for their Hollywood-style performances.

3. Getting the show on the road

WITH THE WORLD at his feet, and American TV crews at his door, it didn't look good for an "Oscar" winner to have the PLO after his head. So, the next day, Anwar Sadat got rid of the Palestine Liberation Organization, at least in Egypt. And that took care of our story out of Cairo for November 22. Apart from the fact that his peace mission had exhausted him (his normal work pace being considerably more leisurely), Sadat was not about to tarnish his new hero-peacemaker image by going before the cameras himself, on such a tawdry issue as the PLO purge. Still without a foreign minister after the previous week's defections of, first, Ismail Fahmy, then Mohammed Riad, it was left to the acting Foreign Minister Butros Ghali to fill in for the President on that night's TV shows at home and abroad.

The Foreign Ministry building – an elegant early 20th-century relic of the King Fuad era – conveniently situated in the heart of Cairo, not far from the ABC bureau, attracted the scrambling world media. Now at full strength, they were on call round the clock to record just such events for millions of viewers, who, judging by the money and manpower being expended for their benefit, were hungry for any post-Jerusalem titbit we could produce. The cool, self-effacing Ghali, with his slight, stooping frame and the dark intense look of the academic intellectual, complete with horn-rimmed glasses, was the antithesis of the ebullient Sadat. In Ghali's debut as public spokesman, his French was better than his English; he was ill at ease in the spotlight; and his delivery betrayed none of the inflexion and pacing of either the born actor or the man of history. In short, "Dr Butros", as we came to refer to him, was bad television. To his credit, the legal expert and ex-economist showed every indication of not giving a damn whether he was good, bad or indifferent television. Sadat did not have to worry about Ghali upstaging him politically or theatrically. "Guess we can't always have Sadat," complained a producer as we screened the Foreign Ministery material. "No," I groaned. "But right now I'd settle for Butros Ghali." In the great media rush to grab Ghali, what we got, in fact, was twenty seconds of pictures showing the acting Foreign Minister rushing between two offices. And what he said, weighing each word, was "no comment" in all its English, French and Arabic variations.

One consolation was that all of us, including CBS and NBC, got precisely the same story. The PLO crackdown had broken late in the day (this would become the pattern of the peace story) but since we had three or four shots of Ghali meeting with Arab League ambassadors that evening, we worked around these pictures to satellite a forty-five-second report.

Well, as a fellow TV correspondent once put it succinctly: "Another day and night: another forty-five seconds." In this case, the time constraints of a daily half-hour show (actually twenty-two minutes), the heavy press of news that day and a lack-lustre, virtually non-existent Butros Ghali standing in for a flamboyant Anwar Sadat, resulted in the bare-bones version which told us that the PLO in Egypt was being eliminated. It was a far more politically significant act than the acting Foreign Minister trying to convince the Arabs that Egypt hadn't sold out; or the speculation of what Sadat would say or do five days hence. What the report didn't tell us, though – couldn't tell us in forty-five seconds – was what Sadat's crackdown on the PLO presence meant in terms of Egypt's traditional and future links with the "sole legitimate representative of the Palestinian people" (1974 Rabat Arab Summit) and what it meant in terms of Sadat's initiative and peace in the Middle East. Even another thirty seconds added to my report, or incorporated into another correspondent's report or analysis, would have been better than nothing.

I would have liked more air-time for the story. Most correspondents on most stories would dearly love to fill the show's entire twenty-two minutes nightly with nothing more than an exaggerated sense of their own self-importance. The high visibility and awesome power of the medium tend to inflate further the already inflated egos of television reporters. But the chicanery in which some daily indulge merely to get their "mug on the tube", i.e. insert their on-camera selves into the top, middle or end of a report, attests to more than the fact that they take themselves entirely too seriously. It tells us that in the business of electronic journalism, the reporter who's seen the most, survives the longest. Having grown up in the less competitive, less star-oriented Canadian broadcasting system, I tend toward the theory that while a reporter should be heard and seen, he or she should be visually injected into a story only if his or her appearance enhances the report, not detracts from it. The living room audience is depressed enough by the day's news without wilfully subjecting it to a superfluous, hair-sprayed sign-off in which the reporter sums up in ten or fifteen seconds on-camera what he or she has already spent sixty seconds saying off-camera. Such gratuitous performances dilute the story and, when they occur, are surely seen by the intelligent viewer as blatant acts of self-indulgence. More precisely, a reporter's presence on-camera is required only when:

a) he or she has something to add to the story and does not want to diminish its impact by overlaying the script with less dramatic, or conflicting, pictures;

b) when no relevant pictures, graphics or other visuals are available to illustrate an otherwise newsworthy story;

c) when the show producers want to emphasize or highlight the reporter's presence on the scene of such stories as natural disasters, assassinations, revolutions, wars or other equally potent events;

d) when a news network has expended considerable time, resourcefulness and money in putting a reporter on location and wants to show the flag, i.e. that we are here (or there); and finally

e) when the reporter has an exclusive. A reporter with a scoop deserves to be rewarded for ingenuity and doggedness with an on-camera appearance. In fact, the occasion begs for it. To hide behind the camera would be a cowardly act.

I was reminded of the impact – positive or negative – created by a correspondent's on-air performance when, the morning after the PLO story went out, I found the following telex cable waiting for me at the bureau:

KAYS WELCOME AND THANKS FOR FINE MAIDEN APPEARANCE
WILL BE LOOKING FORWARD TO SEEING MORE. REGARDS
WESTIN

Five days and four reports after arriving in Cairo, I had received my first *herogram*, for what was, substantially, a rather pedestrian performance. Because the three reaction pieces on Sadat's Jerusalem trip were so visually dramatic, I did not appear on-camera in any of them. The PLO story, on the other hand, was visually weak; consequently, it afforded my maiden appearance and on-the-record recognition. Naturally, I was delighted that the Evening News' executive producer Av Westin was pleased with my forty-five-second debut. When the cataclysmic peace story broke, Westin must surely have had some doubts, whether this untested new Cairo bureau chief – whom he had hired only weeks earlier to produce soft Egyptian news features – could now handle the biggest Middle East story in decades. Even though I was up against more experienced foreign correspondents, it was a sink-or-swim situation that fortunately did not permit me time to worry or fret about whether I was up to the job.

The story had developed such momentum that all one could do was get on with it. This I did with the help and support of a superb team headed by producer-in-charge Pete Simmons, one of television news' finest, most respected field producers. If Westin had no doubts, Simmons did. Since one of his many talents was an ability to consume prodigious amounts of beer day and night and still remain perfectly sober and coherent, I invited him for a drink in the Nile Hilton bar after the nightly satellite transmission. He proved to be perfectly sober, coherent and charming during the first round of Stellas (the local Egyptian beer).

During the second round, he proved less sober, more coherent, and utterly merciless:

"You won't make it," he roared. "I don't know why the f . . . they sent you here. This isn't America or Europe. It's the Arab world where it's tough enough for a western man to operate, let alone a woman."

I let him continue since he seemed to be enjoying himself after an especially frustrating night at the satellite station.

"Furthermore, you can't write. And you're hair's too black for television. I suggest you do something to lighten it, so we'll be able to differentiate between the correspondent's head and the night skyline."

Just when I thought he was winding down his diatribe, he ordered another round and, deciding to soften the blow a bit, added: "I don't blame you so much as I blame the brass in New York for sending a novice on what promises to be one helluva tough story in the months ahead. And a female to boot!"

Simmons then felt the need to stress that he was not a male chauvinist pig, "at least I like to think I'm not," he said. "I'm simply telling you all this for your own good. Don't stay in Cairo. Get them to post you to London or anywhere else. But get the hell out of this madness."

"Have you finished?"

"Yeah, I'm finished. For now."

"Good. Because I'm just about to begin. You want to know why I was sent to Cairo? I'll tell you. In the meantime, better order another round or two because you'll need them."

Fuelled solely by my own rage, I proceeded: "First," I said, "Westin hired me precisely because I'm a good reporter, and because I can write, read and deliver my own lines as good as most and a helluva lot better than some. Second, when the peace story was but a figment of Sadat's imagination, my job as then outlined was to report and ship news features out of Cairo on a regular basis, in addition to the hard news stories if and when they occurred, and if and when the show was interested enough to want them satellited. Third," I continued, "in a bureau without a perm-anently-assigned producer, Westin needed a correspondent who was not only a self-starter but one accustomed to directing and producing stories as well as writing and reporting them – as I have done for more than a decade." As for being a woman in the tough, male-dominated Arab world, I urged him to demolish his largely mythical world, created and perpetuated largely by western men. "You don't know me or the Arabs. I suggest you stick around long enough to find out. The Arab world," I reminded him, "is not a monolith. And if you want a blonde, all-American girl-next-door, I suggest you hire Farrah Fawcett Majors. Otherwise hire another Rupen who at least knows how to light "blacks" in the dark."

The Stellas had worked their magic on Simmons, who seemed to be heavily sedated and probably hadn't heard a word I'd uttered. Since the bartender was dimming the lights for last call, Simmons ordered up another, allowing me a final say:

"Let the audience out there decide whether I'm any good. After all, isn't the audience what the almighty ratings are all about?" It was enough to stir him out of his stupor. "F--- the audience," he bellowed. "You're living in a dream world if you think it's the audience you have to please or cater to. There's only one person you have to please in this business and his name is Roone Arledge, your president and mine. Our audience. Keep him happy and it won't matter what you, me or anyone else thinks. And don't you forget it!"

On that trenchant note, we shut down the bar and shuffled off . . . me suffering from deep depression; Simmons from too much beer and me. We parted at the elevator door – Simmons, to sober up for another challenging day; me, to contemplate suicide by jumping into the Nile from my balcony.

Over the next two weeks, I received the following cables:

YOU'RE DOING GREAT. KEEP UP THE GOOD WORK
REGARDS
WESTIN   (December 6)

KAYS YOU CONTINUE TO DO SUPERIOR WORK
MANY THANKS
WESTIN   (December 8)

DEAR DOREEN
AM VERY IMPRESSED WITH YOUR WORK. THRILLED TO HAVE YOU
ABOARD. KEEP UP YOUR HIGH LEVEL OF EXCELLENCE. KINDEST
PERSONAL REGARDS
ROONE ARLEDGE   (December 9 1977)

Simmons and I celebrated.

With Sadat back in Cairo, our Ramses Street bureau was no longer an oasis of tranquillity, order or efficiency. It had become a microcosm of the overburdened city. If we were to continue accommodating the peace story and the more than two dozen bodies now covering sequels, we would need more than three small rooms; one red, more-dead-than-alive telephone; one news agency ticker (Reuters) that regularly failed to tick; and one neurotic telex that spluttered indignantly each time it was called upon to convey several metres of obscenity-laden messages to London and New York. The day after the most acerbic of these messages was cabled, Simmons received carte blanche to remedy the situation. We promptly abandoned primitive Ramses Street and its red monster for the more opulent, spacious and serviceable quarters of the Presidential Suite at the Meredien Hotel. Here we were on the fashionable Corniche-el-Nil in the heart of Cairo, not far from the presidential compound, the Foreign Ministry, the Egypt TV-radio centre, other government offices, hotels, Cairo's worst traffic bottleneck and our former home, Ramses Street. The view from our fourteenth-floor balconies included Sadat's Giza residence and helipad, directly across the narrow Nile. And since the hotel is situated on the man-made island of Roda in the middle of the Nile, its architect had the foresight and sensitivity to place all rooms and their balconies overlooking the river, providing a panoramic feast of a city whose exotic beauty is often best appreciated from an altitude that allows the uninitiated to absorb its vibrant sights, sounds and smells without being overwhelmed by them; in Cairo the western sensibility can cope better with seduction at a distance rather than rape on the ground.

Our new, temporary bureau came with built-in makeshift studio facilities: two large balconies where the correspondents (we were now three, including Peter Jennings who'd been in Cairo since shortly after Sadat's "ends of the earth" speech) could record their on-camera pieces against a skyline backdrop of "Cairo-along-the-Nile". When all was said and done, though, Cairo-along-the-Nile looked for all the world no different from New York-along-the-Hudson, London-along-the-Thames or any other river-city in the world, especially at night. In the on-camera segments shot in daylight, the intensity of the cloudless Egyptian sunlight virtually obliterated the skyline, and often the correspondent's face with it. The natural light was, in technical jargon, too hot to allow a cameraman to produce an image that bore any resemblance to reality. Where possible, then, we avoided high-noon shooting in favour of early morning or late afternoon.

In the early months following the peace mission, there were usually twice-daily satellite transmissions to New York, booked by the three American networks who split the $3,000 cost: one feeding material for "Good Morning America" and other breakfast shows; the second for the evening news programmes. Since the late "bird" – as we referred to the satellites – flew around midnight or 1:00 a.m., Cairo time, and since it was imperative that our reports contain the latest, up-to-date information, more often than not the on-camera pieces had to be shot at night-time. The result was that Cairo-along-the-Nile, with its brightly-lit mosques and towering minarets, its shimmering waters and silent bridges of flickering traffic dots, came across as "midnight in a desert sky". And when I was included, it was more "midnight in a desert sky with a Bedouin".

The one alternative was to hit the pavement. But shooting in the streets of Cairo, day or night – lighting considerations aside, proved even less effective and considerably more time-consuming than the balcony sets which we dubbed Studios A and B. Under such primitive studio conditions (normal on-location facilities) one has no access to make-up artists, hair-stylists, tele-prompters, kleig lights or any of the other accoutrements of a planned, controlled television scene. And because of the ready access to Egypt's sun, sand, noise, dirt and congestion, plus the eighteen-hour days, we tended to look dishevelled, harried and baggy-eyed, mirroring the frustration of trying to cope in a crumbling city. But the Presidential hotel suite, with its four enormous luxuriously furnished rooms, wall-to-wall carpeting, two baths, air-conditioning and round-the-clock room service, was a start. With the proper psychological environment, Simmons set to work building a functional structure. Within forty-eight hours we had four working telephones, one working telex, a dozen chauffeur-driven cars (mostly Mercedes) providing a twenty-four-hour personalized taxi service; two bright, efficient Arabic-English-French-speaking translators-researchers-secretaries; two Cairo-based, Arabic-speaking freelance camera crews, in addition to the three TV correspondents, one radio stringer, two producers, four camera crews, two editors, the secretary and of course, Hassan. In short, it was a smoothly-running news operation unequalled by our American and European counterparts, not to mention those of our colleagues labouring primitively for the poorer print medium.

With the mandate and the money – including the *baksheesh* that was liberally dispensed to grease the palms and warm the hearts of the under-paid Egyptian public service sector – everything seemed possible. Almost. Instead of waiting hours or days for a long-distance call to New York or our main overseas London bureau, the friendly, polite telephone operators in the hotel and the international operators at Cairo central exchange, now – miraculously – put us through in minutes. Simmons had done what every good field producer does on a foreign story in the Middle East and the Third World, and that's personally to cultivate the goodwill of the local telephone, telex and radio-TV personnel. Without their co-operation and assistance, reporting a story for television would become an academic exercise. But nothing, not money (over or under the counter), political or personal manipulation or temper tantrums, could fix the internal communications system. It was impossible to dial certain districts in Cairo, let alone other Egyptian cities. What circuits existed were either overloaded or worn thin through generations of use, and the infrequent arrival of a dial tone was greeted first with jubilation, only to be followed by exasperation at hearing "Sorry, wrong number." The only consolation was that these monsters were painted anonymous grey instead of fire-engine red. None-theless, the overnight transformation of our news bureau made life much more palatable for those of us destined to hang on for daily developments of Sadat and his peace. Those people included me and Simmons, who by now had developed a new respect and appreciation for each other's talents.

It was as though President Sadat realized the media needed a breathing period to get their act together. He continued to keep a low profile as he plotted his next move behind the heavily-guarded, concrete walls of his Giza residence, which, much to his chagrin, was located next to the large, modern Soviet embassy whose antennaed roof resembled an inter-planetary Skylab. Having taken care of the PLO, Butros Ghali's next job was to find out where the rest of the Arabs stood, now that Sadat felt he had smoothed their way to Geneva and peace. Based on their public reactions so far – vitriolic name-calling and fierce condemnation from

Syria and other hardliners; and an equivocal "wait and see" from moderate Saudia Arabia and Jordan – Sadat knew Geneva was out of the question. And given his thoughts on the matter before Jerusalem, he must have been relieved to wash his hands of it once and for all. He had to know Cairo would be no more attractive than Geneva. In fact less so, given his electric shock solo to Jerusalem. Yet . . .

> Less than a week after President Sadat made his historic visit to Israel, he went back today (November 26) before the Egyptian Parliament in another step toward peace.
>
> President Sadat's speech – his first to the country since he announced he would go to Israel – was televised live from the Egyptian Parliament. And Sadat delivered – as expected – his follow-up proposal for a Middle East settlement. He is inviting all participants in the conflict to talk peace – here in Cairo – as early as next Saturday, if possible. In what seems to be an effort to bypass lengthy Geneva talks, Sadat wants an international discussion to start immediately and to produce results quickly. The President also attacked his Arab critics, especially Syria. He would like to see the Syrians in Cairo, along with Israel, the United States and the Soviet Union. But he made it clear that the talks would go on with or without them. Syria has promptly turned down the invitation. As for the delicate issue of Palestinian representation, the President slammed the door in the face of the PLO and opened it up to representatives from the West Bank . . . which should please the Israelis. After his speech, Sadat flew to Ismailia where a large, enthusiastic public welcome greeted him. The President is expected to stay in the area much of next week, returning to Cairo . . . perhaps just in time for his proposed Cairo peace talks. (ABC Evening News. November 26, 1977)

Rebuffed by the Arabs, Sadat's response was, in effect, "damn you all to hell". As I left the National Assembly with the camera crew I wondered who, if anyone, would come to Sadat's peace parley after he'd insulted half the guests. Then I realized that it didn't matter. At least not to Sadat. The important thing was that he was back in the news, performing peace, holding centre stage, maintaining the "momentum" – to use one of his favourite English words. Unfortunately, Cairo's Kubbah Palace satellite station was not equipped to keep up with Sadat's momentum or ours.

If Anwar Sadat's peace initiative was pure theatre, our TV transmissions of the unfolding drama were vintage vaudeville: a revival of American theatrical entertainment in its heyday, complete with Marx Brothers and magicians. Those of us who day and night played "peace at the Palace" (New York's famous vaudeville theatre of the '30s) seemed to fly on nothing more than a magic carpet, more times than one has a right to recall. The sideshow's opening routine never varied, and the trip from the centre of Cairo to the city's north-east sector was always hair-raising. There, in the middle of dusty dilapidation, stood the multi-acred Kubbah Palace, another monarchical relic that few Egyptians saw in royal times, and fewer still under the more egalitarian-nationalist regimes of Gamal Abdel Nasser and Mohammed Anwar el-Sadat. While it was a magnificent museum piece, it was not a museum but rather a semi-retired official government guest house/hotel for visiting Arab heads of state. Why one decrepit, less than royal wing was converted into a satellite station in honour of President Nixon's hero's welcome in 1974, was as much a mystery to us as it was to its somnolent armed guards. After waving us to a screeching halt at the entry checkpoint, they would, even after three months, refuse to wave us any further. Our forty-five-minute journey to Kubbah (twenty-five-minutes if the driver followed our "dead-or-alive" order) invariably ended with a bayonet-tipped "*Mumnouh!*" (Forbidden) which one came to assume was the only Arabic word these parrots picked up in basic training. Our arrival became a ritual featuring Arabic insults and English obscenities, all from our side of the barrier. We were always asked who we were and where we were going; the spelling of our names bore only a slight resemblance to the Egyptian spellings on the white piece of paper authorizing entry; and our special passes were as unfamiliar to the palace protectors as our daily – sometimes twice-daily-faces. Finally, to win this bizarre game of charades, we had to pretend we were someone other than we were. If they insisted I was Tom Jones, or that Pete Simmons was Carolyn Smith, who were we to argue that we were not and that half the names on their official list had already left Cairo or had not yet arrived, and the other half did not exist? It was obvious that the palace guard simply liked the ring of certain names and sounds, since there was no indication they could either write, read or pronounce them. Once convinced that all was in order, they gave us a typically warm, friendly Egyptian send-off, being consistently better-natured than the foreigners who didn't understand the system. As we charged the few hundred yards to the palace door, I would jot down the next day's false IDs: Simmons would be Ingrid Bergman and I would be Humphrey Bogart and after that we could simply assume the identities of all our favourite cinematic and literary characters. An identity crisis was the least of our problems as we raced up the stairs, tapes in hand, to the first-floor communications centre where Mohammed Wardani, the affable, calm Egypt TV engineer always greeted us as though he were genuinely looking forward to the nervous breakdown ahead.

Cairo traffic permitting, the three network editors had preceded the correspondents and producers and were in the process of pumping life into their respective electronic editing machines, which came equipped with tape decks, monitors, levers, push buttons and all the other unfathomable accessories considered useful in editing videotape television stories. Once everything was plugged in, hooked up and alight, the acrid smell of competition flowed freely through the non-partitioned, unfurnished cubicles that passed for ABC, NBC and CBS editing rooms/studios. That CBS occupied the only room available was offset by the fact that one entire wall and one quarter the space was shared by Egypt TV's satellite console, which was provided to the three networks free of charge. Whatever edge CBS might have enjoyed in the way of physical space was further eroded by the presence of two black antique telephones upon which all three networks depended as their sole means of communication with their New York recording studios. NBC occupied a semi-secluded corridor which sprouted off the main doorway, offering both a degree of privacy and reconnoitering capability, giving their "spies" effortless access to the ABC operation – sandwiched between NBC and CBS and conveniently adjacent to the toilets. That the bathroom appeared not to have been cleaned or visited by a plumber since Richard Nixon's 1974 visit did not deter our competitors from making frequent use of its facilities. Serving as a main thoroughfare, the ABC operation suffered chronic traffic jams which we alleviated periodically by assigning a couple of our own spies to oversee and hear the competing products being assembled under similar slapstick conditions.

These missions were always disguised as legitimate queries about how each network was progressing – time-wise – with their reports and who therefore would be in a position to "feed first on the bird". Learning we would not be scooped (which is what each feared about the other) did nothing to dilute the adrenalin that kept us racing against the clock. Editor, hunched over his machine, fingers flying in search of the best pictures, going forwards, backwards, locating it, locking into an edit, repeating the procedure hundreds of times, would be coaxed, cajoled and comforted by an equally tense producer hunched over him and weighed down with the responsibility of packaging and delivering the required minute or two spot. Having done my bit by now, I would hover nervously in the wings eating a cold, greasy French fry and a cold, under-nourished, over-cooked piece of carry-out chicken that survived the cross-town journey no better than we did. Before dinner, however, the frenetic activity and overriding background noise being generated in our "grand central station" would force me to retreat to the WC, with a long cable and microphone to record my track (a script that is not so much composed as thrown together) on a separate tape cassette which the editor plays on a second Sony, cueing it up simultaneously to the picture cassette so that narration matches video in split second timing. The recording session, during which I would stand as far away from the latrine as possible, hold my nose, take a deep breath and wait for a cue from the editor sitting comfortably on the safe side of the bathroom door, always ended remarkably quickly and without a fluff, on the first take. Whenever New York complained that the track sounded like I was talking out of "the deep end of a barrel", we assured our puzzled colleagues that the hollow ring they were hearing was a perfect reproduction of a bathroom, not a barrel. Always sympathetic, they replied that they could "live with the bathroom" but could we please do something about the "trickling water". "No, terribly sorry," we said, "a malfunctioning toilet is a malfunctioning toilet."

But in an effort to accommodate our long-suffering show producers, we sought a way to eliminate the "strange sounds" emanating from Kubbah Palace, especially as they were noticeably missing from the NBC and CBS reports transmitted on the same satellite line. We tried option two, which took me out of the WC and onto a nearby window-sill where, when I placed my body on the inside and my head and hand-held mike on the outside, the vulgar noises disappeared. In their place was a static, cackle-cackle of walkie-talkies (talkie-walkies to the Egyptian staff) which the networks had imported along with base stations to overcome the local telecommunications problems. As the satellite deadline approached, the two-way walkie-talkie traffic accelerated with ABC, NBC and CBS staffers all trying to communicate with their respective bureaus, several miles away. The varying degrees of success depended on the power of the base station and antennae, and of course on one's proximity to open spaces, such as my popular open window recording studio. New York could never decide which extraneous sound it preferred so we alternated them in the hope that one would grow on them in time. Personally, I found the cackle-cackle of the walkie-talkies less nauseating.

While the editors and producers were still working at breakneck speed constructing their pieces, one of the two black telephones would ring. Taking no chances, a network tape room in New York (ABC, NBC or CBS depending on which one booked the satellite that night) was calling to open up a line to co-ordinate what was usually a one-hour satellite feed. A floating body would be assigned to babble sweet nothings into the receiver on a long-shot chance that a) the telephone line would not be disconnected and b) that New York could hear us, or we could hear them, or both. The shouted monologue that ensued, drove the Kubbah Palace editing teams into apoplexy:

"Hello! Hello! New York! New York! Can you hear me? Are you there New York? Hello! God damn it!! Answer me!!! Operator, GET OFF THE LINE. PLEASE. ..." The bloody line's dead. We've lost the BLOODY LINE!! The phone warmer would slam down the receiver. Five minutes later: "Hello! Hello ... Hello New York! New York!! Can you hear me? I can only barely hear YOU. ... You'll have to shout. Yes SHOUT ... at the top of your lungs. ... scream, shout ... LIKE THIS. Now can you hear ME? (Pause) Bloody hell! Of course we can't F------ call you back. Where do you think we are, Los Angeles, London, Paris? ... Can you hear me? Say Something!! God damn it, we've been cut off again. Operator get off the F------ phone. ... Yes, we're talking to New York ... or trying to. ... You want me to hang up? Because you have a call for me from New York? But I already had New York!!! Ok, Operator, Ok, Ok! Tell you what. I'll hang up if you put the call through and then get off the line. You can't keep interrupting like this!" SLAM.

This screaming performance – repeated several times in the course of the thirty minutes or so leading up to and including the satellite hour – was played against a background of a frantic CBS still trying to finish its report, and a perfectly sane, unflappable Mohammed Wardani. He'd successfully done his bit and produced a network Cairo stand-by logo on his monitors which would show up simultaneously on the New York monitors once the satellite was up and they were patched in. Whether the phones were dead or alive, the network ready to transmit first would rush into the CBS zone and start feeding its report a couple of minutes after the bird was up. If the phones failed to ring again, we fed blind.

Since it was rare to get a "buy" (acceptable quality) the first time around, each report had to be fed several times and in the same haphazard way. Then, when the phones did not fail us, we waited to hear those beautiful words from New York: "Cairo. We have a buy. That's a good night Cairo," which translated means the evening news show received our report and we could leave the satellite station and go home. When the phones did fail us, we good-nighted each other with all the camaraderie of competitors at the finish line. And so another day, another night, another typical peace performance at the Palace. As we picked up our shattered nerves and cassettes, it would be past 1:00 a.m. By 2:00 a.m. we would be back at the bureau. By 9:00 a.m. we would be "staking out" Sadat for another mission impossible.

Many months later – for major news events – the networks were able to bring in and set up a four-wire co-ordination system, with the help of Egyptian telecommunications. This allowed us to talk through a microphone to both New York and London and vice versa, twenty-four hours a day; the same system used by businessmen for international conference calls.

4. Christmas in Ismailia

THE MONTH OF December, 1977 saw Cairo's traffic-flow problem exacerbated by the arrivals of Egypt's new friends, the departures of old ones and the comings and goings of those trying to sort out whoever was left on the fringe. The PLO, Syria, Iraq, Algeria, South Yemen and Libya held a Tripoli Summit called the "Front for Steadfastness and Confrontation" which promptly froze diplomatic relations with Egypt. President Sadat called the Summit "puerile" and having already expelled the PLO from Egypt, promptly kicked out the rest of the Arab hardliners. Some three hundred diplomats representing five embassies packed up and left town. And, while trying to record the Algerians' departure, the crew and I squared off with Algerian security men in a nasty little "steadfast confrontation" of our own. We were hauled off to a police station – located directly across the street from Sadat's Giza Residence – where after contacting the Presidency, our gentlemen interrogators apologized. The Algerians, they explained, were simply a little nervous and angry over their hasty exit. Could we exercise a little more patience and understanding next time? We assured them we could – if the Algerians were ever kicked out again. Hard on the heels of the Arabs were the Soviets and their satellite states who didn't think much of Sadat's peace initiative either. Sadat ordered the shutdown of the Soviet Union's social and cultural centres throughout Egypt, along with consulates in Alexandria, Aswan and Port Said. Bulgaria, East Germany, Poland, Hungary and Czechoslovakia were told to do the same. While the move stopped short of a break in diplomatic relations, it was meant to tell the Soviets they were no longer calling the tune in Egypt and to remind the Americans that peace-hungry Egypt was firmly in the western camp.

Jordan's King Hussein flew from Damascus to Cairo on an Arab house-mending mission and a few hours after he departed, US Secretary of State Cyrus Vance arrived on a similar mission of mediation. Vance – on his third trip to Egypt in ten months and his first since Sadat's Jerusalem visit – told Sadat and the world media that the United States fully supported the peace initiative and wanted to do all it could to keep the momentum going. He would play his part by shuttling off to Riyadh, Tel Aviv and other Middle East capitals. Only hours before the VIPs arrived, tens of thousands of enthusiastic Egyptians poured into the city from all parts of the country. The popular people's march – clearly choreographed by the government – was nonetheless highly emotional and reflective of the genuine support Sadat had been getting from his people since his trip to Jerusalem. The public demonstration which built a human wall around Abdin Palace was just what Sadat ordered and needed after a tough week dealing with his fellow Arabs and the Soviets. As his motorcade swept into the grand courtyard of another royal legacy, the crowds roared, the Republican honour guard snapped to attention and a military band sounded drums and bugles in a manner suitable for this giant among "dwarfs" – which is how from that day forth Sadat would refer to his Arab critics. On entering Abdin, he would acknowledge the acclaim of the crowds for several morale-boosting moments before giving his pep talk. In his speech, he seemed to lose control as the bitterness surfaced for the first time since Jerusalem. Referring to the hardline Arabs, he told his listeners, "The Egyptian people will continue to carry the troubles of the dwarfs on their shoulders," and for his new friend, Israel, there was a word of warning: "Peace, yes. But not at any cost." It was vintage Sadat – the consummate actor – and the people loved it, name-calling and all. But Sadat's real audience was not the agreeable, acquiescent masses before him. His defiant rhetoric was aimed more directly at the Jordanian monarch and the American Secretary of State, at that moment en route to Cairo; and of course, at the western world and the American people in particular, who would see and hear his performance on the news that night. By staging the massive people's rally only hours before his visitors arrived, Sadat was cleverly editing our reports that night: nice, visual up-beat packages mixing cheering mobs and an uncompromising peace speech with pictures of the Egyptian leader meeting with the Jordanian King whom, he hoped, would join his "initiative". While the meeting resulted in "no comment", government sources were saying privately that Jordan hoped to be in a position to join the peace process, after the Cairo Conference.

Secretary Vance's late-night arrival provided the perfect tag-line for the sanguine American television reports: a stay-tuned, coming-up-next teaser. If Anwar Sadat's peace initiative should fail and he kept his promise to step down as President, he would have no trouble landing a job in American television as producer of the evening news. He'd been doing the same job with the Egyptian media for years, with great success.

In order to build his pyramid of peace (Washington-Cairo-Tel Aviv), President Sadat would have to exploit and manipulate the Israeli media as well. It would not be difficult given the hungry, aggressive, enterprising nature of Israeli journalists. Two weeks after Sadat returned home from Israel, an Israeli television producer and correspondent flew into Cairo via Athens, taking the Israelis and Egyptians alike by surprise. They had less trouble with Cairo airport immigration and security than with their own Israeli superiors who refused them permission to go, telling them that if they went to Cairo they were on their own; if they ran into trouble, got themselves killed or fell victim to other embarrassing circumstances, the Israeli Broadcasting Authority would not be responsible. The team left Israel under the pretext that it was flying to Athens and a few hours later it was hard to say who was more stunned, Alex Gilady and Ehud Yaari or their Egyptian camera crew. We found producer Gilady on downtown Adly Street in one of Cairo's two remaining synagogues, filming an event he never dreamed possible in his lifetime. As both the narrator and star in this once-in-a-lifetime story, he became the first Israeli to pray in an Egyptian synagogue; the first to light a candle during the Jewish festival of Hanukah; the first to be greeted by some of Cairo's one hundred and seventy Jews; and the first Israeli television newsman to record it all on film . . . with the help of an Egyptian cameraman and soundman. That only one of the nine Jews present spoke Hebrew did not diminish the tearful enthusiasm of the elderly worshippers for this harbinger of peace.

These Jews – once part of a large, flourishing Egyptian community – now believed that because of President Sadat's Jerusalem trip and the arrival of Israelis like Gilady, they might one day see Jerusalem, after all. As for the Israeli newsman, coming to Cairo was the "warmest, friendliest experience" in a career that had taken him everywhere except to the Arab world. That evening – December 5, 1977 – Gilady and political correspondent Ehud Yaari rushed about the Egypt TV building surrounded by friendly, helpful Egyptians, well aware that they too were making history. Together they assembled the report and in the studio control room, Gilady and Yaari – an Arab specialist – transmitted the first Israeli television report from Cairo via satellite through Paris. Instead of a reprimand from their reluctant bosses, the two intrepid journalists became instant heroes, much to the dismay of their print colleagues who got scooped while trying to outdo one another in filing first-ever reports out of Egypt.

If Yaari and Gilady were the first Israeli-based journalists to report from Egypt, two Israeli women, Tamara Golan and Tullia Zevi – both working for the Israeli daily *Ma'ariv* – lay separate claims to being the first Israeli correspondents accredited to work in the country.

Zevi, Yaari and Golan were joined by about four hundred members of the world media, including a strong contingent of Israeli journalists, who flew into Cairo with the official Israeli delegation to the peace talks. I never saw Zevi again but I was to see a lot of Yaari and Golan over the next four years. And so would President Sadat and Egyptian government officials. In those early days of the peace initiative, the fair-haired, bespectacled Israeli TV Arabist and the red-haired *Ma'ariv* academic turned journalist – often working as a team – gained easy access to every top official who mattered in Egypt. And since they were already on a first-name basis with everyone who mattered in Israel, they quickly became the best-informed peace journalists in town. Yaari's impeccable Arabic (Palestinian-Jordanian dialect) and Golan's exclusively-white wardrobe

(for personal, sentimental reasons) were dramatic accessories to a brilli-
antly incisive, sometimes corrosive style of journalism that neither Sadat
nor his aides could afford to ignore. And having learned the benefits of
leaking news from the masters of the art – the Americans and the Israelis
– senior Egyptian officials like Mustapha Khalil, Butros Ghali and the War
Minister, General Mohammed Abdel Ghany Gamassy, made themselves
available to Yaari and Golan on a daily basis either by telephone or
personally in their offices and homes.

The two peripatetic correspondents regularly got their stories and their
scoops. And the Egyptians got their message out directly to the Israeli
people, over the head of the hawkish Israeli Prime Minister and his
recalcitrant government. This mutual manipulation and exploitation of
news was remarkable only insofar as the manipulators were still officially
in a state of war with each other. And because and in spite of that, Ehud
Yaari and Tamara Golan were well looked after in Cairo in every way!
They stayed at the Shephard's Hotel. (The original, legendary one which
served as a military headquarters for the British during the Second World
War, was set ablaze during the '52 "revolution".) The room service staff
couldn't quite figure out the lady in white. However, they found her polite,
friendly and talkative, especially on the telephone which, in the unlikely
event it was not bugged, proved to be a constant source of fascination to
the chamber maids and waiters. They regularly dropped in to "check-up"
on Madame Tamara with or without their linen or coffee. Golan assumed
they were part-time spies and they assumed she was a Mossad (Israeli
intelligence) agent. And everyone got along just fine. As for her next door
neighbour, Yaari, they were convinced he was a special agent of the Israeli
government. Did he not after all speak fluent Arabic, talk on the telephone
several hours a day to important people like Gamassy and Ghali and when
he wasn't getting information, he was tapping it out on his typewriter, or
listening to Israeli newscasts on his portable radio – in Hebrew, Arabic
and English? The hotel staff was so fond of the charming Yaari that one
or two were always parked outside his door or down the corridor, ready
to rush in with a smile and a Turkish coffee *masbout* (medium sugar), or
more often with "Did you call, Mr Ehud Sir?" noting all the while his
comings and goings and those of his visitors, invited and uninvited, foreign
and Egyptian. Whatever role the Arabian Nights' cast played, they played
it well and not without a touch of humour and sensitivity. No harm should
come to the Israeli. No harm would come to the Israeli. Not in his hotel
room and not in his chauffeured Peugeot (circa 1960) as he travelled
about the city in search of a source and a story.

The Cairo peace talks were a farce. And not a particularly entertaining
one at that. More than half the guests – Jordan, Syria, the PLO, Lebanon
and the Soviet Union – didn't show and those who did – Egypt, Israel,
the United States and the United Nations – gave every indication they

wished they hadn't. But President Sadat, determined not to lose face, insisted that the momentum continue, only to leave the public relations exercise – the selling of peace – to an embarrassed foreign ministry while he retreated to Ismailia to talk "big business" with Ezer Weizman. While the business of peace was being tackled secretly in a cosy presidential hideaway along the Suez Canal, and in Washington where Israeli Prime Minister Begin was outlining his idea of peace to Jimmy Carter, five ambassadorial-level diplomats sat at a round table-for-nine, in a dark wood-panelled oriental supper club staring at one another and the TV cameras, instead of at the preferred belly-dancers who had to be evicted. After the customary five-minute "photo-op" – just long enough to ensure that the media made asses of themselves – we left to do our non-substantive reports on the Mena House front lawn, which the American networks had transformed into a vast garden studio including a mobile, make-shift transmission van for twice-daily live reports. The back lawn was converted into a helipad shuttling delegates wanting to break out of their misery. The flying circus – as we referred to the deployment of supplemental TV troops for major stories – was back in town, spending hundreds of thousands of dollars and hundreds of man-hours for a media event that produced no news but plenty of hazy pictures of the pyramids, in whose shadow we preened and pranced. The one consolation was that the pathetic peace show going on inside was behind closed doors. Oblivious to the temper tantrums, ultimata and surrenders immediately preceding the Conference, the journalists and official spokesmen were content to idle under the palms at the poolside restaurant when they weren't staking out the plate-glass doors for any sign of momentum racing through the hotel lobby.

The best that can be said about the mid-December peace parley was that it was a bad omen: the Egyptians (i.e. Sadat) wanted the name plaques of the five missing peace partners placed on the table as a symbolic reminder to the absentees and the watching world that there would always be chairs for them at the peace table, should they change their minds. But when the head of the Israeli delegation, Eliyahu Ben Elissar saw the PLO plaque, he threatened to go home unless it was removed. After much haggling, the conciliatory Egyptians offered up a compromise: "Palestine". That was no better for the Israelis for whom Palestine was Israel. It took Sadat to solve the dilemma in his own magnanimous manner: no plaques at all. But there remained one more snag and one more Egyptian concession before this parody of peace could begin and end. The Israelis didn't like the colours of one of the nine flags flapping in the light winter breeze in front of Mena House. They demanded it be lowered. Down came the PLO flag . . . and the flags of the four other non-negotiators. Peace by the pyramids, billed as "historic", was a sham; a publicity stunt engineered by Sadat and executed by the media to fill a theatrical gap between "Weekend in Jerusalem" and "Christmas in Ismailia". The international media were so caught up in the momentum of peace that the farcical overtones were lost in the excitement.

Assigned to remain in Cairo, I was spared the disaster of "Christmas in Ismailia", where Menachem Begin failed to produce a sequel equal to Anwar Sadat's no-holds-barred performance in "Weekend in Jerusalem". Having been snubbed by the absence of the Arabs and embarrassed by the nit-picking, intransigent presence of the Israelis at the Cairo Conference – still in process – the Egyptians were not predisposed towards a hero's welcome for Begin on his first trip to Egypt. Having been briefed by the Americans on Begin's counter-offer peace plan, Sadat realized the Israeli leader was not up to playing the hero role, so there would be none of the ceremonial panoply – so important to Begin – that so stirred hearts and minds on Sadat's first trip to Israel, a month earlier. There were no smiles, no embraces, no bands, no bugles, no Israeli flags and no Egyptian President on Begin's arrival at Abu Sweir Airport on Christmas Day, 1977. Only Vice-President Hosni Mubarak, the man good-humoured Egyptians pejoratively labelled *la vache qui rit* (after the bland processed cheese), who could barely muster a smile, let alone a laugh, for Begin whom he was meeting for the first time (Mubarak had stayed behind to look after the shop when Sadat went to Jerusalem). The Israelis, who came bearing gifts – as dictated by protocol – and a little something special for Sadat who was celebrating his fifty-ninth birthday, may have felt like holding on to them as they headed towards their rendezvous with Sadat. Everywhere they looked, he was there – Sadat's distorted face staring out at them from larger-than-life colour posters; primitive hand-drawn portraits of Sadat wearing various military and civilian costumes decorating the streets of Ismailia along with banners proclaiming the "Hero of Peace". But no "Welcome Menachem Begin". That the festive propaganda had been put up days earlier for Sadat's arrival in Ismailia did not dilute the dimensions of the public snub that greeted the Israeli Prime Minister on his first historic trip to Egypt. By the time Begin arrived at the presidential compound, a jovial, gregarious Sadat was oozing with all the charm and warmth of a forgiving father opening up heart and hearth to the prodigal son.

As the talks got underway it was clear neither of them had changed at all. In the name of peace, the Israeli Prime Minister offered up a twenty-six point plan that would have returned much of the Sinai to Egyptian sovereignty, but not the Israeli settlements between Rafah and El-Arish and those between Eliat and Sharm-El-Sheik. In the name of Israeli security, the settlements and an Israeli defence force would have to remain. In the name of Israeli energy needs, the oil fields would be retained. And in the name of justice, Begin proposed "self-government" for the Palestinian inhabitants of the occupied West Bank and Gaza Strip; an administrative autonomy that, in effect, would grant the Palestinians the right to collect their own garbage, control their own sewerage and mind their own business. They would have no legislative, executive or judicial powers and no control whatsoever over the land on which they were living. They would look after themselves. The Israelis would look after the West Bank and Gaza. In effect, Begin proposed de facto annexation of the territory Israel had acquired in the 1967 war; territory that for a lifetime he has considered part of biblical Greater Israel; the land of Judea and Samaria. Begin tied up his peace package with a pretty ribbon: Palestinian "self-government" would be subject to review after a five-year period. And a peace treaty between Egypt and Israel would be signed and sealed until the year 2001 when it would come under review. So much for Sadat's demand for Palestinian "self-determination"; so much for his call to solve the Palestinian problem and get the Israelis to withdraw from the occupied Arab territories; so much for four wars; so much for Sadat's "sacred mission" to Jerusalem; so much for peace.

"You want an Arafat Palestine state?" asked Begin.

"I am not talking about Arafat," Sadat retorted. "The subject is self-determination for the Palestinians. . . . It is in your interest that I continue to be leader of the Arab world. I can finish Arafat off in two weeks. We must have something in hand, otherwise they will stone me." And if Sadat wouldn't get stoned for selling out the Palestinians, the Egyptians would get him on the Sinai: "If I tell my people that Begin wants to leave his settlements in the Sinai and that the Israeli army will protect them, they will stone me. Begin's proposal is not enough for me, especially when I face the whole Arab world." (Haber, Yaari, Shiff, *The Year of the Dove*, Bantam Books, New York, 1979)

The most and the least Sadat wanted out of his second summit with Begin was a "declaration of principles" that would address the Palestinian issue and satisfy the Arabs. He did not get it. What he got was agreement to form two committees, one political, one military; one headed by Egyptian and Israeli foreign ministers, in Jerusalem; the other by Egyptian and Israeli defence ministers, in Cairo. By the afternoon of December 25, the talks were already deadlocked but for the world media, parked at the kerbside, Sadat successfully camouflaged it with characteristic flair: without warning, the Egyptian President jumped into a black Cadillac, got behind the wheel and invited Begin, Dayan and Weizman to join him for a friendly spin through Ismailia. For Egyptian and Israeli security men, it was a nightmare; for the photographers and cameramen, it produced the best pictures of the summit (if they caught up with him) and for the Israelis it was a personally-guided tour of a Canal with which they were all too familiar, and a city they had once devastated. More out of pride than bitterness, Sadat told his passengers: "A million refugees who left due to the War of Attrition have returned to the Canal cities. Ismailia was a pile of rubble, but we rebuilt it. Life here has returned to normal." (Weizman: *The Battle for Peace*) Unfortunately, Sadat's fifty-ninth birthday was not marked by the one gift he so desperately wanted and needed: those "hard and drastic decisions" from Begin.

That the Israelis stayed the night rather than fly home as planned, was not a good sign, as the media speculated, but a last-ditch effort by Sadat to salvage the summit. By the afternoon of December 26, in anticipation of some historic breakthrough, the American TV networks who were sharing a makeshift mobile van were frantically testing a cable laid down by Egypt TV and the telecommunications people in a first-ever effort to transmit live via satellite from Ismailia. That experiment worked little better than the Sadat-Begin summit, or their joint news conference, which papered over the stalemate with jokes. A confident-sounding Sadat went so far as to predict a peace agreement with Israel in two months.

As the media circus and the principal players made their way gloomily back to Cairo and Tel Aviv, Sadat's social secretary tipped off ABC as to the President's plans that evening. He would be attending a private, lavish wedding in his Giza neighbourhood. As we set out from our relatively deserted hotel suite/bureau, the crew and I glanced at the lonely cold cuts passing for a day-late Christmas dinner that ABC News President Roone Arledge had so generously insisted we have, and counted our blessings. One of us mumbled "Merry Christmas to you, too," to no one in particular and out we went in pursuit of Anwar Sadat.

A cloud hung over the double-wedding reception of the son and daughter of Sadat's old family friends. Painful memories resurfaced. The father of the family – General Abdel Hakim Amer – had "committed suicide" in the wake of the ignominious 1967 Arab defeat at the hands of the Israelis. Now his two children were marrying in a double ceremony and though Sadat had had a tiring, disappointing day, he felt a familial, patriarchal obligation to honour the newly-weds with his presence. Determined to find out just how badly Sadat's day had gone, I smothered my aversion to lavish Egyptian weddings acquired on my first night in Cairo and proceeded to fight my way into the wedding of the year. It was hard to say which was more obscene: the opulent elegance of the thousand-guest, upper-class ritual going on inside the multi-coloured marriage tent, or the battle outside between me and Egyptian security. They kept insisting that our little group of five, plus gear, was not on the guest list. I kept insisting politely that there had to be some mistake. Our discreet contact was nowhere in sight, having remained at home for his own protection and comfort. The security detail, including several police officers, the presidential guard and a dozen of Sadat's personal bodyguards, were still unfamiliar with the aggressive, competitive ways of American TV news. So, after their first *mumnouh* (forbidden) they tried ignoring us in the hope we would quietly disappear. I tried convincing them we were glamorous, powerful people. I considered telling them about my fan mail until I realized it consisted of kudos from ABC and one primitively-written letter from a psychopathic sexual pervert in California. To them, glamour and power meant sequins and diamonds and I was sparkling in neither. By the second hour, security realized we were there to stay as they saw me accosting guests to whom I had turned in locating someone who could right this terrible wrong.

From there I moved into a pouting, sulking stage attempting to match security's every contemptuous, arrogant and disdainful gesture. There are times for a reporter to display haughtiness and childish behaviour. This was not one of them. So, in frustration, I started cajoling and threatening in a loud voice, suggesting to a couple of the more insufferably obnoxious types that they would regret their little oversight, that perhaps they didn't realize that the man they were so assiduously protecting might want to talk to ABC, might have something important to say to the American people?

To their credit, they chose to ignore my absurdly presumptuous pitch. At this point, I felt like packing it in and going home to the cold cuts. But I decided to give it a final go. I pulled out my trump card: the guilt trip. Desperate and angry, I started shouting in both Arabic and English that "I have better things to do with my time than cool my heels on a Cairo kerb during the Christmas holiday season. Of course we were invited to this wedding. How else would we learn of it, and now we're simply being treated like scum! Off the street!" Then, in a final flourish of exasperation I asked: "If we're not invited guests, what are we, terrorists?"

Presidential security men get the jitters at the very mention of the word. It did the trick. They were about to send the raving reporter packing when Sadat's chief bodyguard materialized, ending their three hours of terror. He ushered us inside, semi-apologetically: "*Malesh* (never mind). Welcome. Welcome. Please have a seat." All a dreadful mistake. Terribly decent of him, considering we were common crashers. At this point I would have stayed cooped up in that tent until New Year if necessary. For (coup of coups) the dreaded competition, CBS and NBC were nowhere in sight. In fact, the international and local media were probably either too busy writing their summit stories, or pretending it was Christmas, to bother us. My dignity lay in shreds on the doorstep but I had an exclusive on my hands and I wasn't about to let it slip through my fingers.

As guest of honour, Sadat was sitting front-row centre, smoking his pipe, drinking his juice and being entertained by some of Egypt's finest musicians, singers and dancers. The bridal couples were on pedestals left and right of a stage. The crew was disguising our real mission by over-shooting colourful Egyptian wedding cutaways. And I was plotting my next move. It would be tasteless, I thought, to attempt an interview while the festivities were in full swing. It would be equally tasteless to ambush the President on his way out. This was neither the place nor the time for vultures. I would have to introduce myself in advance and seek his permission to pose a few questions on his departure. The President had been seeing and hearing a lot of me that month and since I was going to be in town a while, it was a good opportunity to present my credentials. Unfortunately, Egypt's renowned belly-dancer, Nagwa Fouad, appeared to be monopolizing Sadat's attention. Given the stiff competition, I waited out Nagwa's final undulating movement before making my own. It was a hard act to follow. But it was now or never. Crouching in order to face the seated Sadat, I announced my mission:

"Good evening, Mr President. Forgive me for disturbing you. I'm Doreen Kays, ABC News' new Cairo bureau chief."

He continued to smile, nod and puff contentedly on his pipe, which encouraged me to tell him in my best Arabic that I was an Arab girl whose parents came originally from Lebanon. Egyptians are not especially enamoured of Lebanese accents, even less of Lebanese–Canadian ones. I quickly switched back to English. Lest he forget my real nationality, of course.

"Would you be so kind, sir, as to answer a few questions later, as you are departing?"

"Why not?" He nodded and smiled, enthusiastically, still puffing his troubles away on what I kept thinking of as his "peace pipe". "Yes. Yes, but of course." He finished with a flashing double-wink smile, the one in which he shut both eyelids briefly. It came to be one of his trademarks in American television appearances.

"Thank you so much, President Sadat. You are most kind!"

I was so pleased by his affirmative response that while I was taking my leave I must have taken leave of my senses as well. Why else would my right hand be patting Anwar Sadat's right knee? However innocent or instinctive the gesture, it is *mumnouh* for women to go about patting the knees of strange men. Especially in the Arab world. Especially the knees of an Arab head of state, however magnetic.

Since his face registered neither shock nor offence at my faux pas I have long since decided that Sadat either had the wisdom and discretion to pretend it never happened, or he was too preoccupied with Menachem Begin and himself even to have noticed. In any event, at the end of a long day and night – past midnight – I got my exclusive interview. Anwar Sadat acknowledged that yes, indeed, Begin's peace plan was a great disappointment. On the other hand, he was quick to add that he did not expect peace to come overnight. One had to be patient, he urged. It was the first of many times he would talk of patience for peace over the next four years. It was also the first indication that whatever the obstacles, whatever the results, whatever the cost, he was not going to abandon the five-week-old affair he had started in Jerusalem, however tumultuous it promised to be.

That night's effort earned me one minute thirty seconds of air-time, and a *herogram*.

Christmas in Islamic Egypt can be a lonely celebration even if one remembers to pack a couple of cans of cranberry sauce, a silver bell and some artificial snow spray between the underwear. For the country's Moslem majority, it is business as usual and for the seven million or so Coptic Christians, Christmas is Old Christmas which, according to the Eastern Julian calendar, is January 6. So the foreign Christian community numbering several thousand do the best they can with what they have in the privacy of their own homes, be it Yorkshire pudding, American butter-ball turkeys, gifts, decorated trees, or Santa Claus. Spirited partying could be fuelled by seemingly adequate supplies of spirits bought from embassy stocks or, in the case of journalists, from a downtown Cairo duty-free shop where our allotted monthly quota of thirty-five dollars produced – over an accumulated two or three months – a respectable tradition among friends. But I recall only one such celebration and the Christmas season of 1977 was distinctly not it. That it began in tears and ended in a provocative piece of TV diplomacy places it in the "memorable" category, along with New Year in Tehran, 1979 (the American hostages story) and Christmas-New Year in Algiers, 1980 (American hostages freed story).

The tears surfaced the week before Christmas during eighteen-hour days that in a month of eighteen-hour days differed only in one respect: a telephone call and a cable from the foreign desk in New York, announcing who could go home for the holidays and who could not. Since we were sitting on a breaking story, several bodies would have to hold the fort, including, not unreasonably, the new Cairo bureau chief. Producer-in-charge Pete Simmons, who had been away several weeks from his London base, had a long-standing commitment and request for home leave back in the States. He was freed and while we would miss his strong, steady hand and colourful language, he'd been on the road much of that year and there was unanimous agreement that no one had worked harder or deserved the break more. Among those who found themselves on the "Christmas in Cairo" list was ABC's State Department correspondent Barrie Dunsmore, who was visibly upset at learning the news. My sympathy went out to him as he explained to the love of his life – a Washington-based ABC producer – that he could not be with her as hoped. She was in a Washington hospital suffering from a potentially fatal spinal ailment and Barrie, fearing she might die, desperately wanted to be by her side. In order to hear and make himself heard, he had taken the telephone out on the balcony which provided him no more privacy since his shouts and screams echoed across the Nile and back. About thirty minutes later, in his disappointment and frustration – exacerbated by a bad connection and frequently no connection at all – he slammed down the phone and stormed out of the bureau, virtually in tears. Figuring he might need a shoulder to cry on, I rushed after him, convinced that the best therapy for one's own misery is to share someone else's, at least when one is thousands of miles from home. So he talked and I listened, refraining from playing Polyanna. Dunsmore, a Canadian who had "paid his dues" over fifteen years in Canadian and American broadcasting, had a solid reputation as a respected journalist, one of the best. But his career in the ephemeral world of television had its political ups and downs and with ABC News' new president and mandate, he felt himself in a down period and was thus reluctant to push his case. Being the professional he is, he remained in Cairo where he did some superb reporting, bolstering his image in the eyes of President Roone Arledge, and his career. Eventually he got back to Washington. And eventually his woman-friend recovered.

There was a day's delay before self-pity set in and I realized I didn't much fancy spending Christmas in Cairo myself. Maybe it was the peace charade at Mena House. Or the ritual Friday noon stakeouts at local mosques where we would ambush Sadat, Sadat's bodyguards would ambush us, and Sadat lost in cables and lenses, would sanguinely speak of peace. Or maybe it was that sandstorm on the road to Alexandria.

In fact there are two roads: the Delta Road and the Desert Road, both lethal. The Delta Road – so named because it follows the narrow, fertile Nile Valley all the way from Cairo to the coastal Mediterranean city – is meant to be a two-lane paved highway for two-way traffic. Instead, it is a track of pavement that seems to carry the full weight of Egypt's burdens on its shoulders, including, not infrequently, contorted metal remains and crushed corpses. One does not so much ride the Delta Road as fly it, without benefit of radar, through a maze of cars, trucks, buses, tractors, donkey carts, bicycles, chickens, hens, goats, children, *fellaheen* (farmers) and the day's agricultural produce. The kamikaze way to Alex takes about four hours. If one survives. Personally, I prefer death in the desert to death in the delta, even during the summer inferno.

In winter, sections of the Desert Road disappear in blinding sandstorms as producer Arnie Collins, a camera crew and I discovered as we set out one beautiful afternoon to cover Israeli Defence Minister Weizman meeting his Egyptian counterpart, War Minister Gamassy in Janaklis, near Alex. The road, which begins a few hundred metres southeast of the pyramids and runs parallel to a military camp, did not appear menacing as we sped past a checkpoint and cruised along at ninety miles an hour on to the relatively traffic-free stretch of highway (there are no speed limits in Egypt). We had the additional luxury of travelling in two chauffeur-driven Mercedes which gave us the comfort of enjoying the cool desert surrounding us. The soothing rays of the December sun acted as a tranquilliser and I dozed off. An hour later, I awoke to find no desert, no road, no moving car, no driver, no colleagues. I looked out the car window and realized the desert had turned on us in all its winter ferocity. I stepped outside to zero visibility and spitting sandballs, as big as hailstones, ricocheting off my face. I could hear Collins and the drivers trying to communicate through the swirling sand, and followed their voices. I found them standing between the two cars which had conked out simultaneously, clogged to death with sand. The last thing we needed was a visiting cameraman from Cleveland on his first trip outside Ohio. Apparently, he managed to panic himself into apoplexy at our predicament. "Obviously there's only one solution," he roared. "We gotta find us a garage! A gas station! A mechanic! There's gotta be one around here somewhere!"

Collins and I ignored the "ugly American" who was by now clutching his bottle of Evian in the belief, no doubt, it would save him in any ensuing battle for survival. At one point we considered dumping him in the desert, abandoning him and his bottled water, but our humanitarianism took over and we tackled the real problem: how to get back to Cairo since the road to Alexandria was impassable. It was also deserted. The drivers let their engines cool for an hour and after a little masterly tinkering, the stalled vehicles ignited into sound and motion allowing us to turn around and crawl home.

Back in the bureau, Collins authorized ABC payment to repair the damage: rechroming of two Mercedes cabs. Nothing could be done about Weizman and Gamassy. As for the man from Cleveland, he ran out of Evian and I haven't seen him since.

Maybe that's what it was. Whatever it was, the night after Dunsmore's poignant "Christmas in Cairo" scene, I had just finished writing a script when I found myself unable to suppress the tears threatening to spill on the typewriter, so I raced out of the bureau for a couple of moments' solitude in the hotel corridor. Unfortunately, Dunsmore spotted me and, sensing I was upset, ran after me. "I cried on your shoulder," he insisted, "the least you can do is cry on mine." I did. But if the Cairo Christmas of '77 was not especially happy for any of us, it was a successful one. Particularly for ABC News.

On the morning of December 29, an urgent cable and phone call from New York alerted the bureau to a television interview the previous night in which President Carter told four correspondents that he didn't think much of the idea of a Palestinian state. A transcript of the highlights of Carter's extemporaneous remarks immediately followed. He was quoted as saying that in his opinion "permanent peace can best be maintained if there is not a fairly radical, new independent nation in the heart of the Middle Eastern area". Carter seemed to praise Begin for his flexibility, calling his plan for Palestinian self-rule "a big step forward". As for President Sadat, Carter said, "so far he is insisting that the so-called Palestinian entity be an independent nation". On the basis of these excerpts I was pulled off a military story that had taken three weeks to arrange. That morning, for the first time in living memory, the Egyptian defence ministry was to provide ABC with exclusive access to an army base – more importantly, access to War Minister Gamassy and military contacts that would serve me well in the future. Our cancellation was not appreciated and it was months before the insulted military gave us another crack at their bases. Gamassy, an intelligent, serious man not given to media hype, refused all interview requests from that day forward.

So, armed with the "Carter" cable, I reluctantly went out to "get Sadat". My CBS competitor John Sheahan and his crew were already at the Giza compound gates when we arrived. He was not overjoyed to see us and we engaged in small talk for fear of tipping each other off as to the purpose of our respective missions. During the hour or so it took to gain admission, no other media representatives showed, probably because no one was much interested in watching Sadat receive the latest in a procession of visiting Americans who came daily bearing gifts, scrolls, citations, awards, state rocks and floral emblems. I can't recall who – apart from us – was idolizing Sadat that morning but it was not the evangelist from Kansas who got carried away and kissed the President twice. On the lips. It was on the pretext of recording whatever intimate embrace of the hero of peace was scheduled that we gained entry and found ourselves in one of the Giza salons Sadat used for such occasions.

We dutifully shot some film of the Egyptian leader and his visitor, both of whom performed adequately for our cameras. The visitor took his leave and before Sadat's bodyguards suggested we do the same, we asked the President if he would be so kind as to answer a few questions. He did not appear reluctant so we plunged in with microphones and umbilical cords. It was clear from the thrust of John Sheahan's first couple of questions that he was not *au courant*; that he knew nothing of President Carter's remarks and had come to Giza hoping for an exclusive interview with Sadat on the general subject of peace. I waited respectfully and anxiously before interrupting them:

> KAYS: Can you reply to President Carter's statement last night at a news conference in which he said he did not support your demand for an independent Palestinian state?
>
> SADAT: He did not support me? Very well. He may be taking a neutral position but this is my view and I can't say at all that Carter has agreed with me about this, no. To be fair, no. But this is my view until this moment. . . .

The Egyptian embassy in Washington obviously did not feel President Carter's Palestinian comments were worth writing home about, so I pressed Sadat while at the same time briefing him:

> KAYS: Mr President, President Carter, also at his press conference last night, in not supporting your demand for a Palestinian state, did seem to side with Prime Minister Begin's peace plan . . . for limited self-rule. Does this come as a surprise to you?
>
> SADAT: For sure . . . I don't think anyone would oppose the word "self-determination". This is an appealing word. I don't know why Carter has done this but he has a right to have his own ideas like I have and the Israelis have. But let us hope that in the near future we can try and reach a solution.
>
> KAYS: Perhaps it is just a question of semantics — homeland or independent state.
>
> SADAT: . . . When I met my people yesterday through the television I could say there has been some step that has been achieved after my visit to Jerusalem and the talks in Ismailia

in the field of the Palestinian question. We are now differing or quarrelling among each other in Israel and here in Egypt because they are speaking of some sort of autonomy or self-determination. This in itself is a great progress, a great leap because forty days before my visit to Jerusalem no one knew what would be the fate of the Palestinians. Begin and his government, the opposition and everyone in Israel used to say that this is an Israeli land that has been liberated. If after forty days such a leap takes place and the differences between some sort of autonomy and self-determination, I consider this great progress and a great leap and very encouraging for the future.

KAYS: Aren't you disappointed by President Carter's latest statements?

SADAT: For sure I'm disappointed. For sure because I should like that we put all our efforts towards ending the suffering in this problem in the Middle East and giving the bright future for our next generation. This would take both of us sometime, because we have to reopen the whole issue again.

KAYS: You were talking in terms of two months. You said that an agreement could be signed in two months. Do you now see that this has been delayed and could take much longer?"

SADAT: It may be hindered for some time, but I think I can say that quoting '78 as the year of decision, I'm not exaggerating."

Sheahan then asked the Egyptian President if the American President's statements might make the job of negotiating more difficult.

SADAT: Well for sure, it will make it more difficult for me because Carter himself is a dear friend and he has my full trust . . . but, he is making my job very difficult, Carter is.

Sadat nonetheless added: "We're not going to chuck the whole thing and say we'll go to war. No, we shall . . ."

SHEAHAN OR KAYS: What bothered you most about the President's remarks?

Sadat responded that Carter's comments on the Palestinian question, "the core and crux of the whole problem . . . surprised me most . . . embarrasses me".

We thanked the Egyptian President and scrambled back to our respective bureaux with our story. The foreign desk was delighted; the show producers ecstatic; and the international wire agencies in Cairo, who got wind of our coup, were knocking at the door in an effort to ward off the rockets that would hit them when their New York bosses monitored the evening news that night. The Associated Press operation, which was larger and more aggressive than its major competitors, Reuters and United Press International, requested a transcript of the Sadat interview. We allowed them to screen it and use the information, provided they fully credited ABC News in their story and adhered to a 1:00 a.m. local time embargo (6:00 p.m. EST Time New York), which is when our evening news show hits the airwaves.

In those days the show had a gimmicky show-biz opening which we referred to as "the quad". In lay terms, that means the TV screen was split four ways, leaving four corners for four correspondents to pop into – consecutively – with a five-second introduction to their up-coming story. Over a period of twenty seconds, the viewing audience was given the day's top four stories in capsule form, as selected by a handful of people at the daily morning meeting.That night of December 29, 1977, I provided the show with three optional quad lines, preceding my report, all of which were satellited from the infamous Kubbah Palace in the manner to which we had become accustomed:

1. SADAT SAYS CARTER'S POSITION ON AN INDEPENDENT PALESTINE IS GOING TO MAKE HIS JOB MORE DIFFICULT. THIS IS DOREEN KAYS.
2. SADAT IS SURPRISED AND DISAPPOINTED AT CARTER'S REMARKS ABOUT AN INDEPENDENT PALESTINE. THIS IS DOREEN KAYS.
3. SADAT SAYS CARTER'S REMARKS ABOUT AN INDEPENDENT PALESTINE MAY HAVE SET BACK THE SIGNING OF A PEACE AGREEMENT. THIS IS DOREEN KAYS.

My report – the lead story – followed. But first a commercial break, where ABC had to sell deodorant or dogfood or whatever before we could sell Sadat.

That night I also filed for ABC Radio News, which gave the story big play, as did the AP news agency and the *New York Times*. Next day the paper carried a front-page story under the headline:

SADAT "EMBARRASSED"
BY CARTER OPPOSITION
TO PALESTINIAN STATE

PEACE DELAY SEEN

Egyptian Leader Declares
American Remark Makes
"My Job Very Difficult"

December 30 began with two cables from ABC New York:

URGENT   URGENT   URGENT
MANY THANKS FOR OUTRUNNING THE OPPOSITION WITH SADAT
AV WESTIN

CONGRATULATIONS ON SUPERB PIECE TONIGHT. WORKED WELL
ON PROGRAM. YOUR EFFORTS ARE CERTAINLY APPRECIATED.
HAPPY NEW YEAR
ROONE ARLEDGE

I was not unhappy with the *herograms*. They were great for the morale
and the ego, and a pleasant way to end 1977 after the first six weeks of
my Cairo assignment. The positive feedback meant I was doing my job
. . . staying on top of the story. But it was a shining example of daily TV
journalism at its superficial worst; one I hoped I would not have to repeat.
The public dimensions of this news story distorted the complex reality of
an issue laced with political manipulation. No political story, least of all
one related to the intricacies, nuances and subtleties of the Middle East,
can be sloughed off in such a cavalier manner, without serious repercussions. While television diplomacy in itself is not necessarily bad, in this
case it was unnecessary, frivolous and damaging.

The fact is President Carter said nothing new, substantially. In the past
he had said he supported a Palestinian "homeland". But neither he nor
his administration ever publicly expressed support for a Palestinian "state".
Sadat for his part had publicly asked for a Palestinian "state" to assuage
the hardline Arabs, the Palestinians and the PLO. But it was widely
thought that privately Sadat and his fellow Arab moderates – Saudi Arabia
and Jordan – did not favour a new, radical, independent nation in the
Middle East, any more than President Carter; especially Sadat now that
he'd been graphically denounced by the PLO (this, however, proved to
be an unresolvable debating point).

So, between his November weekend in Jerusalem and the December
TV interview, Sadat switched, publicly, between Palestinian "state",
Palestinian "homeland" and Palestinian "self-determination". It all
depended on his mood and his audience. To the Israelis, of course,
Palestinian "homeland", "entity" and "self-determination" are euphem-
isms for Palestinian "state". And that is anathema to them, as Sadat well
knew.

So if Jimmy Carter and Anwar Sadat were of like mind, what was the
media fuss all about?

It took the respected *Washington Post* to put the story in perspective, on
the front page of its December 31 edition, under the headline:

DESPITE MEDIA
FLAP, POSITION OF
US UNCHANGED

Staff writer Murray Marder wrote:

The uproar that has spun out of Egyptian President Anwar Sadat's
wounded reactions to President Carter's televised comments on the
Palestinian question is a case of polarized media diplomacy colliding

with the fine shadings and the subtle dissembling of professional diplomacy.

This incident, which may require a Carter visit to Egypt to soothe ruffled feelings, may go down in the annals as a prime example of too-swift, too-simplified public diplomacy.

On its face, Carter jarred Sadat and many other Arab leaders by his extemporaneous remarks about a Palestinian state in his television interview. . . .

But the reality is that nothing Carter said in expressing his administration's preference against the creation of a Palestinian state represented any change in the official American position.

The problem was the candour and the timing of what Carter said out loud, the over-hard interpretations put on Carter's remarks by the media, and the media demands on Sadat to react immediately. . . .

President Carter in his television interview on Wednesday with four correspondents was attempting to thread his way through the diplomatic quicksand. But this is always a hazardous course for impromptu comment, and especially so at this extremely sensitive stage of Egyptian–Israeli negotiations, in the aftermath of the deflation of exaggerated expectations built up for the Sadat-Begin talks at Ismailia on Christmas Day.

It was evident to those familiar with the diplomatic complexities that Carter, in response to questions, wanted to commend both Sadat and Begin for their diplomatic initiatives but wanted especially to nudge them forward to continued flexibility.

In the unstructured give-and-take of the interview, which followed Begin's public unveiling of Israel's peace offer earlier the same day, Carter repeatedly commended Begin for displaying "flexibility". That was intended, administration strategists stressed, to encourage more flexibility, not to pronounce an American benediction on the Israeli proposal.

But that is not the way many press accounts that flashed around the world interpreted the brunt of the Carter remarks. Carter was widely reported to have sided with, or to have supported, the Begin proposal, and to have opposed Sadat's call for an independent Palestinian state.

In Cairo, television reporters sought immediate comment from Sadat, who had made television interviews a fixture of what he calls his "electric-shock" diplomacy. . . .

In the *Washington Post*, Marder went on to quote the ABC and CBS interviews/reports, before concluding:

These two TV interview segments were highly condensed and further polarized in press accounts transmitted around the world.

Media diplomacy, ironically, had come almost full cycle. It had been used dramatically by Sadat and Begin to come together; now it was displaying its other, divisive, capacity as well.

In preparing his story, Murray Marder contacted ABC officials in New York, one of whom (Av Westin, I later learned) was quoted as saying proudly of correspondent Kays: "She's a real tiger."

I wish I'd had time to feel flattered. Unfortunately, the performing tiger and the born actor were too busy getting ready for their next television quickie: the arrival of President Carter, to clean up the mess of our hit-and-run TV diplomacy.

5. Hassan, Gumbo and company

PRESIDENT CARTER had already made plans to spend New Year's Eve with another friend and ally in the neighbourhood, the Shah of Iran. Since the Iranian leader was also an old friend of the Egyptian leader, Sadat was delighted that toasts were being raised to the health and future of staunch allies and western alliances and was especially delighted at Carter's last-minute decision to add Egypt to an itinerary that included Saudi Arabia and other friends in the region in need of reassurance. Not that Sadat was feeling unloved exactly.

As 1977 ended and 1978 began, Anwar Sadat was an entrenched media celebrity; the darling of the western world and America's newest hero, the first since Neil Armstrong went to the moon and back eight years earlier. When certain of his fans equated his "ends of the earth" journey to Israel with Man's first landing on the moon, Sadat did not disagree, such was the degree to which his ego was being massaged daily under a halo of fame and glory. A jestful Golda Meir aside, the Egyptian President was nominated for the Nobel Peace Prize, not the Oscar. In any event, Hollywood could not give him the exposure he was getting through the news media.

Time magazine cast Sadat as its "Man of the Year" for 1977 (an individual who in the judgement of the editors has had the most impact – for better or worse – on the course of events over the previous twelve months), complete with a colour cover portrait and a twenty-two-page spread that included an article entitled: "Actor with an Iron Will: An Intimate Look At The Villager Who Became A Ruler". But it was not this article or any other in the news weekly's expansive tribute to an extraordinary man which provided an intimate look at Anwar Sadat. It was a picture; a photograph that better captured, I felt, the essence of the man around whom my life now revolved. The colour photograph was aesthetically stunning – and politically disturbing. There before the great pyramids of Giza, silhouetted against an azure blue sky, stood a handsome, bronze-faced, pin-striped figure, black-booted feet firmly planted on the desert floor – gazing imperially into the unknown. This monumental figure totally overwhelmed those of ancient Egypt. It was a theatrically sublime image of a modern-day pharaoh played to perfection by Anwar Sadat. But this was not an actor playing the role of Pharaoh. It was a Pharaoh playing the role of actor. That prophetic picture haunts me to this day.

The photographer who shot it – David Hume Kennerly – saw it differently. *Time*'s "Man of the Year" is traditionally kept a secret until the magazine's year-end issue goes to press. ABC News, much to the chagrin of Kennerly and *Time* fell upon the secret, breaking it. One of our presidential tipsters telephoned producer Arnie Collins with the news that Sadat had helicoptered from his Barrages residence, about fifteen miles north of Cairo, to his resthouse overlooking the pyramids plateau. Collins quickly dispatched a camera crew – one of the many standing by at the nearby Mena House peace talks – for what was thought to be an important meeting between the President and his aides. Veteran ABC correspondent Frank Reynolds, normally anchor-man for the ABC evening news out of Washington, was in Cairo to cover the peace talks and joined the crew on the short ride along the Desert Road to the resthouse, unobstructed by checkpoint guards innocent of the world of media secrets. Reynolds came across Sadat and photographer Kennerly as they were departing the resthouse (since demolished by President Mubarak) situated on a man-made bluff overlooking the pyramids. The ABC team followed in hot pursuit along the short road leading straight to the Sphinx and the pyramids. By now Reynolds had figured out the photo session and Kennerly was fit to be tied:

"You're not supposed to be here," he roared at Reynolds, who immediately yelled back that he could be anywhere he so desired.

"This is public property," Reynolds retorted with a sweep of his hand at one of the Seven Wonders of the World (not Sadat – the pyramids). Since Reynolds was not budging and Kennerly had to get his historic pictures, Sadat posed dutifully for *Time* and ABC News. The ABC pictures of Sadat silhouetted against the pharaohs' tombs were of dubious quality – virtually unusable – which infuriated correspondent Reynolds but not to the extent that *Time* would be allowed to keep its little secret. That night he went on the air with the "Man of the Year" story. In his book *Shooter*, a piqued Kennerly – used to exclusives from his days as President Ford's official White House photographer – sought his revenge by mildly maligning the absentee mastermind and chief culprit. Producer Collins was thrilled.

A few days later, *Time*'s "Man of the Year" flew to another of his ten official residences to await the personal benediction of President Jimmy Carter, who flew into Aswan from Saudi Arabia en route to Paris. In a hastily arranged early-morning ceremony at the airport's modest terminal building, the two leaders – meeting for the first time since Sadat's peace initiative – took forty-five minutes to clear up their TV-inspired dispute, before appearing in front of the cameras again, this time side by side, in complete accord on the nettlesome Palestinian issue. Carter said it had to be resolved; that the Palestinians must have the right to determine their own future. Whether this meant state, homeland, entity, genuine autonomy or limited self-rule was buried in semantics. By trying to show Sadat he was not tilting toward Begin on the issue, Carter bent in all directions, as the occasion dictated. The highly publicized rendezvous – a cosmetic band-aid applied to a superficial wound – was not the overnight visit Sadat would have liked, but from touch-down to take-off the Carter visit could not have been more successful from a public relations point of view. In addition to the White House correspondents travelling with the American President, the media superstars flew in from Europe and the United States to cover the event, which lasted less than two hours from start to finish. The American networks succeeded, as usual, in getting more mileage out of their mission to Upper Egypt by conducting separate interviews with Sadat once his guest was airborne.

The balloon of euphoria that had been flying over Egypt and Israel finally burst over the Sinai in mid-January 1978. Menachem Begin, ably assisted by his super-hawk Agriculture Minister Ariel Sharon, blew it up with the establishment of dummy settlements in the Western Sinai. Realizing that Sadat would settle for nothing less than the return of all Sinai intact, Sharon, who was responsible for Israeli settlements in the occupied Arab territories, erected "facts on the ground" as a bargaining tool. Egyptian intelligence knew of them but it wasn't until the world media and the cameras discovered these phoney settlements – water drilling towers, old buses and barbed wire – that Sadat finally exploded: "I will not agree to any Israeli settlements on my territory. Let them plough them up," he told his favourite Egyptian mouthpiece, the weekly *October* magazine (January 8, 1978). Sadat's media took over from there, launching a vicious anti-Begin campaign reminiscent of Egypt's worst anti-Israeli, anti-Jewish attacks over the war-filled decades. The cartoonists depicted Begin as a Shylock after his pound of flesh; as a covetous Jew flying over the pyramids listening to a member of his entourage suggest: "That would be a good spot for building a Jewish settlement." Sadat's hand-picked editors spoke for Sadat when they warned the Israelis that their "bloodthirstiness" would conquer them in the end if they ignored peace: "We shall curse the day we ever entertained hopes that so quickly faded."

And Sadat – again through his renowned alter ego, editor Anis Mansour of *October* magazine (January 8, 1978) – finally admitted that "Begin has offered nothing. It is I who have given him everything. I offered him security and legitimacy and got nothing in return. This peace initiative is not the King David Hotel which Begin blew up when he was young. He cannot blow up the initiative without destroying himself and others for hundreds of years."

It was against this backdrop of lost faith and confidence that the political and military committees, agreed upon at the Ismailia Summit, convened respectively in Jerusalem and Cairo.

With Sadat ensconced in his winter villa in Aswan and the world media with him, I was given a week's leave of absence to close up my Brussels flat, which I had not seen since the day I flew to New York to join ABC News. My two-week peace initiative assignment which was meant to be a prelude to the permanent Cairo bureau chief posting had grown to a two months' stay. Since my permanent home was still Montreal, shutting down Brussels meant convincing the rattled landlord I hadn't done a midnight flit by paying the back rent, kissing my friends goodbye and packing my clothes and a few books. As for Montreal, it would have to wait out the peace momentum.

With the political peace committee convening in Jerusalem, in January 1978 I left Brussels directly for Tel Aviv where I was picked up by an ABC News chauffeur for the hour's drive to Jerusalem.

ABC's well-oiled operation was already running at full-steam out of a hotel suite a few floors above the negotiating table and a lobby overrun day and night with journalists, cameras, officials of three nationalities and their bodyguards, not to mention the all-purpose, pervasive Israeli security force. ABC was covered on all sides. Producer Pete Simmons was back in charge; veteran Tel Aviv bureau chief Bill Seamans was responsible for covering the Israeli delegation led by Foreign Minister Dayan; State Department correspondent Barrie Dunsmore for the American delegation led by Secretary of State Vance; and I was responsible for the Egyptians headed by Foreign Minister Ibrahim Kamel. Senior overseas correspondent Peter Jennings had the task of pulling together all the pieces into some comprehensible form for the daily morning and evening news shows. Breakthrough or breakdown, we were ready. There was every indication that these talks would be no more productive than the ones preceding them and by the time they opened the following day, I had a gut instinct which I passed on to my New York superiors. Sadat, I felt certain, was about to do something dramatic, like resign or pull the plug on peace. With nothing more to go on – no tips, leaks, facts, evidence or inside information – I urged New York to send me back to Cairo immediately.

The only way to get to Cairo that night was by chartering a private plane to Cyprus. Simmons and I drove to an airstrip on the outskirts of Jerusalem where we boarded a two-seater aircraft piloted by two Israeli reserve officers. Knowing we were in good hands, Simmons spent the flight dreaming of a Bedouin princess he had left behind, and by the time I had assured him he would see her again, peace or no peace, and had chatted up one of the attractive pilots, we had landed in Nicosia. Here we were met by a charming Cypriot couple who worked on a per diem basis as expeditors for ABC. They put us on a Cairo-bound Egyptair flight which, once airborne, the white-knuckled Simmons was convinced was doomed. It was bad enough to endure a dry flight, but having to share it all with a cargo of chickens was too much. The fact that our fellow passengers were deadly quiet did not appease Simmons.

The next day Sadat broke off the deadlocked peace talks. Two days after arriving in Jerusalem the Egyptians were packing their bags. I do not recall how they travelled home or the company they kept.

In the midst of all this disenchantment with peace, an Israeli dove descended one day onto the campus of Cairo University. Abbie Nathan had been legally and illegally trying to get into Egypt for years to promote his own personal, people-to-people peace projects. The flamboyant Israeli who used to fly peace missions in his own plane had also made several attempts to enter Egypt on foot only to be halted and arrested at the Egyptian-Israeli border. All he wanted to do, he said, was talk to President Gamal Abdel Nasser. Nonetheless he claims to have sneaked into the country seven times in twelve years. But all that was before Anwar Sadat's own peace mission. With the borders still officially closed, the Israeli maverick who now operated a pirate radio station off the coast of Israel called the voice of peace, suddenly found himself welcomed in Egypt, if not by all Egyptians. The voice of peace arrived, bearing an invitation from university students in Jerusalem to university students in Cairo asking them to come and visit. Somewhat taken aback by this impromptu, audacious gesture, Cairo University's elected student council got embroiled in a heated debate over whether to receive the waiting Israeli. Nathan, not surprisingly was rebuffed by a student council which, like most on Egyptian campuses, was dominated by Islamic fundamentalist societies. Undeterred, the voice of peace beckoned anyone who cared to speak, listen or discuss. The camera crew and I, who seemed to have more trouble gaining entry to the university than Nathan, were determined to record his adventure and the reaction of the Egyptians whom he managed to attract with not a little help from the American network cameras.

A large, friendly, curious, seemingly peace-loving crowd soon mobbed the Israeli who, with microphone in hand, proceeded to interview the students, both peaceniks and fundamentalists. Abbie Nathan considered his mission a qualified success. "At least everybody is talking about the subject," he said later as he handed me an autographed copy of the *Peace* record. The album jacket carried a flying white dove in a blue sky and a red, white and blue sticker announced the voice of peace.

1540 KCS . . . SOMEWHERE IN THE MEDITERRANEAN
PEACE THROUGH COMMUNICATION.

Abbie Nathan aside, Anwar Sadat wasn't getting through to the Israelis. So, two and a half months after Jerusalem he went to Washington to test the power of peace through satellite communications. The American media had done its job well. The White House, State Department, Defence Department, the Foreign Relations Committees of both houses of Congress, the business and industrial community, the Jewish-American leadership and the American people – all lavished love and praise on him during a week-long visit that not even the worst winter blizzard in decades could chill. The Egyptian leader gained additional warmth and comfort from the results of scores of public opinion surveys which revealed an historic shift in American perceptions of the Arab-Israeli conflict. The majority of Americans polled showed – for the first time – a declining support for Israel in favour of an Arab country and a feeling that Egypt was more willing than Israel to compromise for peace. And in the popularity/personality contest, Anwar Sadat left Menachem Begin trailing far behind. The fact that Sadat looked like a hero and Begin looked like a villain was a quirk of nature that would have left Sadat's media advisor crying with ecstasy – had there been one. As the man in charge of his own image, Sadat could take double pleasure and full credit for single-handedly changing the image of the Arab in America. Even those critical of Sadat's ways and means towards peace could not deny him that extraordinary feat. In a matter of weeks President Sadat had demolished the popular American stereotype of the "ugly, dirty, war-mongering, deceitful, uncivilized Arab". Having achieved his first Jerusalem objective, he now relied on the new image to sway America into translating his peace initiative into peace. His optimism was based on the belief that since he had delivered, the United States would now force Israel to reciprocate.

That test was still ahead. For now, he contented himself with having won a moral victory over the enemy, a success equal to Egyptian troops storming the Israeli Bar Lev line on the east bank of the Suez Canal in the early hours of the October '73 war. For now, he enjoyed the official and popular acclaim accorded him by America on his first Washington summit since Jerusalem. When Sadat wasn't chatting or dining at the White House or being swept along the corridors of Congress, he was holding court at Blair House, the official government residence for visiting heads of state conveniently located near the White House across Lafayette Square. And it was outside Blair House that I spent much of that blizzardy week from dawn through dark, staking out Sadat, his thoughts, moods, achievements, failures and visitors. Having decided that wherever the Egyptian President travelled I would follow, ABC ensured that I was in place at nearby Andrews Air Force Base to report his arrival and set the summit scene from the Egyptian perspective. As the Cairo-based correspondent I was expected to provide an element of insight into a man and a story born of my all-consuming relationship with both. If anyone could presume to pontificate on Sadat and the inner workings of his mind and peace policy, better it be the reporter who spent her days shadowing him. It made good journalistic sense except at dawn when I was forced to stand outside the Blair House barricade in sub-zero temperatures reporting live what Sadat had said or done and whom he had seen since my last report the night before and what we could expect from him in the next twenty-four hours. As I tried to collect my thoughts and bits of information at 6:00 a.m., all I was certain of was that millions of Americans were preparing to start their day by tuning into the popular "Good Morning America" show and that the late-rising Anwar Sadat was fast asleep. Since the two-hour programme, running between 7 and 9:00 a.m., is a blend of news, weather, sports, taped features, live interviews and commercials – all produced under the aegis of ABC's entertainment division – my live, on-the-scene reports were often supplemented by a pre-packaged report written and edited the previous night and/or a rush to the studios a couple of miles away for a brief question and answer session. The goal of American breakfast TV is to give America something to talk about at the coffee-break. That it does not pretend to provide intellectual nourishment was a comforting thought that sustained me through my forty-five-second servings of quick-mix, instant, disposable news dispensed on a snow-stormed street corner. My contributions to the evening TV news shows and radio were slightly more substantive, especially when played off against reports providing the Washington angle and often the Tel Aviv action or reaction as well, leaving the viewing public with a better chance of something to talk about over dinner that night. If nothing else, my presence in Washington established credibility for ABC News and enhanced my own credibility within Sadat's inner circle. When the Egyptian leader saw me standing on the White House lawn or bumped into me at every turn at Capitol Hill, he could only conclude that the "Barbara Walters Network" was a serious news organization interested in the Egyptian point of view – his point of view – to the extent that it would be given a full airing through its Cairo-based reporter familiar with all its inflections and nuances. That these reports sometimes contained critical details not to his liking was a liability he was prepared to tolerate until such time as it would affect his image in America. But the concentrated media attention being lavished on him during the Washington summit – including the high profile interviews conducted by ABC's Walters, CBS' Cronkite and NBC's Chancellor – were the stuff of Sadat's wildest pre-Jerusalem dreams. And if I helped enhance his image with my twice-daily Washington reports, he helped enhance mine and ABC's, and in the process opened doors granting me greater access to his aides and confidantes; an excellent example of how media manipulation works and how it continued to evolve on the Sadat peace story.

The other networks – CBS and NBC – seeing the advantages of cosying up to the story – dispatched their Cairo correspondents to cover subsequent Washington summits. This one clearly was a success. Sadat departed with America's love, sympathy, understanding and some of its combat aircraft as well. While he did not get the one hundred and twenty short-range F-5E fighter planes he requested, he accepted quick delivery of the fifty he was promised. Calling it a "tenth-rate" plane compared to the more sophisticated F-16s and F-15s Israel was getting, nonetheless he felt it was better than nothing and indeed the start of a serious military liaison with the US, a liaison he craved every bit as much as peace.

As for me, I departed with a tattered Cairo-thin suede coat and a new heavy-duty wool one, purchased at ABC's request for fear pneumonia would set in and curtail my on-camera blizzard performances. Since the coat was a legitimate "in-the-line-of-duty" expense, I regretted the lack of time that prevented me from selecting something more à la mode and becoming than an eighty-five-dollar sale-rack hooded version of Joseph's biblical multi-coloured garment. The blizzard having receded, I hid the coat in my suitcase and flew to New York to brief my superiors on the state of Sadat, Egypt and peace. Having already been given carte blanche to do whatever was necessary to maintain the aggressive and highly competitive coverage coming out of the Cairo bureau, I looked forward to meeting the President, the man who, my friend Simmons had reminded me, was the "only one who matters" in my life.

Up till now Roone Arledge was a publicity picture and the author of much valued *herograms*. On our first meeting I was not unimpressed by my boss or the luncheon he provided on my behalf in the executive dining room of the American Broadcasting Corporation tower in the heart of Manhattan. In the presence of the Evening News' Executive Producer Av Westin and two other executives, Arledge peppered me with questions that belied his popular reputation as a "jock". As a man who was elevated to head ABC News on the strength of his success as head of ABC Sports, Arledge came across as the personification of American dynamism; a shrewd, astute, street-wise, communications leader whose pulse beat in communion with that of Mr and Mrs Average American (whom I have yet to meet). While knowledgeable and intelligent, he suffered no intellectual pretensions that might have distanced him from a mass television audience and the crucial commercial TV ratings system. And the ratings indicated he was doing something right. Under his direction, ABC's share of America's TV news audience had already increased several percentage points, which brought more commercial sponsors, bigger profits for the corporation and increased operating revenues for the news division. Resulting bonuses included a bigger and better Cairo bureau, one whose resources were unequalled by our competitors CBS and NBC, let alone by our European colleagues.

Within six months Arledge had turned a third-rate news network into a major success story, but more importantly – to my mind – he had helped redress the pro-Israeli bias and imbalance that had dominated Western, particularly American, media coverage of the Middle East since the inception of modern Israel. The public was at last getting roughly equal doses of an Arab and an Israeli, at least on ABC News and in varying degrees on the other American networks and in the written press. Admittedly, had it not been for Anwar Sadat and the prospect of peace that he held out, that imbalance would have prevailed much longer.

Having been wined and dined in such fine corporate manner, I could only conclude that I was destined for a long stay in Cairo. However intriguing and fascinating I found Egypt, Egyptians and Sadat, I preferred not to think of the peace story as a lifetime assignment. I thanked Arledge for the superb lunch, the fine company and ABC's continuing moral, financial and editorial support. I said goodbye to the nice, middle-aged man-next-door; the jovial carrot-topped, freckle-faced, bespectacled man who one could perceive as being every bit as powerful as Anwar Sadat, if not yet as influential as Menachem Begin.

In my absence Hassan Bahgat had found ABC Cairo a permanent home. Since carte blanche did not cover an indefinite stay in a E£250-a-day presidential hotel suite, we bid farewell to the elegance, the room service, the spectacular Nile view and moved a couple of miles down the Corniche el-Nil into a E£1200-a-month apartment which Hassan and *baksheesh* had converted into a functional office. The painters who had insisted on two months, finished the job in two weeks; the telephone company which for three years claimed there were no available lines produced three – two local and one operator-assisted long-distance lines – and ultra-modern blue-grey Italian phones to go with them; the bamboo furniture-maker quickly found some bamboo; the telex and two news agency tickers (Associated Press and Middle East News Agency) were installed along with new lighting fixtures and air-conditioner/heating units; the walkie-talkies and base station were hooked up; new stationery, typewriters and calling cards ordered; permanent chauffeurs and Mercedes cars hired; paper clips, pens and notebooks bought; and newspapers and journals subscribed. While the average Cairene could wait for ever for a flat, money, power and influence had given us, in less than one month, one that looked out on the Nile, on one side, and the Egypt TV and radio building on the other. It contained a room for the bureau chief/correspondent, one for the camera crew, one for the producer, editor, editing equipment and tape library, a partitioned office for Hassan, a living room, reception area, two bathrooms, one kitchen and one open-air balcony for on-camera reports.

By Cairo standards we possessed the ideal bureau, which soon became the envy of our CBS competitors located two floors directly above us, as well as many of our foreign colleagues who (lacking financial and human resources) often worked as one-man bureaux out of one-room offices in even more congested parts of the city. The BBC bureau, for example, was manned solely by World Service Radio correspondent Bob Jobbins, and operated from the cramped quarters of the British news agency Reuters. Several other foreign correspondents used Reuters' space too, and a number of Americans worked alone out of their homes. Apart from the three American networks, other foreign television networks with permanent bureaux in Cairo included the French, German, Japanese, Dutch and Italians, who spent much of their time covering other Middle East stories. So, by February 1978 the American Broadcasting Corporation's Cairo news operation held the distinction of being the largest foreign news bureau in Egypt . . . triple its pre-peace initiative size. The motley team of permanent, temporary and freelance foreign and local employees now included the bureau chief/correspondent, two cameramen, two soundmen, two producers, one editor, one office manager, one expeditor/ messenger; three translators/researchers/secretaries; one radio stringer; one "deep throat" purveyor of information whom we dubbed "Gumbo"; one coffee boy/cleaning man and four chauffeurs. In addition, well-placed tipsters were kept on monthly retainers. A London-based roving unit manager/budget controller flew in for extended periods to approve our free-floating budget and to supervise the bureau's ad hoc administration. An expert in the technical, logistical and editorial requirements of ABC's eleven overseas bureaux, he had helped set up the Cairo bureau in 1975 and now served as a valuable and sympathetic liaison with New York management.

A permanent American producer and American editor would eventually replace the revolving ones; the Armenian soundman who would retire from the debilitating eighteen-hour days would be replaced by an Egyptian; some of the temporary local staff would become permanent; and the Bureau's original girl Friday would be replaced by a more efficient young Egyptian alumnus of New York's respected Columbia University's Graduate School of Journalism. The indefatigable Hassan Bahgat, out of driving self-initiative and remarkable ingenuity, had been elevated to new heights and a commensurate salary that quadrupled in line with new responsibilities under the broad title of office manager. Since the early, heady days of the flying media circus and the two dozen chauffeured Mercedes cabs, Hassan had made himself all but indispensable to the ABC operation. Under his deft direction, Cairo's perennially booked hotel rooms were unbooked for visiting television troops and thousands of dollars of electronic equipment and personnel were speedily expedited through Cairo Airport's labyrinthine bureaucracy. If the phones broke down, Hassan would get them fixed, today not tomorrow; if you wanted to know President Sadat's scheduled and unscheduled daily events, Hassan would sniff them out; if you needed to bluff your way past officialdom, Hassan charmed and cajoled with incredible tales; if a news agency ticker went kaput, Hassan would get it ticking again; if the coffee supply ran dry, Hassan would have it replenished; if the chauffeurs complained of no food and no sleep, Hassan would re-juggle shifts to ensure both; if you wanted to buy the best for the least at the *souk*, Hassan would know just the dealer; if you wanted the appropriate Cairo location to shoot a story, Hassan would direct you, often personally; if you ran out of pen and paper, Hassan would pop up with both; if you craved cigarettes or beer, the chain-smoking teetotaller would procure them; if you wanted more Egyptian pounds for your dollars, sterling, marks, or francs than the official rate allowed, Hassan would assure you top rates on the open, thriving black market; if you wanted to know the latest Cairo gossip, the mood of the man-in-the-street or the popular intrigues of a sophisticated but still largely timid populace, this Egyptian barometer could tell you who, what, where, when and how. How you coped with it all was not his concern.

Superman's monthly paycheck reflected his prodigious talents and made him a new member of Egypt's privileged class, in spite of the pejorative and embarrassing connotation this held for a socially-conscious devout Moslem for whom the so-called fat-cats often meant corruption and injustice in a third-world showcase of haves and have-nots. That he might be part of some new economic order – a cottage industry beneficiary of Sadat's 1974 *Infitah* (open door) economic policy (private foreign investment to break the shackles of Nasser's strangling state-controlled guided economy) – presented Hassan with a fierce moral dilemma. It was not his hard-earned prosperity that so troubled his conscience; devout Moslems like most of us – believers and non-believers alike – have a healthy appreciation of the value and benefits of money; rather the dilemma stemmed from other realities. However much Hassan might have thought of himself as an average middle-class Egyptian, he ceased being average the day he and a group of fellow junior army officers plotted to overthrow President Nasser in the wake of the ignominious 1967 Arab defeat. Having failed in his attempt to right the wrongs of what had become a "cruel, oppressive and shameful regime", having failed "to do something good" for his country and countrymen, Hassan spent seven years in prison during which he underwent a profound transformation. He vowed that if he ever got out alive, he would become a true follower of Mohammed, one who did not drink, gamble, womanize or generally exploit life at someone else's expense. Thus it was under a general amnesty granted by Gamal Abdel Nasser's successor that a re-born man emerged from prison one day in 1974. Hassan's calamitous political passions had cost him and his young family dearly. He vowed "never again" to deprive them of his love and protection and the decent life to which they were entitled, and which, according to an Arab's code of honour, he was obliged to provide to the best of his ability. In an effort to make up for past sufferings, his overriding commitment was now to his family; his overriding priority, their welfare. And so he set out to rejoin society as a productive, respectable, law-abiding citizen, under the watchful eyes and ears of Egyptian security.

It was while earning his living as a taxi driver that he chanced upon an ABC News passenger who, impressed with the savvy Cairene, sought out his services up to and including the establishment of the Cairo bureau in 1975. A year into his new life, Hassan had become ABC Cairo's shipper, expeditor and chauffeur, a job which, thanks to President Sadat and his peace initiative, he had now parleyed into one of the best-paying foreign jobs on the Egyptian market; a job that daily required him to play by the accepted rules of a society and a market-place where demand far exceeded supply and where power, influence and money only served to widen the obscene gap between rich and poor; a job that demanded compromises of him. Since ABC News had no trouble qualifying as a member of the powerful and rich in any society, and since Hassan's duties forced him face-to-face with his country's in-built system of corruption, bribes and *baksheesh*, he got us what we wanted and needed, at a price; hotel rooms; airline flights; apartments and telephones, when these would otherwise have been impossible. That all of this and more involved a little wheeling and dealing, a little deception, a little stretching of the truth was justified as a means to a better end; a more peaceful, more prosperous Egypt. Had he not already become disillusioned with Sadat and his open-door regime in which he saw privilege and corruption conspire to make the rich richer and the poor poorer, his new status and success might have been less ironical and less painful. Not that he ever voiced his crisis of conscience. But given his past hardships and his new commitment and motivation to become master of at least his own home; given his realization that he alone could not revolutionize Egypt, could not abolish some of the society's blatant flaws and injustices, perpetrated at the expense of the masses; and given the fact that he was proving to be an able and willing student of the free-enterprise capitalist system, as taught by his American masters, one could hardly fault him for the wisdom of deciding "if you can't beat 'em join 'em".

By 1978 Hassan had apparently resolved his crisis of conscience. Whether in the bureau or out, he continued faithfully to interrupt his ABC duties five times daily by retreating to a corner with his prayer mat, and he continued to the best of his ability to adhere to the tenets of the Koran and the Islamic way of life. He also seized the opportunity to become an entrepreneur. Since ABC required three permanent cars and chauffeurs to facilitate the frenetic lifestyle of its correspondent, camera crew and producer, Hassan – now adept at wheeling and dealing on behalf of the bureau – decided to exercise his skills on his own behalf. He borrowed some money and in partnership with a brother bought two new (cut-rate) Mercedes cabs, and leased them to the bureau at the going rate of roughly one thousand dollars a month. Out of that sum, the drivers – a cousin and an old army buddy – each received an attractive monthly salary (by Cairo taxi standards) while the balance went to Hassan, who paid off the cars and pocketed a profit to supplement his salary.

In time, some of my American colleagues would privately complain about his pervasive flair for business that included a touch of nepotism, as his assistant happened to be a brother-in-law. Since nepotism is an endemic and accepted part of life in the third world, and since our payroll did not cover an assistant, his salary was buried in an exotic choreography of figures – a practice not uncommon in corporate bookkeeping. Hassan, who had honed his shrewd business sense by closely observing the machinations of his main-chance critics, was simply employing the same tactics for the benefit of his extended family, to whom he was equally loyal. Personally, I found this absence of a double standard utterly refreshing and had nothing but admiration and respect for this multi-faceted dynamo and his many qualities, not the least of which was a personal and professional integrity that helped me retain what little sanity I had left after the first six months of the peace story. If peace and America were to bestow prosperity on only one Egyptian I could not think of a more worthy candidate than Hassan Bahgat, the lynch-pin of the Cairo bureau. In fact, ABC's well-paid multi-lingual Egyptian support team was precisely well-paid because it comprised the best and the brightest of Cairo's east-west media hybrids in a market where supply did not come close to meeting the combined demands of the American TV networks. It was luck that found us these gems, these rare Egyptian bodies with their dual mentalities and tongues capable of adapting to a fast-paced, round-the-clock pressurized, aggressive, competitive satellite-style journalism. The "IBM" (*Inshallah, Boukrah, Malesh*) "God-willing, tomorrow, it doesn't matter" mentality was modified into a *modus operandi* in which we attempted not to invoke the will of God or otherwise bother the Deity except in circumstances that threatened to turn today's efforts into tomorrow's disaster. This resulted in us dropping the BM and retaining *Inshallah*.

Whether any of us realized it or not we had by now become a reflexive, well-co-ordinated family of single-minded purpose, dedicated to Sadat's peace story and ABC's news coverage of it. The coverage was second to none in terms of quantity and quality, at least in the eyes of our New York superiors, and judging by the positive feedback emanating informally from other quarters, we were being closely watched by our competitors, electronic and print. Even in Egyptian media and government circles, ABC Cairo by the early months of 1978 had established a highly-visible credible reputation for being plugged in. It was the inevitable result of a highly disciplined, dedicated team effort aided by an esprit de corps fed on success, trust, confidence and an unglamorous daily routine.

My breakfast each morning consisted of coffee, orange juice and the BBC World Service. To arrive at the bureau without having tuned into the Beeb's daily version of the world, which usually included news of the triangle of peace – Egypt, Israel and the United States – was as inconceivable as going to work clad only in a bikini.Once in the bureau I consulted with a producer, Hassan and the rest of the staff; talked to New York and London via telephone and telex (the first of the day's several contacts); read the overnight logs outlining the news shows' story-line-up the previous night on ABC, CBS and NBC; and other cable communications; read the overnight news on the AP and MENA wires; read the English-language *Cairo Press Review* (the Egyptian government's daily digest of the Arabic press) as well as Cairo's English-language daily, *The Gazette*, all of which usually provided material for two or three ABC Radio spots plus questions and answers supplied by me or our freelance stringer Nat Harrison, or both. At this stage another staff member would have compiled, translated and typed ABC's version of news and events culled from the BBC, Radio Cairo, Radio Monte Carlo, Egyptian Television's evening news and our own sources. It was not uncommon to find ourselves quoted as the source of news carried by the three major dailies – *Al Ahram*, *Al Akhbar* and *Al Gomhuria*, as well as the weeklies. The regurgitated news often fell victim to translation and selective self-censorship, but was nonetheless significant on three counts: it enhanced our reputation for aggressive and accurate reporting, especially as denials rarely if ever followed the items; it revealed the double-standard operating in Sadat's Egypt whereby the American/Western free press was permitted to gather news unimpeded by the restraints imposed on the Egyptian media; and it indicated the degree to which the state-controlled local media relied on the foreign media, especially American television, for anything other than the circumscribed version of President Sadat's story. Indeed there were days when I wondered if I were not also Egypt TV's correspondent, so frequent were my appearances and questions on its evening news.

The key to successful reporting cannot be found along the narrow avenues of official information. One cannot live on the pabulum of propaganda alone, Anwar Sadat notwithstanding. In countries like Egypt, where governments dispense only what they dictate is good for the people, it is doubly imperative that the foreign correspondent cultivate alternative sources of information. It is a time-consuming and thoroughly rewarding experience, especially in the Arab world and especially if the relationships are based on mutual trust, confidence, respect and credibility. Without contacts, without someone willing to tell you what he or she knows or able to point you in the direction of those who do, there is no hope of getting even close to the true dimensions and reality of a story. In addition, then, to covering the basics, I set out to cultivate Egyptians in and out of the government, as well as members of the Western diplomatic corps who would be helpful and useful in my pursuit of anything approximating the truth, which in the case of the peace initiative, was particularly perishable once found, given the mercurial nature of the story and its hero.

Although Cairo is among the largest and greatest cities of the world, politically it is a village, and regardless of how often Sadat talked about Egyptian "democracy" and its "freely-elected" institutions, neither existed in the Western sense. Elections and national referenda were rigged to produce the desired and predictable 98.99 per cent (interchangeable with 97.34 per cent or some other equally ludicrous consensus) in favour of Sadat's foreign and domestic policies. The country's ruling elite, traditionally, is a small, well-known clique, as is the opposition – official and unofficial – ever-lingering on the fringes in the hope of a political miracle. Penetrating this powerful country club would not be difficult at the worst of times and I had arrived on the scene at the best of times, a time when the country's ruler was trying to sell peace to Egypt, Israel and the United States, a time of American TV diplomacy, of love in full bloom between Egypt and America. That I was the Cairo face and voice of one of America's three powerful TV news networks, that I was sociable by nature, nosy by inclination, Arab of blood if not birth, and female of sex did not impede my efforts. Admittedly it was ABC's intoxicating power that unlocked the doors to my network of contacts and sources, but it would be an insult to those involved, and not a little naïve, to suggest that mere infatuation with this electronic power kept them open. And while it was hardly my colloquial Lebanese Arabic that prompted these contacts and sources to talk, my Arabness was an important psychological factor that cannot be underestimated. Not to have exploited it would have been tantamount to denying my spiritual and emotional roots, which are as much a part of my background as my Canadian and North American upbringing.

One highly-placed Egyptian with whom I established a good working relationship best articulated, perhaps, the subliminal effects of this ethnic bond. "You may not be one of us, strictly speaking," he said, "but your lack of contempt for us natives and our culture makes us feel you care about this country and its people. At the very least," he said, "you attempt to understand us. So even if you are often critical of what we do and how we do it, we feel you are one of us."

I did not in any way feel that my journalistic integrity or independence was being compromised by his remark, which I took to be more than personal or professional flattery. It was a subtle allusion to some of my colleagues in the Western news corps whose behaviour was often perceived as contemptuous and arrogant; those who could find little positive to say about Egypt and Egyptians in private or public, and whose sole motive in being there apparently was to promote their own careers. For this lot, the Cairo assignment was a step to something bigger and better, a temporary prison in which they were serving a short-term sentence of one or two years. With luck, having "done Cairo" would look good on the curriculum vitae. One could hardly expect the Egyptians, or any other nation for that matter, to appreciate these patronizing, denigrating foreigners who see foreign lands as black or white, rich or poor, good or bad; east or west, civilized or uncivilized – these Westerners and their forebears who through the centuries contributed not a little to the giant inferiority complex from which Egyptians still suffer. Admittedly, to have lived and worked in Egypt during the halcyon days of peace was a challenge to one's physical, emotional and mental equilibrium. But the greater part of that challenge, certainly for the American TV news corps, was not the daily confrontation with over-population and poverty – the decay, filth, noise and congestion – it was the insatiable demands of a media mandate gone beserk thousands of miles away in a controlled, comfortable, structured, technological society. The combined frustration took its toll. Some of us ranted and raved a lot; some withdrew into solitude, and eccentricity; some tranquillized themselves with booze and hashish; others cussed or sulked, and in time allowed the uglier side of their personalities to surface; and many simply supplemented one or all of these defences by taking the easy road to self-preservation, that old stand-by: racist humour; pathetic Egyptian jokes, always at the expense of the Egyptians and often within earshot. The Egyptians coped with these superior creatures in characteristically suitable fashion. They ignored them.

Fortunately this ignorant community was offset by a handful of outstanding exceptions; journalists who possessed an acute sensibility for Egypt and Egyptians and a sensitivity that provided some assurance of insight and analysis beyond the simplistic norm. Notable among them were the veteran Cairo correspondents Volkhard Windfuhr of the German news weekly *Der Spiegel*, and Jean-Pierre Peronçet-Hugoz of the French daily *Le Monde*. Both spoke fluent Arabic and were too busy digging out the more substantial stories behind the story for me to encounter them regularly on my Sadat beat. Other notables included the BBC's Bob Jobbins, Agence France Presses' Nabil Joumbert, Deutsch Press Agency's Peter Fischer and freelance American journalist Nathaniel Harrison. That all of them were highly respected for their distinguished reporting and that none of them is a television correspondent is not surprising. They constituted the ideal of a foreign correspondent: that special breed of men and women whose facility for adapting to foreign languages, peoples and cultures makes them exemplary reporters, interpreters and analysts; a credit to their countries, their news organizations and themselves. It is inconceivable that a foreign correspondent should not have at least a fair working knowledge of the language of the country he or she has been assigned to cover. Yet the vast majority of American journalists – especially TV correspondents working abroad – lack this basic credential. It does not make for an adequately or accurately informed public. The fact that my own credentials were considered special said more about those of some of my colleagues and competitors than it did about any privileged status I enjoyed. In concrete terms it helped give ABC an edge over CBS and NBC.

Given the inherent and contrived limitations of the TV medium and given the fact I was not a veteran foreign correspondent, the Arab factor served as a valuable aid in efforts to dig beneath the cursed tip of the iceberg, if only to uncover an occasional exclusive titbit of news. My contacts and sources would serve me well. And while I do not read or write Arabic, my comprehension of the spoken language allowed me to grasp at least half of Sadat's meandering speeches as well as the radio and TV news. I did considerably better however, with Egyptian TV soap operas – the ones produced by Egypt TV, not Sadat – which are viewed nightly by addicted millions.

The Egyptian with whom I conversed most in Arabic was probably my lovable, long-suffering driver Dessouki, who soon became a surrogate father and trusted friend. Since most of the Egyptians I dealt with professionally spoke fluent, or at least better English than I spoke Arabic, I found the language more useful as a listening device. It came in handy in everyday situations where I was marked as an English-speaker, an Amér-kañi, Bedouin features notwithstanding. It was always comforting to know what the *souk* merchant, the police officer, security guard, airline agent, civil servant or someone's private secretary was about to do to me. And sitting through a minister's phone calls was always enlightening and sometimes productive. Even if I'd had the time personally to cultivate contacts and sources beyond the elite circle of the influential and powerful, in part

I was prevented from doing so by virtue of the fact I was a foreign correspondent. The middle-level bureaucrat and civil servant, those charged with the daily running of the country's civilian and military institutions, be it the Foreign Ministry, the Defence Department or the Interior Ministry, is more inclined to be quizzed by an anonymous and trusting Egyptian than a highly visible untested alien, especially in a political environment that still contained the residue of fear and suspicion from President Nasser's police-state regime. As a result, my news-gathering efforts constituted only one level of what developed early on into a three-tier network of sources and contacts. Two ABC-affiliated Egyptian colleagues had cultivated their own invaluable sources and between us we produced a highly effective and prolific system of information to supplement the official news. Equally important, it produced several scoops or exclusive stories.

The relationship with a source is a delicate one, a constant battle of wits, a game of mutual manipulation in which each party attempts to promote and protect his or her own self interest. To help ensure against the broadcast of false or misleading propaganda plants, we employed the widely-accepted safeguard of reporting a source's information or exclusive tip only if it could be confirmed by two other independent sources. And one rule the three of us were adamant in following was protection of sources, if only out of self-interest. A source threatened with exposure is a dried-up source.

The job of digging out information, which consumed not an inconsiderable amount of time and patience, was without doubt one of the more satisfying aspects of the assignment and went a long way towards building and maintaining the high level of morale on which the bureau seemed to float during the first two years of the peace story. The fact that we were all on a "high" helped obviate the debilitation of what had become an obsessive way of life for all of us. The fact that I was also bureau chief proved to be a burden of almost superhuman proportions, particularly during an early period when I was charged with the daily administration of the bureau and its personnel. I found myself writing cheques and scripts simultaneously, in between supervising such household chores as who should clean the office, when, and how, while buried under reams of paper and figures that passed for the monthly accounts and proved totally incomprehensible to one who had difficulty passing high school maths. The load was lightened somewhat with the eventual arrival of a permanent producer who took charge of administrative and logistical matters. But because ABC – unlike CBS and NBC – believes a one-correspondent bureau should utilize the correspondent as bureau chief, for prestige reasons, and because titles are important in the Arab world, I had no choice but to acquiesce to a role whose title benefits were far outweighed by the tedious, devouring demands which served only to distract me from my more fundamental duties as correspondent.

Fortunately there was Gumbo, otherwise known as Emad Adeeb, a brilliant, enterprising, indefatigable young Egyptian journalist, now working abroad. Quite simply, he was the best informed journalist in Cairo. As ABC's phantom round-the-clock sleuth, he was the reporter behind the correspondent – the one who helped make me and ABC News look good more often than we deserved. With Hassan and Gumbo around, everything was possible and tolerable.

The ideal bureau, then, was not without its shortcomings, not the least of which was the garbage that had to be negotiated at the building's ground level entrance and exit and the elevator that had to be avoided even when manually manipulated by the ever-smiling, ever-confident, ever-obliging, ever-patient Ishmael, the *bo'ab* (doorman). I found the life-threatening mechanical contraption far less dangerous and claustrophobic (I was the only one in it much of the time) than the parking lot abutting the garbage which would have warmed the hearts of Busby Berkeley and Charlie Chaplin. The congested parking lot occupied an opening between Egypt radio/TV, three apartment-office buildings (including the one housing ABC and the Paprika Restaurant) and several dilapidated food and tobacco outlets, including a state-run canteen-style grocery stall which bordered a dirt road that served as a detour between points of the Corniche el-Nil. Getting in and out of the parking lot called for a twenty-minute ritual. At any given moment or hour between 10:00 a.m. and 7:00 p.m. (Friday Sabbath excluded) roughly a hundred cars and a token butane-laden donkey were parked bumper to ass in a space that at best accommodated half the number, squeezed in with the help of some supernatural force which could only have been Allah. Each time a vehicle attempted to arrive or depart, the effort of unclogging the dual entrances/exits involved parking attendants, drivers and idle passers-by who, without benefit of car keys, proceeded to unpark the brake-less vehicles by pushing them to more appropriate resting places where they remained only until the cleared path had to be cleared again, which averaged about every sixty seconds. The donkey got the worst of the verbal and physical abuse in this game of musical places. On days when the district sewer mains collapsed, this movable miracle of a garage was expanded and modified to accommodate the extra load that had filtered through the hub caps and exhaust pipes. In either case I rarely, if ever, arrived for work with clean feet and never left without several hours of reading material. Indeed had it not been for excursions into these feats worthy of *The Guinness Book of Records* I would never have managed my required reading list.

The only possible respite might have been my beautiful flat, an oasis of tranquillity inherited (along with Nadia the maid) from my predecessor, and where I finally installed myself three months after arriving in Egypt. Situated on the fashionable end of the Corniche in what was then – at thirty floors – Cairo's tallest building, the Belmont flat, directly across from the Meredien Hotel, afforded a breathtaking twelfth-floor view of Cairo and the Nile. From a rear balcony I looked out on my Garden City neighbourhood nestled against the distant Muqattam Hills where Saladin built his twelfth century Citadel. And from my two large front balconies I could see the pyramids on a clear day (maybe twice in four years). A hanging veil of dust and haze stood between me and the Egypt of the pharaohs. I settled instead for Cairo by night, which from my privileged vantage point played beauty to the beast of Cairo by day. Unfortunately, during 1978 and 1979 my workload was such that it largely deprived me of even this small pleasure. Leisure time was a good night's sleep.

6. When the chips are down

THREE MONTHS AFTER Jerusalem, Sadat's initiative had stalled. The peace talks were deadlocked and the Egyptians and Israelis were barely speaking to each other, thanks in large part to Menachem Begin's perverse interpretation of peace: expanding Jewish settlements in the occupied West Bank while at the same time refusing to dismantle those in occupied Sinai, which he was prepared to return to Egypt in exchange for a peace treaty. Peace in the Middle East was proving as elusive as ever. Egyptians, then, were shocked but not surprised when Sadat's peace claimed its first victim: *Al Ahram*'s board chairman and editor-in-chief, Yousef Sebai, was assassinated by Palestinian extremists in a Nicosia hotel lobby. Sebai – a former Minister of Information and another of Sadat's alter egos – was also head of the Egyptian Journalists' Union and the Arab Writers' Syndicate. He controlled the Egyptian press, i.e. suppressed the anti-Sadat forces, and one of his rewards for silencing what Sadat constantly referred to as "Marxists and communists" (although several could hardly be labelled as either) was to join the presidential peace party to Israel. By merely accompanying the President to Jerusalem in November, Sebai, along with every other Egyptian peace delegate, was targeted for elimination by hardline Arab and Palestinian militants. An enraged Sadat, in an effort to bring the assassins back to Egypt alive, dispatched a commando unit to Larnaka Airport where Cypriot officials were negotiating with the assassins for the release of hostages. The Israeli-inspired Entebbe-type rescue effort was an unmitigated disaster from ill-fated conception to bloody end. And several Egyptian commandos paid the price. At their mass funeral in Cairo, an angry mob vowed vengeance against the Palestinians and their cause. Banner-waving Egyptians marched through the streets shouting "No more Palestine after today." The emotional demonstrators turned up the volume of their outrage each time our camera zoomed in on them. But it was President Sadat and the Egyptian media who most exploited the historically latent ambivalence of the Egyptians towards the Palestinians. Even though the PLO denounced the Sebai murder as a criminal, cowardly act, Sadat and his media blamed the PLO and Yasser Arafat, whose hands dripped with blood in newspaper cartoons.

It was the first and only popular demonstration of anti-Palestinian sentiment I was to witness in Egypt, and while government-orchestrated, it was also an expression of grass-roots frustration reflecting the mixed feelings and schizophrenic commitment born of seemingly endless and futile battles on behalf of the Arab cause. For apart from the Palestinians themselves – and the Lebanese – the Arabs who have most suffered on behalf of the stateless Palestinians are the Egyptians, in human, economic and social terms. But the PLO rejection of Sadat's peace initiative, the assassination of Yousef Sebai and the subsequent loss of more Egyptian lives, as well as Egypt's growing pariah status in the Arab world, served to stimulate and vocalize the nationalistic tendencies that surfaced in February 1978. But only temporarily, thanks to the Israeli Prime Minister's zealousness. Trapped inside a Holocaust mentality, Menachem Begin seemed incapable of making peace with history, incapable of facing peace in the Middle East, incapable of meeting Anwar Sadat even half-way. Thus, while many Egyptians were now disillusioned with the Palestinian leadership, they were more disillusioned with an unbending Israeli leadership. Against this anti-PLO, anti-Begin backdrop, Egypt's Palestinian community – roughly forty thousand – seemed determined to mind its own business.

There are, in effect, two Palestinian communities in Egypt. One composed of those who emigrated before and after the 1948 Israeli War of Independence, the majority of whom carry Egyptian passports; the other made up of those who were under Egyptian rule in the Sinai and Gaza Strip and who emigrated after the 1967 war and Israeli occupation. They hold immigrant passports and a status entitling them to most of the rights of citizenship. Since they are exempted from Egypt's compulsory military service and were exempted from nationalization laws under President Nasser's socialist regime, the immigrant Palestinians have traditionally enjoyed a rather privileged status. Both Palestinian groups have duplicated the success story of the Palestinian diaspora. Many are owners or joint owners of some of Cairo's most successful businesses, including chic boutiques, restaurants and night clubs. Others are prominent in banking, the import-export trade and the professions. Many Egyptian Palestinians have settled down and simply want to live and die in Egypt. The humiliation they suffered at the hands of the Israelis in the '48 war is a memory many have tried to block out along with Palestine, past and future. As a result they are neither interested nor involved in politics and controversy. Many immigrant Palestinians, on the other hand, because of their fresher experiences and memories, adhere to the philosophy that an "immigrant is an immigrant whatever and wherever" with all its attending mental, emotional and social problems. While Egypt appears to have gone out of its way to treat them as equals, some complain of feeling like second-class citizens whenever there is trouble or they are required to pronounce their identity or produce their passport. The reality of statelessness and injustice ebbs and flows with current events. And in February 1978, given the mood of the Egyptian man-in-the-street towards a Palestinian leadership considered hostile and ungrateful, and given the revived Palestinian issue, Egypt's Palestinians wanted nothing less than to be caught up in the political fray or become the centre of attention, as a camera crew and I discovered.

In the wake of the Sebai and commando funerals, we set out to get the Palestinian angle. What we got – on a Cairo street housing a couple of long-established small Palestinian businesses – was an irate, hand-waving Palestinian blocking the camera lens. He demanded to know why we were snooping about trying to stir up trouble . . . and ordered us to disappear unless we wanted a fistful of camera. The man was absolutely right. We humbly departed. Other attempts to ferret out Palestinians proved equally fruitless that day. As for the families of several PLO leaders living in Cairo, they had adopted such a low profile they became invisible, at least to the media. There were two exceptions, two Palestinian officials untouched by Sadat's purge. One was Dr Sedkey Al-Dajani, a member of the PLO central committee and a professor of political science at Cairo University, who remained highly visible, active and influential. Regarded as a moderate, he maintained good relations with the Egyptian Foreign Ministry. The other PLO representative, Saied Kamel, a vice-president of the organization's political committee, was considered by many to be more Egyptian than the Egyptians including, it seems, by the PLO, which decided to freeze Kamel's membership because he refused to quit Cairo after the rupture over the peace initiative. Having lived several years in Egypt, Kamel and his Egyptian-born wife Mimi continued to be active on the social and diplomatic circuit. Although not as influential as Al-Dajani, the equally moderate Kamel filled some of his hours cultivating certain members of the media partially out of loneliness I suspect, especially the Americans, whom he considered crucial messengers for the Palestinian cause. But since his power within the PLO decision-making apparatus was now limited, his ability to exploit the media (and vice versa) was equally restricted. Nonetheless the Kamels were charming. I liked them and their interesting *mélange* of Egyptian and foreign friends who gathered occasionally for dinner parties that always included a taste of Lebanese cuisine (virtually identical to Syrian, Jordanian and Palestinian cuisine), which my Egyptian friends readily concede is considerably superior to their own. As for a "Palestinians in Egypt" story, it would require time, and by now it had become abundantly clear that I would never have that time, given television's insatiable appetite for the daily Sadat story.

The peace initiative – dead or alive – now had the American networks staking out Sadat's every breath and move. Even without the price on his head, the Egyptian leader had become too much of a political superstar, too much of a celebrity newsmaker, to ignore. And considering that he was born and came of age on American television, American television seemed determined not to have him die off-camera. The daily stake-out was as much a death-watch as a news check-up. But at this pulse-taking stage I confess I was too busy playing the good, energetic, enthusiastic, aggressive, competitive TV correspondent, too much the professional automaton to reflect on frogs and scorpions in all their seductive disguises.

By March 1978, Sadat's November peace initiative found its natural refuge. Since the Americans – both the Carter administration and public opinion, including a significant portion of the Jewish community – now favoured Egyptian magnanimity over Israeli intransigence, Sadat dumped the peace problem into Washington's lap, where it was instantly picked up and sent back to the Middle East in an old familiar wrapper called "shuttle diplomacy". We were back to square one and the go-between. The US assistant Secretary of State for Near East Affairs, Alfred "Roy" Atherton, shuttled between Cairo and Jerusalem as the newly-appointed roving Middle East ambassador in an effort to mediate between the Egyptians and Israelis. Atherton's comings and goings dragged on for weeks and served only to increase the daily movements of those of us dedicated to stake-outs – the three American TV networks, the wire agencies (DPA, AP, UPI, AFP, Reuters and MENA) and a handful of Egyptian journalists. In addition to staking-out the President (wherever he happened to be), we were now spending several hours a day butting out cigarettes in the brass planters at the Foreign Ministry, begging for coffee in the waiting chambers of the Prime Minister's office or blocking the driveway outside negotiator Mustapha Khalil's Zamalek home. The shuttle ritual never varied in its ending. The opening of a door would signal the media stampede of bodies, cameras, cables, tape recorders and microphones in search of nothing so utopian as a breakthrough, just a hint of something more than "no comment" or "it would not be wise at this time to discuss details" or "we had fruitful and hopeful discussions". Our questions were answered by dancing diplomats with career smiles that signalled their departure and another media stampede to get a couple of closing visual shots of the peace negotiators shaking hands and driving away. We rarely, if ever, had need of these ten to fifteen-second moving visuals because the peace shuttle was going nowhere except between Cairo and Jerusalem. It rarely, if ever, travelled via satellite to New York. Indeed, the best part of the Cairo end of the shuttle was watching Roy Atherton's car speed off to the Jerusalem end of his mission-impossible. We could then pass on the stake-out to our Tel Aviv based counterparts, who seemed to enjoy this peace relay about as much as we did.

Sadat's peace initiative was not dead; it was merely in a state of suspended animation and as long as it was being administered to by the Americans, Sadat could remain outwardly patient, optimistic, even benevolent. Although the political peace committee had collapsed after only a couple of days in Jerusalem, the military peace committee, while equally deadlocked on principles of Israeli withdrawal from the Sinai, was not disbanded. Sadat did not expel and Begin did not recall the Israeli military delegation from Cairo's Tahra Palace. True, Defence Minister Weizman was no longer sleeping in King Farouk's bed, but nine other

Israelis were still ensconced in this royal oasis in suburban Heliopolis, communicating the mood of Cairo – if nothing else – via direct telephone and telex lines. Their existence was so low-keyed that at times the media could not confirm their presence.

On one snooping mission, a camera crew and I decided to park ourselves within viewing distance of the main entrance/exit. After thirty fruitless minutes, during which we ourselves were under surveillance by Egyptian security, we were hustled on our way and ordered not to return. To roll up to the grounds of this walled-in national estate (if one approached on plebeian feet, one would probably not get past the security barricade, let alone the iron gate) is to roll from the present into the past: from the decline of Cairo and the decrepitude of Heliopolis into a museum of immaculate green acres and rarefied air, distilled by decades of colonial privilege and monarchical corruption and preserved along with the complex of palace pavilions not as a public museum but as a refuge for native and foreign VIPs. This magnificent if overly-ornate palace-cum-guesthouse-cum-office was a gift from King Farouk to his wife Farida, who may or may not have had a hand in decorating it with suitable quantities of crystal, marble, gilt, French-inspired furnishings and *objets d'art*. Whenever I had the occasion to stake out Tahra Palace I would fill the hours coveting the Persian carpets or amusing myself with the frescoes on the ceiling that depict Farouk's weakness for nubile pulchritude. Most of the time, though, I was relegated to a stoop on the less artistic side of a door where, unencumbered, I thought about the opulence inside and the poverty outside the palace walls. This never ceased to remind me that the "revolution" which rid Egypt of the British and Farouk was not a revolution but a coup d'état, one that more than a quarter of a century later still left an obscene gap between two worlds that rubbed against each other like two stones in search of a spark.

For the time being at least the prospect of peace, however precarious, prevented Egypt's economic and social inequities from igniting into ugly popular manifestations of the kind that shook the country in January 1977. But now, fourteen months later, others were far less patient or sanguine. Sadat's peace initiative, which so far had met with an obdurate Israeli response, fuelled the fears and passions of the most militant of Palestinians. And again the terrorists struck – this time at the heart of Israel. They came in from the sea not far from the Haifa–Tel Aviv coastal highway, where they commandeered two busloads of Israelis before security forces caught up with them. Over thirty men, women and children died in the attack, more than enough to ensure a swift, massive Israeli reprisal.

I remember Operation Litani well: not because Israel invaded South Lebanon in an effort to carve out a PLO-free security zone from its border northwards to the Litani River, but because the invasion was Israel's first serious test of Egypt's peaceful intentions. And because Sadat passed the test with flying colours. That the Egyptians did not react nearly as strongly as the Israelis feared proved, as though further proof were needed, that Anwar Sadat was not about to scuttle his peace initiative, not for anything or anybody, least of all for the PLO, whom he considered an obstreperous stepchild deserving of the Israeli rout, though he dared not say so publicly. If nothing else, the invasion gave the secluded Israeli military delegation something to do after several idle weeks in Cairo. Since the nine-member team was ostensibly left behind as a communications link (and a symbol that the peace initiative was not dead, only comatose) it now found itself with the ironic task of keeping the Egyptians abreast of Operation Litani from beginning to end. Officially, of course, Egypt joined the Arab and Western chorus of condemnation, urging Israel that the sooner it pulled out of Lebanon, the quicker the peace. Nonetheless, privately, Egyptian authorities (the military brass and Sadat) appreciated the briefings on what the Israelis referred to as an incursion.

But with the peace talks deadlocked, the March 1978 invasion exacerbated Sadat's shaky position in the Arab world and further damaged his image with political foes at home. The fact that the Carter administration – which already embraced Sadat's version of peace – now gave Begin and Dayan a rough time when they visited Washington after the invasion, was another public relations coup for Sadat. But little more. It was that reality which prompted Sadat to invite the only Israeli cabinet member he liked and trusted for another tête à tête, one he hoped might save him from further humiliation, embarrassment and isolation. On March 30, 1978 Defence Minister Ezer Weizman, accompanied by Attorney General Aharon Barak, flew into Cairo from where they helicoptered to Sadat's favourite Barrages residence, fifteen miles from the capital, for talks that would be shrouded in secrecy. Indeed the foreign media, barred from entering the residence compound, resorted to a stake-out position on the perimeter several hundred yards away. This point provided us with a shot of an arriving helicopter, a shot of a departing helicopter, supplemented by various shots of the security surrounding us, and of course shots of other TV crews, which are always indicative of desperate situations and useful in fleshing out picture-poor stories like this one. But as I rushed back to Cairo that evening I had more than a picture problem. I had no story. I did not even know for a fact that Ezer Weizman was in that helicopter. Maybe it was Menachem Begin. Or Yasser Arafat. Or all three. Or none. In this case Egypt TV came to the rescue. As the only media witness permitted to record the opening of the "secret" talks, we requested and received a copy of their tape (a common practice that was often reciprocated). By satellite hour that night I was able to transmit the following story . . . with a little help from ABC's Gumbo:

It's the Israeli Defence Minister's first trip to Cairo since the military talks broke down almost two months ago. And the Egyptians would prefer it if no one knew he was back. The

Egyptian people were not even told of General Weizman's visit. Security is the tightest seen here since November. The foreign news media have been barred from the airport, the presidential resthouse outside Cairo and from Tahra Palace where Weizman reportedly is spending the night. Only Egypt's state-run television was allowed to film the handshakes and smiles but for President Sadat there was nothing substantial behind the Israeli smile. Weizman brought no new peace proposals from Israel; no new position on the West Bank and Palestinian issues ... only an offer to solve the Sinai problem. Sadat refused. It was not enough to resume the peace talks. Sources close to the President say he's furious; he feels he's been deceived, tricked by the Israelis who wanted to score a public relations point. Some Egyptian observers say today's meeting wasn't a total failure, at least for the Egyptians. Sadat has proved he's not interested in a separate agreement with Israel. And this will bolster his position among the hardline Arabs. The meeting they say may also force the Americans into the fray.

Tonight, no one, not even the Foreign Ministry, knows whether General Weizman is still in Cairo or back in Tel Aviv. So it's impossible to even speculate on what happens tomorrow.

That script is a classic example of pressure journalism, TV-style, during the Sadat peace era, the inexcusably contradictory references to Weizman's whereabouts being the least of the points meriting further attention. The fact that there was a news blackout on these secret talks meant that any titbit of information would be amplified in the Western media in general and the American media in particular. As it developed, my exclusive information, however meagre, was more than either CBS or NBC News reported out of Cairo that night. It meant a *herogram* lauding our "editorially and pictorially superior spot" but more significantly the source information disclosing Sadat's anger received big play in other news reports on the Sadat-Weizman meeting. While I provided the sexier Sadat element, the written press, which generally spent much less time staking out a story and more time digging for it, was able at least to place the story in somewhat clearer perspective. Reuters and the March 31, 1978 editions of the *International Herald Tribune* and the *Boston Globe* also quoted in full the source information which ABC New York's publicity department had distributed as a press release along with the script. My little scoop notwithstanding, what the Western media reported of this crucial Sadat-Weizman meeting barely scratched the dimensions of the real story and what was brewing behind it, as I discovered long after it mattered.

Most of us were well aware of Sadat's own hardliners in the Foreign Ministry – a brilliant coterie of highly respected diplomats, legal experts and senior career officers who woke up every morning fearful of what

Sadat might have given away the night before. The majority of them – including the Minister of State for Foreign Affairs, Butros Ghali and the Under-Secretary of State for Foreign Affairs, Osama el-Baz (principal author of Sadat's tough, elegant Knesset speech) – were staunch nationalists and pro-Palestinians deeply committed to Israeli withdrawal from all occupied Arab lands as well as a just resolution of the Palestinian problem, i.e. self determination or homeland. The chimerical Sadat often preferred not to deal with such messy, cumbersome realities as cause and effect, which more than ever were impeding his dream of peace. Thus, one of the functions of his Foreign Ministry was to remind him from time to time that there were certain things he could not do in the name of peace. In return, Sadat was able to exploit the existence of his hardliners in his arguments with the Israelis, reminding them that he too had to think of his critics.

Knowing full well that his Foreign Ministry and others would hardly have recommended he go to Jerusalem in the first place and the suspicion that key individuals who remained at the Foreign Ministry may not have backed him solidly on his peace initiative, may have made Sadat more jittery and wary about the orthodox cadre of diplomats in his service. This did not deter him from pressing on. Egypt, after all, was Sadat. But as each day passed without any visible result accruing from his trip to Jerusalem, many of Sadat's own aides and diplomats, along with the equally cautious Saudis and Jordanians, watched his every move and listened to his every utterance with considerable apprehension. As a result the Egyptian leader increasingly kept his own counsel, rarely consulting his ministers or aides on major decisions involving his peace initiative. Sadat knew they were looking for any hint of a sell-out, of the separate deal he vowed he would never make with Israel. Given the abysmal state of peace by the end of March 1978 and Sadat's anxiety that it might collapse, that his "sacred mission" might have been in vain, the latent adversary relationship between the President and his Foreign Ministry surfaced as barely disguisable mutual mistrust. The hardliners privately opposed the Weizman visit, which is partially why the invitation was issued through War Minister Gamassy who, apart from being Weizman's counterpart, was less dogmatic than his Foreign Ministry colleagues. Besides which, the two generals got along well on a personal level and were still communicating through the Tahra Palace open-line. In fact Gamassy and Vice-President Hosni Mubarak (fiercely loyal to Sadat but, one always sensed, more comfortable with the hardliners like el-Baz) were the only Egyptians present during the Weizman talks.

Judging by Ezer Weizman's account of what transpired that day – the only public one available – Sadat was indeed furious and disappointed with the Israelis, especially with Prime Minister Begin, whom he refused to meet again unless and until he was prepared to display better faith. Sadat felt obliged to remind Weizman that there could be no peace without a resolution of the Palestinian problem and that a separate peace between

Egypt and Israel would serve no one's interests. But then he proceeded to outline a new proposal which even by Sadat's generous standards was remarkable. On the issues of the PLO and a Palestinian state, he confided that he was committed to neither, but that if he told Begin as much, Begin would blurt it out to the whole world. All Sadat wanted, apparently, was Israeli withdrawal from the occupied Arab territories, allowing for a few agreed-upon Israeli military points to take care of the security problem. When Weizman insisted there could be no discussion of total Israeli withdrawal from the West Bank, Sadat retorted that it would be enough "if you say you are willing to withdraw". As for the question of sovereignty over the West Bank, Sadat was prepared to leave it open, and let the Israelis keep their settlements there. In spite of Sadat's furore – or perhaps because of it – Weizman was handed more than he bargained for. But as he was preparing to fly home the following morning with his excellent progress report, he received an abrupt summons to report to the President's Barrages resthouse, where an agitated Sadat told him the deal was off. Sadat had changed his mind. After meeting with Weizman the previous day he had apparently received a group of Palestinian officials from Gaza who made it clear they would settle for nothing less than self-determination, which implied a plebiscite or referendum on the future of the West Bank and Gaza Strip, and Sadat admitted he still needed Palestinian support at this stage. While it's not clear who urged him to consider this obvious fact – the Gaza group or the Foreign Ministry – he deferred to political reality and urged Weizman to encourage Begin to be more flexible, to accept a West Bank link with Jordan. The fact that Sadat had candidly admitted he was not in favour of a Palestinian state was not enough to cheer the deflated Israeli Defence Minister. Since a plebiscite was unacceptable to the Begin government, the peace negotiations were back to square one. Weizman returned to Tel Aviv where he immediately ordered his chief of staff to prepare the army for war.

It would be a long time before Ezer Weizman or any other Israeli official would again be mobbed by Egyptian well-wishers in the streets of Cairo. Only two months earlier, a camera crew and I had trailed behind the euphoria that embraced Weizman, his wife and son as they toured the landmarks of a city enthralled with the promise of peace. There can be no people anywhere in the world more peace-loving, gentle, kind and hospitable than the Egyptians. Unlike members of the intelligentsia, who tend to be more sceptical, average Egyptians, no less than average citizens anywhere, tend to give their leadership the benefit of the doubt in the early phase of a major policy decision. So it was with the peace initiative, staged-managed demonstrations of support notwithstanding. That Sadat had the support of his people was reflected in the warm welcome given visiting Israeli officials and tourists, and Weizman was especially popular. I confess I was amazed at the ease with which so many Egyptians seemed to make the transition from enemy to friend after decades of bloodshed, hatred, fear and humiliating impotence in the face of a seemingly omnipotent foe. That Weizman was charismatic, gregarious, spoke Arabic and already knew Cairo from his World War II days as a Royal Air Force pilot, did not hurt. But the firm handshakes that gripped him, the *Shaloms* that assaulted him, the offers of *Ah Wah Masbout* (regular Turkish coffee), pastries and more lavish gifts thrust upon him and his family as they ducked in and out of the winding shops of the ancient, cavernous Khan el Khalili bazaar, were more than mere expressions of traditional Arab politeness and hospitality. They were sincere gestures of goodwill, peace and hope that prosperity could not be far behind. War after all is bad for business, as Weizman was to discover for himself when he descended upon his old wartime haunt – the famous Groppi's Restaurant in central Cairo. The staff fussed over him just like the old days as he took a table and ordered an *Ah Wah*. But the old faces were gone, along with the splendour that was Groppi's in British-occupied Egypt. Weizman barely recognized the grande dame. She had not aged well. Apart from the fact I had never known her in her prime, I did not share Weizman's sadness at the sight of Groppi's. At least, I thought to myself, she is now her own woman. As for Mrs Re'uma Weizman, a handsome woman with a gentle, gracious manner, she seemed perfectly at ease in her new world. It was Sha'ul Weizman who appeared most overwhelmed by the warmth and smiles of an alien people who almost killed him four years earlier in the War of '73. Unassuming and rather shy, he seemed always to hover in the shadow of his flamboyant father. He had no bitterness towards the Egyptians. On the contrary, he indicated a preference to forget the past and concentrate on a future he never dreamed possible. Tens of thousands of young Egyptians with similar wounds and experiences doubtless felt the same way, in those heady days of peace.

There would be a nine-month interval between the second Sadat-Begin summit at Ismailia and their third summit at Camp David. And it would be another four months before President Sadat would again summon Defence Minister Weizman for another round of private talks. In the wake of their dismal secret discussions, Sadat had no choice but to leave the negotiating to the Americans, who had still not given up hope of producing an Egyptian-Israeli Declaration of Principles on Peace, which is all Sadat wanted and needed and failed to get at Christmas. While the Americans continued shuttling back and forth with no visible result, our foreign desk in New York took the opportunity of an anticipated lull in news activity to switch producers in the bureau. On April 10, Arnie Collins was somewhere between Cairo and Paris and Pete Simmons somewhere between London and Cairo when Gumbo walked into the bureau breathlessly clutching the elements of an American-inspired Egyptian-approved draft of the much sought-after Declaration of Principles. Once Gumbo and I had digested its contents and were agreed on the iron-clad credibility of the sources of the leak, I discussed the story at length with the show producers in New York and executive producer Av Westin and made the decision to air it that night. By mid-evening I had written a draft of my report and consulted with New York again on the graphics that were required (maps, names, etc.) to cue with each element of the draft peace plan; without visuals of some kind, the story would be totally unpalatable for TV viewers. Producer Simmons, anticipating a quiet stint this time around, arrived to find me and the staff frantically preparing for the satellite that had been booked for 1:00 a.m. local time – the precise hour the evening news' first edition goes on the air in the eastern United States and Canada. For the next couple of hours the script was revised and rewritten several times before Simmons and I considered it sufficiently comprehensible. Like most TV news reports, it could have been greatly improved, but in this instance substance took precedence over style.

I powdered my nose, combed my hair, straightened my collar, memorized my twenty to twenty-five-second on-camera summation and proceeded to the bureau balcony studio where I stood against the night, the Nile and the noise of the traffic three floors down. The recording ritual that followed, the Cairo comedy, which we preserved for our in-house gag reel, entailed several takes of me and the cameraman monitoring wind and traffic conditions along the Corniche el-Nil waiting for the perfect moment, the moment when two-ton lorries labouring under their Nile Delta produce and the brisk breeze off the river synchronized and passed us by. That moment often took half an hour in coming, during which time, on the verge of completing what had been a perfect take, the wind would sweep my unlacquered hair in my face or a lorry would drown out my voice, causing me to utter words towards heaven and hell that had no place in my story, script or the family TV. Once the environmental elements got their act together, I was able to perform my little bit, trying all the while to look and sound authoritative as I suppressed the urge to sign off: "Doreen Kays, ABC News, Cairo . . . at the end of another fun-filled day and night of glamorous TV reporting." Friends and family often asked why I never smiled more on-camera and never quite believed me when I replied, "Because I rarely have anything funny to say or smile about, given my life off-camera."

On nights like April 10, 1978, though, the on-camera Cairo ritual and other frustrations were absorbed with the adrenalin that keeps a reporter floating on a good story through the next day and beyond. The following exclusive report was finally transmitted, with a minimum of street noise, wind disturbance and profane asides:

> According to highly placed sources here in Cairo tonight, a declaration of principles is being worked out by the Egyptians, the Israelis and the Americans which covers the following points:
> *First*: the right of each country involved in the Middle East dispute – Egypt, Jordan, Israel, Syria and Lebanon – to its sovereignty and security.

Second: a tripartite Jordanian/Israeli/Palestinian commission to oversee the Israeli-occupied West Bank and Gaza for a period of five years.

Third: at the end of five years, some form of self-determination not only for the Palestinians but for the Egyptians, Jordanians and Israelis living there as well. ABC sources say that before Egypt and Israel would agree to such a declaration of principles, the idea of a Jordanian/Palestinian federation would have to be accepted.

Then there's the Sinai. The Israeli settlements would come under Egyptian sovereignty and security ... and Egyptian settlements would be permitted alongside them. The compromise on Sinai concerns two of Israel's strategic airfields. Egypt would give the Israelis access to Etzion and Ofira air bases until 1982. Israel would withdraw from the Sinai within eighteen months and from Al Arish and Ras Muhammed within the first three months.

On camera close: In order to pave the way for the Sinai agreement, President Sadat has re-assigned three of his top hardline generals. But the main problem is still the Palestinians. And for Sadat, only King Hussein can solve that problem. Well there are reports here tonight that the Jordanian leader might meet with President Sadat this week.

For the moment at least the peace momentum is stirring again ... in spite of all the reports of doom and gloom.

ABC's aggressive publicity department immediately released the report, which was picked up by the Reuters news agency. The following day Westin wired this cable:

KAYS THANKS FOR YOUR EXCELLENT SCOOP ON PEACE TALKS WHICH REUTERS IS GIVING HEAVY PLAY HERE. PRO SIMMONS. KAYS SOUND HAS A DISTORTION TONIGHT PARTICULARLY IN "SH" AND "CH" REPEAT SH AND CH LETTER COMBINATIONS. COULDST CHECK MICROPHONE OR OTHER AUDIO EQUIPMENT TO LOCATE THIS NEW SOUND ELEMENT.
THANKS
WESTIN

While Simmons checked out the strange Kays sounds emanating from Cairo (including a balcony inspection of wind and traffic conditions), I took time out to attend a reception at the Foreign Ministry where I was greeted by a stunned Foreign Minister Ibrahim Kamel and his deputy Butros Ghali who graciously declined to deny the existence of a Declaration of Principles. As for my foreign and Egyptian colleagues, they simply shook their heads and grinned at what one colleague so generously characterized as ABC's "endless resourcefulness".

In between enjoying the limelight and trying to find out what else was going on in town Gumbo and I anxiously awaited the public confirmation that would prove us right. It never came. We subsequently learned that our report was accurate, that there was indeed a declaration of principles with all the elements we reported. But in the perishable world of Middle East news, it died shortly after it was drafted. King Hussein never came to visit because the Americans were unable to get the approval of the Saudis and Jordanians on the proposal for a Palestinian-Jordanian federation; and were also unable to persuade the Israelis to relinquish sovereignty over their Sinai settlements.

The proposed Declaration of Principles resurfaced five months later – with some modifications – in the Camp David Peace Accords.

President Sadat's long, hot, stalemated summer began in April just slightly in advance of the Cairo summer. The Israeli invasion of Lebanon and the lack of progress on the peace initiative combined to force an influential group of his peace critics to come out of the closet. During a heated four-hour debate behind closed doors, several members of the Egyptian Parliament's Foreign Relations Committee called for an end to peace negotiations with Israel.

Leila Takla, the respected chairman of the Committee said:

"We have negotiated with the Israelis for the past six months and there has been no headway. Israel still stubbornly refuses to withdraw from occupied Arab lands and allow the Palestinians a homeland of their own. She is not serious about a comprehensive peace ... she continues to demand – and get – more concessions from Sadat. We all want peace but this path will lead only to more blood. Real peace is not just getting back Sinai. It depends on how Israel behaves in the region. . . . The time has come to close the door." Other parliamentarians echoed her sentiments including a Leftist MP – Mahmoud el Kady – who said: "We are in a unique position. We have alienated our brothers and are speaking to our common enemy. If it had borne any fruit it would have been worthwhile but so far it has not and therefore it should end."

The Minister of State for Foreign Affairs, Butros Ghali, tried arguing the peace position by reminding the committee that the negotiations to end the thirty-year-old Arab-Israeli conflict were at the beginning of a long road. "Let us suppose", he said, "we have a sick man and the cancer he bears can only be cured by surgical operation or fifty sessions of electric shock treatment. How can we claim that the shock treatment we opted for has failed if we have given only two out of fifty prescribed sessions?"

The peace opponents were unconvinced and would become more vociferously entrenched in their views as time passed. For now, they constituted a minority and as such were ignored in the Egyptian media for several months and overshadowed by the Sadat forces in foreign media coverage. Takla, who spoke English and French as fluently and eloquently as she spoke Arabic, was ideal for American television interviews not least because she was an articulate, pro-American, pro-Western member in good standing with the ruling establishment, I sought her out frequently as a highly credible voice of opposition representing Egypt's moderate middle-of-the-road political current. However, by merely opposing the peace initiative with Israel, Takla had become a voice in the wilderness whose interviews tended to get lost on the cutting room floor more often than was editorially desirable. In a one-minute or so peace-related story, the Takla nay-sayers fell victim to the keep-it-short TV news syndrome and American television's predisposition toward Sadat and the official peace corps. In other words, when time constraints forced a choice between a sound clip of Sadat or Takla, the latter became expendable. It would have been inconceivable for Sadat to pop up on the CBS or NBC evening news shows saying something newsworthy and not appear on ABC saying the same thing, especially if we recorded the event. In the first year or so of the Sadat peace story, those brave enough publicly to express their opposition were subjected to censorship in the Egyptian media and an unconscious bias in the American media, specifically on the TV networks, who through their obsessive fascination with Sadat and peace – on and off the air – had little time left over for the anti-Sadat, anti-peace initiative forces. Nothing as crude as imposed censorship, mind you, but the overall effect of our early news coverage was every bit as deleterious.

Takla – a Sadat-appointed Member of Parliament – had become a thorn in his side; one he could never quite dismiss, ignore or manipulate. The dynamic former chairman of the Foreign Relations Committee had become too influential, too well known, too highly regarded by Egyptian, American, Arab and European policy-makers for Sadat to silence. It wouldn't look good for democracy. Takla, after all, was and remains one of Egypt's most notable natural assets. Born into a blue-blood family of lawyers and politicians, she followed in the footsteps of her grandfather and father, studying law at the University of Cairo before heading off to New York University and the University of Southern California for doctorates in political science and management law. It was during her student days in New York that the young Coptic Christian first broke with tradition. She fell in love with Karim Darwish, an Egyptian Moslem whom she married, against great family opposition, in a society where mixed Moslem-Christian marriages are rare. The first of two sons was born in New York City and the couple eventually returned to Egypt. By the time of the peace initiative, Darwish was head of Egypt's Police Officers University, while his more flamboyant activist wife had found a comfortable niche in her country's predominantly male body politic. The husbands of famous wives are a special breed. Without the support of her husband, Dr Leila Takla could never have prowled the corridors of Congress or political committee rooms in the Arab and Western worlds, hobnobbing and consulting with powerful men in the glamorous world of international affairs. But even on the Cairo diplomatic-social circuit, Karim never accompanied Leila, who could always be spotted as the one darting about like an unguided missile. This warm, charming, spirited middle-aged woman, who lights up a room more than any woman I know, is a phenomenon; a superwoman who juggles her roles as wife, mother and public figure with an aplomb I have rarely seen in the supposedly more liberated West. Sadat had every reason to worry about her . . . about her connections and clout with the Americans, the Europeans and the Arabs, and about her embarrassing and potentially dangerous condemnation of his peace initiative. He would not tolerate her indefinitely. Nor most of his critics.

One quiet day in mid-April a cameraman, soundman and I set out for the City of the Dead, not so much to see the dead as to report on the living. Cairo's two-square-mile cemetery area on the city's eastern border, which runs north and south of the Citadel, is a medieval heaven and hell resting under the Muqqutam Hills – beyond the Old City. The cities of the dead have to be the liveliest cemeteries in the world as well as the best-maintained suburbs on the sprawling fringes of greater Cairo. These necropolises with their broad avenues and town houses have through recent decades become thriving squatter communities complete with markets, cafés and *mahaels* (shops). An estimated half a million men, women and children live here among the vaulted dead (actually on top of them) in conditions far superior to Cairo's overcrowded working-class neighbourhoods. The squatters, along with the permanent population of *bo'abs* (caretakers, known as doormen) and their families, have set up home in the stone tomb houses which are built around open courtyards. The vaults of these private family properties are usually found under the courtyard and contain separate furnished chambers for men and women, in the Islamic tradition. Families visit on the anniversaries of the deceased's death and on other occasions such as religious feast days. Otherwise the only other indication that these vibrant communities live off the dead is the sight of a gravedigger preparing a fresh burial spot for someone less affluent than the mausoleum dweller.

It was a gravedigger, by chance, who would figure as the central character in the story I set out to report, an economic story that would provide a human portrait rather than an abstract statistical outline of Egypt's desperate economic plight. Mohammed, his wife and three children seemed to embody the heart, soul and mind of ninety per cent of the Egyptian population; of a country with a per capita income of less that $400; of a deprivation more real and more overwhelming than all the talk of peace and politics swirling daily around their unchanging lives. There were moments as Mohammed and his family lived part of their day before my eyes that my eyes could not bear the pain of what they saw. Was it the stoic resilience, the courage of getting through today in case there is a tomorrow; was it the sense of resignation behind the gentle faces that turned into smiles for the *hawagas* (foreigners) and their electronic eye; was it the four-year-old daughter's face dancing with flies, her matted nest of hair that would never shine, her brown eyes that would never sparkle, this born beauty trapped in a cemetery watching me watching her as her mother cooked *foul* (broad beans – the Egyptian staple) over a flame atop a tombstone; or was it the relief that someone had died that day, that Mohammed had a grave to dig, that the noon meal might be more than *foul* and bread after all? Perhaps it was my own surrealistic existence of frenetic privilege along the Nile ten million miles away. I don't know what precisely caused the ache. I know it was not relieved by the E£30 that Hassan and I pressed into the couple's hands – more money than a month of graves – as a token of appreciation for allowing us into their death chamber. As we scurried to our chauffeured Mercedes that would transport us back to the soap-opera world from which we had briefly escaped, I knew the ache would never go away. And by the time I sat down to write my story, I also knew that Mohammed and I shared something in common: both of us dug graves for a living.

After five months in Egypt I had done my first TV report on Egypt. Unfortunately, Mohammed was not a superstar. His story would not be satellited. It would be hand-carried by producer Simmons to London, where it would join the daily satellite booking to New York and be aired the following night on ABC's late-night fifteen-minute Saturday Night News, when the American TV news audience is a fraction of what it is for the prime-time week-day evening news programmes. If Mohammed was not worth a three-thousand-dollar satellite line, the least he merited was prime time. But since I had long adapted to the realities of the TV news system, I acquiesced in the premise that it could take months before the evening news could fit in my feature. Mohammed clearly did not deserve to sit on a shelf for the rest of his life, so if only one American gets to see Mohammed and hear his story, I thought, it will have been worth all the fatuous non-stories that had become a habit-forming part of television's coverage out of Egypt since November 1977.

April 1978 also marked the end of a five-month era for me. The sustained hype of our media coverage had peaked along with the peace initiative and we were now settled in for a long haul stand-by of daily stake-outs. The imminent arrival of a Cairo-based producer meant saying farewell to two rather special European-based field producers, two veterans so different in personality and professional style it was hard to believe they laboured at the same vocation so effectively. Arnie Collins and Pete Simmons had held my hand and guided me through the madness of an event, a time and a place that only the insane could be expected to appreciate. Collins, the tall, soft-spoken Harvard graduate, the telephone voice that six months earlier had asked "how would you like to be Cairo

bureau chief?" had already departed Cairo with his Lebanese wife, Claud-
ette, whom he'd met during a Beirut assignment. I would miss his friendship, his humanity, his class and his ability to inject himself intelligently
and thoughtfully into a story; a talent, alas, that would no longer be in
abundance among foreign-based producers by the time my assignment
ended. Collins would be over-taken by a younger breed whose intellects
seemed to atrophy the moment they came in contact with anything and
anyone foreign. This deterioration seemed to coincide with the advent of
daily satellite transmission of foreign news and the ascendancy of electronic technology over journalism. In addition, the pressure to come up
with a story equal to, or better than the competition, favours the technicians, those whose qualifications seem limited to technical expertise, speed
and physical stamina. Equally importantly, the best, most experienced
network news producers (for personal, financial or professional reasons)
prefer to remain in the United States rather than work abroad, a trend
that grew up with the satellite age when TV news-gathering became a
global, round-the-clock fireman's job, a trend reinforced for some peculiar
reason by the fact that US-based American producers generally earn
more than their foreign-based counterparts, overseas living allowances
notwithstanding. The end result of all this is fewer and fewer TV news
producers with the required competence and depth to assist the correspondent (and the network) in gathering, evaluating and reporting the news.
In short, the *raison d'être* of the foreign news bureau or assignment –
reporting the news – all too often becomes secondary to transmitting
the news. An industrious, competent correspondent can camouflage this
deficiency by simply carrying the full editorial load, leaving the producer
to tackle the technical and logistical side of the story. But if the correspondent is as lacking as the producer, the result can be such vacuous reportage
that no amount of show-biz electronic wizardry can disguise it.

Perhaps the best definition of a field producer, whether he or she is
attached to a permanent bureau or roams the world as a fireman putting
out crisis news, was volunteered by another favourite of mine who, like
Collins, is no longer overseas or with ABC television. "My job," he said,
"is to make your job as easy as possible." Paul Cleveland, like Collins,
Simmons and a half dozen other dream producers with whom I've worked,
share enviable professional traits: editorial and technical competence, intelligence, solid journalistic experience, broad educational background, sensitivity and adaptability to foreigners and their environment, and an ability
to get the best out of each member of the news-gathering team. If I had
to choose a model producer, I would probably nominate my all-time
favourite, the one who taught me to play blackjack a few feet away from
the bar where he almost demolished me that November night at the Nile
Hilton. Once Pete Simmons got used to the fact that I was not a sub-
standard cub reporter in danger of being intimidated by the reality of
high-stakes TV journalism, and once I got used to the fact that he was
not an ignorant, chauvinistic bully who happened to get off at the wrong

stop, a lasting friendship was born of mutual respect and confidence. In addition to the basic credentials, Simmons possessed a few extra weapons that endeared him to his troops and inspired a loyalty and trust bordering on the phenomenal.

During his long stints in the Cairo bureau, unbeknown to him, a cult had grown up around this self-possessed professional who blithely practised what he preached: a little commonsense in a nonsensical world. As the chief liaison between 18 Sahel el-Gelal Street, Cairo and 7 West 66th Street, Manhattan, Simmons served his dual constituency with a competence and integrity that left all of us on both sides of the Atlantic, feeling secure. When confronted with an absurd suggestion, unreasonable request or outrageous decision from anyone fitting his description of "idiot, asshole or incompetent", he buried it all with the dispatch of a confident, secure, individualist unfamiliar with the popular art of sycophancy. That Simmons cared more about his work than his job, that he had a habit of telling New York coolly, succinctly and graphically exactly what he thought, when the occasion warranted, and that he had the necessary clout to get away with his candour meant that if he was sometimes a thorn in the side of his superiors, he was a legend among those of us who looked up to him as our de facto boss. That he treated his colleagues, Egyptians and non-Egyptians, with the same compassion, good humour and understanding was just one more reason why working with him during the early months of the Sadat peace story made the work more rewarding and enjoyable than anyone had a right to expect. His irreverent wit and appropriately jaundiced eye gave us the necessary levity and perspective to surmount the satellites, non-satellites, the stories and non-stories, the wild goose chases, fruitless stake-outs, equipment breakdowns, power failures, telephone disconnections, traffic jams and eighteen-hour days of stand-up junk food dinners. Simmons was fun to work with. And, as I soon discovered, fun to play with.

A couple of days after our showdown in the Nile Hilton bar, my first week on the job, I took comfort in the fact that Simmons and I had at least one thing in common: we were night people in a city that went to sleep every night sometime between midnight and 7:00 a.m. Since we often finished work about 2:00 a.m. we faced a choice of winding down the day by frequenting one of three all-night hotel coffee-shops, taking in the gaudy sights along the night-club strip near the pyramids, or trying our luck at one of Cairo's two casinos. The casino was the odds-on favourite. We figured we might as well end the day the way we usually began it, but before we could start gambling away the rest of the night, Simmons would have to teach me the intricacies of a game of chance that I suspected was a trifle more sophisticated than the slot machines I once played in Monte Carlo. My mentor, a man of infinite patience, was eagerly up to the task but not before we repaired to the casino bar, where it was agreed we would clear our heads of the day's excess baggage. As the Nile Hilton Casino and bar had become the favourite playroom and watering hole of the more adventurous members of the foreign media in need of unwinding from the seven-day-a-week grind of the peace initiative, the aperitifs also provided an opportunity to socialize with our network competitors, some of whom begged to be reminded they were good family men back home who should quit while they were ahead. That one amateur-turned-addict – a cameraman from England – had already parted with two thousand dollars of borrowed chips did not deter Simmons and myself from cockily ambling towards the tables to sort out the winners from the losers, both patrons and croupiers. After this rather time-consuming promenade, we headed for the cashier to cash in our dollars for chips – or rather Simmons did, with the understanding that if I was to learn how to play blackjack it was best I start off by hovering over him until I caught the gist of play and felt confident enough to lose some of my own dollars.

The Nile Hilton Casino is a modern, attractive, airy, well-lit arena of four roulette tables, eight blackjack tables, young American-trained Egyptian croupiers and a mixed clientele of professional high-rollers (mostly wealthy Gulf Arabs) and less affluent amateurs (mostly tourists and, depending on the night, clowns and cowboys like us). Since gambling is not an official Islamic pastime any more than it is an official Christian or Judaic hobby, the Casino is off-limits to Egyptians. All patrons must display their passports upon entry and only hard currency is accepted. The Casino is operated by a US-based franchise and, according to Egyptian law, half its revenues go to government coffers. It was comforting to know that if I were foolish enough to risk throwing away some of my hard-earned salary, with a little luck half of it would find its way into the hard-pressed Egyptian treasury.

We would in fact return to the Casino several times over the next five months, not so much to win or lose – in the end we broke even – but to seek some relief from our gruelling, unrelenting workday/night schedule and to chat with Silver Rich, to whom we had become addicted. Silver Rich was as unreal as his name. He no more belonged to our world than we belonged to his and he was as out of place in Cairo as Menachem Begin would be, which didn't matter since he worked from 4:00 p.m. to 4:00 a.m. and slept the better part of the remaining twelve hours. Silver, who was born in New Jersey but hailed from "Grahame Greene Land", was tall, middle-aged, debonair and meticulous right to the silver streak in his sleeked-black hair. As co-manager of the Casino, his quiet, unobtrusive presence lurked behind every table, every croupier, every potential trouble-maker and every high-roller who threatened to break the house. Under Silver and his partner Alice's direction, voices, let alone scandal, were rarely raised in this gaming emporium that gave every appearance of being the most orderly, efficient enterprise in Egypt. It was at the bar that we managed to attract Silver's attention one night. Curious about the new breed of gambler that had descended on his casino at roughly the same time President Sadat descended on Jerusalem, he approached Simmons and myself during a break in our verbal gymnastics. We were delighted someone appreciated the jousts that were liberally punctuated with sardonic bursts of laughter, leading him to wonder about the nature of our seemingly bizarre relationship. Once we identified ourselves – Humphrey Bogart and Lauren Bacall – he understood. It was the start of a wonderful friendship. Silver entertained us with tales of the gambling world in exchange for stories depicting the no less degenerate world of power, politics and television. But it didn't take long to realize that Silver Rich, who didn't gamble himself, didn't think much of those who did. Even though Simmons and I were amateurs – I had set a two-hundred-dollar ceiling on my losses – Silver undertook a crusade to dissuade me, in particular, from parting with my money, not that he did anything so godfatherly as coach the croupier to prevent that happening. I realized I had two fairy godmothers when one of them made me the charge of the other. The night before Simmons' final departure from Cairo, we paid a sentimental visit to the Casino. Silver was instructed to look after me and I was made to promise that whenever I got lonely or felt the need to escape TV News and everything and everybody associated with it, especially Anwar Sadat, I was to come and visit Silver, who would regale me with stories of the real world. Their concern so touched me I determined to try and live up to my promise. Sensing that Silver would miss Simmons every bit as much as I would and was sure to welcome any word of his welfare and whereabouts, I quietly contrived a stratagem that would keep me in touch with both. That night at the blackjack tables Simmons hit a winning streak and entrusted me with five hundred dollars for safekeeping while he pursued his luck. By 4:00 a.m. he was riding high on heavy winnings and several litres of Stella beer. Two days later an irate Simmons telephoned from London enquiring after the missing five hundred dollars. I feigned innocence and at the earliest opportunity dispatched an envelope to London which prompted another telephone call, this one appropriately obscene. Instead of receiving his five "big ones" as anticipated, he was now in possession of five one-pound Egyptian notes, the oldest and dirtiest in circulation. I made a point of returning to the Casino to brief Silver, who delighted in the ruse and proceeded to spend the next hour talking fondly of a character the likes of whom he was certain he would not see again in his staid den of iniquity. Our little game lasted several months, ending finally in a London pub with the reluctant hand-over of the five crisp hundred-dollar bills.

It would be several more months before I saw Silver again. Not that I never got lonely. Not that I never felt the need to escape from the story. But by the spring of 1978 I had become entrenched as bureau chief/ correspondent which entailed a heavy obligation to the social circuit. It would be another two years before I would indulge in anything resembling a personal, private life. Fun and games would prove as scarce as peace.

Six months to the day after President Sadat returned home from Jerusalem to a triumphant hero's welcome, he turned the first of many screws
on his much-vaunted democracy. Egypt's constitutional freedoms, we were
told, were being "exploited by opportunistic bubbles". They would have
to be removed to save democracy from itself, or more accurately Sadat
from his critics. In a national referendum on May 21, 1978, eleven million
eligible voters – out of a population of roughly forty million – were asked
to approve a clamp-down on the President's political opponents of the left
and right. Of the ten million who voted 98.29 per cent said "yes". At
least, that is what the media was expected to report. The Egyptian media
had no choice. The foreign media did. It's hard to say how many people
actually went to the polls or how many believed that ten million did. But
in Cairo, by now with a population of nearly twelve million and presumably
half the eligible voters, foreign journalists who made individual tours of
various polling stations – those we were able to scrutinize with or without
the approval of the Interior Ministry – failed to see even hundreds marking
ballots let alone millions, although we assumed several thousands must
have voted. Foreign embassies estimated the Cairo vote to be in the
thousands. Furthermore, no Cairene I knew voted and every Cairene I
confronted with the staggering official results the day after dismissed them
with the snickering incredulity that had come to characterize their opinion
of elections and referenda in a democracy which President Sadat turned
on and off whenever it was to his advantage.

In the reports filed and transmitted by the Western media, doubt was
expressed on the referendum results and, more cogently, on the threat to
democracy as perceived by Sadat. The gist of the stories revealed the anti-
democratic warts in Sadat's hitherto enlightened and unblemished image
in the West. Our hero could not and would not tolerate opposition to his
peace initiative. His broad-based popular support, while it had been
chipped away by Israeli intransigence, American impotence and economic
strangulation was hardly in danger of imminent erosion from what he
called "subversive" elements. Neither the right-wing, largely upper-
middle-class New Wafd Party, reconstituted from the remains of the
Old Wafd Party which ruled before the 1952 revolution, nor the small
Progressive Socialist Party, a coalition of Nasserists, socialists and Marxists
(led by Khaled Mohieddin, one of the leaders of the '52 coup along with
Sadat and Nasser) could claim broad grass-roots support although the
Wafdists posed a possible long-term threat. In now silencing them, Sadat
was undermining his own liberalizing efforts to steer Egypt on the road
towards a multi-party democracy. And in a move which merely reinforced
this new image of a heavy-handed dictator, he also reproached those who
had so successfully promoted his good-guy image abroad for now tainting
that image by "distorting the facts" about his domestic leadership. Evid-
ently he felt he could not afford to alienate the foreign media while he
still needed them. So rather than silence us, too, he summoned us to his
Barrages villa for a stern lecture on truth.

After telling the assembled correspondents, cameras and recorders how happy he was to see us all again, he proceeded to spend the next two and a half hours wrapping us on the knuckles for our wayward reporting – not unlike an exasperated headmaster scolding his naughty, impudent charges for straying from the chosen path. Such a disappointment were we to this world statesman and staunch Western ally, this peacemaker whom "the whole world" had come to admire. "Quite frankly," he began plaintively, "I am not happy with what I have read in your papers." The prime culprits, we were informed, were four of the most influential British and American news organizations: the London *Times* and *Guardian*, the BBC World Service and the *New York Times*. Reaching into a heap of papers on a table before which he was seated, he plucked out press clippings and other bits and pieces of evidence to substantiate this purported anti-Egypt campaign of "half-truths" and "false pictures" that included references and questions on the stability of his regime and the collapsing state of the Egyptian economy. Playing the role of the wounded puppy, Sadat reminded us that "censorship ended in Egypt four years earlier" (a half-truth, since this freedom applied only to the foreign media and not the Egyptian media) implying that we, like his critics, were exploiting this freedom by indulging in "misinterpretation".

"If I were against democracy, would I have held a referendum?" he roared indignantly. "This is not Moscow. This is a free country. No one bugs your phones. . . ." (Without exception, each of us assumed our phones were bugged, and as internal dissent intensified over the next three years we had good reason to believe they were indeed bugged.) Because the British media were not as valuable to him as the American media and American support for his peace initiative, he concentrated his attack on the BBC, *The Times* and *The Guardian* in London, chastising them for consorting with his critics whom he did not mention by name, preferring to lump them all together as "opportunistic bubbles on the surface". The most prominent of these irritating "bubbles" charged with infecting us with "false pictures" was the noted journalist and author Mohamed Heikal, once President Nasser's Minister of Information, editor-in-chief of the prestigious daily *Al Ahram* and Nasser's favoured confidante. Heikal was also a close aide of Sadat until 1974, when the two split over the President's decision to freeze the Soviet Union out of Middle East peace negotiations. Following the rupture, Heikal began writing critical articles that appeared in Egyptian, Arab and Western publications, particularly the respected *Sunday Times*, with which he had a contractual agreement for serialization rights to his English-language books. That he also frequently popped up in interviews on the BBC World Service and BBC TV, speaking his mind on the flaws, as he saw them, in some of Sadat's domestic policies as well as the sacrosanct peace initiative, further infuriated Sadat. He felt a personal betrayal that manifested itself in public bitterness. Heikal, who spoke French and English and was courted by the American and British media as a credible voice of opposition – one of less than a handful prepared to talk openly to foreign correspondents – had become public enemy number one.

Heikal, who worked out of his spacious, elegant, book-lined Nile-side flat was the antithesis of a rabble-rousing political radical. Admittedly, he was ambitious and suffered from the loss of power he once enjoyed so abundantly. That Sadat felt threatened by this representative of the Egyptian upper-middle class, and by anyone else who publicly defied him or denounced his peace initiative or other policies, and that he felt the need to silence these critics by pushing through a national referendum to "strengthen democracy" as he put it, indicated more than an insecure, vulnerable leader. It showed up traits in his personality that had lain dormant since his phenomenal peace mission six months earlier, one of which was an inability to separate the personal from the political, a trait admittedly shared by many Arab leaders. Furthermore, the authoritarian who believed in peace did not really believe in democracy; he played at it for the benefit of the most powerful democracy in the world and when his democratic experiment – for that is what it was – got too messy, he crushed it, in the name of a more pressing priority called peace. As the self-proclaimed "father of the Egyptian people", he and he alone it seemed knew what was best for his "sons and daughters" as he so fondly referred to them in his Arabic speeches, talks and interviews. That this patriarchal, patronizing and contemptuous attitude insulted many Egyptians – especially those who were neither illiterate nor ignorant – seemed to elude him. Since his people were not mature enough to cope with democracy, for that is what he and his policies implied, he would have to look after them, to save them from themselves.

If Sadat the dictator didn't much care about the opinions of his own people, he was too astute to ignore the criticisms of Westerners, especially Americans, without whom he figured his peace initiative would surely die, and him with it. His love affair with America, and more importantly with American television, helps explain why the only American target in his attack on the foreign media was the *New York Times*, even though I, for one, transmitted TV reports on both the referendum and President Sadat's predicament at home and in the Arab world. None of the stories – including those most offensive to Sadat – was as critical as it might have been, even allowing for our lack of prescience. The American media, TV News in particular, still tended to accentuate the positive Sadat, not because our producers in New York were unaware of his negative tendencies but because in the words of one: "We know the man's a dictator; that's not especially newsworthy. What's still news though is peace in the Middle East and his efforts towards that end." It was too soon then for the Egyptian leader to have worried about TV sullying his pristine image. Apart from the news shows' format – hardly a vehicle for responsible or in-depth analysis – we had no outlet equivalent to the *New York Times'* daily editorials or leaders. In 1978 commentator Howard K. Smith was still doing his five-minute commentary slotted into the end of ABC's half-hour evening news; a personal analysis on subjects of his choice. Not even that exists today. A critical analysis of Anwar Sadat at this stage would not have been popular either with network news executives or the mass TV audience, popular enough, that is, to get aired. The promise of peace was still far too potent and untouchable.

A news conference immediately followed Sadat's lecture on "truth". As it was several weeks since the media had had an opportunity to query him thoroughly on the state of his peace initiative, the thrust of the questions was predictable. I had prepared a list of eight, only one of which dealt with his internal crackdown and conflicting images, and by the time I was given the floor it had already been answered. So I concentrated on my priority peace question, knowing that with Sadat's rambling style of speech punctuated with dozens of ums and ahs . . ., I would probably be limited to one question.

"Mr President, the Second Sinai Disengagement Agreement with Israel expires – comes up for renewal – in October. If there is still no movement on the peace initiative by then, will October become the real test of your Jerusalem initiative . . . in other words would you be prepared to hold off on renewal?"

The President's response was guaranteed to make headlines. And bury his ugly domestic story. The master manipulator had done it again. He threatened to pull another rabbit out of his hat: if the peace process proved fruitless, said Sadat, he just might *not* renew the Sinai Disengagement of Forces Agreement: "I hope that on the next 23rd of July there will be a surprise." If his overtures to Israel failed to bring a settlement, "it's not the end of the world," declared Sadat, "let us try another way, let us try another system". So for the first time he was serving notice on the Israelis and Americans; they had two months to get cracking, otherwise who knew what might happen, what the unpredictable Sadat might do? It was the old carrot and stick routine. His two-month deadline would coincide with celebrations of the 28th anniversary of the July ('52) "revolution". "The momentum of the peace process now is slackening," admitted Sadat, "but it has not stopped. For now there is a stalemate of sorts. It is not frozen but going in slow motion." Slow motion? My God, I thought, he's even talking like us now.

We filed out and rushed the fifteen miles back to Cairo to write up our lead story. The peace initiative was back on stage for a long summer run.

Less than a week later Sadat's official opposition, the New Wafd Party, was disbanded and its leader, Fouad Serrag-Eddin, excluded from public life. The Progressive Socialist Union Party suspended its activities rather than be gagged by a new law restricting political activity; a law that now prevented what Sadat termed the "pre-revolutionary centres of power" as well as communists (real or imagined) from holding key posts in government, trade unions, industry and the media. The leftists, with three seats in Parliament, released a statement to the media saying: "The bill passed by Parliament is vague . . . it threatens freedom of thought and violates Article 40 of the Egyptian Constitution which prohibits discrimination on the basis of sex, conviction, religion, origin or language and considers all citizens equal before the law." More than forty leftists, including a member of parliament, were now in police custody for having urged a "no" vote on the referendum, a vote supported by Egypt's Lawyers' Syndicate which termed the referendum "unconstitutional". The leftist party also suspended publication of its weekly newspaper *Al Ahali*, which had turned into a powerful weapon against dubious government policies.

Since the 1976 political liberalization programme that opened up the party system in Egypt for the first time following the 1952 "revolution", the official opposition forces (including the conservative New Wafdists with twenty-four seats in Parliament, seven Socialist-Independents and eighteen Independents) represented a tiny minority, albeit an increasingly vocal one, alongside Sadat's ruling National Democratic Party with three hundred and eight of Parliament's three hundred and sixty seats. They had become troublemakers with their allegations of government mishandling of foreign investment projects, questions about the personal integrity of some cabinet ministers and criticism of the government for sky-rocketing food prices, and of Sadat's go-it-alone peace initiative. The first victims of the crackdown, though, were not politicians but journalists – Egyptian journalists working at home and abroad. More than fifty came under investigation by the State Prosecutor, charged with "abusing Egypt and threatening national unity". Those writing from abroad were ordered home for questioning while five of Cairo's most prominent writers were banned from leaving the country, Sadat's former confidante Mohamed Heikal among them.

The story did not make the TV network news shows – insufficient interest.

By the summer of 1978, American network news' obsession with Anwar Sadat – "a man and his peace" – had become a debilitating one for those of us charged with the task of watching him personally. The ABC, CBS and NBC correspondents and camera crews were now covering the Egyptian President with the same attention accorded the American President, but without benefit of the human, technical and logistical back-up enjoyed by our Washington counterparts. The flying circus of extras (human and electronic) that had come to town for the opening acts of "peace" had departed, leaving the three Cairo bureaux with one correspondent and camera crew apiece to stake-out the daily comings and goings of a President who never stayed in one residence long enough to establish the Egyptian equivalent of a White House. The peripatetic Sadat hopped between his several "white houses" whenever he felt the urge to escape Cairo, which came about every three days. And when he wasn't reflecting in one of the resthouses he was criss-crossing the country giving pep talks on peace and prosperity and laying cornerstones of model projects which, as far as I could discern, were largely token symbols of progress meant to augment the highly creative economic success stories that daily filled the press and TV screens. If Egypt were building as many low and medium cost housing units, converting as many hectares of desert into arable land and producing as many goods and services as Sadat's official propaganda machine trumpeted, the country would long since have joined the ranks of the world's most developed nations. The fact that Sadat preferred to view his country from the air rather than from the ground could hardly be attributed to security measures alone. I dare say his penchant for helicopter and jet travel between Cairo and his home village of Mit Abul Kum, his favourite resthouse at the Barrages, his two resthouses in Ismailia, his summer home in the Alexandria suburb of Mamourrah and the scores of cities, towns and villages along the Nile Delta, the Suez Canal and inland, was the most painless – and expensive – way of avoiding the sights, sounds and smells of poverty that would have accompanied him along the narrow, dusty overburdened roadways. Sadat, who was only too familiar with the harsh realities of his poor country, knew that he could not turn the situation around dramatically and quickly enough to make a significant dent. So he literally flew over the immense problem while setting his sights on the more urgent and glamorous problem of peace. His preoccupation with peace at the expense of Egypt's deep economic malaise – including the unfettered corruption that walked through his Open Door policy in 1974 – would cost him dearly.

For the time being, I calculated that Sadat's air travels, not including the longer journeys to his winter home in Aswan, his beloved Sinai and a variety of foreign countries, had him suspended between heaven and earth for more hours than the average commercial airline pilot. This possibility comforted me at moments when I strongly doubted that Sadat had, in fact, ever touched ground when he returned from Jerusalem that November day. Not that I can blame him for wanting to remain in the clouds. And not that the rapacious American networks were idle bystanders in this heady experience.

Having collectively dedicated ourselves to the pursuit of one man and his story, we could do no less than co-ordinate our individual, and at times indistinguishable efforts. Once we realized that our seven-day-a-week coverage of Sadat was turning us into zombies, commonsense overtook our competitive instincts. Since all three Cairo bureaux – now conveniently operating under the same roof – followed Sadat's every public or official outing (in case he might say something or, worse, succumb to heart failure or an enemy's bullet) and since each of us on these occassions inevitably wound up with the same story – visually and substantively – or no story, as was more often the case, we agreed to pool our resources on selected Sadat stake-outs. For example, if the President was scheduled to spend four days in Tanta, Fayoum, Minya or some other Delta town planting trees and meeting party officials, or if he decided to meditate on his roots in Mit Abul Kum for a couple of days, secluded in his compound so as not to be disturbed by the villagers, his relatives or us, we husbanded our energies by assigning on a rotation basis one pool correspondent and camera crew. Nine times out of ten these excursions produced nothing more than a severe case of ennui or a frustrating encounter with local police, blue-bereted presidential guards, Sadat's personal bodyguards or, worse, his press spokesmen, all of whom knew considerably less of Sadat's plans than we did and none of whom seemed in the least interested in accommodating himself to American-style electronic journalism. If we chose to spend our days trailing their *Raïs* (President) that was our business; if the President couldn't resist talking into our camera, that was his business. Their business was to protect him at all times, even when he indicated to his press and security men, less than subtly at times, that he didn't want to be protected. This usually resulted in a nasty scene of pushing, shoving, shouting, swearing and a few bruised ribs courtesy of the muscular protectors, usually outside a mosque, usually on a Friday Sabbath. Our pool system was probably most effective in these free-for-all stake-outs. At the least it guaranteed that two TV correspondents and two camera crews were always physically fit and in reserve back in Cairo. And while the pool crew was out in the field getting bashed about or dehydrated, Cairo was being covered by the other two networks who served as pool for all three. Given the constant comings and goings of shuttling peace negotiators, visiting congressmen and wandering VIPs, the pool system rarely if ever gave us an intended day off but occasionally allowed us a sit-down lunch, if only in the bureau. The arrangement worked for a time.

The Cairo coverage of the Sadat peace story was unique in the degree of co-operation that existed between the three major US TV networks, certainly in the field. Personally I found the pooling of resources for certain Sadat stake-outs not only feasible but necessary if we were to function day after day after day in what could only be described as an abnormal assignment. But when it got excessive, I was often tempted to advise my producer to advise New York to amalgamate the ABC, CBS and NBC Cairo operations under the title American Network News, ANN for short. Instead, I tried to beat this system whenever possible by giving our reports a different look, not visually but substantively.

By working overtime with my network of informants, ABC could occasionally claim credit for something more than the predictable fluff being churned out. If nothing else, coming up with exclusive information and cultivating sources got me through some of the absurdities and frustrations that seemed to multiply with time.

Speaking of stake-outs, Mit Abul Kum and Friday prayers at the mosque topped the "least favoured" list; Alexandria in summer and Aswan in winter were "most favoured."

President Sadat's home village rests in the Delta Governorate of Munifiya at the end of a hair-raising ninety-minute drive from Cairo. To the first-time visitor from outer space, it is neither pretty nor palatable and in most other respects is a typical Egyptian village inhabited by dust, horse manure, flies, mud huts, chickens, donkeys, less-than-spotless children, men in long, soiled cotten *galabayias* and women in traditional layers of black out of which peek colourful house dresses. The village is a victim of the unhygienic Nile and Egypt's pervasive poverty. What distinguishes it from thousands of other villages camped along the Delta is a paved main street along which a presidential retreat nestles between concrete walls on one side, an oasis dotted with real, red-brick houses on the other, and the absence of begging children. The asphalt road, the red-brick dwellings and the lack of little outstretched hands beseeching "*baksheesh*, mister, *baksheesh*?" came courtesy of the village's most famous son, who every now and then touched down on the helipad within his concrete compound to renew his links with the past and the present, if only for the benefit of the foreign media.

Sadat's first autobiography *Revolt on the Nile* was banned in Egypt. His second, *In Search of Identity*, published shortly after his peace mission, (widely ridiculed for its self-serving distortion and twisted history) fused both worlds. By chronicling the story of his life, which began in this poor village along the banks of the Nile, Sadat publicly rhapsodized on one of his favourite themes: the tale of a peasant childhood rich in spirit and love of God; the Abe Lincoln of Egypt whose humble beginnings drove him on to a greatness for which he was destined, an unselfish greatness at the service of his country and people, a people with seven thousand years of civilization behind them, a superior people, and he their destined leader. That this twentieth-century pharaoh saw himself as a common man destined for the uncommon coloured his autobiography and cropped up repeatedly in scores of articles, books and interviews in the West. I sensed it was this romantic, mystically imbued image of himself that he most cherished and cultivated. And as a reminder to the world, Egypt, his family, relatives and the villagers of Mit Abul Kum that his past was alive and well, he would leave a legacy other than a private villa – however modest – that announced his escape to power, fame and wealth; he would leave real red-brick houses for the peasants who would never break out, built with royalties from *In Search of Identity*. Each time I drove into Mit Abul Kum, the construction sign told me so. And each time I thought what a generous, compassionate gesture. But other gestures always marred the purity of the image.

Sadat's trips home occurred usually on special occasions: to celebrate his birthday on December 25; to vote at the village school in some election or national referendum; to pray at the tomb of his younger brother on the anniversary of the October '73 war in which his brother had been a victim; to pray at the village mosque; to visit the schoolroom he attended as a boy; to give important interviews. Each event seemed guaranteed to generate publicity, indeed each event – including the interviews conducted in the privacy of his garden or home – were media events which served to promote the image of local boy makes good and comes home again and again to his roots. These gestures would have been more convincing had they been realized without an army of television cameras, tape recorders, gawking reporters and pistol-toting bodyguards who invariably stood between the *Raïs* and the intended object of his affections, be it the ballot box, the tomb, the villagers, us or God. The Mit Abul Kum experience was further tainted by the endless hours of waiting for His Excellency's scheduled appearance from behind his barricade, which did not always transpire, schedule or no schedule. Without exception, a Mit Abul Kum stake-out, active or passive, always ended in exasperation, exhaustion or both – and if it ever produced news, I fail to recall what it was or how relevant it was to reality.

Only one other stake-out assignment provided as many feet of stock video tape for our Cairo and New York libraries and that was the mosque, or more accurately mosques, depending on where the President was in Egypt on any given Friday. The one opportunity of the week, the Sabbath, when we could have joined the rest of Egypt in a day of rest, became just one more opportunity to shadow Sadat who tended to pray in public more often than not, if only to enhance his image as a devout Moslem. Photographers for the three major Cairo dailies and Egypt TV's presidential camera crew made certain this politically important gesture did not elude the populace. When he happened to be in residence in Cairo, which was not infrequent despite his travels, the American network ritual involved less than discreet surveillance duty across the street from the presidential concrete compound in Giza which had the Soviet Embassy and the Sheraton Hotel as neighbours on one of the city's bustling thoroughfares. Since the Presidency rarely announced where Sadat would pray on a Friday (and since there are one thousand mosques in Cairo), several hours were consumed by a cat and mouse game that started just before noon with our Mercedes parked and ready to go the moment the presidential guards lifted the barrier signalling the exit of the President's car, which depending on his mood was either a Mercedes or a Volkswagen Rabbit in any one of the colours of the rainbow. In the split second it took for the motorcade to speed past us, our well-trained and experienced drivers (CBS and NBC usually spent their Fridays with us) would be on the tail of a car occupied by some of Sadat's personal bodyguards, not necessarily the last one in the convoy. What then ensued was an eighty-mile-an-hour chase through the city with the network cars bumper to bumper and door handle to door handle with the security cars and each other. With the presidential motorcade dodging in and out of traffic in an attempt to shake us off their trail, and the three network cars vying for first place abreast (not behind) the convoy, other Cairene motorists, who of course could never be forewarned about these unofficial drag races had nowhere to flee. That there were no fatalities as a result of these Friday outings was a miracle and damages seemed limited to dented fenders, scraped car paint and abnormally high pulse beats.

On reaching our destination, which invariably was one of the mosques in the vicinity of the pyramids, we were lucky if the cameraman managed to get a shot of the President entering the mosque and some interior shots of him on his knees, forehead bent in prayer. As my growing perversities did not include glaring at supplicants, presidential or otherwise, I always maintained a decorous demeanour outside the mosque midway between the entrance/exit and Sadat's car at the kerbside. Hassan – who usually joined the prayers along with some of the bodyguards, two or three Sadat aides and confidantes and some non-threatening locals who had been screened in advance – always managed to slip out early so as to be in position to assist me and the crew for the contest ahead. The reason we were rarely officially notified of where Sadat would be praying is that Sadat did not want us around, at least officially. But because he sometimes felt the need to say something – usually to the US administration or the Israelis – we were forced into phase two of the cat and mouse game. Unfortunately Sadat's bodyguards refused to learn the intricacies of this primitive game which entailed close observation of Sadat's face upon recognition of our hungry presence. After the first few weeks I for one had become expert at sensing whether the President wanted to talk or rush off to meet with family at a nearby in-law's home. But this was lost on his bodyguards, with whom he rarely spoke, especially the half dozen or so who seemed to have been recruited from the grunt school of infantry combat. Even those with whom we had established a warm, friendly rapport were themselves often overwhelmed by the sheer brute force of their comrades. The mosque stake-outs were the most violent, if not always the most fruitless. In the beginning these encounters yielded several newsworthy interviews which were always picked up by other Western news agencies and the Egyptian media. But by mid-1979 the network correspondents and camera crews came close to mutiny over these hit-and-run battles which our producers back in the comfort of their bureaux did not have the wisdom and courage to end, even though they were becomingly increasingly futile and ridiculous. I especially resented finding myself alone to ask the questions on behalf of all three networks, my colleagues having given up, leaving their cameras and me to do the work. I too eventually cut out, refusing to accompany the crew to Friday prayers, which hardly delighted the cameraman and recordist who rightly felt they were doing everybody's dirty work. I finally suggested to my New York superiors that we wind down Sadat stake-outs in general, and the mosque exercise in particular, on the grounds that our time would be better spent researching and reporting on the country and the people behind the man, of which our viewers had been little informed. They agreed wholeheartedly in principle if not in practice. But by the time the bureau producer felt secure enough to wean himself off his habit (i.e. the fear of missing a Sadat story) it no longer mattered.

That some of us managed to maintain a semblance of equilibrium – though quite frankly I never found time to corroborate this with experts

– can in large measure be attributed to what I shall always fondly remember as "summers in Alex."

It became clear in early May 1978 that Alexandria was a Mediterranean plum waiting to be plucked by a group of newshounds hungry for anything but news. Here at last was a stake-out whose hedonistic potential begged to be exploited. Although every bit as ravaged as Cairo, Alexandria has only one third the population and all the ambience of a city hugged by a fifteen-mile stretch of sand, surf and salt-sea air. At the end of the one-hundred-and-thirty-five-mile northwesterly trip from the capital, before even turning onto the broad Corniche that spans the city, one literally breathes easier, swept along by a sea breeze that whispers relief from the dry heat of Cairo and the Delta. This one-time capital of Egypt, founded by Alexander the Great in 332 BC, tries nobly to remind the visitor of its glorious, ancient and not-so-ancient past. But along the Corniche it is best to look leftwards towards the eternal blue than towards the grey dilapidation of the high-rises to the right, long since ignored by their owners who apparently feel no compunction to cleanse or whitewash their eyesores. The incentive is lacking. Dirty or clean, maintained or not, hundreds of thousands of Egyptians flock to Alex. every summer to rent many of these high-rise flats for the sheer pleasure of draping themselves over the balconies and the beaches below. At night they promenade by the thousands along the café-lined Corniche, blissfully unaware that finer summer resorts with finer corniches exist in this world, along this very same Mediterranean. For to the Egyptian, *Iskandria* (Alexandria) is paradise, a nirvana that bears little or no resemblance to the romantic Bohemia of Lawrence Durrell's *Alexandria Quartet*.

President Sadat's Alexandria was something else; a summer villa in suburban Mamourrah, roughly twenty minutes beyond the Corniche, where he repaired for repose, reflection and a little work for varying periods between May and September. Having moved to his white house on the beach we were obliged to follow. There was remarkably little kicking and screaming as the ABC News convoy first headed north to stake out the beach. Naturally, we would require the best accommodation money could buy, which at that time could only be had at the Palestine Hotel. During the warm weather months it was always booked to capacity. To get a room one had to reserve weeks, if not months, in advance. This was hardly a challenge for Hassan who managed to free four of the best rooms on the strength of a phone call and the mention of *el Raïs* and *el Télévision Amrika*; unfailing passwords that opened doors, with the help of a little *baksheesh* of course. It was not uncommon to unbook a booked hotel room only to find it re-booked upon arrival. The *baksheesh* straightened out any "misunderstanding" and secured the necessary rooms for indefinite stays. At the end of the Corniche there is only one way to turn – to the right along a road that leads to Mamourrah. But only a few yards round this bend one crosses the boulevard and drives up to a checkpoint for a cursory nod from someone whose function is checking ID's but whose talent is traffic control. So moving on, one enters what was King Farouk's Garden of Eden. Palm trees and massive sculpted lions resting on pedestals guide us through what once was the king's private pleasure and today is a public park, acres of wide open green space bound on three sides by tall trees and the ubiquitous concrete wall and straight ahead by only sand, sea and sky. Perched between the sky and the sea are two hotels – the Soviet-built Palestine to the left and across the man-made bay the more historic and colourful Salamlek Hotel, originally a guest house for some of Farouk's friends. Separating the two are public cabanas and a terrace café.

TV news teams do not enter hotel lobbies. They descend upon them like invading armies. And so began three summers of occupation, interrupted only by frequent trips to Cairo, other foreign countries and formal holidays called "home-leave". Sadat's summer retreat was but a swim away from our sandy Palestine oasis and while one could not actually see it, one sensed it was there from the barbed wire installed in the waves, the bobbing frogmen playing charades with the buoys and the soldiers melting behind their beach sandbags. Since there was unanimous agreement among the network news teams that Sadat should interfere as little as possible with our sunbathing schedule, we did not mind the occasional thirty-minute land route to his sealed camp, the sixty-minute battle to enter the camp, the hours spent in waiting rooms on the periphery of the modest white concrete house with its gardens, green acres, tennis court and playground, or (once inside) the additional hours waiting for the fifteen-second photo opportunities and, with a little luck, a question and answer session with either Sadat or his visiting VIPs, or both. As we lounged in the lawn chairs or sprawled on the lawn, our boredom was occasionally relieved by the good humour of our favourite Sadat bodyguards (who with their families occupied an attractive apartment building adjacent to the compound), smiling, white-jacketed waiters serving up fruit juices, coffee or tea and by the President's youngest daughter Jihan, who had an irritating habit of roaring in and out of the compound in one of several European compact cars at her disposal, as though she were preparing for the Grand Prix. Some of us dubbed her the "Princess", though I confess I found her less regal, and more a spoiled brat, pampered and tolerated by an adoring father. That our cameras deliberately ignored her did not discourage this slim, dark-haired beauty from publicly flouncing about at every available opportunity. At age eighteen she had become a source of rumours, gossip and controversy. Of the four Sadat children (he also had three daughters from an earlier marriage, who along with his first wife still live in Cairo, unseen and unheard) Jihan, named after her mother, most resembled her father; the same eyes, the same complexion, the same dramatic flair and the same taste for elegant and trendy European and American fashions. Although married at the age of sixteen – against her mother's wishes – she was rarely seen in the company of her husband, the son of Osman Ahmed Osman, Egypt's best known multi-millionaire, a Sadat confidante and occasional government minister who had a monopoly of the country's construction industry. Young Jihan always seemed to accompany her parents on their travels near and far which lent credence to rumours that her marriage was headed for divorce.

Overall then we tended to prefer the predictability of the Palestine Hotel that first summer: the sun-bathing, the swimming, the omelette and chips lunches in the air-conditioned coffee shop and dinners by the sea at the famous Greek restaurant, Zephyron, in Abou Kir, where we dined on the finest shrimps and fish anywhere in the Mediterranean. When I wasn't working on a story, my bronzed body or deprived palate, I was hunched over the private hotel telex, transmitting and receiving messages and news summaries via the Cairo bureau or waiting for the friendly, obliging switchboard to put me through to Cairo, London or New York, although the feed quality of the phone lines to and from New York was such that ABC Radio could rarely use my radio reports. As for TV, Alex. lacked satellite facilities, so reports (video casettes and recorded scripts) had to be hand-carried back to Cairo for editing and transmission. We saw no reason why these minor inconveniences should abort the Alex. stake-outs. Indeed, so alluring was the assignment that the pool arrangement worked out between the three networks was later abandoned in favour of unilateral coverage. Our respective New York assignment editors, show producers and news executives never queried the transfer of half their bureaux from Cairo to the Mediterranean. Their chief concern was that we cover Sadat and all stories relevant to peace. We did. On a couple of occasions, though, when I would appear on camera, on location, looking like burnt toast, I fully expected a scorching reprimand from the show. That none came I attributed to the compassion or myopia of the show producers. To ensure that everyone in the Cairo bureau had an equal opportunity to cool off in Alexandria's 35°–40° C, schedules were arranged to allow rotation of the producer and researchers to join me, the camera crew and Hassan on the beach.

But by the summer of 1980 our summer stake-out would lose some of its appeal to the monotony of year-round tans and each other's company: our TV "war" stories were no longer amusing, the jokes no longer funny and the shrimp no longer worth the hour's drive to Abou Kir.

Anwar Sadat found no solace in Alexandria in 1978, or in the solitary brisk walks that were part of his daily routine. His orientation towards the West – down to his exercise costume of American tennis shoes, white athletic socks, terry-cloth shirt, matching shorts and brimmed straw hat – belied the anxiety and disappointment he now felt over his American "partner in peace". He did not want or need an "honest broker" but a "full partner". Those close to him indicated in "not for attribution" conversations that the US administration was sitting impotently on the fence watching Sadat slide closer into the abyss. And that reality, plus

Sadat's increasingly vulnerable situation at home and in the Arab world, continued to form the essence of my reports that summer.

The roving ambassador of peace, Alfred Atherton, shuttled between Alexandria and Jerusalem without result; Sadat's two-month deadline (July 23) came and went without the threatened "surprise". In quiet desperation, Sadat would fly to Austria on a last-ditch rescue mission, meeting separately with the trusted Israeli Defence Minister Ezer Weizman and with the seemingly less implacable Israeli opposition leader Shimon Peres. The Cairo-based American network TV correspondents would follow him to Salzburg to transmit dark mood reports heavy on conjecture, light on facts. In fact, Sadat would plead for a token Israeli gesture of goodwill as a response to his peace mission; he would ask Weizman to ask Begin to withdraw unilaterally to the El-Arish-Ras Mohammed line of the eastern Sinai so Sadat could turn El-Arish into a centre for a Middle East peace parley, and Mount Sinai into a tri-faith symbol of peaceful co-existence. He would build, he said, a complex housing a mosque, synagogue and church at St Catherine's Monastery, even before a peace treaty was signed. The Egyptian President would return to Egypt and I would fly on to England to cover a more formal eleventh-hour attempt to save the peace initiative. The Egyptian and Israeli Foreign Ministers and the American Secretary of State would lock themselves inside Leeds Castle in Kent (for security reasons) in negotiations that they themselves considered unpromising, if not doomed, from the start. Protected by medieval moats and a news blackout, Ibrahim Kamel, Moshe Dayan and Cyrus Vance tried haggling their way out of the impasse while members of the international flying media circus were left with little to do but bump into each other in the pastoral English countryside and reminisce about the good old days in Jerusalem eight months earlier. The American network superstars took turns standing on the wrong side of the moat telling the cameras and America no more than they already knew. Clearly Sadat's peace was bogged down. Everyone went home to wait.

Back in Egypt, cameraman Rupen Vosgimourakian, having already decided he'd had enough of the Middle East (more than thirty years), finally packed his family and bags and moved to the Paris bureau. A fresh-faced Canadian replaced him.

As for the Egyptian President, he was back in Alexandria smarting from Prime Minister Begin's public rebuff of his Salzburg request. There would be no hand-overs, hand-outs or give-aways in the Sinai or anywhere else. Fine, said Sadat, and swiftly retaliated by finally expelling the Israeli military delegation from Cairo's Tahra Palace. There would be no further Egyptian–Israeli talks, said Sadat, unless Begin agreed in advance to full withdrawal from the Arab territories occupied in 1967. The Cairo press stepped up its vitriolic six-month anti-Begin campaign and Sadat's domestic and Arab critics came into their own.

A week later, US Secretary of State Vance arrived at the Alexandria "white house" carrying the future in his hands: an invitation to a summit meeting with President Jimmy Carter and Prime Minister Menachem Begin at Camp David. President Sadat accepted on the spot.

Some of the most important decisions of Sadat's life had been made during the holy month of Ramadan, the most notable being the surprise launching of the October '73 war, which Egyptians call the Ramadian War and Israelis the Yom Kippur War, as it struck during both religious observances. President Sadat received the invitation of last resort shortly after the start of Ramadan, which always falls in the ninth month of the Islamic year. Since it follows the lunar cycle and calendar, we were into a series of scorching summer Ramadans that made fasting from dawn to sunset an especially arduous, sixteen-hour experience for the devout. Millions of Egyptians were abstaining from eating, drinking, smoking and sexual intercourse. Given the 45°C temperatures, a paralysis set in, considerably slowing down the nation's productivity and raising the level of general irritability. In a country where productivity can ill-afford a slow-down and where tempers rarely flare, the holy month of Ramadan exacts a certain toll on believers and non-believers alike. The feasting that went on between sunset and sunrise did not diminish my admiration for Islamic self-sacrifice, although trying to maintain a normal, Western style work schedule during this somnambulant month involved endurance of another sort. Having resumed our stake-out in Alexandria, there was little to do after Vance departed except report on Egypt's pre-Camp David position and keep an eye on the more reclusive Sadat, who would spend this prelude fasting, exercising and pondering – in solitude – the future of peace in the Middle East and, equally important, of his regime. Sadat once told a German interviewer that he always felt better, physically and mentally, during Ramadan than at any other time; that his mind became so clear he felt almost high; that he was closer to God, understood better what He wanted and what He expected from him. "Then I see the light," said Sadat, "and know which path I must take in order to fulfill my mission. A mission, does that sound strange? Doesn't everyone have a mission?" (see Anwar Sadat *The Last Hundred Days* Muller/Blaisse, Thames and Hudson, 1981)

On the eve of the summit it must have occurred to Sadat that his fellow-summiteers, Menachem Begin and Jimmy Carter, were similarly imbued with a sense of the divine; that all three, to varying degrees, considered themselves men of destiny. This certainly did not elude some Egyptians, including the devout, who found no comfort in Begin's biblically inspired Greater Israel mission, less and less comfort in Sadat's mystically inspired peace mission to Israel, and a scepticism of the still untested Carter, the evangelical, born-again Christian from Plains, Georgia. That Sadat might become mystically inspired during his solitary deliberations, whether in Alexandria or at Camp David, now privately disturbed some of his aides and made them somewhat apprehensive about a summit scheduled to convene at Ramadan's end. While they themselves worked round the clock on Egypt's position paper outlining a comprehensive peace that would satisfy the Arabs and Palestinians and adhere to the tenents of Sadat's own peace initiative, at least as demonstrated in his Knesset speech, they wondered what divinely-inspired position Sadat was evolving. Those of us in contact with Sadat's closest aides – none could be said to be really close – received this message of foreboding, this sense of impending doom cloaked in the discretion of a diplomatic jargon polished under successive one-man regimes. There was no mistaking their fear of an eleventh-hour sell-out. It was palpable; as tangible as the August heat.

It was time for a change of scene, a change of pace, a holiday. After ten days of self-indulgence on the island of Crete, followed by ten days of Swiss and German tranquillity, I felt unwound and uncluttered for the first time since I arrived in Cairo. I was ready to join the presidential plane on its Paris stop-over en route to Washington and Camp David.

The Arab Republic of Egypt's Boeing 707 was filled to capacity with Sadat's entourage of aides and ministers making up the official nine-member delegation, a large detail of security men and bodyguards, press and information spokesmen, the chief editors of the major Egyptian press organs, the superstars of the Egyptian media and, of course, the Cairo-based correspondents of the three major American TV networks, the two major American news weeklies, *Time* and *Newsweek*, as well as a network pool camera crew.

It was another Sadat flight into the unknown, only this time there was none of the excitement, euphoria and theatricals that marked the trip to Jerusalem. The Egyptian officials, tense and anxious, kept to themselves much of the time, concentrating on the reams of papers that constituted Egypt's peace policy as it would be presented by President Sadat to President Carter during their first working session. Notably absent was the esteemed War Minister General Gamassy. He had been dismissed by Sadat. No reason given. Of all the President's men, Gamassy was surely among the ablest and most popular with Egyptians, Americans and Israelis alike. He was known to favour peace, albeit one based on honourable terms. Many of us lamented his disappearance from public life.

Osama el-Baz, the most brilliant, most influential, most militant member of the negotiating team, took time out to brief us in his impeccable American-accented English acquired during student days at Harvard. His totally uninhibited use of American colloquialisms and jargon made him a popular, sought-after government spokesman, second only to the President on matters dealing with peace, the United States, Israel, the Palestinians and the Arabs. That el-Baz was the antithesis of Sadat in word, deed and manner lent an element of intrigue and drama to what was otherwise a bland, predictable arena of power largely populated by obsequious insiders.

In his no-nonsense straightforward style, el-Baz broadly laid out for us the familiar Egyptian position that was as comprehensive as it was problematic. But on the gut issues of "land and sovereignty", Egypt, he said, was not prepared to compromise. Nor, he repeated adamantly, would Egypt or Sadat agree to a partial settlement; a separate peace treaty with Israel. "We are going into this summit with a sober realization of the complexity of the problem facing us . . . we are not overly optimistic. . . . Sadat is seeking more than a Declaration of Principles, he wants a broad outline of a peace agreement endorsed and supported by the United States." But el-Baz stressed that such an agreement would "not be signed at any cost". As for the Israelis, el-Baz was unequivocal in stating their intentions: "They will be out to neutralize, even negate the US role . . . and we should assume that the Israelis will be the first to leak information to the media during the talks." And leaks, he pointed out, "will determine the outcome of the summit".

The official Egyptian position, as drawn up and delivered by el-Baz, did not of course take public account of the vicissitudes of the electric-shock school of policy-making; of the one man more than capable of throwing away the position paper if the going got tough; our fellow passenger who had secluded himself in a private compartment behind the cockpit. To ensure that Anwar Sadat was indeed on the same plane, we requested a brief audience with the President. His press spokesman, Saad Zaghoul Nassar, who had trouble gaining access to the President and more trouble speaking on his behalf – which is apparently why he was appointed to this paper-thin post – clearly lacked the clout to gain us entry to the inner sanctum, so we begged and pleaded with senior officials, one of whom finally gave us the nod. With camera crew in tow, the five American correspondents approached the Egyptian leader who had used his rehearsal time well. Spiffily dressed as usual in a dark pin-striped suit, dragging nonchalantly on his pipe, he was of smiling good cheer, relaxed, hopeful and seemingly determined to come out of Camp David intact, preferably in the company of a peace agreement, although he did not say so in so many words. Our brief interview was little more than a glossy photo opportunity, fifteen seconds of actuality footage on that night's evening news shows. The stakes were too high this time for TV diplomacy. Sadat refused to show his cards. At least we had an edge on the President's own aides and negotiators, most of whom he managed to ignore throughout the flight. He did not, however, neglect the editors-in-chief of Cairo's three major dailies (*Al Ahram*, *Al Akhbar*, *Al Gomhuria*), the government-run news agency (MENA) or his party's weekly organ *October* magazine. These men were responsible for the propaganda campaign to be waged around Camp David to counter what the Egyptians feared would be a massive Israeli public relations effort to blame the Egyptians for intransigence should the summit appear headed for failure. Egypt was equally determined not to come out the scapegoat. The two editors with whom I was on friendly terms because they were the most personally approachable and professionally accessible were *Al Akhbar*'s Moussa Sabri and MENA's Mohammed Abdul el Gawad. Sabri was a personal friend of Sadat since the pre-revolution days when they escaped together from prison. (In 1974, Sadat publicly admitted to complicity in the 1946 assassination of politician, Amin Osman, and earlier was also involved in an attempt on the life of a former Prime Minister, Mustafa el-Nahas.) Sabri was undoubtedly the most loyal of all the President's men and knew more than most what was on his boss' mind. Sadat and Sabri saw each other frequently, apart from daily phone chats that increased during the hours leading up to the newspaper's late night press-roll. Apart from the fact that Sabri cleared his front page with the President every night – an act which was dismissed by most Western and Egyptian journalists as sycophantic – and along with the other editors was under orders from Sadat to cultivate the foreign correspondents (i.e. discourage us from straying from the chosen path), I found him likeable and informed. By Camp David, we had consumed dozens of cups of thick black coffee in his office and were on a first-name basis. The relationship was based on the fact that we respected each other's power base and Sabri had no illusions about influencing the direction of my reporting. I sensed he did not always like what I said in my reports or how I said it, which made for a healthy adversarial relationship: "You're an *effritti*," (little devil/monkey/ mischievous) he once told me, alluding to one of my exclusive stories, to which I gratefully replied: "Thank you, Moussa, my father always said so, even when I was a child. Thank you for the personal and professional compliment." He had the wisdom and discretion never to ask how I managed to get my hands on certain inside information and he was always more amused than angry whenever I cornered Sadat with an uncomfortable or embarrassing question.

After chatting with Sabri, Abdul el Gawad and everyone else who might be able to shed some light on what might ensue in the days ahead, I wandered to the tail of the plane where a few of Sadat's senior bodyguards were immersed in an exciting game of cards that resembled a popular Middle Eastern card game played occasionally by my father and his friends in Canada. I turned down the offer to join on the grounds that I never gamble, even with marbles. Why destroy an image? As it was, all of us were about to participate in the biggest Middle Eastern poker game in history. And, as we prepared to land at Andrews Air Force Base outside Washington, the two men who most preoccupied my thoughts were Anwar Sadat and Osama el-Baz, neither of whom I would see again until this open-ended summit ended. And whatever its outcome, neither of these men – the principal Egyptian players – would ever be the same.

As Senior Under-Secretrary of State, el-Baz was the Foreign Ministry's third-ranking diplomat. But in reality he carried more weight than Foreign Minister Ibrahim Kamel and Minister of State for Foreign Affairs Butros Ghali combined, especially in the peace negotiations with Israel and the United States. While all three were ideological hardliners on matters relating to Egypt's Arab and Palestinian obligations and commitments, Kamel, an intelligent, soft-spoken ex-ambassador to Bonn, was labouring under two handicaps: Sadat was his own foreign minister conducting his own foreign policy and Kamel was the fourth man to hold the job since Sadat embarked on his peace initiative ten months earlier. Ghali, an extremely competent career diplomat, with an acute legal mind, was more regarded for his expertise on the French-speaking world and, with his French education, was himself more of a francophile than an anglophile. El-Baz, apart from being a brilliant draftsman and jurist was also a tough-talking, hard-bargaining, negotiator who'd honed his talents in numerous dealings with the Arabs and Americans and felt equally at home in both worlds. What he lacked in physical stature he more than made up for with an intellectual acuity and depth that could intimidate any opponent. This forty-seven-year-old stick of dynamite was a workaholic who rarely slept and yet seemed always clear-eyed enough to stare out foe and friend alike. One of his most distinguishable traits was his bluntness of manner and speech which, in a country where polite diplomatese seems to be the national language, I found thoroughly refreshing and endearing. One always knew where one stood with Sadat's chief foreign policy advisor. He did not suffer fools or idiots gladly. The game we played – for that is what a relationship between a journalist and a government official is – was a mutually beneficial check-mating of ideas and views waged on a friendly, first-name basis. Without exception, our meetings at the Foreign Ministry were always insightful, productive, enjoyable coffee breaks, at least for me. I made it a point never to take notes during these background briefings on the basis that people tend to talk more when not faced with frantic scribbling. These chats did, however, produce copious notes on the drive back to the bureau. I made an exception on one occasion when el-Baz provided me with all seven of his official and unofficial telephone numbers, not that I could always reach him at any one of them. When I did succeed, sometimes late at night or on the Sabbath, he was always courteous, unhurried and good-humoured. His irreverence towards the trappings of diplomacy and avoidance of all public social functions were simply two more attributes that turned me into an early admirer. Nor did he fret much over his detractors: those who privately accused him of being an opportunist who rolled with Sadat's punches and policies, a professional survivor who compromised his ideological principles rather than follow so many others out the door. In fact, el-Baz – a protegé of Ismail Fahmy, the foreign minister who quit over the peace mission to Jerusalem – was and still is a clever pragmatist, an exemplary technocrat whose talents and contributions were of more value and impact operating from within the system than from without. It was hard to visualize this man retiring into oblivion at a time when his president and country were turning the Middle East upside down. Someone, after all, had to forewarn the tempestuous Sadat of the political, diplomatic, legal and moral dangers and conse- quences inherent in some of his thoughts, decisions and deeds – not that he had become prone to taking advice after November '77. I always sensed that el-Baz felt frustrated, even violated, by Sadat's often precipitous leadership; by certain domestic and foreign policies that were ill-conceived and not always in the best interests of Egypt, the Middle East or peace.

Now, as the Egyptians were preparing to confront the Israelis and Americans on one of the most important issues in world history, I wondered if Sadat would buckle under in deference to his hero image in the West and to Jimmy Carter, whom he regarded as his friend, supporter and political saviour. And if he did, how el-Baz would go about salvaging the remains of a tough position paper whose details remained secret. With the words "Never. Never. We will not accept a partial settlement, a separate peace treaty with Israel," ringing in my ears, I stood on the windy, humid tarmac at Andrews Air Force Base, watching the Egyptian President and his aides board helicopters that would deliver them to the woods of Camp David.

Of the three leaders, President Carter was the one who could least afford failure. His political status at home and abroad could not withstand a major foreign policy defeat. If he failed to meet his objective – a framework agreement for peace in the Middle East – his prospects of a two-term presidency would be severely diminished. And because the Egyptians and Israelis were worlds apart in their concept of peace, the prospects of failure turned the summit – Carter's own idea – into a desperate political and personal gamble. This reality would not influence Prime Minister Begin, who had no political interest in saving an American president more comfortable with Sadat's perceptions and proposals for peace than with Begin's tunnel vision. For this same reason President Sadat could be expected to pull out all the stops to save the politically vulnerable Carter, not to mention his own peace initiative and divine destiny. Given the high stakes at play, President Carter was in no mood for media circuses and peanut galleries. There would be no TV diplomacy, no public posturing, political grand-standing or propaganda ratings points. Setting no deadline for the summit deliberations, Carter was determined to stay holed up with Sadat and Begin for as long as it took to hammer out an agreement. There was no escaping Camp David; or the dimensions of the US President's commitment and self-sacrifice.

The presidential retreat built during the Second World War as Franklin Roosevelt's "Shangri-la" is part of a forest in the foothills of Maryland's Cacoctin Mountains, about an hour and a half's drive from Washington. Presidents Truman and Kennedy rarely retreated to this rustic refuge but President Eisenhower, who fancied the place, nonetheless found it was more like his grandson David than Shangri-la and renamed it in his honour. Now, on September 5, 1978, the fate of the Middle East would be decided in log cabins with woodsy western names like Aspen (Carter), Birch (Begin) and Dogwood (Sadat). Holly (the conference hall) and Laurel (the dining room) were there to break the monotony, not the impasse. Could the mighty Aspen get the Birch to concentrate on the forest rather than the trees? Could the Aspen save the Dogwood from the Birch's dangerous myopia? Would Dogwood go bonkers in a claustrophobic environment where prolonged confinement might remind him of Cairo's Prison Cell 54? (see Sadat's *In Search of Identity*)

As this sylvan drama unfolded in seclusion, the media would have to perform the soap opera without two of the best performers in the business. We would have to wait for the personal published memoirs to find out who said what to whom and how in the battle of Camp David. The imposed news blackout was so successful and the information plug so tight that nothing of substance concerning the actual negotiations leaked out. While the situation was apparently going from bad to worse and on the verge of collapse more than once, while Dogwood moved briskly among the rustling leaves, stretching his track suit, puffing his pipe and fuming, Aspen, wearing faded jeans or shorts, ran around or cycled between Dogwood and Birch, who refused, it seems, to even remove his tie, let alone jog.

The casual setting aside, this was not a holiday in Shangri-la. Nor was nearby Thurmont, a sleepy community in rural Maryland which several hundred members of the world media transformed into a press centre. The media commandeered every available motel, hotel and guest house within two hours' driving distance of Camp David. ABC Television News took over one entire motel, converting half of it into a miniature Washington bureau, complete with editing rooms. Topping it off, literally, was our own satellite dish floating in a Goodyear-like dirigible a couple of hundred feet above the roof. Sometimes it steadied itself long enough to transmit clear pictures and reports back to the Washington bureau; sometimes it bobbed about sending out reports trimmed with black lines, white waves and grey dots; sometimes it simply gave up.

The blackout prevented us from reporting news, but not from reporting our daily quota of summit information. We could always count on President Carter's press secretary, Jody Powell, getting up on the stage of the Thurmont Legion Hall to refuse to characterize the negotiations, leaving us to speculate whether they were going well, badly or not at all. But Powell did tell us who Carter saw that day and for how long, leading us to conclude that Begin was being a problem – hardly a revelation – but it filled up a few seconds of airtime. There was also Sunday, September 10, when Carter let everyone out of camp for a guided tour of Gettysburg National Park and Cemetery, just over the Maryland border in southern Pennsylvania. It was here in 1863 that Confederate forces suffered a devastating defeat in a crucial battle of the Civil War. And judging from my observations the outing was not a reward for good behaviour. Sadat and Begin did not appear to be on speaking terms and their aides seemed more comfortable with the battlefield cannons of Carter's history lesson than with each other and the battle for peace. It was when the journalists, especially the TV network superstars of various countries, took to interviewing each other at the Thurmont Legion Hall that I decided to head back to Washington, more specifically the Hotel Washington, where most of the Egyptians could be found when they weren't commuting. There at

least I could exchange rumours and gossip with the diplomatic correspondents of *Al Ahram* and *Al Gomhuria*, the husband-and-wife team of Hamdy
Fouad and Hoda Tewfik and other Egyptian journalists who breakfasted
daily in the hotel coffee shop. I could also monitor the shopping expedi-
tions of Sadat's official press spokesman, who had nothing better to do
than join the bodyguards in buying out Washington. My only encounters
with Saad Zaghoul Nassar were in the elevators, where the goodies-laden
official attempted to engage me in impromptu news briefings between the
lobby and the ninth floor. He always cut such a pathetic figure and was
at times so obstructive on his home turf that I now stubbornly refused to
tell him what little information I had. The Egyptian Minister of Information, Morsi Said el-Din, was considerably more popular with the foreign
correspondents for the simple reason that he was more *au courant*, more
understanding of our needs and demands and less sycophantic, which is
why, we concluded, he was promptly fired on his return to Cairo. The
official rumour-mill preferred to attribute his dismissal – which he first
learned from the newspapers – to a life-long love of women and booze,
about which, we were told he was neither as discreet nor as hypocritical
as was deemed desirable and necessary.

Had it not been for Morsi and Sharifa Ahmed, an exeptionally bright
member of the State Information Service in the Egyptian embassy in
Washington, both of whom tried to be as helpful and pleasant as possible,
the five foreign correspondents who'd travelled on Sadat's plane specifically to cover the Egyptian end of the Camp David Summit, would have
been completely cut off from Egypt's position and movements. Not that
either knew much more than we did of the battle raging inside the camp.
Both Morsi and the Embassy's press attaché Mohammed Hakki were,
however, in daily telephone contact with the Egyptian delegation at Camp
David, but Hakki proved as smooth and secretive as any politically-wise
government servant. Mid-way through the summit three official Egyptian
documents were leaked to me. The first outlined the position of Egypt,
Israel and the United States heading into the summit; the second detailed
the possible results of the summit; and the third predicted the Arab
campaign Egypt would undertake in the event of failure. As the summit
dragged on it was in the Egyptian interest to leak such documents and,
given the dearth of news and information, I was grateful to receive an
exclusive story. Then, eleven days into the summit, Moussa Sabri, who
had been filling the front pages of *Al Akhbar* with stories of doom and
gloom to prepare the Egyptian people for impending disaster, telephoned
me at the Thurmont Legion Hall press centre. "Sadat has ordered a
helicopter," the depressed Moussa confided. "He's flying home. It's hopeless. Only a miracle can possibly save the summit." I reported the news,
attributing it to a highly-placed Egyptian source, well ahead of the rest of
the media. Having locked themselves up for eleven days and nights,
Carter, Sadat and Begin were back to square one. Having neglected the
rest of the world far longer than was prudent, the President of the United

States had failed to break the Egyptian-Israeli deadlock; there would be no Middle East peace agreement. Not that President Sadat didn't do everything possible to facilitate his efforts. He would make several concessions in the hope that Carter could deliver Begin. But, as Carter later admitted, Sadat would trust him too much; Begin not enough. (See Jimmy Carter *Keeping Faith*, Collins, 1982.) Nonetheless, he would exploit the assets and liabilities as he found them; Sadat's flexibility against the militancy of his aides led by Osama el-Baz, and Begin's intransigence versus the flexibility of his ministers and aides with whom he consulted constantly, unlike Sadat, who tended to meet with his negotiators only long enough to hear them out and then to tell them what he had already decided unilaterally.

But as Camp David verged on collapse, Carter seemed to succumb to a touch of paranoia. There were moments – day nine of the summit to be exact – when the American President feared for Sadat's life, in a camp that was as secure as a maximum security prison. Carter says he had trouble sleeping that night. . . .

> I was worrying about President Sadat and whether he was safe. We were dealing with some extremely emotional subjects for the Arabs, and it was obvious that some of his more militant advisors were deeply committed to the goals of the Palestine Liberation Organization and other radical groups. Sadat had been and was making decisions with which they strongly disagreed. I could not forget the heated discussion I had observed on Sadat's porch. I remembered that earlier tonight Sadat's views on whether Israel could make decisions on Palestinian refugees coming into the West Bank had been directly misrepresented by one of his key advisors, who professed to speak for Egypt but had not even discussed the issue in question with his President, and I recalled that tonight when I had wanted to see Sadat, his aides told me that he had uncharacteristically retired early and could not be disturbed. In the middle of the night, about 4:00 a.m., I got up, talked to the Secret Service agents and to Brzezinski and directed that security around Sadat's cottage be strengthened and kept alert. Later my concerns seemed groundless, but at the same time I was greatly relieved to see Sadat in good shape the next day. (Carter *Keeping Faith*).

I have great difficulty vizualizing Osama el-Baz – the aide whom Carter discreetly avoided mentioning – trying to overthrow Sadat in a bloody or bloodless coup in the forest surrounding Dogwood. El-Baz and his colleagues, militant ideologues though they may be, were far too loyal and sophisticated to indulge in such a primitive putsch, and one so visible. Begin in Birch was a mere hundred yards or so away and, given the state of the negotiations, Camp David must have been crawling with insomniacs. I prefer to give the former President the benefit of the doubt: his fears were the result of fatigue, isolation and the reality that he was on the verge of losing the biggest gamble of his political life. As it turned out, Carter's worries were simply misdirected: I had received word and I reported that Foreign Minister Kamel had resigned, though this would not be confirmed until after the summit. And the next day – day eleven – Carter found that Sadat and his delegation had had enough. Their bags were packed. They were flying home. As they waited for the helicopter that would take them to Andrews Air Force Base, Carter approached Sadat with his last remaining card, one that would capitalize on Sadat's chief weakness: his international image as a peacemaker. According to Carter:

> I explained to him the extremely serious consequences of his unilater-ally breaking off the negotiations: that his action would harm the relationship between Egypt and the United States, that he would be violating his personal promise to me, and the onus for failure would be on him. ... He was adamant, but I was dead serious, and he knew it. I had never been more serious in my life. I repeated some of the more telling arguments. ... He would be publicly repudiating some of his own commitments, damaging his reputation as the world's foremost peacemaker and admitting the fruitlessness of his celebrated visit to Jerusalem. His worst enemies in the Arab world would be proven right in their claims that he made a foolish mistake. I told Sadat that he simply would have to stick with me another day or two – after which, if circumstances did not improve, all of us simultaneously would take the action he was now planning. (Carter *Keeping Faith*)

Sadat unpacked his bags.

Two days later, just before dusk on Sunday, September 17, the heavens opened their gates and the thunder roared as the word came down from the mountain-top: breakthrough. And in the scramble to cover history, hundreds of us poured out of the Thurmont Legion Hall only to be inundated by the heaviest rains to hit the Maryland – Virginia – Washington district in months, if not years. The media were ordered to head back to the capital and the three TV networks were advised to prepare for an important announcement, live from the White House. At the best of times the networks are loath to interrupt their commercially profitable prime-time programmes. And that particular Sunday evening was the worst of the year for history to force itself on one of America's most competitive industries. It was the official opening of the autumn entertain-ment programming schedule – the single most important event of the television year in which the three giants pour millions of dollars into rival productions, each hoping to attract the biggest audience and the largest share of the ratings, not just for opening night but for the next twelve months. ABC would have to pre-empt its extravagant *Battlestar Galactica*; CBS, the Emmy awards, television's pat-on-the-back version of Holly-wood's Oscars; and NBC, the last segment of a Dino de Laurentis's four-hour production of *King Kong*. Not even Anwar Sadat starring in "Peace in the Middle East" could compete, dollar for dollar, with King Kong or space wars. On the other hand, who else could have made "Peace in the Middle East" possible, and what else but war or peace could pre-empt the US networks' multi-million dollar season debut?

Unfortunately, Camp David would not deliver us Middle East peace. The two framework agreements as presented by President Carter to millions of Americans certainly constituted an historic and unexpected victory, complete with heroes. Yet it seemed the Egyptian President had just signed a separate peace agreement with Israel, something he vowed from the day he went to Jerusalem he would never do; something, he repeated ad nauseam, he could have achieved years ago without the risks of his Jerusalem mission. Under Carter's masterful persuasion he had defied his critics, his own negotiators, and his principles by agreeing to sign a peace treaty within three months without any commitment from the Israelis to withdraw from the Arab lands occupied in 1967. Indeed the deliberate ambiguity of the second framework agreement, dealing with the future of the Palestinians and the occupied West Bank and Gaza, left little doubt but that Israel agreed to return all the Sinai to Egypt in return for holding onto the West Bank and Gaza.

Little wonder that Menachem Begin promptly dubbed Camp David "The Jimmy Carter Conference"; that during the televised ceremonies in the East Room of the White House the hero who smiled least was Anwar Sadat; that an exhausted, beaten Sadat fluffed his TV lines, calling the US Senate the "Knesset" and Camp David, "Waterloo"; or that the latest casualty to fall by the wayside of Sadat's peace was Foreign Minister Kamel, conspicuous by his absence. It was a painful performance; a mockery of a man and everything he had believed in only ten months earlier. That this courageous Arab leader should end up burying his courage at Dogwood, Camp David, was no less shattering for all its anticipation by those of us who had followed him every inch along the road. I was torn between tears of pity and tears of anger. I chose instead to rush back to the bureau where our live coverage of this historic event was in process and banged out the forty seconds allotted me for the likely reaction back home. "Yes," I gushed, "the Egyptian people, who had been prepared for the worst, would now give Sadat a hero's welcome on his return to Cairo." It would be left to the pundits and more senior colleagues to dissect and analyse the peace agreements and their consequences for Carter, Sadat, Begin, the Middle East and US interests in the region. Given the nature of instant TV analysis, and the novelty of peace – fake or genuine – I didn't hold my breath. Not that ABC News asked me to. The Cairo and Tel Aviv correspondents were not called upon to participate in any on-air discussion of the matter. As for President Sadat, over the next couple of days he managed to tell ABC's Barbara Walters, CBS's Cronkite and others how satisfied he was with the results of Jerusalem and Camp David, vigorously denying he had struck a separate deal with Israel. Whatever it was, he predicted that it could be wrapped up, not in the scheduled three months, but in two months. At the same time Prime Minister Begin was publicly confirming that he was up to no good. Contrary to the agreements and to President Carter's word, he made it clear that he had not agreed to freeze Jewish settlements on the occupied West Bank and Gaza beyond three months.

And on that portentous note, Sadat departed Washington. The return flight to Cairo resembled a wake. I took one look at Sadat's chief mourner and foreign policy advisor and decided to delay paying my respects long enough for el-Baz either to recover or shoot himself. The mood deteriorated during our two-day stop-over in the friendly Moroccan capital of Rabat, where King Hassan couldn't bring himself to join Sadat in a joint news conference, and Jordan's King Hussein didn't show up as planned. The Egyptian leader, trying to hide his disappointment and anger behind a happy face, got testy over one of my questions dealing with the Camp David Accords. When Sadat was faced with a question not to his liking, he pretended not to hear it. He performed this charade with me in Rabat, all the while indicating he had never lain eyes on me before. After repeating my question three times, he answered with a heavy dose of anti-Arab polemics. My CBS and NBC colleagues and I prepared our reports for the satellite booked that night. Thirty minutes to the transmission, NBC backed out of the bird. CBS and ABC soon followed. As a result there were no reports outlining the Egyptian President's first brush with reality: the negative reaction of a moderate Arab leader. Back in Cairo, Sadat got the predicted – and well staged – hero's welcome which of course got satellite coverage. Two weeks later when el-Baz agreed to see me, I figured he'd been battered enough without me having a go at him, so I restricted myself to one indelicate question: "Are you able to sleep at night?" I asked as gently as possible. "Yes," he replied in his usual confident, controlled, jaunty manner, "I sleep very well at night."

I didn't believe him; he knew I didn't believe him and that was the end of that. Clearly he now faced another, greater challenge and simply wanted to get on with it: how to link the peace treaty he was going to help negotiate and draft, with the second agreement for Palestinian autonomy on the West Bank and Gaza; in other words, how to turn a *separate* peace into a *comprehensive* peace. I wished him luck.

7. The pride of the peacock

I N AN EFFORT TO stress that the two Camp David Accords represented a comprehensive Middle East peace rather than a separate deal, the US administration made certain that the historic record should begin with: I: "A framework for Peace in the Middle East covering the future of the Occupied West Bank-Gaza Strip areas" whose main provisions called for:

• A five-year transitional period of civil self-rule for Palestinian inhabitants.
• Withdrawal of Israeli military forces in the West Bank-Gaza Strip to garrisons in specified locations.
• Negotiations involving Egypt, Israel, elected representatives of the Palestinians and Jordan, if it would join, to determine the final status of the areas.
• No new Israeli settlements to be established during the negotiations.
• Security arrangements which may involve United Nations forces, special security zones, demilitarized zones and early warning stations to be negotiated.
• An exchange of letters covering the status of East Jerusalem. Contents unknown.

Only then were we treated to the agreement most cherished by the Israelis: part II: "A Framework for the Conclusion of a Peace Treaty between Egypt and Israel covering the Sinai and bilateral relations" whose main provisions called for:

• An Egyptian-Israeli peace treaty to be signed within three months.
• Phased Israeli withdrawal from all of the Sinai to begin within three to nine months after signing of the peace treaty. Final withdrawal to be within three years.
• Israeli airfields in the Sinai to be returned to Egyptian civil control.
• Various security zones to be established in the Sinai.
• Normal relations between Egypt and Israel to be established at the completion of the first major Israeli withdrawal.

In presenting the Accords, White House officials hastened to add that the issue of Israeli settlements in the Sinai would still have to be considered by the Knesset within two weeks. Furthermore, there was no linkage between the two Accords, which meant that Israeli withdrawal from the Sinai and normalization of relations between Egypt and Israel were expected to proceed regardless of progress in the negotiations on the West Bank and Gaza. So much for the Palestinians; the "core and crux" of the problem.

Camp David was a great bargain for the Israelis. And a recipe for disaster, not peace. One brave American senator who refused to be blinded by the media hype was the Democratic member from South Dakota, James Abourizk, a respected, often rebellious voice on US government policy in the Middle East. Less than forty-eight hours after the Camp David "breakthrough", he stood on the floor of the US Senate to denounce what he called a "warmed-over" version of the Begin proposal of December, 1977, which had now become a rolling bandwagon driven by the euphoria of an historic moment:

> . . . We are asked to support the final separate peace agreement between Israel and Egypt that contains, in my view, the seeds of destruction of untold numbers of people in the Middle East, and the suffering of untold millions more.
> . . . With respect to settlements on the West Bank, while President Carter has said there is a freeze during the period of negotiation on new settlements, he has also said there is *no* prohibition on the expansion of existing West Bank settlements, a practice which in fact, Israel has undertaken in the past to avoid the appearance of new settlements being established.

Abourizk then went on to point out that the Camp David summit agreement on settlements was in total contradiction to the US government's previous position and in fact, in total violation of the Geneva Civilians Convention of 1949, a treaty ratified by the United States, Israel and Egypt:

> . . . Article 49, paragraph 6, of that convention specifically states that "the occupying power shall not deport or transfer part of its civilian population into the territory it occupied." Article 47 of the same convention states that protected persons in the occupied territories cannot be deprived of the benefits of the convention by any change introduced as a result of the occupation of a territory, into the institutions or government of the territory, nor by annexation, as in the case of Jerusalem, nor by any agreement between the authorities of the occupied territories, for example, a Quisling government, and the occupying power. We have always claimed the settlements were illegal, based on that convention, that is until now.
> The key point, however, is the concept of self-determination, or the lack of it, provided to the Palestinians in this agreement.

The words of significance that run all the way through the document are the words, "by agreement of all the parties". "All the parties" refers primarily to Israel, Egypt, Jordan and the Palestinian "Administrative Council".

Thus it is provided that all the parties must agree on the procedures for establishing the so-called self-governing authority in the West Bank and Gaza. Israel is given the right to veto those procedures. Israel is also given the right of veto over a number of other actions, such as:

1. Which Palestinians other than those from the West Bank and Gaza may be included in the Egyptian and Jordanian delegations.
2. The nature of the so-called "self-governing authority" to be exercised in the West Bank and Gaza.
3. Which refugees displaced by the 1967 war can return to the West Bank and Gaza.
4. Any decision made by the Palestinians on the grounds of security for Israel, which provision eliminates what little was left of the label "self-rule".
5. The final status, following the five-year interim period, of the West Bank and Gaza. Specifically, and this is the most important point, Israel can veto a Palestinian decision establishing an independent Palestinian state.

Senator Abourizk admitted that this interpretation was confirmed to him by Secretary Vance, who went one step further in saying that not only could Israel veto such a state but that Israel "very likely would exercise such a veto" to prevent a Palestinian state from coming into being. So, concluded Abourizk on the floor of the Senate:

The dreaded hour has finally arrived, the separate peace treaty between Egypt and Israel, which President Sadat swore would not come from him, and for which Israel had hoped for so long a time. It is a revival of the "Begin plan" of last December which was rejected out of hand by President Sadat. It is the exchange of a great deal of sand in the Sinai for the elimination of Egypt as any kind of negotiating threat. It is the ratification of the expansionist dreams of Israel.

Now, with the inclusion of President Carter, what was reprehensible last year has now become a "great victory". The continued denial of self-determination for the Palestinians is given a sheen and a gloss designed to cover what it really is – an Israeli occupation under a different name, but this time with a Quisling government to make legal what was previously illegal. What other name can honestly be given to such an arrangement, conceived by the occupying power, Israel, and approved by the

United States and Egypt, the only two powers who might have prevented it?

This action not only denies the right of self-determination to the Palestinians but its result can only be large-scale disruption throughout the Arab world. Without Egypt, the military balance will be tipped overwhelmingly in favour of Israel. Too weak militarily to threaten, or even to negotiate on an equal basis, the remaining members of the Arab bloc will, in all probability, suffer deep divisions amongst themselves. Radicalism and all that comes with it, will be greatly encouraged, since it is the only real alternative left to people who have been denied a normal political outlet. The upheavals will reverberate throughout the Middle East, and the cost in human suffering in that part of the world simply to raise President Carter's popularity rating here at home will not, I think, be worth it. (Press Release, September 19, 1978)

Had Abourizk been a professional clairvoyant rather than a maverick senator, his cogently perceptive analysis might have received the media and congressional attention it merited. Indeed, had Abourizk been a "Jewish" senator from New York rather than a Lebanese senator from South Dakota, his accurate reading of Middle East politics, encompassing the Arab equation, might have been taken more seriously. All that's certain is that one did not require five years' hindsight to realize that the man knew what he was talking about: a separate deal between Egypt and Israel; one that harmed the interests of the Arabs, the Palestinians, the Middle East, a genuine comprehensive peace, and ultimately, of course, the state of Israel itself, not to mention US interests in the region. And it was while Anwar Sadat was in the process of compromising those interests at Camp David that he lost yet another foreign minister. Ibrahim Kamel resigned then and there because he could not square Egypt's actions with his conscience. Shortly after, Sadat seemed to have trouble distinguishing between conviction and cowardice when he told his party magazine *October*: "I forgive him, because he could not bear the terrible pressure on his nerves." (October 8, 1978). Kamel was and remains as emotionally stable as most of us and considerably more than some of us. Rather than add to Sadat's troubles, not to mention skewered interpretations, Kamel retired silently to the Egyptian countryside to become a gentleman farmer. Once the Israeli Knesset voted for the removal of the Sinai settlements and the Egyptian cabinet gave its rubber stamp to the Camp David accords, the Israelis lost no time in proving Abourizk, Kamel and everyone else free of illusions, absolutely right. Publicly and privately various Israeli officials, including Prime Minister Begin, talked of a Palestinian "autonomy" that fell considerably short of "self-determination". They left little doubt that since they were about to hand back Sinai at great "sacrifice" and "risk", there would be no more give-aways, no parting with "Judea and Samaria" (the biblical West Bank and Gaza), no dividing *Eretz Israel*. If Sadat pretended not to see and hear, his two most important Arab allies – the Saudis and Jordanians – were not fooled.

Immediately following the summit, the American Secretary of State Cyrus Vance was dispatched to Riyadh and Amman to solicit their much-needed support for Camp David. King Khaled and King Hussein rebuffed him. Both Carter and Sadat had underestimated the political realities facing these two staunch, moderate friends. For them, Camp David violated the basic principles that formed the foundation of the Arab consensus for a comprehensive peace. To have embraced the agreements as the more politically secure Sadat had done, would have been suicide; possibly the end of two pro-Western regimes in the region. Sadat had to make do with the only Arab support he was likely to get: Sudan, Somalia and Oman, hardly a pyramid of power in the Arab-Israeli conflict.

For all his on-camera bouyancy, optimism, and "I don't need them" defiance against his fellow Arabs, there were public off-guard moments when Sadat seemed more detached than ever from those around him; when the actor stopped acting long enough – a few seconds – for observers to detect a man not quite at peace with himself. One example came the day after we arrived back from Camp David. Sadat's only son, twenty-one-year-old Gamal (named after Gamal Abdel Nasser) was married in a lavish ceremony that culminated with an opulent reception for hundreds of glittering guests, including Cairo's high society, social and political. The star performer that evening was neither the father of the groom nor the bride but one of the Middle East's most popular, glamorous singers, Lebanon's Sabah, who had made Cairo her base since the Lebanese civil war of the mid-70s. While her voice might lack the beauty, clarity and elegance of her chief rival Fairuz, Sabah is a mesmerizing artist, a tall, blonde, svelte symphony of seduction and heartache whose repertoire stretches from the plaintive to the playful. Like many Arabic performers, she seems to have an eternal quality about her, not least because she does not appear to have aged either physically or vocally since my childhood. This exotic creature had formed part of my early musical education and having seen her perform on stage years ago, I was looking forward to seeing and hearing her again. But first I would have to stake-out Sadat, smiling graciously in the receiving line. Trying to forget my first Sadat wedding experience, the camera crew and I planted ourselves about ten feet across from the President and Mrs Sadat in the foyer of their Giza residence as they greeted the guests, who then descended steps leading towards a garden converted into a green and white marriage tent. That evening I spent several hours observing Sadat's facial expressions, gestures, behaviour and mood. After the first rush of guests, the line trickled, opening up an almost embarrassing gap between the President and us. When he was not on he was distinctly aloof, at least in our presence, and on this occasion he was both aloof, uncomfortable and nervous. Or so it seemed to me during the lulls in handshakes and embraces. Even though we were hardly strangers to Sadat, he seemed to go out of his way to pretend we were not there, preserving him on tape for posterity or the evening news. Thinking he might be insulted by our poor social manners, I suggested to a colleague that the situation was not only awkward but slightly ridiculous: "I think it might be in order for us to congratulate the President and Mrs Sadat on the marriage of their son," I offered. He did not think much of my idea so I plunged forward, with him shamed into following. Mrs Sadat was typically gracious and charming; the President acknowledged our best wishes with a weak handshake and an even weaker smile. My colleague was right. It was a rotten idea. But one does not write news reports based on feelings and instincts, especially if there are no pictures to convey the felt mood. In any event, Sadat was too polished to be anything but exuberant while our cameras rolled, and he always knew when the cameras were rolling. Sabah was the best part of the evening.

I confess that in spite of my own deep misgivings about the Camp David Accords, in spite of the blatant and growing evidence to the contrary, privately I still wanted to give the Israelis the benefit of the doubt, still held a stubborn, naïve hope that they wouldn't, couldn't get away with their nefarious intentions; that the Egyptians and Americans wouldn't let them consummate this mockery of peace. It was a little like falling in love with a man everyone has warned you about, a man whom you know to be up to no good but in whom you want to believe just a little while longer. "The verdict's not in yet," I would argue with Egyptian friends, colleagues and critics, which always got me pathetic looks even when I legitimately played devil's advocate to liven up discussions.

In October, 1978 the Egyptians and Israelis, in the presence of the Americans, closeted themselves in Washington's Blair House to draft the peace treaty that Sadat so glibly said could be wrapped up in two, not three, months. The conference turned into a marathon haggling session. Before Osama el-Baz left for Washington, he was adamant about negotiating "linkage" between the treaty and the agreement on the West Bank and Gaza, and under Sadat's auspices, the Egyptian negotiators – led by the new Foreign Minister, General Kamel Hassan Ali – remained steadfast in their demands, chief among them being linkage and a fixed deadline for Palestinian self-rule on the West Bank and Gaza. Since they were being accused of a sell-out, of making a separate deal, at the least the Egyptians felt the need to placate the Arabs.

I took to calling el-Baz regularly at his Madison Hotel room for progress reports and reaction to Israeli or American statements. Apart from the fact that he was far more accessible at a distance of several thousand miles, our long-distance chats were invariably valuable and newsworthy. He got the Egyptian message across and I got exclusive information, thanks to the laxity of my fellow Cairo-based correspondents – television and print – who either didn't bother to find out where the Egyptian delegation was staying or didn't care. By now, ABC's "Evening News" had become "World News Tonight" under a revised format that included three anchor-star correspondents, one of whom was Peter Jennings, who went on the air nightly from his London base. As the presenter of all our foreign news, Jennings was able to incorporate various items as "readers" – stories not worth satelliting, but worthy of mention. By keeping in daily contact with Jennings, I was able to pass on all my useful titbits, which, though insufficient to stand up as a full-blown on-air reports from Cairo, were newsworthy enough for Jennings to read and graciously attribute to me. I didn't care who reported my little scoops as long as it was ABC, so loyal and competitive had I become. As a result of our team effort, ABC's unique format, Jennings' special interest in the Middle East (which meant my stories had a better chance of being aired) and my contacts with el-Baz, we consistently and regularly beat our competition with more and better information on the treaty talks (not that we did more than scratch the surface, and not that we could affect the outcome). As the conference went from crisis to crisis and verged on collapse, Anwar Sadat and Menachem Begin were named co-winners of the Nobel Peace Prize.

The October 27 announcement came too late in the day to scramble for a Sadat reaction. So the following day, after playing cat and mouse with presidency press contacts all day, Hassan got an exclusive tip: Sadat would be calling Begin to congratulate him, and ABC would be permitted to tape yet another historic Middle East moment. It was dark by the time we reached the President's Barrages villa, and since there wasn't a reporter, photographer or camera crew in sight, we were thrilled with the prospect of beating the pants off everyone. As the camera crew and I waited confidently in the car, Hassan approached the security guard to advise him that ABC had arrived and should be promptly ushered through. The President was waiting for us. The guard looked puzzled, picked up the phone and thumbed through some sheafs of paper. A few minutes later he reported back to Hassan: "There must be some mistake," he said, "ABC has already entered. Their correspondent and camera crew are already inside. And my instructions," he went on calmly, "permit me to allow ABC and only ABC to enter. Sorry." Not nearly as sorry as we were. By now we had joined Hassan, who was ranting and raving at the diligent guard with the bayonet, informing him that he had let in the wrong crew and that whoever it was, it was not ABC. Shoving our IDs in his face, we refused to leave until he lifted the barrier. And after much commotion and more phone calls, we were admitted past the first barrier, searched at the second barrier and escorted into the villa and a small room where we found a sheepish NBC crew setting up its camera and lights. NBC, which had moved in months earlier to occupy the flat adjoining the ABC bureau, had become rather nosy neighbours with a habit of keeping their front door ajar to track our comings and goings, as well as those of CBS directly above us – not that it ever seemed to improve their catch-up performance. Fearful they would miss a story and under pressure from their New York desk, the veteran bureau chief – a bizarre character from Brooklyn who had converted from Judaism to Islam at some point in his Middle East career – had hired what we jokingly called his network of flunkie spies – about eighteen junior clerks whose duties, as far as CBS and ABC could determine, were to monitor our daily activities. Our competitor's clandestine operation, complete with attempts at toying with our satellite transmissions and tri-network pool arrangements, was a source of continuous consternation and amusement. Since ABC Cairo was still considered to be on top of the story, NBC eventually took to shutting its front door more frequently, diminishing the possibility that it was their intelligence ear that had got them through Sadat's front door that night. They had driven out to the compound simply to try their luck, not knowing that we had made exclusive arrangements to record the Sadat-Begin phone call. As the guard at the gate was expecting ABC, and NBC sounded like ABC, NBC did not protest the warm welcome they received. In the same situation I would have done the same thing. It was a fluke and they were well ensconced by the time we arrived. What ensued was a pushing-shoving-shouting match between two normally civilized correspondents and a parallel war between Hassan and his counterpart. As both camera crews went about their business, the verbal slinging grew louder and more unpleasant as we demanded that NBC be ejected forthwith. The NBC correspondent refused to budge. We were still at it when President Sadat walked in to witness the nasty competitiveness of American TV news. It was time to stop fighting and start talking, so still flushed with anger I started chatting up Sadat unobstructed by my rival who, having done me out of an exclusive, was by now perfectly content to play second fiddle. Sadat, who had placed his call to Begin, waited for the phone on his bare desk to ring by rehearsing his unbounded joy over the great news that he and his friend Menachem would now share the peace prize of peace prizes. If Sadat were to share the coveted Nobel with anyone he would have preferred it be Jimmy Carter, but you'd never guess from the bonhomie that crackled back and forth over the Cairo-Jerusalem line. Shouting at the top of his lungs (the line can't have been that bad) Sadat beamed his congratulations to Begin. This was followed by spurts of guffaws and bursts of love, hope and peace. In the interview that followed, Sadat allowed that President Carter should indeed be sharing the Nobel because "really . . . really, he is the real hero".

Sadat turned the question and answer session into the media event he had intended. It was a dramatic piece of fluff unmarred by provocative revelations or comments. Predictable pap or not, it was a good TV story. As we rushed out of the compound for the high-speed ride back to Cairo, we were accosted by the news agencies and other media members, who, having long ago reluctantly accepted the primacy of the US networks, set about getting the story from us, with the proviso, of course, that they credit us. Among those standing out in the cold was the apoplectic CBS team. They would have nothing to offer up on the bird and were dreading the rocket (cable) that would be fired from New York. Back in the bureau, we learned that our Tel Aviv crew had been selected as the American network pool crew to tape the Begin end of the historic phone call. So the New York show producers of the three networks quickly agreed that the Cairo material would also be pooled. It was the only decision all day that made any sense.

As for Anwar and Menachem, tens of millions of Americans watched their latest peace performance on the evening news shows.

The following day, Sunday, October 29, I said to hell with it, all of it, and took the day off; my first in thirty-two days. It was time for a little Mozart; time to stop chasing phantom heroes and a mythical peace. If only for a day.

The "spirit of Camp David" soon became a euphemism for a tragi-comedy with farcical overtones. In an effort to keep Egypt from jumping into bed with Israel, the Arabs made Sadat an offer they hoped he couldn't refuse: five billion dollars to remain a virgin; a pay-off in exchange for a sell-out.

I remember it as the "Saturday night bribe". The Arabs, who had gathered in Baghdad, dispatched three envoys to Cairo whose arrival coincided with a major speech Sadat was giving in the People's Assembly. As they were welcomed by a protocol official at the mid-town Sheraton Hotel, Sadat was warming up for his response, live on television. Knowing that the Arab emissaries were closeted in their room with nothing better to do than watch TV, the Egyptian leader gave them the performance of his life! No one could deliver a sarcastic line better than Anwar Sadat. Staring straight into the camera, the hospitable host greeted his guests in the third person: "I welcome them . . . but they will not meet me or any Egyptian official," he began sardonically, pretending they were a thousand miles away rather than a couple of kilometres. Then he told them why: "Because what matters to Egypt is morals and values." Egypt, he reminded them, was "not like other countries with a hundred million dollars making it decide one way, a hundred million another. . . . No, not all the billions of this world could buy the will of Egypt." Still addressing them in the third person and by now alternately pointing his forefinger and pounding his fist on the lectern, Sadat said that unlike (Syria's) Hafez Assad or (Jordan's) Hussein, *he* could not be bought with cheques. The rest of speech was devoted to "snakes . . . dwarves . . . paralytics" and "war profiteers who think that money is everything". Sadat's message sent his guests packing.

Having spent the night listening to the speech on the radio while simultaneously watching the Arab envoys come and go from the comfort of a ninth-floor hotel corridor, I figured the only Egyptians with whom they'd come in contact were bodyguards, room service waiters, hotel receptionists and airport personnel. My report beamed back to New York via satellite that night showed an indignant, irate Sadat defending his

May 1979. President Sadat, the author and other media foot soldiers aboard the "El-Hourriya" during peace treaty celebrations along the Suez Canal. (Photo courtesy Bill Foley of Associated Press.)

Spring 1978. The author getting acquainted with some of the women and children of Sadat's Nile Delta village of Mit Abul Kum.

1978. The author and Sadat in a typical "hit and run" TV interview.

March 26 1979. Author's long-range view of the Egyptian–
Israeli peace treaty ceremony on the White House Lawn.

President Sadat greeting the Cairo masses upon his return
from Washington and the signing of the Egyptian–Israeli
Peace Treaty. March-April 1979.

Summer 1979. Israeli Television's Ehud Yaari and ABC's Kays waiting for Begin and Sadat to emerge from an Alexandria summit.

The "father of the Egyptian family" mediating a dispute in Upper Egypt.

A group of Sinai children happily back in Egyptian hands. May 1979.

May 1979. The BBC's Bob Jobbins, the author, ABC cameraman Rick Hull and some of the media "peace" troops parked
on a tarmac in the Sinai capital of El-Arish waiting for a plane
out . . . to report history.

October 6 1979. Military Parade. President Sadat takes the salute from the same spot where he was assassinated two years later.

Egyptian journalist Nabila Megalli with the author the night of the "man in a peaked cap" coffee-cup reading. February 1981.

Author fetes farewell home-made "hafli" for ABC Cairo team on eve of her first departure in February 1981. L to R Antar, Fabrice Moussous, Hossaim El-Sharaky, Nat Harrison, Dessouki, Mustapha Labeeb, the Author, Aly Ashmawy, Hassan Bahgat, Hanzada "Honey" Fikry, Mustapha Shalaby, Emad "Gumbo" Adeeb.

honour and "principles" in the face of those he considered to be unscrupulous wheeler-dealers The report ended with the departure of three humiliated Arab messengers representing the defeated "snakes, dwarves and paralytics". The parting shot in my story was a slamming door and screeching tyres as the Arabs beat a hasty retreat back to Baghdad. I wondered if those briefcases contained any of the billions of bribe money. I also wondered about the billions Sadat would get from the Americans in exchange for the Camp David peace.

Estranged from the Arabs, Sadat found little comfort in the arms of the Israelis, who by now had made it clear they were marrying him, not his family. In case there was any doubt on that score, the Israelis kept right on expanding existing settlements and planning more than eighty new ones on land whose sovereignty – according to Camp David – was to be negotiated by all the parties concerned. No, the peace treaty would be on Israeli terms or no terms at all. Seeing the negotiations in jeopardy, the Americans expressed their "concern" and "regrets" over the settlements issue in particular, and Israeli intransigence and bad faith in general; hardly sufficient to break the logjam. Sensing he was not likely to get more than verbal and moral support from the United States, Sadat moved quickly to produce yet another compromise: he would accept a link between Israeli withdrawal from the Sinai and a definite timetable for Palestinian autonomy in Gaza – that part of Palestine Egypt had administered until the 1967 war. Still no deal. My first anniversary in Cairo came and went. The first anniversary of Sadat's Jerusalem peace initiative came and went.

In twelve months the Middle East had gone full circle. And I for one wanted off the merry-go-round. I boarded a first-class Air France flight to Paris, booked into the Bristol Hotel on the Faubourg St-Honoré from where I slept, ate, drank, walked and shopped myself back to normality. All in a weekend. At a cost of only two thousand dollars. The fat surrounding my brain was now evenly spread around my waist, hips and thighs, which I covered under a new white wool coat that in Cairo would have to be worn under a plastic bag. As for the pure-silk violet dress with the ruffled collar and cuffs, I bought it to remind me there had to be more to life than stake-outs, satellites and Anwar Sadat.

Two days later I found myself on a train, whistle-stopping with Sadat through Upper Egypt. While chatting with the bed bugs one night and waiting to return to Cairo so I could go to the bathroom, I realized that my weekend in Paris was a figment of an overactive imagination. A fantasy. An hallucination. The moment I got home I rushed to my closet. Hanging there was a white wool coat and a violet silk dress with ruffled collar and cuffs. Then I rushed to the WC.

December 10 came and went, without Anwar Sadat flying to Oslo to pick up his half of the Nobel Peace Prize. Since there was still no peace treaty, let alone peace, an enraged Sadat sent a deputy (aide and in-law Sayed Marei) to share the limelight with co-winner Menachem Begin, who had the *chutzpah* to show up at the ceremonies. The Egyptian media, speaking for the President and many other Egyptians, felt Sadat and Sadat alone deserved the honour; that Begin should share it was an insult. In fact, it was black humour.

December 17 – the three-month deadline for the signing of the peace treaty – came and went.

December 25 – Sadat's birthday – came and went.

December 26 came and went. But not without a traditional turkey dinner with all the trimmings which I prepared for the homesick troops. But there was no peace on earth, goodwill towards men that Christmas 1978. And no happy New Year. Only 1979.

The Carter administration was so absorbed with the Arab-Israeli problem in 1978 that it failed to notice the dramatic transformation taking place in another part of the neighbourhood. By mid-January 1979 the tyranny of the Shah of the Iran finally caught up with him and America – more than a quarter of a century after the CIA had installed him on the Peacock Throne. The western world's Persian Gulf policeman was overthrown by the repressed masses in a revolution that should have surprised no student of political science or history, let alone the US government and the Central Intelligency Agency. Propping up tyrants in the name of security, stability and peace has long been a staple of American foreign policy; a bankrupt policy in which peace is invariably short-lived and the tyrant invariably replaced by less friendly tyrants. By the time America woke up to the reality of Iran it was too late to save the monarchy from collapse or the Shah from himself; too late by several years. So the Shah flew into exile or, as the Egyptian media preferred to put it, left on "an extended holiday".

His first stop was Aswan, where he piloted his own Boeing 707 to a touchdown. And as the world media scrambled to record the event, I stood on the tarmac trying to visualize a similar scene thirty years earlier when the Egyptian "revolution" toppled King Farouk. As one of the young Free Officers who had helped overthrow the King, Anwar Sadat was standing by in Alexandria the day Farouk's yacht slipped out of the harbour into exile. Now, with the same sense of pride and history, and in the role of head of state, Sadat was preparing a royal welcome for a freshly deposed monarch who was linked to Farouk more closely than even their fate of exile indicated. The first of the Shah's three wives was a sister of Farouk. But it was not this lowly ironic moment that had prompted Sadat to embrace the Shah in his humiliation. According to Sadat it was time for honour, friendship and ethics, which, he implied, were in short supply in the world of expedient politics. When I asked a close Sadat aide on the tarmac that day: "Why, why with all of Sadat's and Egypt's troubles, did the President welcome yet another problem?" I was told without hesitation that Sadat felt it would have been cowardly and dishonourable to have done otherwise. Just because the Shah had suddenly become an untouchable was all the more reason for not shunning the man, who, I was reminded, had supported Sadat during and after the '73 war. So he had. Furthermore, he had also visited Sadat a year earlier to express his support for the Jerusalem peace initiative. And given Sadat's new pariah status in the Arab world, no one knew better than the Egyptian President how it felt to be deserted by friends in an hour of need.

Political friendships aside, life and politics and Anwar Sadat were a little more complicated than all of this suggested. And as the Shah was planning to spend only a few days of his "holiday" in Aswan, the journalists on hand were being paid to report the facts, not psychoanalyse Anwar Sadat, however more intriguing that assignment would have been. So we left him to his public altruism and went about trying to record and report the story. As much as I had always loathed the Shah and his imperial rule, I confess there were moments on that Aswan tarmac on January 17, 1979 when I felt sorry for this pathetic creature who through stupidity, self-delusion, callousness, selfishness, blindness and weakness had destroyed countless thousands of lives. That he should now pay for his sins and shortcomings was as morally comfortable as it was inevitable. This pity was largely stimulated by the fact that the man I saw that day was finally stripped of all his armaments, real and psychological, and all the maniacal arrogance with which he had come to be identified. In their place was a small, pale, timid shell, a walking ghost of the past, supported by a robust, confident ruler, a man who still had a country and such accoutrements as an heroic image, imperial bearing and haughty manner. The Shah must have seen some of his former self in his friend that day. And Sadat could not but have been reminded that ". . . there, but for the grace of God go I . . ." for Sadat subsequently let it be known that the United States had acted dishonourably in abandoning a long-time ally on whom it had lavished love, attention and billions of dollars. He realized he could face the same fate.

Now, rejecting the counsel of senior aides, the Egyptian President kissed his old friend on both cheeks and together they slowly inspected a military guard of honour. Mrs Sadat and the still beautiful, ever-regal ex-Empress Farah Diba followed in a valiant attempt to put a normal face on the event. The entire ritual resembled a funeral. Not even the warm, hospitable, loving Sadat could make it seem otherwise. The Shah betrayed little emotion at the sound of the Iranian national anthem and the sight of Iranian Embassy officials who no longer worked for the King of Kings. The Shah appeared grateful as he smiled and waved to the enthusiastic, largely rent-a-crowd. It had been a while since people in the streets had turned out to demonstrate in his support. The two men then posed for pictures on the Nile River boat that would ferry them the few hundred yards to the elegant Oberoi Hotel, now empty of guests and out of bounds to the rest of the world. The Shah spent his first night in exile chatting privately with Sadat for a couple of hours before the two were joined by their families for dinner. He could not have asked for a more gracious or attentive host. Sadat chose to move into the hotel with his guest rather than occupy his nearby villa. Apart from the fact that it made good security sense, it was a kind gesture, and a typically defiant one.

The following day while the Shah was strolling the grounds of the island hotel on the Nile, looking rested, even relaxed as he waved to us bobbing about in our floating *feluccas*, President Sadat was at the airport greeting yet another guest and former head of state, President Gerald Ford, who had planned his visit long before the Shah had planned his. The three met but refused to talk to the media. The only substantive titbits I could get my hands on that day were included in a one-minute, fifteen-second report of the following source information: The Shah was in daily contact with his supporters in Tehran. Sadat had assured the Shah of his full support, and in the event that the Shah would not return to Iran, Sadat invited him to take up permanent residence in Egypt . . . if he wished. My sources also claimed that Morocco's King Hassan and Jordan's King Hussein tried telephoning the Shah in Aswan. It wasn't much, but it was more than some of my competition managed to produce. And our sail in the graceful *felucca* – the traditional Egyptian river boat with a triangular sail – was memorable if somewhat less exciting than Cleopatra's *felucca* experience with Mark Antony.

The media's first priority was clearly the Shah. Since the Nile separated us, we were in for an indefinite nautical stake-out; what you might call a satellite-age version of a Cook's turn-of-the-century steamer tour up the Nile. The choice of river boats at our disposal unfortunately did not include luxury steamers, as romanticized by Agatha Christie, or their modern-day equivalent, as popularized by the package tourist. From our base at the New Cataract Hotel, which we had all but taken over along with much of Aswan – a sleepy, sparsely populated oasis of unpolluted beauty and tranquility – about a dozen of us set out like vultures ready for the kill. Needing something less romantic than the windguided *felucca*, and at the risk of blowing our tourist cover, Hassan came up with a vessel big enough to accommodate all of us and flexible enough to steer clear of the security net (which we assumed contained enough holes for us to slip in and out of without entangling ourselves in naval frogmen, rubber dinghies and merchant mariners). Upon being informed we would make this little cruise, however dangerous, worth his while, our obliging veteran Nubian helmsman looked utterly fearless in his flowing white *galabayia*. He was to head for the Shah – wherever he might be – stay clear of security and take orders from Hassan. Our fourteen-by-six-foot wooden craft was a cross between a raft and a fishing boat, but it had an engine with enough horsepower to get the job done. Or so we cockily assumed as we set off for our cruise along a two-square-kilometre stretch of the Nile designated as our stake-out zone: the Oberoi Hotel and the man-made island on which it is situated.

Since neither the Shah nor the Egyptian government wanted to turn his exile into a crass media event, we were on our own. If the Shah chose to stay in his room and draw the curtains for several days, our viewers would have to make do with picture-postcard scenes of the Nile; if he went sightseeing at one of the ancient temples indented among the curves of the Nile, we would have to sightsee with him. We couldn't take our eyes off the hotel, especially during daylight hours, although we did not dismiss the possibility that the Shah had a penchant for seeing ruins in the dark. Not that it mattered much – on day three of our cruise, we got arrested, all of us, including our Egyptian media companions who were relying on us to get a story. Something resembling a coast guard forced us back to our launching pad, where uniformed officers proceeded to strip the Nubian pilot of his licence and ID and to confiscate our presidential credentials, after which he slapped us with a fine. Our collective indignation did not impress the industrious military and civilian authorities, so we lapsed into quiet and nonchalance and designated Hassan as our sole negotiator. We were most concerned for the innocent pilot, who had been merely following instructions. They could lock us up if they liked, but we were not about to leave the Nubian high and dry without his bread and butter. So for more than an hour Hassan pleaded, cajoled and no doubt threatened the officers with the power of the mighty American media. Whatever Hassan promised and however he persuaded, he got us off the hook, off the boat and off the stake-out. And having retrieved his licence, our intimidated Nubian sped off never to be seen again.

Day four was more adventurous and more productive. We decided to strike out on our own. No more collective, conspicuous stake-outs. Word got out that the Shah and Empress were going sightseeing. We knew not how, where and when, although we were fairly certain the couple was not headed for the colossal temple of Abu Simbel a plane's ride away with its seventy-foot statues of Ramses II. Rushing out of the New Cataract we bumped into a spare NBC crew who, we later discovered was headed for Abu Simbel via the five-hour land route, on a hot tip generously provided by a competitor. That it was shaping up into a competitive day was confirmed when Hassan, the crew and I reached our destination after a thirty-minute drive. Operating on a hunch that the Shah was going to the Philae Temple a few miles further along the river, we had driven to a fishermen's dock with the purpose of renting a boat for our excursion to Philae. With no time to lose we arrived in a puff of dust just as CBS was executing a sharp, high-powered turn out of the village harbour. If CBS had a head start on us, we figured we could still beat NBC to the story. We negotiated a deal for the two remaining boats and pilots and sputtered off to the Greco-Roman temple where we hoped to find our exiled tourists. It was a balmy winter day with blue skies, a gentle Nile breeze and a sun warm enough to tan a cheek and burn a nose. But as we entered Lake Nasser, a motor launch charged towards us at full throttle, obstructing one of the world's most beautiful landscapes. Egyptian security ordered us to turn back. When we explained our mission, beseeching their co-operation, they became even more emphatic about the need to secure the

Nile River passageway to the temple site. At least we had the right ruins. Rather than push our luck we apologized for being in the way and obediently turned around. One of the joys of Lake Nasser and that part of the Nile is the abundance of little coves, nooks and crannies. We would hide out in one of them until we either saw or heard the Shah's vessel, which would no doubt be part of a security flotilla. Having secured a hideaway and silenced our outboard motor, we luxuriated in the self-satisfaction of our prospective coup. Every ten minutes we would lift anchor and inch forward silently for a peek. Roughly thirty minutes into our clandestine operation we spotted two fishing boats engaged in a similar game of hide and seek. We got close enough to spot cameras. We cursed our luck and waved to CBS. We did not wave to NBC who, to their credit, were renting boats long before us. What seemed like hours later, the Shah's boat rippled by and we were off in hot pursuit. By the time we were in sight of Philae, the Nile was infested with frantic security guards determined this time to do battle with the American networks, at least CBS and ABC. NBC was already ashore. And so was the Shah. For longer than we cared to document, we watched NBC shooting exclusive pictures of the Shah and the Empress, and as we screamed "foul" at this gross injustice, the Shah and his Egyptian hosts heard the commotion. Permission was granted to invade the temple. By now we had become a media flotilla incorporating grateful Egyptians and aggressive French photographers. Our cameras followed the Shah and Empress as they walked alternately hand-in-hand and arm-in-arm through the site where Cleopatra once walked about 300 BC, its ruins – flooded by the waters of the Aswan High Dam – in the process of being salvaged. And that night on the evening news I talked of royal tourists inspecting this monument to kingdoms past, looking at carvings and hieroglyphics inscribed on the temple walls; a melancholy journey, perhaps, as their Egyptian guide told them tales of former kings and queens.

After five days in Aswan, the Shah was sufficiently rested and relaxed to move on, to Morocco, and an odyssey that would end fourteen months later where it had begun. With the Shah gone, Gerald Ford by now in Damascus and President Sadat still in winter residence, we too were able finally to rest, relax and reflect.

It was during a langorous afternoon at the hotel pool that I realized how powerful we – American television news and ABC in particular – had become on the Sadat assignment over the past twelve months. The most dramatic example of this power came during the flight from Cairo to Aswan.

Hassan, the crew and I were sitting abreast of one another, content at the prospect of spending a couple of weeks or more in the Nile winter resort, when suddenly the Egyptair pilot announced his regrets: because of President Sadat's impending arrival in Aswan, the airport was sealed off to all commercial traffic. We would be landing in Luxor – the ancient city of Thebes – instead: "Sorry for the inconvenience," he signed off, "we'll be landing in fifteen minutes." Hassan and I froze in our seats, and gaped at each other incredulously: "This is impossible, Hassan, we can't land in Luxor. They can't do this to us!" How the hell are we supposed to cover Sadat's arrival if we don't arrive as well? "Impossible. We cannot go to Luxor. Do something, Hassan, please," I pleaded as though he were God. Hassan, his face contorted with panic, bolted out of his seat and marched forward towards the cockpit, while I tried consoling myself with visions of the Valleys of Kings and Queens and the glories of the Middle Empire which I had yet to see. Less than five minutes later, Hassan was back in his seat looking like a man who had just threatened to hijack the plane unless his demands were met. Before he had a chance to explain what he had said and to whom, the pilot was back on the intercom with another announcement: "Ladies and gentlemen, sorry to bother you again. It seems we will be landing in Aswan as scheduled, after all. I repeat," he intoned clearly and calmly, "we will be landing in Aswan, not Luxor, shortly. Enjoy your trip. Thank you." As our fellow passengers – about a hundred package tourists – sent up wild cheers and claps of relief (they weren't ready for Luxor either) I grabbed Hassan's arm in an effort to prevent myself from rolling in the aisle with laughter. I managed to get control of myself long enough to ask him what precisely had he told the pilot. "I told him we were ABC News and that we're flying to Aswan to cover Sadat's arrival and that if we weren't there it would be an embarrassing situation for *everyone*," said Hassan, beaming like a cocky child used to getting his own way. "I also reminded him that *el Raïs* would be expecting us. That's all," he concluded.

That was more than enough. The pilot, seeing the wisdom of Hassan's argument, quickly radioed the Aswan control tower explaining the VIPs aboard and within seconds was given permission to land. And land we did, on a remote runway about a kilometre from the main terminal, where we were met by Dessouki and another ABC chauffeur and car. Somehow they had been informed by airport officials and provided with an escort to meet us. As our baggage and camera gear were being off-loaded from the cargo hold directly into the car boots, a woman passenger from Florida who had been sitting in front of us turned in an enthusiastic embrace to announce: "I watch ABC TV News faithfully and I see you regularly on the evening news. I knew ABC was powerful," she gushed, "but God I didn't know you were this powerful . . . thanks for getting us to Aswan. Bless you."

I patted her on the shoulder: "Thanks, don't mention it. I didn't know we were this powerful either," and I waved goodbye. "Enjoy your holiday", I shouted, " . . . Oh! and stay tuned when you get back home."

As we stepped into our Mercedes, we waved goodbye and thank-you to the pilot, crew and other passengers, who were so impressed with the whole adventure they didn't seem to mind the fact that it would be at least a couple of hours before the airport was re-opened and they could disembark. When we met up with our media colleagues outside the airport terminal, those prepared to believe our escapade received the news with a mixture of admiration and envy. That was the day Hassan – the hero of the hour – became a legend, if only within our powerful inner circle of Cairo crazies.

By March 1979, Iran and Israel were under the hypnotic spell of two self-styled saviours, each determined to rescue his people from the infidel. Menachem Begin and the Old Testament ruled a Jewish homeland; the Ayatollah Khomeini and the Koran, an Islamic republic. The Western media, particularly the American media, while only slightly more familiar with the Bible than with the Koran, portrayed the fundamentalist Jewish leader as benignly devout and the Islamic leader as malignantly fanatic. Because Begin was "one of us" (i.e. Western and democratic, albeit only where Jews were concerned) his religious fanaticism was a comfortable, acceptable form of twentieth-century nationalism; a sacrosanct policy that had no room for the non-Jews of the world, especially those called Palestinians with an historically legitimate claim to the same turf. In order to keep the Palestinians from ever regaining even a third of Palestine (the West Bank of the Jordan River and Gaza) Begin popped up regularly on television quoting God to justify eternal Israeli sovereignty over "Judea and Samaria". By dragging God into this man-made political and human tragedy, which he seemed intent on perpetuating through his expansionist –colonialist rule, Menachem Begin was engaging in cheap-shot politics, transparently destructive to Israelis and Palestinians alike. Such, then, was the reality and background of the deadlocked negotiations on an Egyptian-Israeli peace treaty more than three months after the "great victory" called Camp David. Menachem Begin was still holding out for the non-Palestinian deal he had signed in Washington, all the while thumbing his nose at Jimmy Carter and Anwar Sadat by furiously building and planning more Jewish settlements in the occupied West Bank. Sadat, faced with a last opportunity to redeem his honour with the Arabs and Palestinians, was also holding out in an effort to show he was a man of his word and that Camp David was something more than it was.

Unlike Sadat, Carter had elections to think about as he watched his one presidential achievement collapsing around him. He finally admitted that his effort at Middle East peace-making was "one of the most difficult, frustrating and discouraging experiences" he'd ever had. He seemed angry and exasperated with the truculent Begin, but it would require more than harsh words and indignation to save both Carter and the peace treaty. It needed apparently, another Camp David-type compromise. With little to lose and again against the advice of several White House and State Department aides, the American President flew to the Middle East in a last-ditch effort to save Camp David and his political future.

On March 8, Carter arrived in Cairo on a visit that President Sadat referred to as a "reflection of American ethics and dedication to peace".

But Osama el-Baz, together with other members of the Egyptian negotiating team and senior officials feared the worst. Since Sadat had proved himself infinitely more accommodating and malleable than Begin, so far as pleasing the Americans was concerned, they had every reason to worry about the psychological pressure on which the Carter mission was predicated and to which Sadat was prone to succumb. The arrival of the flying media circus, led by American televison's celebrity correspondents, merely reinforced Egyptian apprehensions about a theatrical do-or-die performance. Before Carter and the TV superstars arrived, I was called upon to set the scene in this satellited report for the breakfast crowd tuned into the popular "Good Morning America" show:

> One thing President Sadat does not expect is a confrontation with President Carter. Apart from the fact that the two men genuinely like each other, there has been – up to this point at least – a meeting of minds over what kind of peace treaty the Egyptian leader can sign. So, Sadat now is counting more than ever on Carter to come through. So far, no deal has been struck to ensure a treaty is just around the corner. And I'm told, the big question Sadat will ask of Carter is not "what about the timetable for Palestinian self-rule," but "what does self-rule mean?" Sadat will demand full Palestinian autonomy within a certain period of time, if not on the West Bank at least as a start in Gaza. And what Sadat expects Carter to do is convince the Israelis of that. What, in short, he expects out of Carter is not just a peace treaty but a peace treaty that does not have Arab sell-out stamped all over it.

Later in the day I was joined by other ABC colleagues, including the London-based foreign desk anchorman and senior overseas correspondent. Peter Jennings could always be counted on for a fair presentation of, and equal time for the Arab or Palestinian cause to help offset the overwhelmingly pro-Israeli, pro-Zionist bias in the America media's coverage of the Middle East. Unlike many correspondents, I did not mind having my brain picked by Jennings because I knew that the culled facts and perceptions were more likely to result in a soufflé than in scrambled eggs. I always felt secure when Jennings was in town, even if he frequently stole my story and the best lines of every script.

The following day, *Al Akhbar*'s editor-in-chief Moussa Sabri, speaking on behalf of Sadat, repeated the task he had performed at Camp David: preparing the Egyptian people (and the American delegation) for the worst. He wrote in the daily's March 9 edition of a Menachem Begin using every trick to escape the "cage of peace". To better appreciate the outcome of the Carter mission, I quote here from Sabri's editorial in which he accuses Begin of:

Conducting an odious campaign to ruin Carter's reputation, warning him day after day that the Zionist forces can vanquish him even in the White House, robbing him of his second presidential term; while the American administration has accustomed us to acting, growing enthusiastic, and going the whole way with us . . . and then just as surely retreating step by step in the face of Zionist terrorism. For this reason I received the news of Carter's visit to Egypt with great caution, especially after Begin announced he had agreed . . . to new American proposals. . . . When Begin agrees to proposals, it means he thinks he can fulfil his dreams of clinging to the land, that he figures Egypt will make a separate peace with him, that he imagines self-rule for the Palestinians will become a word without substance."

Careful not to blame Carter for the lack of a peace treaty, Sabri, still speaking as Sadat's alter ego, went on to denounce the Israelis for not rising to the responsibilities of peace, of failing to overcome the past, of exploiting the "Zionist octopus in America, Europe and the Soviet Union to obstruct all steps towards peace!" (*Al Akhbar*, March 9, 1979).

It is safe to say that this anti-Begin, anti-Zionist diatribe reflected the views of a broad spectrum of Egyptians, and the editorial was meant to cushion what was being portrayed and perceived as an inevitable failure.

In the course of day two of his talks with Carter, Sadat emerged to display his true persona, the one that never ceased to amaze his critics and admirers alike (albeit for different reasons), the one that announced "we are on the verge of an agreement". That evening I was allotted forty-five seconds in Jennings' report to make sense of the apparent contradictions. This is what I managed to say:

Tonight, some of President Sadat's own men are a bit baffled and worried. They're not sure what to make of his "we are on the verge of an agreement" comment. Was Sadat sounding optimistic to avoid future blame for a possible failure? Was he putting pressure on President Carter so *he* won't fail? Or was Sadat giving a serious signal of which way he is leaning in these talks? In reality, the talks – I'm told – are not going all that well. Two Egyptians are giving the Americans a hard time: Sadat's Prime Minister and his number two negotiator (Osama el-Baz). They drafted the counter-proposals. Both want Palestinian self-rule defined now. Both want a time-table. Their problem could be Sadat himself. In the end, he's the one who decides if there will be a treaty.

The new American proposals that President Carter laid before President Sadat all but eliminated the "linkage" issue over which the treaty had been deadlocked for six months. In true Camp David style it was to be tucked away as a joint Begin-Sadat letter to Carter attached to a peace treaty; a non-legally binding document whose implementation depended on the one thing in short supply since Sadat embarked on his peace mission sixteen months earlier: Israeli goodwill. Menachem Begin would ensure its swift burial, and both Carter and Sadat knew that. The timetable for Palestinian autonomy, the so-called link between the Egyptian-Israeli treaty and Palestinian self-rule on the West Bank and Gaza, called for negotiations to begin on an elected self-governing authority one month after Egypt and Israel ratified their peace treaty, and were to be completed within a year so that elections could be held "as expeditiously as possible". The letter of "linkage" also called for full US participation in all stages of the negotiations. Since there was no legal guarantee that the negotiations would be wrapped up in a year, Sadat would be at the mercy of the Americans – and only the Americans – to deliver the Israelis into "autonomy".

Realizing that this proposed "linkage" was a sham, Sadat tried holding out by offering up his much-talked-about "Gaza first" option. If he couldn't have a timetable for autonomy on the West Bank, then he hoped to have it applied in Gaza, as a start. He did not appear as keen to compromise on two other contentious issues: the Israelis wanted full diplomatic recognition between the two countries in exchange for handing over the first slice of the Sinai; and they wanted special access to Sinai oil supplies, now that they were faced with an oil shortage as a result of the Iranian revolution and the loss of those Sinai oil wells under treaty terms already agreed. Sadat preferred to bind full diplomatic recognition to progress on the autonomy talks and while he himself did not object to selling the Israelis Sinai oil, he opposed any preferential deal. Remarkably, the American proposals and Egyptian counter-proposals would not be leaked to the media or the public during Carter's visit. We were left to guess and speculate, even as hundreds of thousands of Egyptians were brought out to cheer the American President and Sadat as they travelled by train in an open-air, 19th-century presidential car through the Nile Delta all the way to Alexandria, where more crowds were assembled along the fifteen-mile Corniche. If the crowds were bigger for Nixon, Carter didn't do badly by the show of popular support for America that Sadat managed to produce.

In one respect this motorcade resembled all the others I covered in Egypt. If they all tended to look, sound and feel the same it was because my vantage point never varied: the back of a pick-up truck that moved so erratically it rarely succeeded in keeping abreast or in front of the open-air VIP limousine. In an effort to get moving and still pictures of these emotional displays of grass-roots support, TV cameras, cameramen, photographers and American TV correspondents (the written press was never permitted to compete for the limited space available) were herded like cattle into two pick-ups whose drivers were instructed to cruise just fast enough as to be a jump ahead of the President or Presidents we were attempting to film or tape, and slow enough so that the pictures would be in focus. The quality of the footage was always interesting and frequently blurred, not least because each of us was constantly angling and elbowing for the best positions in the pen. The fact that I always had to ad lib several on-the-scene radio reports into my tape recorder merely added to the frantic jostling, pushing and shoving. I always emerged from these pick-up truck assignments bruised, frazzled and coated with layers of dust, dirt and sand. It was always amusing to appear on camera later with hair so matted I did not have to waste time trying to put a comb through it.

A look at President Carter's hectic schedule indicated that most of the business he had to conduct with President Sadat must have been wrapped up on the first day. When he returned from Alexandria he addressed the Egyptian National Assembly and, like any tourist, had his picture taken at the pyramids, albeit with the country's President. On Saturday, March 10, Carter flew to Jerusalem to make his final pitch on behalf of Sadat and himself. Although the media was still not privy to the substance of proposals and counter-proposals, a sense of foreboding permeated coverage of the talks in Cairo and Jerusalem. As anticipated, Begin rebuffed Sadat's counter-proposals. He saw the demand for a liaison office in Gaza as an embryonic Palestinian state, and he was still adamant about a preferential oil deal with the Egyptians. Clearly he wanted nothing to do with timetables for Palestinian autonomy anywhere. The following day President Carter accepted the unprecedented honour of chairing an Israeli cabinet meeting. After the platitudes were duly recorded and the TV cameras ushered out, the reality of failure apparently stirred Carter's anger and bitterness. He pleaded angrily with the Israelis, who flatly refused to sign anything and Begin told him so in no uncertain terms. If there remained a shred of doubt in Carter's mind, that evening Begin swept it away. During a state banquet he was unequivocal about the Israeli position as he announced that there could be no peace treaty until serious problems were resolved. The next day Carter addressed a noisy session of the Knesset in which militant right-wing members of the Likud coalition government became so impassioned over Carter's pleas for peace that one – the ever fanatical Geula Cohen – had to be evicted. Those of us tuned into Israeli radio's live coverage of the session on our transistor radios back in Cairo were only slightly less discouraged than the Egyptians. This was followed by a meeting between Carter and the Knesset's Foreign Relations Committee, and another one between the Israeli cabinet and US Secretary of State Cyrus Vance and National Security Advisor Zbigniew Brzezinski; none of which were hopeful enough, apparently, to forestall the Americans' departure set for the following morning. Carter would say goodbye to Begin at breakfast before flying to Cairo for an airport briefing with Sadat.

At the proverbial eleventh hour, Moshe Dayan, Ezer Weizman and other ministers who had been quietly but feverishly working behind the scenes in an attempt to salvage the mission, sat down for more talks with the Americans – private talks which the world media knew nothing about.

So by Monday night, with the situation looking every bit as hopeless as it had Sunday night, and with Carter preparing to pack his bags, reports of the collapsed peace mission were being beamed via satellite to America's evening news shows. ABC's Barbara Walters, CBS's Walter Cronkite and NBC's John Chancellor led the rest of the world media in grim accounts of the death of peace, only sixteen months after all three had declared its birth from the same King David Hotel. Although Begin told reporters of "substantial progress", the Americans saw things differently and Carter's press secretary Jody Powell's pessimistic word carried the night. The Carter mission, then, had failed. So had the Sadat mission. The Middle East was back to square one.

Cairo's three major semi-official dailies went to press that night reflecting a deep depression and anger over the Israelis, saying they, alone, would have to bear the blame and shame of an aborted peace. Early the next morning, the world media, including those of us standing by to cover the Carter-Sadat farewell meeting at Cairo airport, were preparing to report on the most dramatic funeral in the history of Middle-East shuttle/TV diplomacy. By 10:00 a.m. of Tuesday, March 13, I left the bureau, tiptoeing through the garbage and around the car bumpers in the parking lot, and climbed the few steps to the Egypt Radio and TV building where the American networks had rented makeshift cubby-hole studios for the occasion. As I settled into my four-by-four I counted two blessings: CBS and NBC on either side of me were no better off, and the blurry black and white reception on my TV set indicated that Egypt TV's mobile cameras were in position on the airport tarmac, fifteen miles away. In preparation for their live coverage of the Carter-Sadat meeting, the cameras zoomed in and out on various members of the assembled media circus and other props, such as a carpet that I presumed was red, not that I would probably ever know or that it mattered much, although a lime green, orange or black carpet might have made for more colourful colour reportage. Since this was not the sort of assignment one could rehearse or script, I could only hope that the technology would work as I adlibbed my way through the Egypt TV sound and pictures which ABC and the other networks were plugged into via a New York-Cairo satellite line. My only link with the events on that airport tarmac was the TV monitor which would show me what was happening, and a little button in my ear (not unlike a regular hearing aid) which would tell me what was happening. This audio plug in the ear would provide me with actuality sound of the airport scene, plus the voice reports of my colleagues, who would be reporting live on-camera from the VIP tarmac into our weekday "Good Morning America" programme which would be on the air by the time Carter arrived. My two-way audio feedback also plugged me into the GMA producers in New York and Washington, from whom I would receive my instructions and with whom I could communicate with the aid of a microphone. As an ABC sound technician wired me up and plugged me in I thanked him for my hearing and speaking ability and said goodbye.

For the next indefinite while I would not even see the man who was holding me together, or his machines to which I was physically attached. The "studio" wasn't big enough for both of us, so he crouched outside the green felt partitioned cubicle, switching knobs and stabilizing the Cairo end of the New York hook-up, while I stared at the TV set and my few notes which had to be transformed into a script at some point.

The situation that day was not abnormal. It was typically fraught with the tension of acute vulnerability. There was no guarantee that men or machines would co-operate or that the live coverage would not drop dead in mid-sentence or picture. Under such circumstances, where the primitive and the sophisticated conspire to put us all in our proper places, I always assumed that if the home TV screen didn't go deaf and dumb and blank simultaneously, there was a good chance of losing either sound or video, which was just as traumatic, particularly when you have to worry about your competitors and the ratings. Producing remotes or live feeds out of Egypt required strong nerves and nimble minds. I had long since learned not to fret over technical imponderables, especially those about which I knew next to nothing. By leaving such matters to God and his expert technicians I was better able to concentrate on the pressures and tensions of actually reporting the unfolding story – challenge and risk enough, especially when you're not there to see and hear for yourself. And on that March day I was not there – at the Cairo airport – for the simple reason that should the ABC-CBS-NBC satellite transmission line break down somewhere between the airport and New York, I could provide back-up narration and commentary from my Egypt TV position (as well as report the Egyptian angle). This assumed, of course, that Egyptian television, which was feeding American television the airport pool video into and out of the central control room a floor above me, did not itself fall victim to break-up, breakdown or blackout. Satelliting news from far-flung corners of the globe as it's happening usually means flying by the seat of one's pants on the wing of that little bird. Operating on a wing and a prayer has been known to cause ulcers, nervous breakdowns, alcoholism, lost jobs and worse. If you survive, your career is assured until the next kamikaze mission. If you don't, it is still better than being an ulcerated lush in a straitjacket.

As Air Force One, carrying the President of the United States, rolled into view at Cairo airport, this high-wire act got underway in earnest. I was cued for action: "Stand-by, Doreen," which I did while Jennings, Walters, Donaldson and others did their "here he comes", "there they stand" and "here's what it all means" numbers. I was then called upon to produce a forty-five-second narration over the video being transmitted live; my contribution to the unfolding disaster being the Egyptian position past, present and future. There were several opportunities to panic; several moments when either the audio went silent or the TV set went blank, interruptions of an otherwise perfect transmission just long enough to threaten sanity. In short, everything seemed to be proceeding according to expectation, if not plan. While Presidents Carter and Sadat were having their farewell session inside the VIP terminal, without benefit of TV cameras or journalists, the three American network morning shows were literally playing it by ear, cutting back to Cairo only for live inserts into their regularly scheduled news segments until such time as the principal actors re-appeared. During these inserts, and on five minutes' notice, I was requested to expand my forty-five-second scene-setter into a seventy-five-second rendition, which was not difficult to execute given sixteen months of information and trivia stored in my brain. The difficult part was trying to read my own writing. Since my claustrophobic off-camera chamber made no allowance for a typewriter, I was forced to write my scripts longhand and to narrate them without sounding as though I had just picked them out of the dustbin. New York had no complaints with either the material or the delivery, but by now I was rather looking forward to being called upon to ad-lib should Carter and Sadat ever emerge from seclusion. It seemed to take an interminably long time for two men to say "I'm sorry". They had been together roughly two-and-a-half-hours when Egypt TV was ushered into the terminal to record a scene that popped up on my TV monitor with such abruptness that seeing it was not believing it. Within seconds, our alert producers standing by in New York noticed the same extraordinary pool pictures on their monitors. They patched into the video material and we were soon on the air – scooping our competitors. Executive-producer of Specials, Jeff Gralnick, was shouting into my ear from New York while I myself was still trying to absorb the bizarre drama on my black and white TV:

> Doreen, you're on . . . tell us what's happening. Are you seeing the same pictures we are . . . who's Carter talking to . . . what does it all mean? . . . nice and easy does it now. . . . Cue. . . !

And so over the video, but with no actuality sound of a beaming President Carter talking on a telephone with a distinctly unsmiling President Sadat at his side, I reported (on gut instinct) that the only person Carter *could* be talking to was Israeli Prime Minister Begin and that judging by the smile on his face he must be announcing some good news; there must be a breakthrough, I continued, more confident by the second, swept up in a moment none of us had been led to expect. Yes, there must be an agreement after all. Sadat and Carter must have clinched it. When Sadat himself took the receiver from Carter, I felt more certain than ever that the phone call was not to Amy Carter, the President's sub-teen daughter back in Washington, although I refrained from saying so on the air. I was already out on a limb, no need to commit suicide. Besides I hadn't survived the past sixteen months of this assignment only to be dismissed for flippancy in the face of history. In fact, when our live coverage ended and we were off-the-air, Producer Gralnick congratulated me on my performance, especially the reference to Begin which he informed me he was able to illustrate simultaneously with live footage of a happy Israeli leader talking on the telephone to Carter and Sadat. The use of split-screen Jerusalem–Cairo images made for superb television. I also learned that the two-hour-long "Good Morning America" show had long since passed by the time I was ad-libbing live. I was too absorbed to realize that producer Gralnick had joined the act precisely because we were into a "News Special".

The official moment of truth came soon enough. Carter and Sadat walked out of the terminal and along the carpeted tarmac to microphones set up on a dais. Funnily enough, Jimmy Carter was no longer smiling, perhaps in deference to the stone-faced Anwar Sadat. Carter was brief and to the point as a hush descended over the assembled media and VIPs.

An agreement had indeed been reached on the terms of a peace treaty.

He did not go into detail.

President Sadat said nothing.

His silence spoke for him.

Once again Sadat had rescued Carter from political humiliation. And the private consensus among the professional Sadat-watchers in Cairo was that the final surrender must have come during that airport meeting.

Little did we know that the capitulation had occurred before Carter ever set foot in the Middle East. According to the former American President (see Carter's *Keeping Faith*), Sadat had assured him that his pending visit would be a "complete successs". "From then on I felt I had a guarantee from President Sadat that my mission would not fail – or at least, that a failure would not be caused by differences between him and me." Carter then goes on to reveal that the very day he arrived in Cairo, "over the opposition of some of his advisors, Sadat accepted the troublesome texts, and within an hour he and I resolved all the questions which still had not been decided after all these months." *Within an hour*, then, Sadat had caved in. Why? Partly, one suspects, because his desire to please Carter, save him from possible political defeat, keep his peace partner in the White House, necessitated nothing less than more of the same moral collapse that had saved Camp David. Carter himself admits in his diary of March 8, 1979 that "in my private visits with Sadat he emphasized again and again that his main concern was about me, and that he wanted my trip to be a 'smashing success' ". Given Sadat's unbounded generosity and the prior Israeli Cabinet approval of the US proposals (treaty texts), the American President had every reason to feel confident as he left for Israel, although Israeli Defence Minister Weizman cautioned him by saying: "What the Israelis fear most of all is peace itself."

Menachem Begin, who personified that fear, succeeded in dashing Carter's hopes during their first encounter. In his memoirs, the former American President explains his frustration. He was convinced Begin did not want a treaty, did not want full autonomy for the Palestinians on the West Bank and that he was obsessed with keeping all the occupied territory except the Sinai. Even after compromises had been worked out on language, Begin was still holding out the morning Carter was leaving for Egypt to brief Sadat. In the hotel lobby, Carter made a final desperate plea, asking Begin to give him some room for manoeuvre. He asked Begin if he would accept the American proposals provided the references to Gaza were deleted. Begin agreed, indicating that Carter had a deal. When Carter arrived for his now-famous Cairo airport scene and embraced Sadat, he told him, "You will be pleased." Sadat responded, "My people in Egypt are furious at how the Israelis have treated our friend Jimmy Carter." The Egyptian President's ingratiating words signalled the sweet victory ahead.

It was while I was wondering if the technology would continue to co-operate that President Carter and his team met with Sadat, and his advisors. The Egyptian President had quickly overruled the dissenting voices and accepted the entire package.

Mission accomplished. Surrender complete – well, almost. Once the nettlesome advisors had left, Sadat agreed to put some icing on the cake for his friend. The main ingredients included an early exchange of ambassadors, the offer of a pipeline from the Sinai oil wells to Israel and a cooling down of the anti-Begin rhetoric in the Cairo press. Whatever remained of that "comprehensive peace" for the Middle East on whose behalf Anwar Sadat once gambled so boldly and pleaded so passionately and eloquently, was now officially buried in a back file of speeches, documents and policy papers on some dusty library shelf.

This peace treaty was not even the cornerstone of a comprehensive peace, as the official propaganda touted. No, Carter and Sadat knew Begin too well to believe it was that. I felt the urge to sub-title the:

TREATY OF PEACE

Between

The Arab Republic of Egypt

and

The State of Israel

Another Lost Cause – Another Missed Opportunity

What I did instead, on request, was a five-minute world commentary for ABC Radio, reflecting the views of Egyptians:

> This is Doreen Kays, ABC News, Cairo, with commentary for the American Entertainment Radio Network.
>
> Now That Peace Is Imminent, Many Egyptians Are Asking themselves . . . 'Will It Be More Trouble Than It's Worth?'
>
> I'll have a comment right after this: (*commercial break pause. . .*)
>
> The Egyptians have mixed emotions about peace. Now that they're face to face with it. They're hopeful. Also apprehensive. So is President Sadat. The peace treaty with Israel that will be

signed within a few days is not quite the treaty Egypt had in mind when Sadat set off on his courageous one-man peace mission to Israel sixteen months ago. Sadat wanted a comprehensive peace – one in which Israel would be forced to withdraw from all occupied Arab land, and one in which the Palestinians could decide their future and preferably have their own homeland. It was too much to hope for, given Israel's emotional and biblical ties to the West Bank – especially Jersualem – and given her security fears.

So, at the eleventh hour, the Egyptian leader was forced to accept a compromise. Technically, Sadat is getting a treaty with Israel linked to Palestinian self-rule. But it's not the iron-clad, binding link he and his tough negotiators fought for, for so long.

The draft treaty, then, is pretty much what most realistic Egyptians have long expected it would be: a peace that looks like a separate deal . . . and once it's implemented . . . probably will be. And that's a problem for Egypt and Sadat, internally and externally. The Egyptians have gained peace with Israel, and lost peace with the Arab world. Egypt's bank-roller, Saudi Arabia, threatens to cut off its billion dollars in annual aid. The Arab hardliners, who think Sadat is a traitor, threaten to boycott and blacklist Egypt . . . kick her out of the Arab League and the Arab family. And the Palestinians promise to make life even tougher for both Egypt and Israel. President Sadat is already trying to blunt the onslaught that's coming. He's sending goodwill messengers to reason with the moderates, at least. But perhaps only time, another war or a Palestinian state will heal the rift that will bring Egypt back into the Arab fold.

Inside Egypt, war kept the lid on. Peace won't. Not every Egyptian loves Sadat or his peace deal with Israel. Critics from the Marxist left to the Muslim right think he's made a pact with the devil and Western capitalism, corruption and decadence. Egypt is not Iran. Sadat is not the Shah. But Sadat is worried that what happened there can happen here. In the eyes of the devout, Sadat – by making peace with the Israelis and love to the Americans – has made a mockery of the Koran and the Islamic way of life. So, discontent is simmering beneath Egypt's calm surface. Peace, directly or indirectly, could mean instability from within and without. One member of the government I think best characterized the peace treaty for Egypt. "We have cured the cold", he says, "now we must cure the leukemia." In other words, there will be no peace in the Middle East while there is no home for the Palestinians.

Ten days later, on March 26, 1979, I was in Washington to witness the

signing of the peace treaty between Egypt and Israel. It was a media event
guaranteed to win the hearts and minds of peace loving peoples everywhere. Except, perhaps, where it mattered most. Like the few hundred
assembled on the White House lawn that morning, I wanted to believe I
was participating in a first step, an historic start as I watched Anwar Sadat
and Menachem Begin embrace and clasp hands. But I knew better and
so did my two colleagues – White House correspondent Sam Donaldson
and Tel Aviv correspondent Bill Seamans – as we stood on wobbly crates
trying to project a note of reality into the live television coverage of this
latest Middle East fantasy. We had seen too much and heard too much
over the past tortuous months to ignore the flaws of this achievement.
Even as we talked into our microphones and stared into our cameras, off-
stage across the street in Lafayette Square – right on cue – a chorus of
Palestinian extras shouted angrily in the background.

At the same time the handsome Arab hero of the western world, in his
eloquent remarks commemorating love, peace and the brotherhood of
man, managed – by design or accident – to omit an entire page of his text
– the one calling for Palestinian justice. His peace partner, the brave
defender of the Jewish homeland with elastic boundaries, proved a warrior
to the end. Predictably, he was somewhat less accommodating than Sadat.
His history lesson called for an Israeli future for "Judea and Samaria".
Standing centre-stage between Anwar Sadat and Menachem Begin was
an exhausted but jubilant Jimmy Carter. However the audience interpreted
this historic drama – an especially rich experience for the symbolists –
there was no denying the American's President's pivotal role; a role no
other US leader (with the possible exception of Richard Nixon) had ever
dared take on; one admittedly into which he'd been shanghaied by Anwar
Sadat. Jimmy Carter after all had set his heart on an international peace
conference involving *all* the parties concerned (the US, USSR, the Arabs,
Israelis and Palestinians) when Sadat had suddenly bolted out of the blue
with his one-man "electric-shock" diplomacy. Having run into a brick
wall and too stubborn to admit his go-it-alone initiative had failed, he
pleaded for American help on the premise that only US intervention could
provide the leverage necessary to unblock the Israelis. The astute Israelis
saw no reason to budge. Their prime objective was a peace treaty with
their most formidable Arab enemy state. Begin did not want to solve the
Palestinian problem and since that had become rather clear early on in
Sadat's initiative, the Palestinians, Saudis, Jordanians and Syrians opted
out of the peace negotiations. Without their co-operation and participation
there could be no comprehensive peace. It was left to Jimmy Carter to
finish what Anwar Sadat had started, for better or worse. The result was
the Camp David peace accords and the Egyptian-Israeli peace treaty.
Given the United States' historic relationship with Israel, and the endemic
domestic pressures exerted by a powerful Jewish electorate which have
hamstrung every American president since the birth of Israel in any and
all attempts – however feeble – to tackle the Arab-Israeli conflict, and

finally, given the historical and psychological make-up of Begin and Sadat, Carter did the best he could. That he failed to do better is a commentary on Israel's power to hold America hostage in the Middle East, and Anwar Sadat's obsessive need for American approbation, rather than an indictment of Carter's own political ideology or personal powers of persuasion.

As the cameras zoomed in one final time on the three peace-makers, I could still hear the noisy protestors in the background. Central casting, at least, had done its job well. Another fine piece of theatre.

By now President Sadat was feeling more at home in Washington than in Cairo. As the only Arab leader strong enough and courageous enough to buck the tide of history and politics, he had become the darling of America's power barons, showered with the love, adoration and support reserved for foreign friends and allies who, having paid their dues, are entitled to all the privileges and benefits of membership in the western world's most exclusive of clubs. His three previous trips were mere warm-ups for the one that would now ensure him his rightful place in history; which place, depending on which history. As I followed him faithfully from one public adulation to another over four days, there was no time off-air or on to reflect on the effects of this love feast on a leader whose *search for identity* would end in the corridors of Congress, the White House, the State Department, the Pentagon, the Chamber of Commerce and on the screens of American television. That would only become clear to me in the following months back in Cairo.

For now Sadat basked in the glory of such luminaries as Henry Kissinger, David Rockefeller and other super-power giants of politics and business. Fêted by the Senate Foreign Relations Committee and the House Foreign Affairs Committee, he would not be forgotten when billions of dollars in economic and military aid were being doled out to deserving clients. Indeed, by putting his signature to the peace treaty, there would be a bonus of hundreds of millions, tacked on for good behaviour. And when he wasn't attending luncheons and dinners he was lobbying with the best in the lobby business, the men he considered the world's principal movers and shakers in terms of American foreign policy in the Middle East – Washington's most powerful lobby – the leaders of the Jewish community who controlled a block of votes sufficient to elect or defeat a President. He now charmed and flattered the presidents of the World Jewish Congress and Zionist organizations who had once been his *bêtes noires*. There were more invitations for honorary degrees from some of the country's respected universities; a sculptor's conception of a Sadat bust; a key to the city of Pittsburg; a chat with America's most esteemed and influential members of the Fourth Estate, the tone of whose columns and commentaries Sadat had succeeded in shifting from a top-heavy pro-Israeli anti-Arab bias to a pro-Egyptian, pro-Israeli balance.

And, unless the public relations got to be too much for him, he was scheduled to receive a group of Israeli student representatives studying in the States. Egyptian student representatives seemed to fare less well. Sadat was scheduled to speak with them, but via the telephone. For some inexplicable reason they were in the mid-west state of Illinois. Could no pro-Sadat students be located in the District of Columbia or bussed in from New York? I was too busy covering the rubber-chicken circuit to pursue such questions. That night there was a Chamber of Commerce dinner to honour the Arab phenomenon and it was there before a distin-guished gathering of "Who's Who" in American business and finance that Sadat made his pitch for post-war Egypt. He asked the more than two hundred senior corporate executives for their technology, know-how and money. He implored them to come to the ancient land of the Nile with their private investments and joint ventures to help re-build Egypt from top to bottom, not that he put it quite so bluntly. Some, in fact, had heeded his previous calls and gone to the land of the Nile only to return mummified in layers of red-tape. When one executive asked Sadat about his country's legendary bureaucracy, the Egyptian President replied: "You are right. Yes I agree. Something will have to be done about that. I will put Mustapha onto that problem immediately. And for sure he will tackle it." A confident Sadat turned to his latest prime minister, the respected and long-suffering Mustapha Khalil, who at that moment looked as stunned as the rest of us at the news of this monumental task to which he had just been assigned; cutting through the red tape would be akin to dynamiting Egypt and rebuilding it all in seven days.

Fortunately, Jimmy Carter showed up that night to lend political and moral support to the man he called "my brother". But, significantly, his personal pitch ignored Sadat's latest dream, the one – appropriately enough – he labelled the "Carter Plan"; a fifteen billion dollar package modelled after the US Marshall Plan that helped rebuild Western Europe after the Second World War. A month earlier, while the peace process lay in ruins, the Egyptian President was already making post-peace plans. He then announced publicly that he wanted the United States, West Germany and Japan to pour as much as fifteen billions into Egypt over a five-year period. The collective lukewarm response to this grandiose scheme forced Sadat to cancel a planned sales trip to Japan. As for the US and West Germany, they were already committed to more money than Egypt could efficiently absorb. More than two and a half billion dollars, almost two billion of which constituted half of Congress' aid package to Egypt over the previous four years, were still in the pipeline, blocked by major projects that require time to plan and build, by the decomposed state of Egypt's infrastructure, the thicket of red tape and the shortage of trained management, skilled labour and technicians who, having given up on the Egyptian economy, were by now commuting lucratively to Saudi Arabia and the Gulf countries.

But Carter Plan or no Carter Plan, Anwar Sadat would go after prosperity much the same way he went after peace: with a vision that far exceeded his grasp of reality.

Before Prime Minister Khalil could get around to playing Hercules with the Egyptian bureaucracy, he had another impossible role to perform on behalf of the *Raïs*: selling a peace treaty that was "not a separate peace" to the regime's own hand-picked loyalists. Such allegations, charged Khalil, were "baseless and utter lies". Speaking to the ruling National Democratic Party's three hundred and twelve members of parliament, Khalil insisted that under the terms of the treaty, "the Arabs will regain East Jerusalem" because "Israel will withdraw its forces to the 1967 borders and East Jerusalem will again be part of the West Bank" (of the Jordan). In fact the future of East (Arab) Jerusalem was completely shelved in the Camp David accords and the peace treaty. Yes indeed, said Khalil, the treaty was a triumph for Egypt and the Palestinians. It "will give us back all our lands . . . all our rights and the Palestinian rights". As for those problematic, not to mention illegal, settlements in the occupied territories, Khalil said, "Washington supports Egypt's insistence that all Israeli settlements will have to be dismantled," so that a Palestinian state could eventually be established in their place.

That Mustapha Khalil – a sober, realistic, honest man not normally prone to wishful thinking – should now indulge himself in myth-making was indicative of a regime forced by reality onto the defensive, within its own councils. The next day in the Knesset the Israeli Prime Minister demolished Khalil's pipe-dream of a peace treaty with a lethal dose of vintage Begin: "Dr Khalil. Dear and honourable Dr Khalil, please note this: Jerusalem, the united, the one and only, is the eternal capital of Israel. It will never be divided, and this is how it will remain for generation upon generation. Dr Khalil, a state called Palestine will never be established in Judea, Samaria and Gaza." The Israelis also duly noted the American-Egyptian "insistence" that Israel dismantle its settlements by announcing plans for ten new ones. Coming on the very eve of the signing of the peace treaty this provocative, even obscene, act could not hope to compete with the media event being staged in Washington.

Just for good measure, Israel outlined its own interpretation of Palestinian "autonomy". The self-rule called for under the treaty would apply only to the *inhabitants*, not the *land*; that would continue to be controlled by Israel along with the water, security, taxes, customs and just about everything else of political and economic substance. The Palestinian inhabitants would be allowed to collect their own garbage and look after a few other day-to-day chores of life, not that the Israelis put it so graphically. They didn't have to. The message was sufficiently clear: Palestinian self-rule would be stripped of all power and meaning. There would be no full autonomy on the West Bank and Gaza, treaty or no treaty. Menachem Begin made the only territorial concession to peace he would make in his lifetime; he would give the Sinai back to Egypt provided he got to keep the West Bank and Gaza. That is the deal he made. That's the deal he planned to implement. And if Sadat and the Egyptians didn't like it, it was a little late for objections. Besides they were too overcome with the novelty of peace.

A few days after the deal was signed and sealed in Washington, Begin found himself at last in Cairo, face to face with tens of thousands of peace-loving Egyptians who had long been led to believe there could never be such a day. Surprised and overwhelmed by the affectionate cheers that greeted his motorcade through downtown Cairo, Begin at one point pushed protocol and security aside by jumping out of his car and submerging himself in the flesh of peace. The Egyptian and Israeli security men panicked at this impromptu display of dare-devilry that happened with such speed that even the swift-moving media failed to scramble in time. Only the ABC camera crew was on the spot to record the mob scene that scooped our competition and highlighted the night's satellite report for "World News Tonight". The Egyptians (some of them at least) had taken Menachem Begin into their hearts, just as Anwar Sadat told him they would. And quite genuinely. The fact that the Egyptian media's virulent anti-Begin campaign had been called off, and the latest Israeli version of peace halted at the border, may have accounted for the more effusive moments of joy, but even without the official manipulation of emotions and doctoring of facts, a majority of Egyptians welcomed both the peace treaty and the Israelis. It meant an end to wars, and Egyptian sovereignty over all Egyptian land for the first time in twelve years. That was good enough for most. For Sadat and Begin the visit was a second honeymoon, an opportunity to sweep sixteen months of bad faith and bitterness under the carpet, and since Begin was the partner most responsible, he tried making up by agreeing to return the Sinai capital of Al-Arish to Egypt several months ahead of schedule. This symbolic goodwill gesture was prompted in part by the delirium that had an ecstatic Begin exclaiming at journey's end, "I have more friends in Egypt than in Israel." His friends did not seem to include Prime Minister Khalil, who developed a case of the diplomatic blahs severe enough to keep him away from all official functions honouring Begin. He recovered from his sudden "illness" only after the final farewells at Cairo airport.

For the tens of thousands who came out to embrace Begin at least as many stayed home, no less piqued than Khalil, but unlike their Prime Minister, some did not intend to remain silent. If the modern Egyptian society – traditionally torn between its paternal Arabness and maternal Egyptness – was ambivalent toward its peace with Israel, the rest of the Arab family was not. For them Sadat's peace was a separate peace. He had betrayed the family and would have to pay the price. This time there was no equivocation on the part of Egypt and the US's two moderate holdouts. At another Baghdad summit, Saudi Arabia and Jordan joined the hardliners in denouncing a brother who had vowed never to do what he did. As punishment the Arab nations severed diplomatic relations with Egypt and left her to her new alliances. Embassies closed and ambassadors departed. This historic rupture was deep and widespread, its consequences reaching far beyond the diplomatic arena and into the lives of millions of Egyptians.

In May 1979 I drafted several versions of a word and picture documentation of Egypt's isolation in the Arab world. The following version – the shortest, at three minutes, six seconds in length – was aired on "World News Tonight". Neither the original version, which was twice as long, nor this one could afford to provide the viewer with the proper perspective and analysis necessary to evaluate and understand Egypt's alienation from its roots. That the evening news show was forced to settle for three minutes indicates there was no time for more facts, let alone an arrangement into a meaningful context:

KAYS ON CAMERA & PAN PIX FOR: 25 SECONDS:

VOICE/OVER PANORAMIC CAIRO SHOTS: Cairo. For a thousand years the heart, soul and mind of the Arab world: its political, diplomatic, religious, intellectual and cultural centre. Today. A symbol of treachery in the eyes of the Arabs. And President Sadat, the traitor who made peace with the enemy. Embraced Israel. Jilted the Arabs. So, today. Cut-off. Isolated. Egypt, like Israel, has fallen victim to the Arab boycott:

ARAB LEAGUE EXTERIORS: The Arab League. The twenty-two-member group Egypt founded in 1945. Its Cairo headquarters. Shut down. Its staff, mostly Egyptian, idle.

AL AZHAR MOSQUE EXTERIORS: Al Azhar Mosque. Seat of Islamic learning. Suffering the banishment of Egypt from Islamic conferences. And the Islamic family.

EXTERIOR PLO OFFICE: The PLO Office. Hard to tell, though. Its flag down. Its representative, Saied Kamel, suspended. Now requesting a visa for a private visit to the US.

FILE FOOTAGE ARMS PLANT: The AOI. The billion-dollar Arab arms industry. Saudi Arabia wants it liquidated. Egypt, a partner with the Saudis, Qatar and the United Arab Emirates, supplies the factories, technology and fifteen-thousand workers.

AIRPORT EXTERIORS WITH ARAB AIRPLANES ON TARMAC: Cairo International Airport. A suspension of all Arab airline operations ordered. Egyptair prohibited from flying through Arab airspace. Effective mid-July. Some carriers cut the lucrative Cairo route the day Prime Minister Begin's plane touched Egyptian ground. The airlines don't want to cut flights. But they may have no choice.

BOOKSTAND: Egyptian newspapers, magazines, books, films, TV serials. Banned from Saudi Arabia and Jordan.

BLDG. EXT AND NEWSPAPER: *Al Ahram*. The Arab world's most influential newspaper. A twenty-two-million dollar microfilm deal with Kuwait. Cancelled.

HOTEL EXTERIOR: Hotels. The booming Arab summer trade. Dried-up.

LUXURY BUILDING: Hundreds of luxury flats. Empty.

FILE FOOTAGE OF F-5s: The 50 F-5s the US is selling Egypt. Saudi Arabia may not foot the bill, after all.

FOOTAGE OF THAT MEETING AT BARRAGES VILLA: Potential American investors. Concerned. During a recent meeting with President Sadat, they asked about the Arab boycott:

(SADAT SOUND/BITE INSERT)

KAYS ON CAMERA CLOSE:

ON LOCATION DOWNTOWN CAIRO IN FRONT OF MEA OFFICES: Whether Egypt can afford to pay the high price of isolation, economically or psychologically, depends on how long the Arab boycott lasts. And how deep it actually goes. Many are pessimistic. But many, like Sadat, feel it will be half-baked. And short-lived. That it's all just a family feud, in the Arab tradition. Middle East Airlines, for one, agrees. It plans to use any suspension of operations to re-decorate its Cairo offices. Middle East Airlines is hanging in. It *knows* Middle East politics.

My three-minute-long report was considered to be a luxury, not the bare-bones account it was. Of the several facts I would like to have included was one dealing with the problem of who would now pay for those American fighter planes. According to my original draft, if the Saudis back out:

President Sadat promises to go on US television. To appeal to the American people to pay. A kind of subscription 'Planes for Peace' campaign.

It's doubtful Sadat was actually planning a sixty-second TV ad campaign in which he stood under a wing of an F-5 and pleaded for one-dollar contributions. Nonetheless I felt the American people should be ready for this appeal if, when and how it materialized. More importantly, Sadat pretended not to care about an Egypt dishonoured, disowned and disinherited. But the more he reminded the "dwarves, paralytics and hypocrites" that he didn't need them now that he had real friends (almost as rich), the more he revealed his true feelings and nature. Deeply hurt, he sought to bandage his wounds while displaying a venom towards the Arabs that bordered on the pathological. After years of trying to cut down the Zionists and Jews, Sadat would now dump his annual quota of rhetorical vindictiveness on the Arabs, whom he now considered the vilest and lowest of creatures, a distinction he formerly reserved for the British, Americans, Russians and Israelis, depending on his political mood and ambitions. His long, rambling prime-time televised speeches – tediously repeated for the benefit of those who didn't get the message first time around – became hours of vitriolic contempt for an enemy that now wore a new face and name. It would prove to be too much and too soon for the Egyptian psyche that had been tossed about like a salad under Sadat's leadership. The masses – literate and illiterate – would become dizzy and disorientated by their President's sudden shifts and changing postures, political and economic. Having rid themselves of the eternal Israeli enemy – at Sadat's behest – they were now being introduced to a new enemy more invidious than the last because it was family.

One suspects that the Egyptian strain in Sadat always tended to dominate the Arab one, but it now surfaced with a vengeance that only served to further alienate him from his Arab roots. At the same time, being visibly drunk on America and the West did not enhance his image with a population that, however homogeneous and Egyptian, was not as ready to dismiss its Arabness and the Arabs as some accident of nature best ignored in favour of a foreign saviour.

Neither the Americans nor his aides could dissuade him from his intemperate public attacks on the Arabs – particularly the Saudis – which were both strategically harmful and illogical. For while he was railing against them he was also desperately lobbying to become America's new Gulf policeman, the region's anti-Soviet watchdog. In one breath he would insult the Arabs and in the next inform them he would come to their rescue ... whether they asked him to or not. In the aftermath of the peace treaty even the Egyptians turned him out. His speeches could no longer be taken seriously. His general tendency toward excessiveness would be his ultimate undoing. He simply never seemed to know when or where to stop. He was creating monsters, one after another. In the end a hydra-headed one would devour itself.

If Anwar Sadat's pastime was old American cowboy films, his hobby was democracy. My, how he loved playing democracy. It was so quintessentially American. By modifying the rules slightly, he was able to create an interesting variation on the standard game; a neat, tidy version in which he far preferred his rules to the rather messy ones in which the Americans, Israelis and others indulged. Sadat's game of democracy was unique. It was not Western, Eastern, Oriental, Arab or Egyptian. In fact, it was quite anti-Egyptian. It was based on the premise that a people born of seven thousand years of civilization – as Sadat himself constantly reminded us and the barbaric Arabs – was not up to the rigours, responsibilities and dangers of thinking for themselves; they were too vulnerable, innocent and unstable to make free and honest choices concerning their government, their leadership, their future. Since the Egyptians were not yet ready for freedom and democracy, since they were not even capable of playing the game by his rules, he was periodically forced to silence those players who had the temerity to pretend the game was real. The observers meanwhile – more than forty million of them – were given a heavy dose of pabulum in the hope they wouldn't notice these noisy aberrations of democracy. And all of this to prevent the game from collapsing into anarchy. So we were told.

Admittedly it was a dicey game to play. Sadat was the only one allowed to cheat, and if and when some of his fellow players attempted to criticize one of his moves or challenge his incessant rule changes, he'd launch into a tirade about how a handful of irresponsible riff-raff was abusing him and his democracy, following which he'd call off the whole charade and start from scratch with new rules and players; actually one rule, one player and one pliant peanut gallery. All of this would be approved, of course, by the people, whose voices would be heard loudly and clearly through national elections and referenda that tended to attract about ten per cent of the country's eligible voters, yet 97 to 99 per cent of its grassroots support!

If Sadat could not prevent his humiliation at the hands of the ungrateful Arabs and the duplicitous Israelis, he could and would prevent his people from questioning his authority and his peace treaty. If nothing else he was still master of his own home. His well-stacked National Assembly would dutifully rubber-stamp the treaty into law. Of the almost four hundred parliamentarians who voted on this critical *fait accompli*, only thirteen deputies said "no"; thirteen dared to criticize the terms of a peace treaty which to their mind was "separate" and therefore lacking. That was thirteen "no" votes more than Sadat was prepared to tolerate. These dissenting MPs, of various political persuasions, had made a mockery of the President's Parliament, where opposition on matters of war, peace, bread and butter, constituted a threat to the social peace and security of the state. Their treachery would not be permitted to further contaminate and subvert the national interest, the national good, the national will, as perceived and dictated by the only man seemingly qualified to judge such issues. Thirteen renegades had been allowed to slip through the electoral process to "exploit democracy". They would have to be snuffed out.

To prove to the United States and Israel that his mythical democracy sprouted more than gossamer wings, to prove to them and the Western democracies that his people supported his treaty, Sadat cranked up the Interior Ministry machines for another of his "popular" mandates. On April 19, 1979 the Egyptian people were asked to vote "yes" or "no" to the peace treaty. They were also asked to approve the dissolution of a Parliament that had just given its overwhelming endorsement to the treaty – and still had two years to run. Of the roughly thirteen million eligible to cast a ballot, 90.2 per cent did so and 99.95 per cent of them voted "yes" to the peace treaty. The foreign media chose to reject the official count of the magic markers. In our reports we expressed scepticism based on past experiences, our own random and individual polling observations and the eye-witness accounts and man-in-the-street reports which filled private conversations. If the average Egyptian assumed all his elections and referenda were rigged – including this one – which accounted for the traditionally low voter turnouts, we were hardly in any position to refute the knowledgeable evaluations of the voters and non-voters. Not that those of us in American television, at least, went to great lengths to dissect Sadat's bogus democracy in public; the underlying assumption being that the man was a friendly dictator, no worse than most and better than some. . . .

What was especially disturbing about the peace referendum was that of all of Sadat's popular mandates, this was the one that may not have required his intervention. The grassroots support for peace – even on Sadat's controversial terms – was probably genuine, broad and sincere enough to carry the treaty in a free and honest vote. Peace had too much going for it to be rejected by a population whose *raison d'être* seemed to be leading the Arabs into eternal battle against the Jews of Palestine. There had to be more to life than suffering, poverty and death, and peace promised them that hope. By falsifying the results, Sadat betrayed a lack of faith and trust in his people's own judgement. He also betrayed his own insecurities about the kind of peace he signed. He could not take the risk of having it rejected by a people too primitive to know what was good for them. That was the implication. Sadat's contempt for the Arabs now seemed matched only by his contempt for the Egyptians. How else to explain the national election that was engineered to follow the referendum? If 99.95 per cent approved the peace treaty, 99.9 per cent approved dissolving Parliament. If the referendum was a laughable fraud, the election was a crying shame. In addition to knocking out those thirteen misguided missiles who had voted "no" to the peace treaty, Sadat banned all debate on the treaty during the election campaign. There was nothing to discuss or debate, he argued, since all but five thousand of forty million Egyptians had already approved the treaty. This little twist of democracy was on a par with the one he executed during his last "reform" of freedom and democracy, when he stripped the small leftist and rightist opposition parties of all their powers. No sooner did they dissolve themselves than Sadat announced the birth of his own "official" opposition, the Socialist Labour Party, whose membership was to be recruited in part from his ruling National Democratic Party. That remarkable announcement was followed seconds later by another in vintage Sadat style: in an effort to encourage the NDP party faithful to enlist in the SLP – though not all of them, mind you – he astounded them by declaring that he, the President of the NDP would take the lead. He would become the first member of his very own opposition party. And he did right there and then. There were many red faces in the room that afternoon. Anwar Sadat's was not one of them.

After a tepid debut, the Socialist Labour Party went on to become something more than Sadat had envisioned. He did not intend that they take him at face value and actually perform the role of an honest opposition. By the time of the May, 1979 elections the party itself was not yet a thorn in the President's side, although one of its leaders posed a threat and would have to be eliminated before election day. The vice-chairman of the SLP was none other than the esteemed former chairman of the National Assembly's Foreign Relations Committee. As one of the early opponents of the Sadat peace initiative, Leila Takla had fallen out with the President and was no longer sitting in Parliament as one of his appointed members.

Now a member of the Socialist Labour Party, she was asked by her party to run for election in the Cairo suburb of Heliopolis where – if allowed a free vote – she was virtually assured of winning the seat, given her high visibility, credibility and long-standing popularity on the Egyptian political scene. It soon became clear to Takla that neither Sadat nor Mrs Jihan Sadat welcomed her back in Parliament. To prevent Takla from taking Heliopolis and to avoid the public controversy that would ensue from a blatant manipulation of the district polls, the plan was for Takla to run and lose. So, while encouraging Takla to run for election, Mrs Sadat sponsored her own NDP candidate – a little known female, one guaranteed to tow Sadat's line in Parliament. The salons of Cairo went to work turning up the pressure on Takla to back off. Other groups deceived by Jihan Sadat's apparent friendship towards Takla encouraged her to hold firm, but in the end the pressure got too hot for Takla and when Jihan Sadat went campaigning for her NDP candidate in Heliopolis – thus enlisting all her charm and influence – Takla and her supporters smelled foul play. Takla figured sooner or later they would get her. She did not run. Jihan Sadat was deprived of the pleasure of seeing Takla run and lose. At the time, Takla chose not to publicize the incident.

On election day itself, the Egyptian President succeeded in wiping out twelve of the thirteen official troublemakers, including Khaled Moheiddin, leader of the disbanded National Progressive Unionists. Sadat made sure that his former comrade-in-coup (one of the twelve young officers who helped overthrow King Farouk) would not be back in Parliament to taunt him about the short-comings of the peace treaty. Nonetheless Moheiddin was proud to announce that while he lost his seat, he received twice as many votes as all those allegedly cast against the treaty in the national referendum.

The only one who managed to escape the regime and get himself re-elected was a popular politician by the name of Mumtaz Nassar. He beat Sadat's electoral machine by sheer show of force. His supporters – some of them toting guns – were prepared to fight it out in the event that their candidate was rigged up as a loser. The adjusted vote was readjusted to reflect his natural support. By the time the Moheiddin and Nassar examples of democracy came to media attention – the following day – it was too late. I had already done my TV report on the election results, and,

given the American network news consensus in New York on domestic·
Egyptian politics, I knew the incidents would not merit a second report,
for two reasons: the first was that the defeat of a dozen anti-peace MPs
in Egypt – regardless of how they lost – would not be considered satellite
news to an America enthralled with Sadat and his peace with Israel.
Secondly, on any given day there exists a plethora of American domestic
political news competing with foreign news for twenty-two minutes of air-
time. In addition, those who decide what's news, and that includes the
correspondent in-the-field at some stage in the daily TV news line-up,
operate within a news "mind-set" that is formed almost by osmosis. Had
there been dramatic visuals (Nassar's boys spilling blood or threatening
to – what in TV news jargon is known as "bang-bang" pictures) the story
would surely have become news.

Sadat's Egypt could not hope to compete with Sadat's peace on prime-
time TV. Now that the Egyptian leader had a fresh "popular" mandate
and *his own* Parliament again, he could stop playing democracy for a while.
He had neither the stomach for it, nor the flair. He much preferred the
game of peace in which he could play the international hero. A few days
later he would have another opportunity. This time from the sand stage
of the Sinai.

The State Information Service requested that the Egyptian and foreign
media be at Cairo West Military Airport promptly at dawn the morning
of May 19, 1979 if we hoped to make the latest flight into history.
Two coffeeless hours later, a groggy, irascible collection of jaded history-
watchers was herded into a C–130 transport for a cross-desert trip that
had not been made since the 1967 Arab-Israeli war. We were headed for
the dusty, blistering Sinai capital of El-Arish, which the Israelis were
handing back to the Egyptians well ahead of their scheduled first-phase
withdrawal from the occupied territory. Even without the presence of
Anwar Sadat and Menachem Begin, who would be watching the military
ceremony on TV from their respective living rooms, the official handover
promised to be an emotional event. After one-and-a-half years of hearing
and talking about peace, finally we were to see a sample of it. Indeed the
first glimpse came as we disembarked: there on a well-maintained airstrip
built by the Israelis twelve years earlier, were Israeli and Egyptian soldiers
and airmen laughing, chatting and mingling like lost brothers organizing
a family reunion. One perfect moment of peace, so pure and simple, so
naked and vulnerable, so sublimely untheatrical, I wanted to wrap it up,
take it home and press it like some exotic butterfly between the pages of
a book of poetry. But there was no time. We were still a bus ride away
from peace.

The lowering of the Israeli flag and the raising of the Egyptian one
tended to be anti-climactic. But for the millions not privy to my private
moment of peace, the pictures of the official ceremony conducted by

senior officers at a military post on the outskirts of the town, were dramatic enough. One alone was spectacularly moving: an Egyptian soldier, overcome with joy at the sight of the Egyptian flag flying once more over El-Arish, wrapped his arms around the flagpole and wept . . . like a clinging, sobbing child who had just found its lost mother. It was a moment made for television, unlike the esoteric airstrip scene that could not have been captured in a couple of seconds of moving pictures; a shatteringly beautiful moment of one man's agony and ecstasy; a TV frozen frame of peace.

I would have liked to devote my report to a "profile of the unknown soldier", but in the scramble to report live for the morning show and to get supplementary footage of the happy people of El-Arish, it was all I could do to catch the C–130 back to Cairo in time for that night's satellite. In any event there was no place for it in the evening news line-up. The El-Arish segment – the lead story on the show – called for an opening report on the ceremony itself followed by standard back-to-back accounts from the Tel Aviv and Cairo correspondents. My colleague Bill Seamans focused on Begin at home and showed an angry group of Jewish settlers in the El-Arish area whose passions over the loss of the land threatened to spill into violence. My sixty-second report similarly featured Sadat but for once I sensed he was being upstaged . . . by an Egyptian no one knew or would ever see again:

> V/O PIX: For President Anwar Sadat, it was a twelve-year dream come true. And he watched it all materialize live on television from his summer house in Alexandria. He called it a turning point in history. This ceremony, said Sadat, sends a lot of messages to those who oppose peace. But for today . . . Sadat basked in the emotion of getting back the capital of his Sinai:
> (Here, Sadat says: "This is a very moving moment. I am extremely happy."
> V/O PIX: But Sadat's moment of emotion was nothing compared to the emotions of his own people . . . the people of El-Arish who could not contain their joy. Some went wild at the sight of an Egyptian soldier . . . others simply broke down . . . and wept. . . .
> PICTURE AND SOUND OF THE UNKNOWN SOLDIER.

A week later, one day after the Israeli occupation forces moved out of El-Arish, Sadat, his entire cabinet and government moved in, to celebrate and to give thanks. Resplendent in his white admiral's uniform the Egyptian leader – who had not seen the capital since his army days twenty-seven years earlier – knelt on the carpet-covered sands of Sinai and facing Mecca touched his forehead to the "sacred" soil in a prayer of thanksgiving. Then at a public rally that included a popular delegation from Cairo, Sadat kissed the Egyptian flag and once everyone else had done the same, he hoisted it. All that was left was a jubilant motorcade into the heart of the northern coastal town where thousands cheered him as the liberator of Sinai. It was another dramatic made-for-television event, one seen by hundreds of millions around the world that night. But just barely.

By mid-afternoon of May 25, several hundred people had to be transported back across the desert to Cairo and there were only so many C–130s to go around. Someone in the Ministry of Defence made up a last-minute ad hoc list of passengers that did not include the sizeable contingent of domestic and foreign media. Since we did not exist, neither did the C–130 that was to ferry us and our stories back to civilization. Transport after transport landed and took off – with Sadat's official party, the cabinet, the government, the popular people's delegation and sundry hangers-on allowed to participate in history – as we sat on the concrete tarmac floor. Seething with rage at being subjected to another cliff-hanger, we demanded to know if and when we would be given the opportunity to go home so as to report this historic event to the world. At one point the BBC's Bob Jobbins marched at the head of a delegation of tired, dirty, hungry, thirsty, professional recorders demanding to know who had seconded the media's C–130. Ranting and raving in his best, most authoritative broadcast voice, Jobbins reminded the bureaucrats on hand that all of us – press, radio and TV – had deadlines to meet and if a transport plane didn't materialize within an hour there would be no international coverage of *el-Raïs'* one-of-a-kind celebration of peace; the implication being that heads would roll and they wouldn't be ours. At that point we were informed that our C–130 was somewhere over the Sinai ferrying VIPs back to Cairo and with a little patience it would surely return for us. When we suggested that Defence Minister Kamel Hassan Ali be contacted immediately about this breach of responsibility we learned that the no-nonsense General already knew of the impending media fiasco and, enraged, had ordered a transport to be placed at our disposal as promptly as one could be found.

Not even ABC's Hassan could perform his magic that day. Shortly before dusk we grabbed our cameras, recorders, notebooks and the souvenir peace posters which had served as cushions during the five-hour wait on the runway, and made a dash for a C–130 coming in to land. Taking no chances, every remaining body at the airstrip wanted to board what was doubtless the last flight in or out, resulting in a stampede in which several of us came close to being rubbed out of existence. With no corpses on the runway, our over-loaded transport rumbled along gaining enough speed finally to get its belly airborne. As some of us perched on top of the sliding metal door hatch at the rear, drawing up our last wills and testaments, we relaxed for the first and only time that long Sunday.

There would be other memorable flights to the Sinai and near-missed satellites and deadlines, but two months later when Hassan, the crew and I decided to do a progress report on El-Arish, we chose to cross the desert by car, an extraordinarily beautiful five-hour trip through a time tunnel. To see the Bedouin encampments dotting the emptiness mile after mile after lonely mile was to see that war, peace, Egyptians, Israelis – it was all the same to the Bedouin. In the Sinai capital of El-Arish itself, though, life had visibly changed in eight weeks, and not for the better. Peace had not yet brought the promised prosperity.

That same day – May 26 – that Sadat inaugurated the return of the Sinai capital, Prime Minister Begin and American Secretary of State Cyrus Vance inaugurated the first session of the Palestinian Autonomy Talks in the Israeli coastal town of Beersheba, not far from El-Arish. But in spite of the public bonhomie, the talks would drag on through 1979, bogged down, as expected, on the very meaning and interpretation of "autonomy". It was a foregone conclusion among many that the one-year target date for completion of the talks would not be met, further reinforcing the "separate peace" signed. In all the excitement of El-Arish and Beersheba, Sadat typically got carried away and declared the Egyptian-Israeli borders officially opened. Only the Egyptian bureaucracy stepped in to prevent the President's latest act of spontaneous combustion from being implemented until normal and diplomatic relations were established nine months later.

The Sinai festivities marked the beginning of a five-day national celebration that included more pomp and ceremony, this time along the length and breadth of the Suez Canal where Sadat, still decked out in his white naval costume, acknowledged the hoots and hollers of a flag-fluttering flotilla from aboard the presidential yacht – the *El-Hourriya* – (Freedom) as he sailed from Port Said to Ismailia. The American TV networks and the Egyptian media joined Sadat for the five-hour peace cruise aboard the yacht, the same vessel that helped open the Canal more than a hundred years earlier. Bruised and isolated in the Arab world, Sadat took comfort in the carnival-like welcome organized along the Canal banks; thousands of cheering townsfolk and troops of the Second Army poised to remind him of the past, of vicious wars fought, of cities decimated and already rebuilt under his regime. Of all Egyptians, those of the Canal cities seemed most grateful to be free of war for the first time in thirty-one years. Given the warm reception and his expansive mood, it was a good opportunity to query Sadat on his "open borders" initiative so full of controversy and contradiction, and the future of the Palestinians and peace. But after talking into our cameras and recorders for almost thirty minutes, his fudged answers were easily swallowed up by the pretty pictures that dominated that night's TV reports. After this latest three-month-long portrait of hero worship, this one-dimensional image of omnipotence, one could hardly blame the American and foreign public for its continuing love-affair with Anwar Sadat. But unlike his popularity abroad, his popularity at home was too fragile to survive the post-peace treaty rule of a god in love with himself and his own image of greatness. Since I had played a not insignificant role in creating, pampering and coddling this benevolent image, I thought it only fitting to request a souvenir for my personal scrapbook; a group shot of Sadat surrounded by some of the American media regulars covering the peace cruise aboard the decks of the *Freedom*.

The result was nothing less than comic: a man in a white uniform so imperially detached from the motley group of plebeians around him that one could not help but be left with the impression he had been superimposed by a deft graphic artist once the print was safely out of the darkroom. Anwar Sadat did not belong in this scene; he looked as uncomfortable as any man of "destiny" being forced to rub shoulders with the common, the ordinary, the real. We were not celebrity names. We were merely the troops, a necessary evil, a nuisance, and as such he saw no need to engage us in idle chatter or chit-chat before or after the photograph was snapped. Indeed, for eighteen months he had been treating us like nameless marionettes manipulated by the greater forces of history; mechanical dolls every ready to perform at his pleasure, not unlike the Egyptian masses. This was not the charming, warm, generous, charismatic figure so familiar to Western television audiences. This was the cold, aloof, private Sadat around whom the world should naturally revolve; the one I saw virtually every day.

I stopped laughing at my souvenir long enough to study its tragic overtones. A week later the black and white print hung in a black frame in my office under the mental caption:

BEWARE DANGER AHEAD

Weary from the peace celebrations Sadat retired to Alexandria for the summer to await his next international media event: another summit with Begin whose outcome was so predictable I was able to write and record a three-minute twenty-five-second radio commentary on the meeting a full day before it convened. In that broadcast of July 10, 1979: "Peace", I said, "is a problem. And Anwar Sadat and Menachem Begin meet by the seaside to talk about it."

The two-day summit made the morning and evening TV news shows, and so did Begin's emotional encounters with some of Alexandria's two hundred Jews in a local synagogue and the friendly Egyptian mobs outside. So moved was Begin with the welcome that he announced to Sadat, "today I have seen the reality of peace". That reality, however, was not real enough to transform the summit into anything more than the smashing public relations success Sadat had planned. While the Americans and their special envoy Robert Strauss – an international trade negotiator and fast-talking Democrat politician from Texas – were left to extricate Sadat from his Palestinian problem, the Egyptian leader was free to exploit further the theatrics of peace.

I took one look at my assignment list for the month of September and realized that Sadat had moved from international peacemaker, world statesman, hero, TV super-star and Nobel Laureate to Hollywood impres-ario. He had booked Frank Sinatra and Elizabeth Taylor into the pyramids.

Having devoted the better part of my adolescence to trying to make myself look like Liz Taylor, with nothing more to work on than black hair, thick black arched eyebrows, a black beauty mark northeast of my chin and pink lipstick, I gave up the inimitable violet-eyed raven look in favour of ethnic Mediterranean, a tarty cross between Gina Lollobrigida and Anna Magnani, requiring little more than a few spit curls, a hot temper, a bosom and a low-cut blouse. After more than twenty years, the prospect of coming face to face with eyes that had caused me so much grief was about as appealing as becoming a teenager again. As for Sinatra, I wasn't sure I was ready for "Ole' Blue Eyes" either, especially "Live . . . at the Sphinx".

Taylor arrived first. It had taken seventeen years and a peace treaty for Elizabeth (Cleopatra) Taylor to set foot in the Land of the Nile. No longer blacklisted and boycotted for her pro-Israeli sympathies, her films no longer banned, Hollywood's famous pharaonic queen was thrilled to be in Egypt as guest of honour at the fourth international Cairo film festival. The American actress, who upstaged a handful of Israeli film celebrities trying to make their own history, was mobbed by more than a thousand movie fans and local film stars as she officially opened the festival at a downtown Cairo cinema. At a gala bash later, Taylor, who had met President Sadat earlier in the day, confessed that in spite of the official ban on her films all those years, a few Egyptians had indulged in the forbidden: "I think the Sadats probably saw every film I ever made." And with that eight-second political titbit extracted from the crush of sequins and chiffon, I returned to the bureau to rest up for scene two. The actress' long-time secret fan had offered her his private plane to fly to the ancient port city where Queen Cleopatra lived and died, and where the Alexand-rian scenes of the epic film were shot in 1962 using a double for the blacklisted Taylor. As she surveyed the harbour for the first time and wandered through the Roman amphitheatre, the silver screen's Cleopatra decided real life in Egypt was better than the celluloid version. Finally the pyramids brought her back to Cairo where the hungry paparazzi badgered and angled for that shot of shots: "Cleopatra and the Sphinx together at last. . . and for a split second ancient Egypt and modern Egypt seemed to come full circle. . ." or so I reported without even a blush. All those years of reading *Motion Picture* and *Modern Screen* had finally paid off. I was now ready to blather and gush my way through the sick Sinatra joke that followed.

Whereas Taylor's visit was a promotional piece of political fluff, Sina-tra's was a two-megaton political bomb sponsored by none other than Egypt's First Lady in co-operation with the crassest consortium of Ameri-cana ever dumped on a Third World market. This vulgar striptease act imported from the cultural and commercial bowels of the world of international jetsetters was a naked display of how far the Egyptian leader had removed himself from reality, his village roots, his poverty-stricken people, his Egypt, his "values", all in the name of peace and prosperity. The Sinatra extravaganza had all the ingredients of a media event, another made-for-television visual vignette with a spectacular setting; a pleasant counterpoint to the heavy dose of day-to-day socio-political reality thrust upon the viewer for a full twenty minutes or so, at the end of a long hard day. How refreshing to end this daily litany of doom and gloom with a touch of American glamour set to music against an exotic backdrop freshly discovered thanks to a miracle of peace.

And so my first contribution told the story of how one Anwar Sadat finally got to meet one of his biggest fans. . .

> KAYS V/O PIX OF SADATS & FRANK & BARBARA SINATRA AT GIZA RESIDENCE: And it was hard to tell who was more impressed: Sadat or Sinatra. The singer said he felt "goose bumps." The Egyptian leader said . . . "so much has happened in the Middle East . . . and now we have Frank."
>
> V/O PYRAMID PREPARATIONS PIX: As they chatted . . . workers were setting the stage and Sinatra organizers were doing what organizers do best: worrying and wondering . . . a bit awed by the setting if not exactly the set. If it all worked, they thought, it just might become the eighth wonder of the world.
>
> V/O SINATRA REHEARSAL PIX INCL. FAULTY SOUND SYSTEM AND SWIRLING SAND: At rehearsal today, Sinatra worked on a few numbers with the band. He felt a little intimidated though it wasn't the shaky sound . . . or the sand. How must it feel to have to perform with the Sphinx looking over your shoulder?
>
> (SINATRA ON CAMERA) sound up Sinatra: "I feel small".
>
> V/O REHEARSAL PIX: After almost fifteen years on the Arab boycott list, Ole Blue Eyes – a long-time supporter of Israel – was asked to come to Egypt to perform a benefit for Mrs Sadat's favourite charity. It will be a one-of-a-kind performance. For Sinatra *and* the Sphinx. A peace performance at the pyramids."

And off I went to cover this "one-of-a-kind" show.

> UP SOUND ON TAPE SINATRA SINGING "CHICAGO, CHICAGO" FOR 2 OR 3 SECONDS
>
> KAYS V/O PIX SINATRA ON STAGE AT PYRAMIDS: Sinatra. Yes. But a long way from Chicago. Sinatra. Live at the pyramids . . . in his first performance ever in an Arab country. With the inscrutable Sphinx looking over his shoulder, 'Ole Blue Eyes' belted out the old favourites before a benefit dinner

audience of eight hundred American fundraisers who paid as much as thirty thousand dollars a table to hear him sing . . . and to contribute half a million dollars to Mrs Jihan Sadat's personal charity.

MRS SADAT FRONT ROW CENTRE AUDIENCE: Sinatra was clearly at home in his new environment.

SOUND UP SINATRA JOKING ABOUT CAIRO TRAFFIC: (A joke about a tomb to the unknown pedestrian.)

KAYS V/O PIX: Then, 'Frank', as President Sadat now refers to him, paid tribute to the Egyptian leader:

SOUND UP SINATRA: "He's a great cat . . . his quest for peace is the eighth wonder of the world."

KAYS V/O PIX: Sinatra wound up his hour-long midnight show . . . the way he ends every show:

SOUND UP SINATRA. UP SOUND ON TAPE SINATRA SINGING "My Way" for :03 seconds. . . .

It was enough to make the Sphinx smile or topple from his pedestal in shame.

The most accurate and succinct account of the whole extravaganza cropped up about eight months later in the respected British journal, *The New Statesman*, in an article by the historian Desmond Stewart. As he saw it, Egypt was now part of the "American Cosmos" what with the once-blacklisted cosmetic giant, Revlon Inc., footing the bill – half a million dollars – for the jet set party. Among the more than four hundred party-goers, he reminds us, were some of what he called the "same rich-raff previously photographed at Persepolis" which for those of you who don't follow these things, was the bash the Shah of Iran threw in 1971 to celebrate two and a half thousand years of Persian monarchy.

A dinner table for six (from which to better hear Sinatra sing) cost thirty thousand dollars. And that was simply the headliner. Other sched-uled events, he pointed out, included a pool-side Balmain fashion show (in the shadow of the pyramids) which featured such couturier collection pieces as gold, fig-leafed bikinis. Stewart calculated that the two and a half thousand dollars it cost each jetsetter to partake of this exotic act of charity equalled nine years' wages for an ordinary Egyptian.

The Sinatra-Balmain-Revlon performance was a charity benefit the proceeds of which were intended for Jihan Sadat's personal charity – the Wafa Wal Amal Society (Hope and Faith Centre for the Handicapped and War Wounded). I'm not sure that it was ever recorded or revealed by how much the charity benefited.

It should be noted though that Wafa Wal Amal had long been a source of ugly rumours centred on alleged corruption. The rumours which were never substantiated, nonetheless tended to reflect on Egypt's First Lady. These persistent rumbles merely contributed to the widening gap between the ruling elite and the ruled.

In addition, the Sinatra show coincided with the ninth anniversary of President Nasser's death and while President Sadat did not himself attend the show, neither – for the first time – did he attend the commemorative service for his predecessor. This did not pass unnoticed by those Egyptians who retain fond memories of Nasser or by those less willing to bury their recent Egyptian and Arab past.

The Americanization of Anwar Sadat, then, was mentally noted by his temporarily silenced political critics and by Cairo's growing fundamentalist movement – still seething over the outcome of the Haifa Summit, held the previous week.

This eighth tête-à-tête between the Egyptian President and the Israeli Prime Minister brought Sadat back to Israel for the first time since his Jerusalem peace initiative. The visit to the port city of Haifa, which was "twinned" to Alexandria during the Begin visit that summer, was intended to create a big splash. It did. The waves rippled all the way back to Egypt where Sadat's arrival via yacht was being televised live. As the slick white *El-Hourriya* berthed at the dockside and an Israeli military band sounded bugle and drum, President and Mrs Sadat beamed their way down the ramp. So, alas, did a tanned, beautiful, younger Jihan wearing what appeared to be a strapless sun dress. From my vantage point several hundred metres away I could not see the shoe-string straps that I later learned held up this chic creation, not that it mattered much in terms of Islam's code governing female dress and behaviour. Not believing that the daring Jihan could be that daring, I gave her the benefit of the doubt: no sooner had I decided I was too far away to see the material that covered her bodice and shoulders than I saw the two Jihans imitate the President in the friendly, casual Western custom of greeting friends and hosts with a warm peck on the cheek. Since their hosts were predominately male and Israeli, and the guests distinctly Arab and female, the gesture had the impact of a slap in the face whose sting would surely be felt in Islamic Egypt where life, politics and traditions were undergoing change of cataclysmic proportions.

These two cultural-social-religious gaffes would prove to be mere appetizers to the political feast that lay ahead. It was love at first sight between the people of Haifa and Sadat, who stopped his motorcade and plunged into crowds of enthusiastic Israelis. So moved was he by this demonstration of warmth and affection, and so determined to overwhelm Menachem Begin with his own warmth and affection (in the hope this would later pay dividends of greater Israeli flexibility, if not in the Palestinian autonomy talks then in the Sinai withdrawals), that he outdid even himself. He announced to a group of Israeli newspaper editors that he was going to pump the sweet waters of the Nile into the Sinai, right on up into the Negev Desert, as an act of good neighbourliness. During his sessions with Begin he also agreed to sell Israel two million tons of oil a year, as it had so adamantly demanded, at a price to be determined. In return Begin agreed to withdraw from Mount Sinai ahead of schedule to allow Sadat to stage his planned Peace Festival there on November 19th, the second anniversary of his pilgrimage to Jerusalem. Sadat would have dearly loved to open up those borders and exchange ambassadors well ahead of the treaty timetable, but this was the one and final concession his Foreign Ministry wanted no part of. Some of his aides, infuriated by their leader's magnanimous, conciliatory, good-guy image, felt he had already far exceeded the bounds of diplomacy as practised by even the most seasoned of international allies.

Sadat made an attempt to push Begin on the issue of Palestinian autonomy and the future of Jerusalem. The fact that Begin refused to budge beyond bilateral relations did not seem to disturb the buoyant Egyptian President, who departed Haifa on a cloud. The way he saw it, the world around him was in great shape: the Arabs were in greater disarray than ever, which pleased him no end; the Sinai was looking better and more accessible by the day; and for the moment he was getting on beautifully with the courtly, Talmudic Begin, who had caused him so much grief in the past and who he knew was capable of causing him as much in the future. The appearance of peace was what now counted for Sadat and it was looking good.

In an eleven-minute radio perspective on the Haifa summit: "What Now?" I reported it as the best of the lot. Cosmetically. On a scale of ten it rated nine and a half. The eighth Sadat-Begin summit, I sardonically suggested, should have been sub-titled: "We told you so . . . ain't peace grand?" I then went on to outline, assess and analyse what I saw to be Sadat's current plans, problems and predicament with regard to the Israelis, the Americans, the Arabs and the Palestinians. In fact it was his growing Egyptian predicament that should have most concerned Sadat, the media, and me.

By the time Sadat landed back in Egypt, storms were brewing behind the scenes on several fronts in varying degrees of visibility: outraged whispers over young Jihan's immodest dress and behaviour at the Haifa dockside filled the gossip mill; and while the dinner-party crowd swallowed hard on this latest breach of presidential commonsense, devout Moslems and religious militants simply choked in disgust at this display of Western taste and morals. More vocal Egyptians chose substance over form and devoted their energies to something they considered slightly more durable than sundresses and Israeli kisses: the ancient, sacred waters of the Nile. Sadat's offer to hand Israel a part of Egypt's most treasured heritage leaked out of the Israeli and foreign media fast enough to create the torrent of protest that greeted him on arrival home. The loudest noise was coming out of Sadat's own loyal, official opposition party – the Socialist Labour Party – whose weekly newspaper *Al Shaab* (The People) screamed: "The Nile Is Threatened." That was more than enough to set Cairo abuzz over its leader's latest great step forward. Forced on the defensive, Sadat went about setting the record straight in typical fashion. Speaking through his media alter ego and sometime philosophy guru,

October magazine editor Anis Mansour, Sadat dismissed the fuss as just rumours. According to Mansour, whose chief talent seemed to be transforming black into white and evil into good and vice versa, depending on the day's political surprises and flip-flops, what Sadat had in fact proposed was that "in the name of Egypt and the holy Al-Azhar the Nile water should become a *zemzem* (the sacred well in Mecca) for the faithful of all three religions". This, argued the agile Mansour, would prove yet again Egypt's commitment to peace. Just to ensure there was no more misunderstanding, Sadat later revealed that what he really had in mind was to pump Nile water to Jerusalem as a way of bringing the Israeli and Palestinian people together, so everyone could live in peace.

Israel did not get the Nile.

On October 22, 1979, the deposed and exiled Shah of Iran was admitted to Sloan Kettering Hospital in New York City for treatment of malignant lymphoma.

On November 4 – in protest – Iranian militants seized the American embassy compound in Tehran and took more than fifty Americans hostage. For the next four hundred and forty four days, "America Held Hostage" would become the longest-running media event in the history of US television news.

The Iran story was now the multi-million-dollar, best-selling story. American lives were in danger in revolutionary Iran. The President of Egypt (representing "good" Islam) lost no time in attacking the leader of Iran (representing "bad" Islam). Anwar Sadat called Ayatollah Khomeini a "lunatic", thus further endearing himself to a bewildered and angry America.

On November 9, the Egyptian leader, in an unprecedented request, summoned the three Cairo-based American TV network correspondents and their cameras to his Barrages home to deliver himself of a message to the American people and its government. An hour or so after my colleagues and I arrived, Sadat made his entrance, one that appropriately set the tone and mood of his wrath. One could only assume that the actor in Sadat had been rehearsing during our long wait. In my two years of Sadat-watching I had not seen him more irate or agitated, not even when attacking the Arabs. Boiling with rage over the Iranian hostage situation and not content to stick to Iran and Khomeini, he sweepingly condemned the world and Islamic leaders: "For shame," he roared, "shame on the world, shame on the Moslem leaders . . . they will suffer the same fate." What so enraged Sadat was the bad name he felt Khomeini was giving Islam; that demanding the return of the Shah to Iran was a crime against Islam: "I am really infuriated," he reminded us, "Islam teaches love, brotherhood. It does not teach what this man is doing." Seeing him so inflamed and concerned over the fate of the hostages and Islam, I asked if he was prepared to mediate with Khomeini to help resolve the problem.

Predictably, this sent his blood pressure soaring to even greater heights: "Never! Never!" he bellowed, " . . .that lunatic . . . he is a lunatic." Perspiring heavily by now, the Egyptian President went on to predict the early fall of Iran to the "leftists, the communists". And his only advice to the US was "don't give in". As for the man without whom this criminal state of affairs would not have been possible, Sadat said he was awaiting word on his offer to fly the Shah to Egypt, doctors and all.

Two hours later the President's message was being transmitted via satellite into millions of American homes. Two hours after that his "lunatic" quote was moving on news tickers round the world to be replayed and repeated before being retired into history. Sadat, then, was back on centre stage playing the good guy; lined up on the side of God, the Koran and America in a world growing more simplistic and polarized by the day. That night, like so many other nights in Cairo, we – the CBS, NBC and ABC correspondents – had done our bit; the Sadat piece was good, hard-hitting, grabby stuff; our respective show producers loved it; we were good-nighted, to use the jargon of the electronic bird-age. Never mind that our reports probably served no other purpose than to reinforce existing opinions, perceptions and prejudices on a highly complex and emotive issue. Such disturbing notions have a tendency to lie down and roll over with the TV correspondent at two o'clock in the morning.

Playing in tandem with the hostage story was the Moslem fundamentalist story. Media attention was now focused on a serious new threat to the status quo variously perceived as the rise of Islam, the revival of Islam, terrorist Islam, fanatic Islam, militant Islam, barbaric Islam, the kook-fringe of Islam. More to the point, the compelling media question surroun-ding this threat – all the more intimidating because it defied comprehen-sion by an ignorant, Christian-Judaic America – was, could it happen in friendly, pro-Western Islamic countries like Egypt, where so much was at stake. President Sadat would go on to declare ad nauseam that he would permit "no Khomeinis in Egypt; no mixing of politics and religion", forgetting that Islam is precisely politics and religion, that it is not merely a religion but a way of life and as such should govern every aspect of a Moslem's behaviour. One did not have to search further for an answer to the question. Indeed, Sadat's reassuring words to America would have the opposite effect on Egypt's growing community of frustrated, disaffected fundamentalists; they would further exacerbate and alienate him from that critical segment of the population. In an effort to expand its coverage of the volatile hostage issue beyond the restrictive morning and evening news programmes, ABC News, which was first on the scene in Tehran, kept its lead by introducing a nightly half-hour news special entitled "America Held Hostage", devoted entirely to the crisis and, presumably, to its causes, implications and ramifications; presumably, because I rarely saw the programme tapes and had no way of knowing whether the extra information increased or diminished public understanding and insight, especially in the early aftermath of the hostage-taking.

In answer, then, to the question of potential similar trouble in Egypt, I offered "The Blind Sheik" to "America Held Hostage":

V/O PIX: They come from miles around to see him. Every Friday. Faithfully. They come. Thousands of them. To hear him, some even to record him. By the time the noon call to prayer sounds, his followers are packed shoulder to shoulder into Cairo's Il-Malek Mosque . . . overflowing into the surrounding courtyards and alleyways. All eyes are focused on the Blind Sheik as he's led on to centre stage.

Then Sheik Abdel Hamid Kishk leads the way, alone. At forty-six, he is Egypt's leading Islamic fundamentalist. Sheik Kishk: a household name throughout Egypt. He is the country's popular voice of opposition; the outlet for hundreds of thousands, if not millions, of the poor, the working-class and the devout Sunni Moslem purists. When he gets too loud, he gets thrown into prison. Nasser silenced him twice. Sadat twice. Sadat is too politically astute these days to jail his popular critic again. A new set of unwritten rules, a gentleman's agreement, seems to be in effect: Sadat has made it clear he will not tolerate any Ayatollahs in Egypt. He tolerates his sheik because his sheik has agreed not to rock the system.

The renegade clergyman usually wraps his criticisms in parables: when he attacks Sadat's domestic and foreign policies he never mentions Sadat by name. But his messages elude no one. Not the uniformed police standing guard outside his mosque, and certainly not the ever-present, less than discreet, intelligence agents.

But Sadat is not the Shah. Egypt is not Iran and Kishk is not Khomeini:

Sadat is not an aloof blue-blood. He helped overthrow Egypt's own monarchy back in '52. He is popular, charismatic, publicly devout; prays at a local mosque faithfully every Moslem Sabbath. He travels regularly to meet his people, shake their hands and solve their problems. His wealth is not ostentatious. He is more a benevolent dictator than a ruthless tyrant.

As for the Egyptian people, they are patient and passive. Historically not a volatile nation. And unlike the Shi'ites of Iran, the Sunnis of Egypt are less rigid, more flexible in their interpretation of the Koran.

The Sheiks and the mosques are government guided and controlled. Even the maverick "blind sheik". With the turbulence in Iran and elsewhere in the Moslem world, Kishk is careful not to enflame. He attacks the West for failing to understand Islam. In an interview he urges Khomeini to leave revenge to God. And attacks the Ayatollah for giving Islam a bad name. He condemns him for holding Americans hostage; urging Khomeini to concentrate instead on his Islamic revolution and republic. He warns Khomeini of the most dangerous threat: the communists.

Sheik Kishk's thundering, spell-binding sermons are heard throughout Cairo and Egypt via the most popular medium: audio cassette. Khomeini used the same method to transmit his messages while in exile. Kishk is a magnetic performer. Something of a pop figure.

KAYS ON CAMERA OUTSIDE MOSQUE: The Blind Sheik is really Egypt's fourth estate. He provides the checks and balances which the semi-official press often cannot provide. He is a bellwether of popular mood. A necessary evil. And potential troublemaker. No one knows that better than President Sadat. If trouble should erupt in Egypt, one day, over economic or domestic issues – as is possible – that gentleman's agreement between Sadat and his sheik would probably crumble. Islam, be it Sunni or Shi'ite, is after all more than a religion. It is a way of life. That's why the popular Islamic fundamentalist leader – the blind sheik – is so closely *watched*.

Twenty months later he was back in prison.

By the end of 1979 it was impossible to assess how many of Egypt's roughly thirty-five million Moslems were fundamentalists and how many of them were fanatics. All that one could safely assume was that Sadat's rule was antagonizing Egypt's right-wing religious community. Inviting the Shah into such a delicate environment would prove to be another stage in Sadat's progressive disintegration.

On November 18, I received word that the Shah was coming to Egypt and went on the air that night with the following exclusive report:

ABC News has learned that the Shah is expected to arrive in Egypt the first or second week in December – *if* he does not require further surgery and *if* his doctors permit him to leave the hospital.

Highly-placed Egyptian sources tell me the Shah will stay in the winter resort town of Aswan, where he spent his first few days of exile last January, as guest of President Sadat. But it would be for a few weeks' convalescence. Only. He has no plans apparently to take up permanent residence here. Anwar Sadat has repeatedly offered his old friend and supporter political asylum, and his parliament, at least, backs up the invitation:

UP SOUND ON TAPE SADAT: "My plane is ready to go ... to bring the Shah" ... said Sadat, who was highly indignant over the abandonment of the Shah which he found to be "very, very dangerous".

Only a couple of days ago, Sadat confirmed to me that his plane is *still* ready, anytime, to fly the deposed Iranian leader to Egypt ... for asylum, medical treatment or convalescence. Concerning treatment, one of Egypt's top cancer specialists told ABC that the Shah could be adequately treated. The country's cancer institute in fact specializes in the very type of cancer – lymphoma – from which the Shah suffers.

The prospect of the Shah returning to Egypt – for any reason – did not sit well with Sadat's opposition, or for that matter with the Carter administration which was more sensitive to Egypt's political problems than Sadat was.

On November 30 I reported:

... President Sadat denies reports that the US may be discouraging the Shah from coming to Egypt for fear it might stir up trouble for an already troubled, isolated Moslem leader. In fact, tight security is being enforced, especially on university campuses, where some Islamic fundamentalist groups are under close surveillance. ...

Two days later the Shah flew to Texas – not Egypt as originally planned – where he remained a short period before flying off to another exile villa, this time in Panama. While Sadat secluded himself, a government spokesman assured us the invitation was still open; furthermore, Egypt could look after itself and any trouble that might erupt as a result of granting the Shah political asylum. Unofficially, Egypt breathed a sigh of relief, so did the US. Last minute White House diplomacy had saved Anwar Sadat from himself, at least for three months.

The second anniversary of the Egyptian President's peace initiative came and went. There was no spectacular International Peace Festival as planned for Mount Sinai. Nor did Sadat lay the cornerstone for his proposed multi-faith complex housing a mosque, synagogue and church. The selected site turned out to be too close for the comfort and solitude of the Greek Orthodox monks living in the centuries-old St Catherine's Monastery. All was not lost, however. Israeli Prime Minister Begin kept his word and returned the southern Sinai desert area two months ahead of schedule, allowing Sadat to pray and give thanks at the foot of the biblical mount where God is said to have spoken the Ten Commandments to Moses. It was another historic, emotional moment, albeit in splendid

isolation. Jimmy Carter and Menachem Begin couldn't make it. Representing the United States was a twenty-member delegation headed by
Middle East Envoy Bob Strauss who, after learning that the Palestinian
autonomy talks were less fun than presidential election campaigns, was
quitting the job so he could go home to try to get President Carter re-
elected. Representing Israel was a batch of Israeli reporters and photographers. Representing the world media was the ever-dependable Cairo-
based foreign news corps, led by the three American TV networks. For
some reason Walter Cronkite and Barbara Walters couldn't make it either.

With the Palestinian autonomy talks still arguing over the meaning of
"self-rule", Sadat needed a distraction from his separate peace and the
prosperity he was promising, but knew he couldn't deliver, short of divine
intervention. The Iranian revolution, the hostage crisis, the growing instability in the region and the threat that all this posed to American strategic
interests was ripe for exploitation. Sadat could now prove his worth to the
United States. He would offer them military "facilities" to help defend
all the Arab countries and their oil, never mind that his fellow Arabs no
longer considered him a friend let alone protector. This triggered more
trouble for the Egyptian leader at home. No matter how much Sadat
insisted he was offering facilities, not bases, it still looked like bases to
most Egyptians. They had not got rid of French, British and Soviet
troops only to welcome American troops. The facilities/bases offer was just
another political hot potato Sadat insisted on juggling with in typically
theatrical fashion. If nothing else it would guarantee him continued appearances on American television and the international stage. Unfortunately,
his obsession with America and external threats to peace and stability in
the region obscured the far more dangerous internal threats facing him
and his regime; the major one being economic. By all appearances the
rich were getting richer and the poor were getting poorer.

As 1979 ended Egypt was quietly rotting away, its domestic problems
and injustices devouring the masses. It was a seemingly endemic situation
that played into the hands of Sadat's political and religious critics. If the
Sadat regime were to crumble it would crumble from a cumulative pile
of irritants, the most glaring of which was the sheer reality of day to day
life; a life that was getting worse not better except for a privileged few
who flaunted their wealth in the face of those who hadn't a hope of sharing
in it. The obscene gap between rich and poor could not be narrowed by
utopian promises of prosperity or millions in American aid. For whatever
reason, Sadat refused to dirty his hands; that would have meant grappling
with corruption at the top and all the other nasty little inequities that keep
a country of haves and have-nots flourishing. It's as though he had long
ago decided Egypt was a lost cause – at least in his lifetime – which helps
explain why he went for the more glamorous, short-term gains of "electric-
shock" therapy.

At a meeting of top ABC News executives and foreign correspondents
in London, my assessment of Egypt's plight and Sadat's future resulted

in a request for an economic story. Upon returning to Cairo I set about finding a typical Egyptian family to illustrate in simple human and dramatic terms how more than ninety per cent of Egyptians live. A family portrait was more easily executed than a rich-poor montage of Cairo, given the amount of time I could devote to the story and the challenge of shooting on location. The result was the story of Khairy El-Shahat:

His name is El-Shahat. The Arabic word for beggar. Khairy El-Shahat. He's poor. And illiterate. But no beggar. He works. Night and Day. 365 of them a year . . . struggling to stay on his feet. His day, in fact, begins at night. At Cairo's Nile Transport Company which he guards from eleven to seven. After time out for a bite to eat – some cheese, bread, tea, a smoke and a few laughs with the boys – El-Shahat, night watchman, watches. And waits for morning. And his other jobs . . . as office boy and when lucky, as cleaning man, messenger, handyman, film extra, jack-of-all-trades. He'll do anything. Anywhere. Short of beg or steal, to feed his family. Some are better off than El-Shahat. Others worse off. But his hand to mouth existence is typical . . . *of millions* of Egyptians.

Even with the moonlighting – and most are not so lucky – El-Shahat cannot make ends meet. All he can do is keep moving from night to day and job to job. Like he's been doing for thirty-five of his forty-six years. Even if he doesn't seem to get anywhere. Even if his life seems to get worse, not better. In Cairo these days, it's survival of the rich . . . and the fit. El-Shahat thanks God that at least he's fit.

As night watchman he earns the equivalent of twenty-seven dollars a month. As office boy in a downtown movie company, twenty-five dollars a month. *Seven hundred dollars a year.* Twice as much as the average Egyptian wage. That's little comfort as El-Shahat heads for the cinema office. Over a solitary breakfast – more cheese and bread – the rich and glamorous, like his actor-producer boss, stare him in the face. So does the movie poster depicting Victor Hugo's *Les Miserables* . . . the story of a man who *stole* to feed *his* family. El-Shahat prays it never comes to that. And steals a few winks instead, whenever he can. In another section of Cairo, his wife daily pinches piastres as the cost of food steadily rises. The family can still afford vegetables. Fruit: never. Meat: once or twice a month. Fish: even less.

At the end of his sixteen-hour day, El-Shahat heads home. On foot. To save the eight-cent bus fare. And during the forty-minute walk he thinks of his hard luck.

Twelve years ago, he thought he married the ideal woman. Two husbands had divorced her for failing to produce children. Just the economical wife he wanted. Today – four children later

– he laughs at Fate's cruel trick. For most poor Egyptians, birth control is still a sin.

So, home to El-Shahat is one cramped room. In a building that could collapse any day. At five dollars a month, it's all he can afford. He prays for more space. Two rooms. And dreams of three. But that means roughly three-thousand dollars in key money, plus furniture. And triple the rent. As for the government's new low-cost housing plans: only couples married after 1975 need bother apply.

He praises President Sadat. And peace. But curses the bureaucrats and government officials. Who ignore him. His hopes for the future? His children. Their education.

All that economic projects, statistics and budgets mean to millions like El-Shahat is: a monthly income of fifty-two dollars. Monthly living costs of eighty-three dollars – half of which goes for food.

He desperately wants to emigrate. The only way *out*, he says, is *out* of Egypt.

In addition to this three-minute, forty-five-second version, a tighter, shorter script was also shipped to New York, along with the tapes that contained powerful visuals to illustrate the story. It was an ideal profile for television; a perfect melding of pictures and words whose impact could not be duplicated by the print medium. Indeed, of the handful of feature background stories I had the luxury of reporting out of Cairo, this one would prove the most professionally and personally satisfying: it was a slice of life in Egypt, life as it was being lived not by Anwar Sadat but by real people; those fated to be dismissed as the "masses", like so many incurable lepers in whose name a better world was being constructed, somewhere beyond the grave.

"El-Shahat" arrived in New York on November 4, the same day the hostage story broke. The Egyptian masses couldn't hope to compete with the American hostages. Periodically I tried selling "El-Shahat" to the show producer who had commissioned it with such urgency and enthusiasm, before America was "held hostage". Having given up on the prime-time flagship "World News Tonight" I peddled it elsewhere. Finally the executive producer of the "Sunday Evening News" agreed to dust it off for a look. He bought it on the spot. Nine months later.

8. Malignancies

ONCE THE EGYPTIAN-ISRAELI peace had been consummated, Egypt ceased to be a hot news story. Having losts its seductive powers over American television, it settled into a humdrum relationship that, barring another Sadat electric-shock treatment, would have to depend on the occasional peace-related event for its survival. The love affair, after all, had been with Sadat not Egypt – the country or its people. If there had been little interest in exploring the stories behind the story during the era of media hype there was even less interest now. Had I produced a Sadat exclusive – positive or negative – or a juicy scandal documenting corruption and the corrupt or some equally riveting "ABC News has learned" report, I might have been able to keep Egypt in the news more often than the three or four times a month to which it had been reduced. As I was still expected to stake-out Sadat day and night in what could only be labelled as "save-your-ass" protective coverage, there was virtually no time to devote to investigative or background reporting. By the end of 1979 this hopeless situation had begun to erode bureau morale; the phenomenal esprit de corps that had fuelled us through our peace successes was collapsing into petty office politics nurtured on frustration, fatigue and the non-story. No longer the centre of foreign news, the Cairo troops longed for one of two solutions: a holiday from Anwar Sadat so we could either search out more significant Egyptian stories, or temporary assignment to a breaking story that would at least guarantee a change of scene and an on-air story at the end of a twelve- to eighteen-hour day.

The hostage story was custom-made. It was the hottest media event to hit the neighbourhood since Anwar Sadat. Every self-respecting foreign correspondent, cameraman, TV news producer and photographer wanted to be in on the action and, while I did not volunteer for Iran, I was delighted when the call came through, if only to escape Cairo and my stand-by duties. The Cairo producer, cameraman and editor had long since joined ABC's heavy duty operation at Tehran's Intercontinental Hotel by the time I arrived to celebrate a new year. America was thrilled with our presence there. Iran was not. Three weeks later the Western media was expelled en masse.

If any country in the region was falling apart it was Turkey, not Iran. By February 1980 anarchy had become a way of life and death for forty-five million people held hostage by daily political terrorism of the left and right. Two-thirds of the Western world's defence buffer between the Soviet Union and the oil-rich Persian Gulf – Iran and Afghanistan – had defected, and the remaining third, Turkey, was disintegrating after almost two decades of violent vendettas.

ABC dispatched me to Istanbul to do backgrounders on a country that not even martial law had prevented from sliding into chaos. With the help of a top-notch producer and camera crew, I came up with three reports that I felt provided some insight into a country traditionally all but ignored by the foreign media. Given the luxury of a week's shooting schedule, we were able to focus on three critical themes: political terrorism, a bankrupt economy and the geo-politics of a NATO country on the verge of civil war, revolution or military take-over. If aired on three consecutive nights on the evening news, the reports could not fail to inform, given the dearth of television information on a foreign crisis whose political implications and repercussions for the United States and Western Europe were far greater – if less emotive – than the dramatic hostage crisis being played out in neighbouring Iran.

The New York show producers, facing the daily dilemma of too much news and too little time in which to convey it – a juggling act of priorities exacerbated by the hostage story – were forced to combine the three background reports into "one giant good piece" as it was characterized by a senior producer. I counted my blessings and gave them the benefit of the doubt. It was not good enough. How naïve to hope that television news could cope with even a poor facsimile of comprehensive reporting.

Seven months later I was back in Turkey covering a hard-breaking news story: the military takeover.

In the troubled world of 1980 the Western world could count on at least one "oasis of peace and tranquillity", as Anwar Sadat liked to brag in his three-hour speeches, now devoted to all-out war on the Arabs, Khomeini and, of course, the Soviets. Two months after the Soviets moved into Afghanistan, Sadat wanted to punish them by expelling much of what remained of the Soviet presence in Egypt: two to three hundred civilian specialists. Seven diplomats were left to hold the fortress-like embassy in Sadat's Giza neighbourhood; just enough to prevent a total rupture in diplomatic relations. However, for practical reasons Egypt found it still needed their expertise and so the Russian presence was not noticeably diminished. At the same time, he reinforced his support for the United States and the Carter Doctrine by repeating his offer of military facilities to help combat any Soviet threat to the Gulf. If 1979 was the "year of peace" for Egypt, he now held out 1980 as the year that would mark "the end of all our troubles". But, alas, what should have been the happiest, most trouble-free day of the year – the day Egypt and Israel would establish diplomatic and normal relations – was too embarrassing for the Egyptians even to mention. February 2 was a non-starter. It did not happen. This is how I reported that historic day:

> KAYS V/O PIX Egyptian television's evening news said it all: a lot about Israel getting out of two-thirds of the Sinai; absolutely nothing about normal relations with Israel. Not one word. President Sadat and most Egyptians, quite frankly, would rather not think about it let alone talk about it. And the media reflects Cairo's feeling about edging closer to Tel Aviv. The ambivalence is glaring: the *Jerusalem Post* on sale side-by-side with *Al Ahram*, which barely mentions this historic day. The reason Egyptians are all but ignoring this latest stage of peace . . . is anger and embarrassment over the lack of progress on the Palestinian issue and Jerusalem.
>
> Open borders, direct flights and mail, business and trade deals; in short, many of the signs of normal relations are lagging; delayed by the reluctant Egyptians, not the eager Israelis.
>
> Neyazi Mustapha, a Cairo millionaire and head of the Egyptian-American Chamber of Commerce admits the two sides are indeed talking business. But, he adds, until there's peace in the Middle East, there cannot be normal business relations. . . .
>
> (UP SOT MUSTAPHA FOR 30 SECONDS . . . explaining why there's no movement on the future of the Palestinians)
>
> KAYS V/O PIX . . . If the Egyptians feel uncomfortable, so must the Israelis . . . desperately searching for an embassy to open by Monday. Security and politics have locked them out of temporary quarters in a downtown hotel. But there's still hope: a couple of grand old villas . . . a few blocks away.
>
> Cairo still can't telephone Tel Aviv but . . . maybe next week, says the operator. The telex . . . that's working. ABC proved that today when our two bureaux communicated directly and quickly. According to Cairo's leading magazine, normal relations will really get moving on February 15 . . . two weeks late. That's mostly propaganda.
>
> In the meantime the Egyptian beer drinker will continue to wallow in his beer. Israeli beer. Smuggled onto the market weeks ago.

While Israeli's first ambassador to an Arab capital was still packing his bags for Cairo, Israel lodged its first diplomatic protest against Egypt. A top Sadat aide and deputy minister, Hassan Tohamey, told a Kuwaiti newspaper that Israel was built on plundered Moslem soil and he predicted its collapse. As for the Jews, the staunch Moslem considered them treacherous, hypocritical people. Sadat's long-time advisor was reacting to a book, *Year of the Dove*, written by three Israeli journalists – including TV correspondent Ehud Yaari with whom Tohamey was in frequent contact. He claimed the book insulted Egypt and quoted Prime Minister Begin describing Sadat as a "degenerate". When told that Israel was lodging a diplomatic protest over his remarks, Tohamey replied: "Phooey to them. I think I'll take the Israelis to court. It will teach them a lesson."

Finally, by the end of February, peace took another step forward with the opening of the Israeli embassy in Cairo and the arrival of Ambassador Eliahu Ben-Elissar. When Ben-Elissar presented his credentials to President Sadat, the Egyptian leader again stunned his aides when he told the new envoy: "Elie, you are the right man in the right place at the right time." The semi-official press, the foreign ministry and the intelligentsia saw him as the wrong man in the wrong place at the wrong time and over the next year they would let him know as much. Ben-Elissar, a rather suave charmer in his late forties, is Polish-born and shares Prime Minister Begin's hawkish view of life. Unfortunately, on the eve of his arrival, he antagonized official Egypt by publicly repeating Israel's right to settle the West Bank, a right which, technically at least, was currently the subject of negotiation in the moribund Palestinian autonomy talks. Israel's chief diplomat in Egypt symbolized Israeli intransigence and bad faith on the Palestinian question and as such was considered a bad choice; one that guaranteed that the normalization of relations would be conducted in a chilly, even hostile environment. The embarrassing search for an embassy was just the beginning. The Israelis were forced to settle for temporary quarters in a cramped villa on a busy thoroughfare in the Dokki section of Cairo. And the day Sadat welcomed the ambassador as a wonderful chap, demonstrators – banned from staging a protest – instead burned paper Israeli flags and hoisted Palestinian ones. The anti-Israelites represented more than a fanatic fringe: Sadat's official opposition party, the Marxist-leftist party, the Moslem brotherhood, Moslem fundamentalists, the syndicates and associations grouping Egypt's doctors, lawyers and journalists and thousands of university students. All boycotted normal and diplomatic relations with Israel. Several artists and intellectual acquaintances refused to have anything to do with the Israelis professionally or socially, either out of their anti-treaty convictions or fear of reprisals and ostracism from their peers. When the US news weekly *Time* held a cocktail reception at the Nile Hilton to introduce its new bureau chief, a couple of Israeli embassy officials showed up, but none of their Egyptian counterparts.

One middle-class Egyptian colleague – a devout Moslem – described the anti-Israeli sentiment more graphically: "I feel like I've been raped," he said bitterly, "made love to against my will." One respected *Al Ahram* journalist resigned so as not to have to refuse assignments in Israel, not that there would be any permanently based Egyptian correspondents in Israel. Tel Aviv's first and only permanent man in Cairo – Israeli TV's Ehud Yaari – was never certain Egypt wanted him to get comfortably settled. Before normal relations, he enjoyed great freedom of movement and wide-ranging official contacts. After the embassy opened, however, he had trouble getting his visa renewed and his freedom to report and film was curtailed considerably. As a result Yaari decided to commute between Cairo and his Jerusalem home.

It was the Israeli ambassador who would bear the brunt of the cold-shoulder treatment. By March the Ben-Elissars had still not been invited into an Egyptian home and Mrs Ben-Elissar, keen to entertain on this historic diplomatic assignment, was advised to be patient. Unable to locate suitable living quarters the ambassador and his wife spent 1980 at the Nile Sheraton entertaining each other, and their friends and families from home.

At the embassy itself, few Egyptians were requesting visas to visit Israel and, with business slow, the ambassador was left to amuse himself as best he could. At the Foreign Ministry meanwhile, the Minister of State for Foreign Affairs, Butros Ghali, found himself working overtime: none of his fellow diplomats wanted to deal with the Israelis.

By March, then, embassies were established, ambassadors exchanged, borders opened, telephone, telex and mail links hooked up and El-Al flights to Cairo a reality. Peace had arrived kicking and screaming; a peace that would remain flawed long after I departed in 1981; a cool, formal, polite, suspicious, ambivalent, uncertain and unfinished peace. The Israeli diplomats and their families and staff would not have an easy time of it. Apart from the problems entailed in adapting to any new country and culture, they were having to adapt to an Arab country – one isolated from the rest of the Arab world – and one that snubbed them diplomatically.

At the time, I reported all this at length for ABC Radio, whose variety of programming included the luxurious eleven-minute-long, personalized commentary outlet called "Perspective". Roughly comparable to the BBC's "From Our Own Correspondent", it offered an ideal supplement to the brief daily news reports. While "Perspective" was not broadcast in prime time and did not command a massive audience, its select market of faithful listeners were addicts of foreign and current affairs and "Perspective" invariably elicited requests for transcripts and, frequently, highly favourable listener comments.

I spent an equal amount of time trying to convey the same story to television viewers, but with predictably less success. Having decided to profile the lonely life of Israel's first ambassador to an Arab country, I set out with a crew on a day-long shooting schedule that included an interview with the ambassador, footage of him at work – so to speak – in an office which embarrassed him. General interior and exterior visuals of the embassy and staff were followed by pictures of the Ben-Elissars at home, in the streets of Cairo and celebrating Passover with the embassy staff. A nice little portrait of Israel's First Couple in Egypt. Apart from the unflattering home-in-a-hotel sequence, in which they refused to co-operate, the ambassador and his wife were charming and obliging throughout the long, dusty day that included a couple of hours in Cairo's hectic *souk*, the Khan Khalili bazaar, which is where the Ben-Elissars felt they were most assured of a proper and warm welcome. Being an old political hand, more than adept at campaigning, Israel's senior diplomat and attractive dark wife were warmly welcomed by the merchants, all of whom tried outdoing one another with Arab hospitality, as much for the benefit of the camera as for the ambassador, who in any case was not exactly a household name or face. Having established that Ben-Elissar liked strong Turkish coffee, medium sweet, I ushered him to a nearby outdoor cafe for his sixth cup of coffee and an interview which he knew in advance would not be sweet: the bitter reality of his lonely, painful existence; a side of peace we could not visually document; the ugly half that nonetheless would show through by the conspicuous lack of footage showing the ambassador dealing with his Egyptian counterparts. His occasional meetings with Sadat did not count, for reasons that by now should be obvious. Refusing to be drawn into further controversy, Eliahu Ben-Elissar was a paragon of diplomacy and patience – while at the same time confessing he did not feel at home in Cairo. Mrs Ben-Elissar, for whom I felt a personal sympathy, handled her interview with the same aplomb. As we left the *souk*, I thanked them effusively for their time and co-operation, suggesting we would doubtless be in touch soon enough.

Too soon, as it turned out. For technical reasons, much of the footage was unusable and would have to be reshot. There is nothing more irritating than having to ask a subject to give the same impromptu performance twice, especially a dignified diplomat who, while he may have had all the time in the world, did not particularly want the world to know it. I explained my dilemma and the ambassador and his wife obligingly trotted through their paces all over again the next day, including the tedious bazaar scene and interviews. If nothing else they deserved actors-of-the-year awards. Bowing and scraping my thanks once more, I made a mental note to send flowers as a token of appreciation for endurance beyond the call of diplomatic duty. This time the camera co-operated and I was able to assemble a report that adequately conveyed the diplomatic deep-freeze, at the same time putting peace in its proper perspective. It was shipped to New York where it was received with the enthusiasm reserved for most shippers and promptly set aside for the day a hole would open up in somebody's show. The story which I considered a vital peace story in that it showed the warts everyone, except the Egyptians, wanted to ignore, never made air. Another victim of more pressing news.

Perhaps it had something to do with the ex-Shah of Iran, who thought the Panamanians were about to kill him on the operating table or, worse, extradite him to Khomeini, if the CIA didn't poison him first.

The future of the deposed monarch had by now become a problem of critical, even paranoid, dimensions, one the intrepid Anwar Sadat would embrace with all its political risks. Sensing his life was in jeopardy, the former Iranian dictator accepted the Egyptian leader's long-standing offer of medical treatment and political asylum without actually acknowledging the latter. The first indication that he was finally headed for Egypt came the morning of March 23, 1980, when the Cairo daily *Al Akhbar* printed a sympathetic front-page portrait of a desperate man overcome by cancer and the fear that, if the disease didn't get him, something or somebody else would. By adding that the surgery required to eliminate his cancerous spleen could not be performed in a Panamanian hospital, the article seemed to be preparing Egyptians for the possible coming of the former Shah, and I passed on my assessment to New York. That evening I was tipped off (via ABC's correspondent in Panama) that a plane was standing by to fly the ex-Iranian leader out of the country, destination unknown. I immediately contacted Prime Minister Mustapha Khalil at his home, as well as the President's press secretary; neither would confirm or deny the information which I offered them as fact. Encouraged, I then contacted two unimpeachable sources – one in his office, the other at a cocktail reception – in an effort to confirm the tip. Again, rather than ask if the ex-Shah was coming to Egypt, I told them that ABC News was going on the air that night with the news that he was coming. This prompted a hasty invitation to the office of one source, who over a cup of coffee confirmed the information in his usual elliptical manner: not wanting to mark him as the "leaker", or even as a prime suspect, I asked my source if I could proceed with plans for a Roman holiday I had cancelled several times and was in dire need of . . . that week.

"No," he replied sheepishly, "I wouldn't leave town if I were you. The next forty-eight hours will be interesting and busy."

I still needed at least one more source collaboration and by the time I returned to the bureau, my cocktail leaker was on the phone: "He's coming all right," said the voice, ". . . unfortunately. Tomorrow morning. As early as seven o'clock."

There was just enough time to consult with the show producers in New York, assemble a few more facts gathered by the Egyptian staff and write and record my on-camera story for the midnight satellite that had been booked – unilaterally.

The Shah story led the show with a report out of Panama back-to-back with the report out of Cairo. ABC's scoop was a good example of swift, aggressive transcontinental team-work, but there was no time to fondle the *herograms*. Sadat's latest problem was due to land in a few hours. By then the foreign and Egyptian media would join us and the story at the Maadi Military hospital.

As Sadat ushered his guest/patient through the main lobby that morning, it was apparent that the Shah's health had seriously deteriorated in the fourteen months of shuttle exile. He was paler, weaker and several kilos thinner than when I last saw him in Aswan and, alongside the robust and confident Sadat, his shrunken frame betrayed the distance the cancer had travelled since it was first diagnosed, secretly, seven years earlier. There was little doubt the Shah would spend the rest of his days in Egypt.

Two days later, several hundred militant Moslems responded by demonstrating against the Shah and Sadat on the campus of Cairo University. The fundamentalists belonged to the then vague organization called The Islamic Groupings and considered the Shah a corrupt enemy of his people and Islam. According to one spokesman, "What happened in Iran could happen in Egypt one day because Sadat's government is attempting to suppress the feelings of Egyptian Moslems." Plainclothes security police arrested several demonstrators and in an effort to prevent our cameras from covering the protest, detained ABC's Hassan Bahgat, whose only crime seemed to be his Egyptian nationality, or so we argued in attempts to get him released. "If you have to arrest anyone in the media," we told the authorities, "arrest us." An embarrassed Ministry of Information intervened, Hassan was freed and that night the anti-Shah, anti-Sadat protest was aired on American television.

The Cairo disturbance was just a warm-up. Two days later an anonymous telephone caller tipped us off about trouble in the Upper Egyptian capital of Assiyut. Night had already fallen as the camera crew set out on the four- to five-hour car journey into the heartland of fundamentalism and traditional hotbed of Coptic Christian-Moslem tensions. That same night, through means equally surreptitious, we learned that the Shah was being operated on. Extraordinary security surrounded the military hospital in Maadi and the renowned American surgeon, Dr Michael Debakey, had already arrived at the urgent request of President Sadat. The bureau's Hanzada Fikry, Hassan and I decided not to leave the bureau until our tips and suspicions were confirmed, and I alerted the show producers in New York to stand-by. At precisely 1:00 a.m. (6:00 p.m. EST New York) as "World News Tonight" went to air with its first edition, Fikry was being issued a medical bulletin from the press centre. As she translated it simultaneously from Arabic into English, I rewrote it and at the same time reported it live – via telephone hook-up – directly into the news show which was ready to flash stills and file footage over my voice report:

> The former Shah, who was admitted to Cairo's suburban Maadi Military Hospital on Monday, was operated on tonight. The official medical bulletin just released says Houston surgeon Michael Debakey performed the surgery which removed the former Shah's cancerous spleen. Sources told ABC News Debakey was assisted by a team of six doctors and a support team of ten Egyptian and American surgeons and specialists.
>
> The official medical bulletin reports the former Shah is in "satisfactory" condition. ABC sources say the former Shah is now in intensive care and will be given radiation treatment for one month followed by chemotherapy . . . indefinitely.

We had killed the competition while they slept in their beds, and New York was ecstatic. Once more the media were forced to play catch-up. The next morning a weary ABC camera crew arrived back from Assiyut with exclusive pictures guaranteed to bury the competition and enrage the Sadat regime. That night (Saturday, March 29, 1980) we scored our latest "Shah" coup with this report:

> KAYS V/O ASSIYUT DEMONSTRATION: "The Shah must leave. The Shah must leave," they shouted ... several thousand Moslem students in the Upper Egyptian capital of Assiyut. Riot police fired tear gas almost the moment the demonstration started, which, coincidentally, was the very hour the former Shah was secretly being prepared for surgery two-hundred and fifty miles away in Cairo.
>
> The anti-Shah anti-Sadat protest – the country's second this week – followed two hours of speeches denouncing the deposed Shah's presence in Egypt, and President Sadat for being his protector. The tear gas succeeded in dispersing the protestors quickly and without major trouble. The demonstration lasted about ten minutes, just long enough for the secret police to briefly detain the ABC camera crew taping this exclusive footage. Egyptian authorities are sensitive about the anti-Shah elements that have surfaced since the deposed Iranian ruler arrived last Monday.
>
> DR DEBAKEY NEWS CONFERENCE PIX: Today ... Houston surgeon Michael Debakey, who performed last night's successful operation on the former Shah, had nothing but praise for the assistance and co-operation of Egyptian doctors ... and Egyptians in general:
>
> SOUNDBITE DEBAKEY: I think it reflects the truly great humanitarian character of the Egyptian people that is symbolized in their President, Anwar Sadat.
>
> Debakey says that now that the former Shah's spleen has been removed he should be able to go on living for an indefinite period of time ... in spite of his lymphatic cancer.
>
> SOUNDBITE DEBAKEY: He should be able to lead a pretty normal life, physically and every way. He should be able to go back to being physically active the way he was and play tennis and do things like that.
>
> Dr Debakey says the former Shah should be out of the hospital ... in another ten days.

Egyptian medical sources were more candid than the kindly Lebanese-American doctor. In spite of the successful surgery, they admitted, the

Shah's cancer had spread throughout the lymphatic system with the result that he might have only weeks or months to live.

Certainly some Egyptians shared their President's compassion towards the dying, stateless Shah, especially in the wake of the hostage incident which had hurt Khomeini's popularity within mainstream Islamic Egypt. More importantly Sadat's bold act of generosity won him points in the West, but it cost him far more where it mattered most, for in addition to Egyptian fundamentalists, strong opposition was being expressed by the official opposition party and the intelligentsia, in fact all the same elements of Egyptian society who were protesting and boycotting diplomatic and normal relations with Israel. Sadat's gesture was a political risk he could ill afford at a time when his domestic troubles and alienation already posed a threat. Of all his opponents it was the fundamentalists he could now least control and silence. Not that he didn't try.

The Assiyut rampage in which, according to the grapevine, scores were killed, injured or arrested, was studiously ignored by the shackled media on the premise, no doubt, that what an impressionable, immature population doesn't know won't hurt it. There was the little matter, however, of that ABC footage and report that made its way to America and back. It would have to be denounced and denied. The job fell to Sadat's devoted Minister of the Interior, Nabawy Ismail, who rose in Parliament to dismiss the ABC fracas as nothing more than a feud between militant Moslems and Coptic Christians. By so cheaply and ludicrously exploiting a festering fringe problem which just happened to resurface at the same time, Sadat and Ismail were seen to be playing with fire. For years Egypt's Coptic community of roughly six to seven million had complained of random harrassment by Moslem extremists that included the burning of churches and abduction of Christian girls. Government blending of the two problems was unfortunate and provocative: the head of the Copts, the activist Pope Shenouda III, added to the mix by protesting against the lack of government action and protection of the Christian minority. He called for a boycott of Easter celebrations and he and his monks retreated to a desert monastery where they became unavailable to receive Sadat's traditional Easter greetings. A joint Moslem-Coptic committee was set up to investigate grievances but at the same time Sadat's Moslem critics privately accused him of hyping up the sectarian rift – even collaborating with the Copts – in an effort to deal a final blow to the real culprits, the fundamentalists.

Sadat was enraged and embarrassed by all this extra baggage being dumped on him on the eve of his latest Washington Summit with President Carter; a summit aimed at heading off a more immediate threat to the Egyptian leader: the collapse of the Palestinian autonomy talks. If his domestic problems had temporarily diverted attention from his "separate" peace – the first anniversary of the treaty, March 26, passed virtually unnoticed – a far more important date would not be ignored by his critics, internal or external: the May 26 one-year deadline for completion of negotiations setting up a Palestinian self-governing authority on the West Bank. With two months remaining they were no further ahead than the day they started. Indeed, they were a sham. So, one year after he'd gone to Washington to sign the Egyptian-Israeli peace treaty, Sadat was back in the Rose Garden with only the fragrance of the magnolia blossoms to remind him of sweeter days. Although he would exude his usual charisma, confidence and optimism as he moved from one applauding audience to another, he was anything but sure of himself or the Americans. In fact he was downright nervous and anxious, and for good reason. His friend and peace partner Jimmy Carter was having his own problems, which had the effect of boomeranging on Sadat. Given the pressures of a presidential election year in which Carter was up for re-election to a second term, the American President was forced to perform a diplomatic flip-flop on a UN resolution condemning Israel's settlements policy on the occupied West Bank; changing the US vote from "yes" to "no", which further eroded his credibility at home and abroad. Realizing that he now faced a weak and ineffectual American leadership, the best Sadat could hope for was a survival of the autonomy talks beyond the May 26 deadline, the survival of Jimmy Carter in the White House beyond November, and the survival of Anwar Sadat until then. Whatever Carter's shortcomings, as author of the Camp David Accords he had a stake in preserving his only foreign-policy success; a commitment Sadat knew would not be shared by the incumbent's likely opponent, Ronald Reagan. So Sadat spent much of his two-day visit discreetly campaigning for his favourite candidate, which prompted some good-humoured café advice from the folks back home: "Anwar could ensure Jimmy's re-election: loan him the electoral genius who never lost Sadat an election; send him Interior Minister Nabawy Ismail to rig the American elections," was the most popular suggestion doing the rounds. Unfortunately, by now Sadat was living in his ivory tower insulated from his people and their pungent jokes.

Democracy's untidiness, in fact, threatened to stain his visit. The American-Egyptian Coptic community hit Sadat with a nasty public campaign on behalf of their "harrassed" compatriots in Egypt. There were large advertisements in the Washington press and a vocal demonstration near the White House. When I queried a confidante as to how Sadat was taking this latest affront to his dignity, he hinted that el Raïs was apoplectic. As for Pope Shenouda, he apparently was finished; a marked man. Sadat, according to the Coptic confidante, was never going to talk to Shenouda again, never, not after the gross insults. And he didn't. Shenouda was added to the growing list of enemies of the state (i.e. personal enemies of Sadat). Sadat's "Islamic tolerance" had its limits, like everything he preached.

No matter how far he travelled these days, he could not avoid his restless countrymen, or ex-countrymen, who now dared humiliate him in front of his foreign fans. He cancelled a tour of American cities and rushed home to look after his problems including the convalescing Shah, but not before granting ABC News correspondent Barbara Walters the ritual up-beat interview. So comfortable had he become with fame and the famous that he shifted from the cosy use of "Bar-ba-ra" to the more intimate "Barb!" a touch of Americana – inadvertent or calculated – that said more about Anwar Sadat than all the interviews combined; an Anwar Sadat America didn't know, didn't want to know, never would know.

The Washington summit, which had been a plea for time, resulted in an extension of the deadline for the Palestinian autonomy talks, a paper victory that Sadat hoped would tide him over through the November US elections when a strong President Carter would be back in the White House, ready to battle with the truculent Israelis, perhaps in a sequel to the Camp David summit. If there was ever to be a breakthrough on the Palestinian-West Bank issue – a dubious prospect at best – the next opportunity was now at least a year away, light years away given Sadat's worsening predicament. Until then he was on his own; a hostage of America's quadrennial foreign-policy paralysis and a lame-duck president fighting for his own political survival, who, unlike Sadat, could not afford to ignore critical constituencies. About all Sadat could do to help out the beleaguered Jimmy Carter was to continue to offer moral support and, of course, military facilities, should the US attempt to rescue the hostages in Iran. Two weeks after the Washington Summit the Americans tried just that and failed miserably.

On the morning of April 25 I listened incredulously as the BBC World Service announced the abortive rescue mission; a bizarre tale of tragedy in an Iranian desert; a humiliating disaster of sandstorms, failed helicopters, freak accidents and death. No one would be more disbelieving and disappointed than Anwar Sadat, since Egypt's Qena airbase was used as the staging area and command control centre for the clandestine operation. Not that Sadat ever directly confirmed the Egyptian role. Calling the debacle "hard luck", the Egyptian President told the media he hoped it would not discourage further rescue attempts; that Egypt was standing by to help should the Americans decide to give it another try.

The fate of the captives in Iran and the ignominious failure to free them by force would plague Carter and further jeopardize his re-election chances. US credibility as the Western world's strongest military power took a bruising: Egyptians wondered how a superpower ally which botched such a limited operation could be counted on in large-scale military situations. In addition, Secretary of State Cyrus Vance, who opposed the mission from the outset, resigned; a loss compounded by the loss of the eight American servicemen who died in the desert. I flew to Zurich to report on the return of the bodies and as I looked at the flag-draped coffins parked on the airport tarmac I felt certain there would be no more daring rescue attempts.

With the Camp David peace process on hold, an insecure President Sadat decided to take care of some unfinished business at home. Having already emasculated his parliamentary and political opposition, it was time for another referendum; popular approval for a sweeping dose of preventive medicine that was in fact a national anaesthetic.

Dispensed as constitutional amendments, the new reforms were denounced as "unconstitutional" and none was more ridiculed or unpopular than the Law of Shame or, as it was known by its diverse critics, the "law of sham" or "act of shame". As drafted by Sadat's obedient Parliament, the Law would "protect the political, economic, social and moral rights of the people" as well as traditional "values of the Egyptian family". Anyone fostering or advocating a doctrine that went against divine teachings or encouraged youth to stray from established popular, religious, moral or national values; anyone setting a bad example in a public place; anyone broadcasting or publishing false or misleading information or news which could inflame public opinion, generate envy, hatred or threaten national unity and social peace; anyone broadcasting or publishing scurrilous words or pictures which could offend public sensibilities or undermine the dignity of the state; anyone endangering public property, squandering public funds, abusing power, directly or indirectly influencing the prices of basic commodities and accepting bribes – all would be guilty of shameful crimes and handed over to Sadat's hand-picked Prosecutor-General who was answerable only to the People's Assembly and its Committee of Values. Big Brother had the power to ban the guilty from all public and economic life, or banish them to internal exile, or prohibit them from leaving the country for a period of five to ten years. The only provisions that might have made the law respectable – those dealing with bribes, the market-place and corruption – drew the biggest laughs.

There was more: something for everyone: for the fundamentalists Sadat offered up the *Sharia* – Islamic jurisprudence – and a hundred-and-thirty-two-member *Shoura*, or consultative council, to ensure that Islamic justice would not be ignored in formulating legislation. Sadat topped off this reformation of Egyptian society by declaring himself President for life.

The Law of Shame, which Sadat had the audacity to equate with the US Declaration of Human Rights, fooled no one, not even his "honest" opposition – the Socialist Labour Party which protested the pill of shame before being force-fed it. As for the prospect of an Islamic legal system, it inflamed Egypt's seven million Christian Copts. And it was difficult to find anyone, in Cairo at least, who was enthralled with the idea of Sadat for life.

Like it or not, 98.56 per cent of the electorate naturally loved it all on referendum day. Or as one Cairene explained the official ballot result: "Perhaps the silent majority votes at home . . . by computer."

The transparent aim of the Law of Shame was not to protect the Egyptians from themselves, but to protect Sadat from the Egyptians. Even so, it did not merit attention on evening news shows in America. The real story in any case was not the latest bogus referendum, or even Sadat's growing fears and problems that compelled him to draw the noose ever tighter. The real story – certainly for the West – should have been: why Sadat was in this highly explosive situation? What did it mean in terms of his future and that of Egypt and peace in the Middle East? The answers did not fit into a ninety-second or three-minute slot of a TV news show. It required considerably more time both off and on the air, and I had neither the time nor the mandate to produce a one-hour-long documentary look at a hero and his warts. Not, mind you, that the dark underside of a demi-god would have made for popular fare on commercial, prime-time television.

Quite frankly, by the spring of 1980 I was too weary and disenchanted even to propose an in-depth study. All I wanted was out. Out of Cairo. Out of the debilitating Sadat story. Hoping I would choose Cairo for life, ABC re-opened my contract, stuffed more money into it and asked me to stay on two more years. I got the salary to which I felt I was more than entitled; they got another year. Only the prospect of a transfer kept me from resigning.

Having made himself President for life, Sadat decided he might as well become Prime Minister as well, so he could "devote ninety-five per cent" of his time to what he admitted were Egypt's "appalling problems". To pacify the masses – for the summer – he handed out a special bonus to public-sector workers; a ten per cent pay hike to public and private sector employees, and he raised the minimum monthly wage from E£15 to E£20. He also cut import duties on such wares as video casette recorders and reduced the cost of more than a hundred commodities, few of which the masses were in the habit of consuming at any cost. He also abolished martial law, which had been in effect since the 1967 war. At the same time he warned the Christian and Moslem extremists to cool it and vowed to clamp down on all fanatic groups, especially on university campuses. All of this was taken care of in one four-hour speech. As for the remaining five per cent of his time, the Israelis would fill the gap nicely.

One week short of the Camp David target date for agreement on Palestinian autonomy, a bill was tabled in the Knesset to formalize Israeli control over all Jerusalem, including the occupied Arab sector. Sadat had already suspended the negotiations when they became deadlocked in early May, only to resume them again at President Carter's request two days later. Now, with the prospect of Israeli annexation of East Jerusalem, Sadat put the talks on hold again, charging the Israelis with undermining the atmosphere necessary for reaching a just solution. He also fired off urgent messages to President Carter and Prime Minister Begin.

When I asked him if he considered this latest Israeli gesture a "slap in the face", his latent fury and frustration found an appropriate outlet: "No, I don't consider it a slap in the face as you put it," he roared into the microphone. "If I did I would do something about it." Just as I was wondering if he knew what he was talking about, indeed if he understood the English idiom I had employed, Sadat suddenly turned repentant, calmed down, waved his hand as though to dismiss the whole business, sputtered a few "uhms" . . . and "ahs", broke into a smile and then admonished me gently for trying to "pull my leg". "Yes, I know you are just trying to pull my leg," he repeated with a chortle. "You mustn't do that," he pointed his finger at the naughty little girl. Realizing that the President was having a little trouble with idioms, I decided to set the record straight. "Excuse me, Mr President, but no, I was not trying to 'pull your leg', sir. Perhaps . . . I was 'twisting your arm'?" He puzzled over that one and chose to end this hit-and-run interview in the garden of his Suez Canal home. I should have levelled with him and admitted that in fact all I was trying to do was "nail him down"; "put him on the spot". Fortunately I realized in time that while the Egyptian leader's English had improved dramatically during his two and a half years in the international limelight, he had yet to master the language's idioms and slang expressions, and considered myself lucky to have ended up without a "slap in the face". Many fun-filled moments would subsequently be spent considering the catastrophic repercussions of a man who thinks you're pulling his leg when you're twisting his arm and twisting his arm when you're pulling his leg.

At the very least, we figured we had all been "taken for a ride".

By the end of May, 1980 the on-again, off-again Palestinian autonomy talks were on again. President Sadat refused to be seen as an obstacle to peace, preferring to leave the label to Prime Minister Begin. This did nothing to diminish Egypt's critical state – internally and externally – and I was able to convey at least that much – in capsule form – in the following report for the "Good Morning America" breakfast TV show:

> KAYS V/O PIX: Halfway through Egypt's battle for peace, Anwar Sadat has paused to shift gears.
>
> Convinced there can be no major breakthrough on Palestinian autonomy until after the US presidential elections, the Egyptian President is now concentrating on the homefront.
>
> By naming himself Prime Minister, he's now personally directing what he calls: Egypt's battle for prosperity.
>
> What it is, in fact, is Egypt's battle for stability.
>
> That battle against the poverty of the majority and the religious fanaticism of the minority. Both are potentially explosive.
>
> In an effort to keep the lid on, at least for a while, Sadat is lowering prices, raising wages, abolishing some taxes and outlawing religious fanaticism on the campus, in the mosque, and in the pulpit.

To appease Islamic fundamentalists, he's attacked the religious leaders of Egypt's seven million Coptic Christians, accusing them of exaggerating recent troubles. And he's made the *Sharia* – the Koranic Code of Law – the principal source of law in the country.

But President Sadat's battle for stability goes beyond Egypt's borders. . . . In addition to Israel's intransigence on the Palestinian issue Sadat feels threatened by American impotence, Soviet infiltration in the region and Egyptian isolation in the Arab world.

He's offered the US military facilities so it can intervene if trouble strikes in the Gulf or Middle East. And the US is speeding up delivery of billions in military hardware.

KAYS ON CAMERA CLOSE: But until the West, and the US, and Israel can give Sadat more of a hand with his external threats, the Egyptian leader is tackling his internal ones. He's playing for time. And trying to survive this American election year.

Again, a complex story reduced to its most simplistic form. One of the many details that eluded mention was the latest casualty of Egypt's sorry state of affairs: Mustapha Khalil, whom Sadat replaced as Prime Minister and whom Defence Minister General Kamel Hassan Ali replaced as Foreign Minister. It was not so much that Khalil's dual portfolio became too much for him, but rather, like his predecessors, he could no longer tolerate Israeli bad faith in the peace progress. And so a weary, disgusted Khalil asked to be freed of his onerous duties as foreign minister. Sadat took over the prime ministership, for cosmetic political reasons; to show that none other than the President was now taking charge personally. Unfortunately, with Sadat at the helm, the economy would drift even further into chaos and into the hands of a notorious bureaucracy.

The quiet, voluntary exit of Mustapha Khalil highlighted another dangerous reality: one by one, Egypt's best and brightest were falling by the wayside. By the summer of 1980 the only men at the top who commanded any respect from political observers and those on the fringe of power, could be counted on less than one hand: Vice-President Hosni Mubarak, the Minister of State for Information and Culture and Secretary of State for Presidential Affairs, Mansour Hassan; those two valiant Foreign Ministry die-hards Butros Ghali and Osama el-Baz; and the still untested new Foreign Minister, General Kamel Hassan Ali. Even this elite group of honest, dedicated professionals was at the mercy of one man and his autocratic rule which made a mockery of government and mincemeat of considered opinions and policy recommendations. Sadat had retreated into his own counsel and the comfort of a few sycophantic cronies and in-laws that included Egypt's best-known multi-millionaire, building contractor, Osman Ahmed Osman. There was no longer any room for the Mustapha Khalils of Egypt.

By the time President Sadat retreated to Alexandria for the summer he was a helpless, friendless giant, a victim of his supporters, enemies and himself. Alone and lonely, he could no longer hide his anger, bitterness and sense of betrayal in a world that was not unfolding as he thought it should. His only solace were his grandchildren and the American TV networks whose devotion and concern never flagged. One fine day – the day Jordan's King Hussein was visiting President Carter in Washington – we requested and were granted entry to Sadat's seaside compound, a signal that the *Raïs* wanted to get something off his chest. After an hour of shop-talk with the bougainvillaea, I spotted the President leave his villa holding hands with a grandson who had been born the day Sadat made his pitch for peace in the Knesset. He had reason to cherish this symbolic child, who on this particular day seemed to be serving as a prop for granddaddy to talk to the cameras without seeming to. Still playing the role of aggressive hit-man, I sauntered towards Sadat and little Sharif as though I were the next door neighbour on my way over for a cup of sugar and the latest gossip. Playing right into Sadat's hands, I mumbled something inane about a fine day for a stroll in the garden and asked if the child was indeed the same one born that fateful day in 1977. Sadat was jovial and receptive. As the cameras continued to roll on this colourful vignette I moved from family affairs to Middle East affairs, and the man Sadat seemed to like about as much as he liked Hafez Assad of Syria and Khomeini of Iran. Mention of the Carter-Hussein meeting sent Sadat into the rage he'd been waiting to vent for days. "Nothing will come out of the White House talks," he snapped sarcastically, "because Hussein is nothing more than an auctioneer and opportunist." Looking straight into the camera's eye, he directed a few words to the King (whom he assumed would be glued to his TV set that night) asking him to jog his memory back to the days of the Camp David summit when he telephoned Sadat to say he was leaning towards joining the peace process. "The reason he changed his mind," roared Sadat, was "money, millions of dollars in Arab aid; the Arabs bought him off." It made for a good, strong television piece that night and New York loved the Sadat-Sharif scene. Unfortunately the days of media diplomacy were over. Sadat knew well enough the real reason King Hussein did not join Camp David. He had no mandate to speak for the Palestinians and furthermore Camp David fell far short of Palestinian autonomy or self-determination, as the Israelis had been proving from the day the accords were signed. To resort to childish insults at this late stage was useless, even counter-productive; the act of a desperate man unable to admit he may have been wrong and unwilling to admit openly what he thought privately: that the Americans, yes, Jimmy Carter, had let him down, had not done enough to prevent him from suffering humiliation at home and in the Arab world. The Americans had allowed the Israelis to make a fool of him. That's what he thought and did not have the courage to say as bluntly as he said everything else. In any event he was in too deep to do anything but continue to ingratiate himself with the Americans, in whose basket he had dumped all his eggs, and to continue to support Carter, whose re-election chances he did not want to jeopardize.

Three days later, in another act of desperation, Sadat went over Prime Minister Begin's head and appealed directly to the Israeli people. In an Arabic interview with the Cairo-based Israeli TV correspondent, Ehud Yaari, he urged the Israelis to start facing the possibility and reality of a Palestinian state:

> The whole world is with the Palestinians in establishing a state . . . in their right to self-determination. And establishing colonies in other people's lands is something the world rejects.

Further pleading his case, Sadat told the Israeli people:

> You are facing one of two options. Either you stand before the whole world including the Palestinians and try to escape this tough decision or – and this is what I'm asking – you sit and think how are we to live together in this area; how you will live; and what are the guarantees Israel would seek when the Palestinians' state is established. But if you want to challenge the world's desires, I cannot say anything to you.

In appealing to the Israelis to choose between a Palestinian state or a solitary battle against the world, Sadat re-introduced a leader we had not seen in a long time. Since Camp David and the signing of the peace treaty he had deliberately avoided mention of a Palestinian state for fear of making Prime Minister Begin even more inflexible in the autonomy negotiations. But with the talks hopelessly deadlocked, if not dead, and the Palestinian cause picking up support, Sadat obviously felt he had nothing more to lose. When Yaari told me about the interview I requested and received a copy of his tape and wrote a report for the evening news on what I considered to be a significant about-face. I'm not sure the story ever made air. Even if it did, the viewer was not seeing Sadat's worsening predicament in quite so comprehensive a context; in fact no context whatever, only sporadic spot news reports which, seen in isolation, constituted just one more sixty-second look at Sadat.

During this period the problem of the Shah had gone into remission. In the three months since his cancer surgery, the former monarch had been convalescing with his family at Kubbah Palace, the same palace that served as our frenetic satellite centre in the early days of the peace initiative, though not the same annexe. He had regained some of his strength and spirit and was planning to join the Sadats in Alexandria when he suffered a setback; complications that included high fever, pneumonia, internal bleeding and loss of white cells. The chemotherapy he'd been receiving since the removal of an enlarged spleen was no longer controlling the lymphoma or cancer of the liver, and the Shah was being attended by Egyptian and French specialists. President Sadat, a regular visitor, continued to monitor his old friend's deteriorating condition. By mid-July the Shah was back in hospital for more surgery, this time to drain fluids from the lungs and lower chest cavity. His critical condition forced the three American TV network correspondents to abandon Sadat in Alexandria and return to Cairo, where each of us hooked up with a second camera crew flown in from other overseas bureaux. The Shah stake-out was in fact a round-the-clock death-watch. The crews adjusted admirably by staking out the best sun-bathing slots at the Meredien Hotel pool, while I kept myself busy sorting through all the conflicting medical reports, rumours and Egyptian newspaper stories circulating, all for reasons of their own. The absence of official medical bulletins from the Maadi Military Hospital resulted in four-way traffic of misinformation. Even as the Shah lay dying, the diagnoses varied from slight fever to coma: the up-beat Egyptian doctors contradicted the visiting French doctors; the Shah's official American spokesman contradicted the doctors; and the Egyptian press, with a mind and public of its own, tended to make all the experts look like mere caretakers. One daily claimed the Shah was not holding his own, indeed was technically dead and attached to a life-support system. When this was vigorously denied by ABC's own medical sources at the hospital, I decided the patient's condition was precarious to say the least and took to calling his chief spokesman Robert Armao, as late as midnight some evenings, to ascertain as best I could, if only from the tone of his voice, whether the Shah was alive or dead. Not only was he alive but apparently completing his memoirs with the help of Armao and his associate, Mark Morse. Two days after Morse told me about the memoirs – the morning of July 27 – I was still at my flat when Hassan telephoned from the bureau to report the Shah was dead.

According to our medical sources, senior members of the Egyptian team whose credibility had by now been well established, the Shah had died an hour earlier (10:00 a.m. Cairo time) after haemorrhaging from an abscessed pancreas, one of many complications resulting from the chemotherapy. Convinced that the information was reliable and accurate, Hassan and I agreed that it should be broadcast immediately and attributed to the sources by name. I spoke with one of our two radio stringers, Milly Ardin, who was standing by in the bureau, and urged her to report the news promptly to ABC Radio and to notify the TV foreign desk. This she did within seconds thanks to our direct-dial long-distance line. As the news was being broadcast in America I rushed across the street to the Meredien Hotel where the French (and by now American) doctors were staying, as were Morse and Armao, although the latter happened to be out of the country at the time. About an hour later, the camera crew and I were able to intercept a couple of the doctors returning from the hospital. By now, a handful of competitors had joined us and with official confirmation in hand, we rushed back to the bureau anticipating a satellite transmission for the morning show. Unfortunately, there was no satellite and no morning show. It was the Sabbath in America, something we tended to forget even after all those Cairo Sundays. ABC Cairo, though, claimed another scoop. We were the first news organization to report the death of the Shah, by a comfortable margin. Several hours later I transmitted the following report via satellite for the Sunday evening news:

> KAYS V/O PIX AND FILE FOOTAGE: Death came one month to the day after the deposed Iranian monarch re-entered Cairo's suburban Maadi Military Hospital. Cause of death: "shock to the circulatory system caused by a general deterioration in his health". At his bedside: the former empress, his four children, other family members and French and Egyptian doctors. There are no official medical details but the former Shah's seven-year battle with cancer ended when a sudden haemorrhage put him into shock.
>
> According to a senior member of the medical team the ex-monarch's last words before slipping into a coma were, quote: "please agree on something to save me". One of his American spokesmen, Mark Morse, who helped the Shah complete his memoirs only three days ago, thinks the deposed ruler sensed his death was at hand. Morse was with him in the final hours:
>
> SOT MORSE: He was lucid almost to the end.
>
> V/O SADAT PIX: President Sadat who flew back to Cairo from his summer home in Alexandria consoled the family, saying they are "my family now". A grief-stricken Sadat had no apologies, only praise for the man he called Egypt's friend:
>
> SOT SADAT: We received him and we will farewell him.
>
> KAYS ON CAMERA: The farewell is scheduled for Tuesday. And as requested he will be buried at Cairo's El-Rafei Mosque where his father was once buried. But in spite of his request for a simple funeral, President Sadat says there will be a state funeral for the deposed Iranian monarch with quote: "full honours and due respect".

This was followed by truncated versions for the late Sunday news and the on-going "America Held Hostage" programme which followed the news. It had been a long, but professionally satisfying day. The Shah's death was precisely the sort of story in which the medium of television excels; a story of immediacy, drama and history. And what made this breaking story so personally rewarding was that the ABC Cairo team had gained and maintained a strong competitive edge from beginning to end. Speed plus accuracy equals good TV news and since we were fast, first and right, we had fulfilled our mandate one more time.

By the morning of July 28, the American networks' flying circuses joined us in reporting the end of this human drama; the burial of a disgraced, exiled monarch whose rise and fall remained a fresh source of grief and anguish for tens of millions – Iranians and Americans alike. The controversy, hatred and bitterness that his decades-long rule generated would not end with death. And indeed it was hard to believe that the ex-Shah himself did not die a bitter man, one who felt betrayed by America, his very life-line. Robert Armao who once worked for Nelson Rockefeller before serving the Iranian in his last days, claimed in an interview that Monday morning that the Shah harboured no bitterness in his soul, while in the next breath admitting to me that he died a lonely, shattered man, who might have lived longer had he not been forced to leave the United States. Only one thing was certain in my mind. Bitterness or no bitterness, the death of the Shah of Shahs was a blessing for Egypt and President Sadat. His presence in the country was a political burden Sadat insisted on carrying in spite of his own shaky existence and against the advice of his ministers and closest aides, not to mention a concerned US administration which did not relish the thought of an Egypt in turmoil. For many Egyptians, then, it was an appropriate, just and timely end.

But by Tuesday July 29, the pathos of human tragedy overshadowed power and politics. For a few hours what could only be characterized as a "pathetic" drama was played out in the hot, humid streets of a dusty and decrepit old quarter of Cairo. A perspiring, grim-faced President Sadat, resplendent in field-marshal's uniform, walked briskly, proudly and defiantly at the head of the funeral procession as it wound its way from Abdin Palace to El-Rafai Mosque, half a mile away in Old Cairo. In front of him moved the Shah's horse-drawn coffin draped in the red, white and green imperial flag of Iran; alongside him, the Shah's black-veiled widow and family flanked by a former President – Richard Nixon – and a former monarch – King Constantine of Greece. Sadat was the only head of state present. The only countries represented were France, Britain, China, Israel, Morocco and the United States, the latter in the person of Alfred Atherton, who had by then become US Ambassador. As the mourners approached the mosque against a backdrop of wall-to-wall security, the absence of ordinary Egyptians along the route was a reminder that while this farewell was being conducted with full military honours and a twenty-one-gun salute, it was not in any sense a "popular" ceremony. The threat of assassination attempts directed either at members of the Pahlavi family or Sadat made that possibility even more remote. In the mosque itself, the Islamic service conducted by a Shi'ite priest began with prayers from the Koran and ended traditionally with the body of the deceased, wrapped in a simple white shroud, being lowered and laid to rest on its side in a tomb alongside those of Egypt's two former kings – Fuad and Farouk – and a few steps from the spot where the Shah's father once was buried. It was all over in two hours. Mohammed Reza Pahlavi, the self-proclaimed King of Kings, was dead. And Anwar Sadat, the only head of state who dared bury him, was still alive and well. There was no doubting the Egyptian President's stubborn courage. Not once but twice within fourteen months he gave the fallen ruler refuge, at great personal and political risk.

After the Shah had wandered sick and rejected from one country to another; after Morocco, the Bahamas, Mexico, New York, Texas, Panama ... only Sadat would publicly offer him the medical facilities, the home, the permanent exile. When the Shah was not being operated on or treated for cancer, he and his family lived a secure, secluded life in Cairo's Kubbah Palace, the same palace the deposed monarch honeymooned in with his first wife, Fawzia, sister of Farouk. Sadat told the Pahlavis it was theirs for as long as they wanted to stay. The former empress Farah Diba now chose to make Egypt her home in exile.

Richard Nixon, whose excesses drove him from power, is a man intimate with disgrace. After a private meeting with Sadat in Alexandria, Nixon turned to a tense, nervous Sadat and said: "I came to Egypt to see an old friend who's dead. And to see an old friend who's alive." After both men lauded each other's courage, one was left with the impression that Sadat felt some bitterness towards the Americans for abandoning a friend, and not a little uneasy about the possibility that he could be as politically expendable one day.

At the time I chose to report rather effusively and at length in a radio "Perspective" about Anwar Sadat's courage, highlighting his gesture towards the Shah which I attributed solely to Sadat's finer moral instincts. This commentary elicited a response of profound gratitude and praise from a listener in the American South, a black female lawyer, that was only slightly less excessive than my own interpretative analysis. Of all the radio "Perspectives", "Commentaries" and news reports, and of all the TV reports I transmitted out of Egypt this was the only one I would want to disavow; a shameful eleven-minute-long tribute to a mythical, one-dimensional god. The more I thought about it the more I determined to stay away from funerals; clearly my emotions had run away with me.

It would be nice to believe that Sadat's courage towards the discredited Shah was motivated solely by "friendship, loyalty, compassion, Islamic mercy and gratitude" (for past favours) as he himself claimed. But the man was too shrewd, too political and far too Machiavellian to have acted purely out of humanitarian impulses. Surely as much as anything he wanted to help out the Americans, who were in a tight bind; by taking the troublesome Shah off their hands and out of Panama he hoped further to ingratiate himself with Washington. That Washington might have preferred less Sadat-style magnanimity; that it did not want to resolve one problem at the expense of another; that President Carter himself was strongly opposed to the Shah's decision to go to Egypt did not in the end deter Sadat. He knew this brave gesture would be popular with the masses. He was right: grassroots America loved him now more than ever.

With President Sadat's attention focused on domestic matters and President Carter absorbed with his nomination battle at the Democratic Convention, Prime Minister Begin decided to fill the peace-gap by officially annexing East (Arab) Jerusalem. Four days after Sadat buried the Shah – and on the very eve of a resumption of ministerial-level talks on Palestinian autonomy – Israel pushed through the law formally making Jerusalem the eternal, undivided capital of Israel. When the bill was tabled two months earlier, the US consoled Sadat with assurances that it was a mere formality that would be shelved indefinitely rather than acted on hastily as feared, which accounted for Sadat's mild rebuke at the time.

But with the dirty deed done and his American partner politically crippled, an embarrassed and furious Sadat retaliated by telling the Israelis to stay home, not to bother showing up in Alexandria for the scheduled peace talks. Israel's latest provocation was justifiable reason for Sadat to freeze, suspend or break-off these so-called negotiations that made a mockery of peace and the "future of the occupied West Bank" that includes Arab East Jerusalem. He could also have retaliated by recalling his ambassador from Tel Aviv or by breaking off normal relations with Israel. Not surprisingly, he chose to dismiss these bona fide diplomatic options for three basic reasons: he did not want to hurt President Carter's nomination and re-election campaign; he did not want to jeopardize the return of the remaining one-third of the Sinai still in Israeli hands; and he did not want to tarnish his image as a peacemaker, preferring as always to leave the role of spoiler to Menachem Begin.

What he did instead was "postpone" the autonomy talks indefinitely and mail Begin a ten-page letter asking him for assurances, public or private, that the law did not pre-empt discussion of the question of Jerusalem and its one hundred and twenty thousand Arab inhabitants. If it did, then the negotiations would be rendered meaningless, even by Sadat's standards. The onus was on the Israelis: they could kill off the dying Camp David peace process. Or save it. No assurances were forthcoming.

One month later – to the day – Sadat agreed to resume the talks. Indeed, one hour after telling a group of Egyptian professors that he would not resume the negotiations on Palestinian autonomy so long as Israel did not change its Jerusalem and West Bank policies, he did just that during a meeting with roving Middle East ambassador Sol Linowitz, the ineffectual successor to Robert Strauss. In an attempt to rationalize this latest flip-flop, embarrassed Egyptian officials explained it was not a resumption of actual negotiations but rather "preparatory talks" for a three-way Carter-Sadat-Begin summit to be convened as early as November, after Carter's re-election, or so a confident Sadat was anticipating. That night I quoted a high-level Egyptian source admitting the whole exercise was nothing more than . . . "Anwar Sadat performing a political PR service for Jimmy Carter." Yet one more time.

In spite of Linowitz's angry denunciations to the contrary, it would all be confirmed that same night by none other than the President of the United States himself. A jubilant Carter – with fresh cable in hand – announced the good news at a campaign function: his Camp David peace process was still alive. There was nothing, it seemed that Sadat would not do for the American President. In the meantime the Egyptian press was ordered to stop comparing Menachem Begin to Hitler.

In September 1980, however, average Egyptians were more concerned about their future than the future of Jerusalem, the Palestinians or Menachem Begin. In a country that does not produce enough food to feed itself; where the rich ten per cent of the population consumes ninety per cent of production and the poor, ninety per cent of the population consumes ten per cent, the profiteering problem that settled nicely in the middle over the years had become critical. Black-market middlemen in effect were stealing from the poor to sell to the rich, further inflating the soaring cost of food, especially meat and especially beef which at three dollars a pound had more than doubled in one year. In an effort to drive down the prices and control the rampant corruption in the market-place, President Sadat ordered a ban on the slaughter of all cattle and the sale of all meat during the month of September. This meatless month had the effect of flooding butcher shops with more turkeys, rabbits, pigeons and eggs than the poor consumer could afford to buy: with no meat in the meat shops the price of several other staples rose sky-high. The greedy middleman now concentrated on siphoning off these and other subsidized items from government-run stores for sale in private sector shops. Furthermore, the meat ban itself was not without its exemptions: tourists, foreign residents and rich Egyptians still enjoyed their meal of meat whether at de luxe hotels, first-class restaurants or at home, proving that where there's money, there's a way. The black market simply moved underground or door-to-door. In short, meat was available if you knew the right butcher. A few of the lawless meat merchants were caught, fined or jailed but the main culprits – those at the top – were untouchable and the public knew it. Egyptian television dared to venture out to interview men and women in the street; the result was a mixed-bag reaction of outrage, ridicule, scepticism, cynicism and general resignation. The poor went on eating what they always ate: beans, lentils, cheese, vegetables, bread and fish, although with no meat and precious little chicken available, the price of fish rose by thirty per cent.

The majority of Egyptians saw President Sadat's crackdown as a political rather than economic band-aid; a symbolic fight against fifty per cent inflation, and corruption, a bone without much meat; and that's how I reported it for radio and television.

They survived September and the following months . . . without meat on their daily menu. "Prime Minister" Sadat was left with a serious credibility problem.

The outbreak of the Iran-Iraq war in late September could not have come at a better time for President Sadat. Unable to do anything about the peace problem until after the US elections and unwilling and/or unable to come to grips with the roots of his domestic problems, he now had the

opportunity to expound on his favourite topic: the geo-politics of a turbu-
lent region and the policeman's role, vacated by Iran, he so desperately
sought to play in the strategic game of East versus West. Although Sadat
chastised the aggressor, Iraq and its strongman Saddam Hussein, he saw
the war as one way for the United States to get rid of the Ayatollah
Khomeini. In an interview with American television correspondents in his
native village of Mit Abul Kum, Sadat warned the US administration:
"By God . . . be vigilant this time. Don't offer everything to the Soviet
Union on a golden platter." It was a variation of his oft-repeated theme
of an America held captive by its "Vietnam complex"; a complex he found
dangerously isolationist and unbecoming a superpower. Washington, he
did not hesitate to imply, was weak and wishy-washy. To help remedy
this intolerable situation, Sadat now faced our cameras to pronounce
Egypt responsible for and ready to "preserve the security and balance of
power in the region". Egypt and the US, he said, were consulting each
other on this very matter and while refusing to divulge details he admitted
contingency plans were being studied in the event that the Iranian-Iraqi
conflict threatened the oil-rich Gulf. Having conveyed that comforting
message to an oil-conscious TV audience I was dispatched to the Strait
of Hormuz to ensure that should our oil tankers go up in flames on the
low seas, America would hear about it and see it in living colour, just in
time for dinner.

By the time Hassan, the camera crew and I arrived at Oman's stunning
Muscat Intercontinental Hotel, our NBC neighbours, having beat us to
the story by a week, had wrapped up whatever there was of it and were
now trying to beat the 45°C heat by staking-out the swimming pool's tepid
waters. While they cooled off, we entered the sauna sphere of this tiny
Gulf country of one and a half million inhabitants, looking for trouble in
land and off coast. All we found was peace, beauty and British efficiency
throughout the sultanate. Until 1970 Oman had been almost totally cut
off from the outside world and any form of development. But ten years
later, after Sultan Qaboos's paranoid and reclusive father Sultan Said was
deposed by the British, a modern oasis was carved out of the desert with
oil revenues and British expertise, civilian and military. Indeed, regular
British officers command each of the three arms of the forces and British
expatriates are visible everywhere in government, including the Ministry
of Information, where I spent a considerable amount of time begging for
a helicopter and/or ship to find the tip of the war I'd come to report. The
Omanis and their British advisors finally obliged and for the next week
we flew over and sailed through the blue waters of the Strait of Hormuz,
two hundred and fifty miles north of Muscat in search of "bang-bang".
All we found was a strategic passageway with little traffic and less trouble;
hardly surprising given the fact that insurance rates for the war zone had
soared by three hundred per cent and thirty-five oil tankers were anchored
off the Omani capital. In spite of that, oil supplies were apparently moving
in and out of the Persian Gulf at only a slightly reduced rate: normally

eighteen million barrels of crude passed through the Strait daily – about forty per cent of the western world's oil imports. Threats that Iran or Iraq might block the Strait – cutting off supplies – seemed to diminish with each passing day, along with the prospect of transmitting any more stories beyond the half-dozen already satellited. With all quiet on the Hormuz and Omani fronts, NBC left town, CBS· arrived and we, along with the BBC World Service man and a handful of other foreign journalists, stayed on to keep an eye on a still-volatile situation. Towards the end of week two – spent at poolside – our bodies, already hash-browned by the Egyptian summer, resembled skewered shish-kebab that had been left on charcoal overnight.

A frantic phone call from the Cairo bureau came just in time. It was my mother, whom I'd invited to Egypt for a pleasant visit and then deserted, fully confident that her fluent Arabic would keep her company until my return. She did not sound as though she was having much fun.

Normally coherent in either Arabic or English, the lady at the other end of the telephone seemed to be making no sense whatsoever; something about a "Nadia". Since I didn't think she was calling to chat about my devoted maid's cleaning talents, I asked her to calm down and start from the beginning. The connection was already playing havoc with her message:

"Doreen, dear," she began again in Arabic, "Nadia is not what you think she is."

"What do you mean?"

"I mean, she . . . is . . . no simple servant."

"I know, that's why she's being paid E£75 a month which happens to be more than double what any other maid in Cairo earns."

"Doreen, where have you been these past three years? My God, have you spent any time at all in your own apartment?"

"I think you know the answer to that. That's why Nadia's been such a godsend." By now Mum was in tears and trying valiantly to remain coherent: "Doreen, I don't think you quite believe what I'm trying to tell you. I'm not hysterical and Nadia is not a maid," she sobbed. "She's been using your flat for other things. . . ."

"What do you mean, using my flat for other. . . . Oh my God! No. . . ! Hold on, don't go away . . . I want to get Hassan on this line." I ran next door: "Hassan, come quickly to the phone, my mother's living with a whore. Dear, sweet, honest, faithful Nadia's a prostitute, nothing but a goddam *charmoutta* operating out of my flat!" I screamed.

A speechless, red-faced Hassan ran back with me, grabbed the receiver and after five minutes of a first-hand account, controlled his rage long enough to assure my mother: "Don't worry Mrs Kays, I guarantee you'll never see Nadia again. Please put Honey (Hanzada Fikry) on the phone!" "Honey, listen closely. I want Nadia in that bureau promptly at eleven o'clock tomorrow morning. Tell her I want to talk to her. Don't tell her why. I'll be calling back at that hour." I was too angry, too humiliated at my own naïvety to do anything more than offer my mother a few comforting words and the hope that since I was idling my time away at the pool, I might be back in Cairo shortly.

Having hung up the receiver, Hassan and I just stared at each other incredulously. Neither of us wanted to believe this sordid little drama. "I'm ashamed to say I should have known Nadia was no better than the company she kept," fumed Hassan, "that Nagwa, the Nagwa who cleaned and cooked at the bureau until one day she was gone suddenly? Well I fired her and the reason I never told you why I fired her was because it was too ugly and shameful and I figured you had enough problems without this one. She was up to no good, that woman."

"What do you mean, Hassan?"

"I mean she tried soliciting in the bureau."

"Pity she didn't solicit me," I fumed. "What else has been going on in the neighbourhood sex market? On second thoughts, spare me the graphic details. I've got more important things to attend to – like get myself out of this hotel stake-out. I'm calling New York. If I'm no longer needed here, I'm heading back to investigate the thriving prostitution racket in Apartment 23 at the Belmont!"

Promptly at 11:00 a.m. the following morning Hassan was on the line to the Cairo bureau and a surprisingly calm, if frightened, Nadia, who knew her game was up but didn't know why or how and dared not ask. The revulsion and embarrassment the devout Hassan felt over the whole messy business were no match for his rage, which he expressed with all the military precision and authority of an ex-army officer: "You will return to the flat," he commanded in Arabic, "under the escort of Dessouki and Hossaim, where you will pick up any personal belongings as quickly as possible, following which you will be swiftly escorted home where you are to remain until I return to Cairo."

"You are not to go anywhere near Miss Doreen's flat, or the Belmont Building, or the district of Garden City, or the ABC bureau. Is that clear?"

Sweet Nadia asked but one feeble question. "When are you returning to Cairo, Mr Hassan?"

"In a day or a year. It's none of your business."

Clearly he was not about to waste his time either enlightening or interrogating a low-class whore. That could wait.

Two days later New York agreed that there seemed to be considerably more action in Garden City than in the Strait of Hormuz and we all flew home.

At Cairo airport I was picked up by the still faithful Dessouki, who drove me straight to my red-light district where for the next seven hours I sat at the feet of two veteran Middle East hands – my mother, and a neighbour's elderly maid – listening to tales of Nadia's thousand and one days/nights overlooking the Nile. It all began with my sharp-witted mother suspecting that the virtuous maid did more than dust and iron away her life. For one thing there were the constant knocks on the door that began in the morning and continued through late-afternoon or quitting time whichever came first; knocks never followed by guests ushered into the flat. In between the phantom traffic, domestic chores and gossip on the back stoop were the badgering questions: when was Madame planning to leave the flat today and why did she not wait for chauffeur Dessouki twelve floors down at street level, on such a lovely day?

At best a Westerner would have thought nothing further of these helpful hints and at worse, would have obliged the servant and taken the elevator pronto. Not my Beirut-bred mother. She sensed the maid's nose was out of joint and worse that she was overstepping her boundary: the servant was acting like a mistress whose turf was being threatened by an interloper. Nadia did not mind Miss Doreen's guests staying a couple of weeks but those who had the audacity to stay two months and remain indoors at all hours cramped her lifestyle. Nor she did appreciate having her weekly grocery list and itemized monthly household expenses scrutinized by someone who could read and write Arabic, especially as it seemed she herself was illiterate and not the actual author of the accounts.

In addition to the plumbers, carpenters, electricians, traffic cops and US embassy chauffeurs serviced by Nadia in *my* boudoir, there were Nagwa's Saudi clients in the flat below to be kept content and clean, which entailed a little extra laundry and pressing accomplished with the help of my suds, my iron and my ironing board. One can only assume the Saudis struck the best bargain. When not scrubbing, cleaning and executing quick fixes six days and nights at the Belmont, Nadia filled some of her spare hours in an alternate brothel across the river in swank Zamalak, where the clientèle tended to take more time plugging leaky taps, if only because they were trained as professors not plumbers. It was here that the illiterate English-speaking Nadia, posing as ABC News' bureau chief, made the acquaintance of a university lecturer. Impressed with her professional calling card – the same one I had given her one unsuspecting day – he invited her one evening to assist him with some papers and in the process of trying to kill two birds with one stone discovered his lady of the night could not cope with Arabic, let alone English – which happened to be the language he was most interested in that night. An enraged professor threw her out.

Bad enough that I was missing out on all the fun; that half of Cairo probably thought ABC News as the American Body Corporation; that an ABC bachelor producer's flat which Nadia also found time to sweep and swab was spared the brothel traffic; that she subcontracted some of her domestic chores because she had neither the ability nor the time for them; that her little "sister" was her daughter; that her one and only "first marriage" to a "homosexual" was in fact her fourth; that her one and only "first" abortion – a result of the week-long fourth marriage – almost killed her; that I took pity on the "victim" and paid for her "one and only" abortion; that Dessouki, Hassan and I managed to save her life by placing her in the care of a reputable doctor and hospital; that she had long ceased being a "victim" of life – a poor, fifteen-year-old country girl come to the big bad city to help support family – and was now nothing more than a thirty-ish diseased heap of deception and decay. Bad enough, then, that Nadia was a pathological liar and a fraud. But that she was also a heartless one devoid of human emotion and common decency was something that not even I – the bleeding-hearted liberal – could forgive or forget. That she and her friends performed a funeral song and dance over the tragic road death of Aida Hakki, our beloved and beautiful thirty-three-year-old ABC Egyptian staffer with whom Nadia's part-time ABC producer-employer was romantically involved – was a perversity and obscenity of which I would never be able to cleanse my Cairo home. This was no run-of-the-mill rip-off artist. And as her gullible, former absentee employer/landlord, I set aside my wounded pride and rage and went out in search of officially-sanctioned retribution. Having endured seven hours of painful testimony I approached Hassan the next morning and demanded that the police be contacted and the case wrapped up within forty-eight hours. The sooner the Nadia episode was disposed of, the better for all of us.

Since I did not trust myself in her presence, Hassan was left to administer a humiliating dressing-down in the full privacy of the bureau, while I lounged at home in a bed that now had me crawling with imaginary and real bugs. Fortunately I had inherited the bed – along with the maid, from my predecessor, so one was as disposable as the other. Twenty-four hours after Hassan contacted the Garden City vice-squad with a threat that the ABC bureau chief was on the verge of contacting high officials, the Belmont was abuzz with news of the morning's police dragnet. Nadia was finally located in her own flat on the wrong side of Giza.

The *bo'abs* were herded into the police station, roughed up and threatened with their licences before being booted back to the Belmont, where they quivered for a full day. Nadia and Nagwa were treated with all the respect and rich language reserved for the Arab world's *charmouttas* before being shoved into a jail cell. While they were left to languish in the company of their poorly paid jail-keepers that night, I was visited by Hassan and two handsome plain clothes detectives who looked as though they enjoyed their work. What, they kindly asked, did I now demand of them . . . now that the culprits had been nabbed, were being punished and forbidden to trespass the lucrative radius of the Meredien Hotel-Belmont building.

Since Nadia had a penchant for policemen, I began by reminding them that some of her customers came from their ranks and that I was not predisposed towards trusting officers of the law, whatever their rank. So as not to insult them further I announced I was not a crusader and had neither the desire nor the interest in cleaning up Cairo's traffic in prostitution; that I happened to believe the profession and those who indulge it serve as honourable, useful and powerful tools in the cause of national unity and social peace; that I have nothing against prostitutes –

although I hastened to add I wouldn't want my daughter marrying one – and that I prefer to live and play in the privacy of my own flat. To ensure that my flat never again be turned into a bordello or a target for a pimp's revenge, I suggested they put my flat or the Belmont premises under surveillance – however cursory – until I departed Cairo in three months. I didn't suggest that they were wasting their time and mine and that they had no intention of doing any more than they'd already done. The following morning – having paid off their jailkeepers – or vice versa – to prevent further harrassment and physical abuse – Nadia and Nagwa were freed from their prison; their names having entered a black list to be filed away until the next time. Rather than risk the talents of a new maid, I would seek refuge in Algeria.

9. Death and burial

NOT EVEN ANWAR SADAT could save Jimmy Carter. On November 4, 1980 his friend and partner in peace lost the presidency to a mediocre Hollywood has-been whose view of the world tended to be as black and white as his 1940s B films. If the complexities of the Middle East promised to elude Ronald Reagan's intellectual and ideological grasp, Sadat could at least take comfort in the fact that the new man in the White House was a muscle-flexing cold warrior whose anti-communist, anti-Soviet obsessions outmatched even Sadat's. Whereas Carter had been committed to peace, Reagan was committed to containing the Soviet threat, and for a man who thought America had gone soft on the commies, it was a fair exchange. For Sadat, the important thing was to maintain his newly-forged links with the Americans, to make Egypt an indispensable ally in the battle of East versus West. Even if Carter had been re-elected, Sadat now knew that the chances of peace stretching beyond the Egyptian-Israeli border were remote, and that it was best to focus his interests and energies on making Egypt as competitive and dependable a military partner as Israel. Indeed, by making peace with America's most powerful ally in the region, Sadat was well on the way to strategic respectability. Washington was delivering or promising billions in military hardware. American AWACS (Airborne Warning and Control System) reconnaissance planes were flying missions out of Qena Air Base. Egyptian military facilities, including the Ras Banas Base on the Red Sea, were at the disposal of the Pentagon. The American and Egyptian air forces were staging joint manoeuvres with a US squadron of F-4 Phantoms. More sophisticated fighters like the prized F-16 would eventually join the Egyptian arsenal replacing the ageing Soviet MiGs for which Sadat by now had nothing but disdain. And by mid-November 1980, combat-equipped American troops and airmen from the newly-formed Rapid Deployment Force were staging mock battles with their Egyptian counterparts in Egypt's Western Desert. The operation called "Bright Star" involved airlifting fourteen hundred troops, and tons of equipment and supplies from the United States, a task that took four and a half days; hardly a rapid deployment of military might. Nonetheless, at a cost of twenty-five million dollars, it was a valuable lesson in logistics for the fledgling RDF that might be called upon one day to airlift thousands of troops to defend the Persian Gulf–Middle Eastern region from a Soviet threat or regional crisis.

Set up by President Carter in the wake of the Iranian revolution, the seizure of American hostages in Tehran and the Soviet invasion of Afghanistan, the RDF and its first exercise was an ideal showcase of Sadat's new status: while the Americans would dazzle the Egyptians with their superior weaponry and performance, the Egyptians would show the Americans how to cope with desert terrain and weather conditions similar to the Arabian peninsula – for example, how to land their helicopters blind in the flat, powder-fine landscape, a challenge for pilots used to landmarks in the deserts of the southwestern United States. In the process, the Americans learned something else: that Sadat's unbridled embrace of the US military stopped at the barracks door; that the Egyptian generals and commanders, while warm and hospitable, were sensitive to foreigners and still bitter over their Soviet experience. Now determined to be masters of their own bases they did not want these joint manoeuvres accompanied by all the fanfare and publicity preferred by their American counterparts, if not by Sadat as well. The result was friendly co-operation and compromise – at least from my vantage point on the mock battlefield. Coverage of the troops' arrival in Cairo was restricted to the RDF's own military camera crew, whose tapes were dubbed and distributed to the American TV networks under the watchful eye of an Egyptian military censor. As for the exercises themselves, local and foreign media coverage was limited to two days out of fourteen – the two most dramatically visual – which to my mind was more than sufficient. Overall, the visiting troops, sensitive to Egypt's political complexities, were model guests who kept as low a profile as possible.

By the end of 1980 it was hard to camouflage the American presence in Egypt. Cairo was now home to the largest US diplomatic mission in the world: in seven years the embassy staff had grown from six to more than eight hundred – more than half of whom were administering the billions in economic and military aid. The compound, situated a few blocks from the British embassy in Garden City, could no longer contain all the people and programmes, and plans were underway for a new high-rise embassy to accommodate the American stake. The prospect of a higher profile was enough to make some observers and diplomats a trifle nervous, including the distinguished career diplomat Herman Eilts, who had served as US ambassador to Egypt from 1974 through mid-1979 when he left Egypt and the foreign service to join academia in Boston. In a farewell newspaper interview, Eilts – while admitting that Egypt was not Iran – cautioned against ignoring history and the potential dangers of so great an American presence. He warned, "It could get out of hand. It is a mistake." As the year ended, the problems of Sadat's Egypt would again be sidelined by the continuing ramifications of America's painful mistakes in Iran; its past commitment to another man and his regime. Revolutionary Iran was now signalling that those fifty-two American hostages held captive for more than a year might have served their purpose, and serious negotiations, with the Algerian government as mediator, were under way to free them, if possible by January 20, inauguration day in Washington – the end of the Carter administration and the beginning of the Reagan presidency. The ruling ayatollahs did not want to have to start from scratch with a new team that promised to be less conciliatory under the hard-line, conservative Republicanism of Ronald Reagan.

With Sadat and Egypt in a holding pattern somewhere over purgatory, I was delighted to be shipped off to Algiers where I would spend Christmas, New Year and the next month reporting the tedious daily negotiations that constituted President Carter's last-ditch efforts to bring the Americans home.

The monumental legal, financial and political problems that had to be resolved before the hostages' release – including the transfer of eight billion dollars in frozen Iranian assets from US banks to an Algerian escrow account at the Bank of England – were stretched out by the Iranians to ensure a tension-filled drama timed to climax on Inauguration Day. In an apparent effort to humiliate President Carter and deny him the least victory in his final hours in the White House, the Iranians – with their eyes on the clock – stalled the departure of the plane carrying the hostages out of Tehran until they were certain Jimmy Carter had handed over the reins of power to Ronald Reagan. Half an hour after the official transition, at roughly 12:30 p.m. Washington time on January 20, 1981, the fifty-two Americans were finally on their way home and the world media standing by in Algiers would be the first to see them during a brief courtesy stopover. American television would remain on the air with live reportage throughout the day and night, which meant President Reagan was upstaged yet one more time in his long career.

Ironically, my first and only glimpse of the hostages as they embraced freedom that winter night at Algiers airport was provided by a television monitor at the Algerian Radio and TV centre, several miles away. It did not diminish the impact of this made-for-TV human drama; the only drama I can recall that played fourteen and a half months with all the leading players hidden off-stage.

The most challenging assignment in almost two decades awaited me on arrival back in Cairo: permanent reassignment. After more than a year of pleading with a reluctant ABC, I was being set free from the debilitating "Sadat story" and transferred to Paris as requested.

Now as I faced the actual task of packing my bags for good I found myself emotionally immobilized. I could not leave Egypt any more than I could remain. For three years I had given it my all – and then some – and in the process had burned myself out. It was not so much that I wanted to get out of Cairo – I needed to get out of the Cairo assignment; needed to put an end to an all-consuming commitment that was impossible to sustain physically or emotionally and one I could no longer justify professionally or personally. It was not just showbiz TV-style journalism with its hit and run sixty-second view of the world, its inherent superficiality and distortion, its frenzied competitiveness, and insatiable appetite for cardboard heroes; not the three-year stake-out of the chameleon Sadat; not Egypt's political, social and economic climate that under the rule of its despotic hero-villain had become depressed and oppressive; not the daily frustrations of Cairo's poverty, dirt, noise and ten million plus inhabitants; not the crippling work load; not the short-comings of the two successive "permanent" producers; not the lack of a personal, private life; not the absence of anything remotely resembling a home-life as so graphically illustrated by the Nadia incident; not even the absence of a lifestyle with proper eating habits and some form of relaxation from the pressures and tensions of a seven-day work week – it was not any one of these realities. It was all of them combined – a conspiracy of forces – that got between me and the story.

Unlike the frog by the River Jordan, I had no compelling reason to surrender to scorpions, no desire to self-destruct nor any sadistic urge to watch Anwar Sadat commit suicide, especially as I had contributed in no small way to his pharaoh's complex.

It was time to leave, time to save myself, at least. I set a deadline – three weeks – in which to pack and crate three years of a love-hate relationship that was as privileged and enriching as it was tortuous and destructive.

I would miss Egypt and the Egyptians – some of whom I had come to know and love, especially the bureau staff: Hassan and his extended family, Honey (Hanzada), Dessouki – my surrogate father-cum-chauffeur, Gumbo, and our many hours of political discourse and passionate polemics. Without their professional support and personal understanding and friendship I would not have remained even three months. I would miss my small circle of Egyptian, American, Canadian and foreign friends as well as a precious handful of Egyptian contacts, sources and officials. I would miss Silver Rich and some of the other colourful characters who in the good old days had blessed me with their laughter. I would miss the "El-Shahats" who had touched my life more deeply than all the "El-Sadats" of the world. And I would miss the beautiful and tragic Aïda – the bureau's girl friday – the one whose car slammed into a lorry parked illegally on the shoulder of the Cairo-Alexandria Delta road, one night just before dawn; and the equally beautiful and tragic five-year-old Anwar – son of the bureau's *bo'ab* – the one who drowned in the Nile one day while playing.

I knew I would see most of them again; I knew I would return to work and/or visit and until then I would remember all the happy moments of a love-affair that could not last; the psyche would successfully block out the rest.

On D-Day – February 12 – Dessouki, another burnt-out case, picked me up and drove me to the airport. Along the way we talked of his plans to retire from network television; it was time to go home again, to the Delta and a wife and children to whom he had become a stranger these past years. He had saved almost enough money to buy himself a little Peugeot taxi; knowing he had hung in this long for my sake and as a small token of my appreciation for a devotion beyond the call of duty, I urged him to accept my gift: "Go out and buy your new life, now, Dessouki, today not tomorrow."

As we rolled up to the departures entrance, the well-organized Hassan had clandestinely organized a farewell that promised to be tearful: the bureau's Egyptian troops were all lined up to kiss the bureau chief goodbye and to wish her godspeed. I smiled and thanked my way through the receiving line, proud of my restraint, until I got to Dessouki, who proved my undoing. We embraced like two sobbing souls who had been to hell and back; two survivors who shared secrets we would take to the grave. Finally, there was only Hassan. He would rescue me and guide me through the final steps just as he had done so many times since that November day in 1977; the only other person who knew enough to understand why I was leaving, who knew enough about frogs and scorpions in all their disguises. Over a cappuccino in the VIP lounge we reminisced and talked of the future. We laughed over his reminder that during my life with Anwar Sadat I never once had the luxury of a sit-down one-to-one interview; that whenever he agreed to speak at length from the comfort of an armchair, showbusiness dictated that he be interviewed by a network celebrity. A sardonic Hassan did not think I would miss the "power, the fame and the glamour" I was leaving behind.

Imitating Sadat, I assured him, "for sure, for sure" I would not miss the "power, the fame, the glamour", that I would be quite content to lose myself in the anonymous charms and joys of the Left Bank of the Seine; that it was better to drown in beauty than be devoured by false gods.

"That's why I chose Paris, Hassan. I'm going to give the wonderful world of TV news another year, probably not more. So I plan to visit you sooner than you might think. There's a story to be done here – a little unfinished business – and I'm coming back to do it."

"*Inshallah*, you must come back to report that story, Doreen, if only to make some sense of the last three years."

As Hassan walked me silently to the tarmac gateway I did not even try to thank him. We shook hands, parted, waved goodbye. I made no attempt to halt the tears or two that escaped. Nor did Hassan. He turned briskly on his heels and walked away. Only an eternity ago and but a few yards away, he had welcomed me to Egypt.

Hassan: the beginning and the end. Alpha and Omega.

I looked forward to meeting myself again.

No more Cairo persona; no more bureau chief/correspondent; no more ugly mask. I dumped them overboard.

One month and $30,000 in moving expenses later, I was happily installed in the Paris bureau's sunny kitchen, a pleasant enough place to work except at lunch hour. Either the bureau had not anticipated my arrival, hoped I wouldn't show up, had no room for a third correspondent, or was flat out of funds. In any case I was without desk or typewriter, which given the beat designated to me by the bureau chief – fashion shows and Third-World contacts – did not cause me to panic. My ambitions fell somewhat short of "haute couture correspondent"; as for the Third World, in this case, Africa: it does not exist for American TV news except on days when the earth moves under it and the tremors are felt in New York or Washington – an event adequately covered by any "fireman" correspondent in the usual hit-and-run in-depth sixty-second backgrounder on the evening show.

During our fifteen-minute get-acquainted session, the bureau chief warned me that France (and several other countries) were his domain. I assured him he had nothing to fear from my underinflated ego. I didn't tell him why I had come to Paris. The man appeared to be suffering from high-blood pressure and other ailments. Besides, I had other things on my mind; some "unfinished business" to attend to in the Middle East, and the individual best able to help just happened to be in town: ABC News executive Av Westin – the same Av Westin who more than three years earlier had sent me to Cairo and would subsequently proclaim that I "owned the story". No one was in a better position to buy or reject my untold tale. As former executive-producer of the evening news, Westin was now executive producer of the weekly hour-long magazine show "20/20" and ABC News' vice-president for programme development. That he was generally accessible and responsive to correspondents' ideas and proposals made him an especially attractive target of frustrated foreign correspondents whose isolation deprived them of the substantive give and take of the New York-based decision-making process.

Over a leisurely dinner, I exploited Westin's patience and interest by compressing a three-year-experience into a four-hour long impassioned monologue on the current state of Egypt and its pharaoh-king and the threats facing both; a portrait clearly at variance with popular American perceptions as created, conveyed and perpetuated by the media, especially television. I proposed an hour-long documentary exposing the paradox of Anwar Sadat, whose policies and style – foreign and domestic – had made him a hero in the West and a villain at home. In short, a candid, unvarnished, balanced look at Sadat and his Egypt; a multi-dimensional image of reality in which the voices of opposition and sources of discontent could be publicly aired through the medium most cherished by Sadat himself – American network television. How and why Egypt was smothering to death politically and economically; how and why despair had replaced the early hope and euphoria of peace; how and why Sadat had turned from benign dictator to dangerous despot; what this explosive situation meant for the future of Sadat, Egypt, peace, the Middle East and US interests in the region, was my subject. To produce this TV perspective these and other questions had to be asked and answered.

"Can you get the opposition to talk – on camera?" asked Westin.

"Yes, I think I can – a handful of his more vocal critics are ready to come out in the open, despite the repressive climate and inherent dangers."

"Can examples of corruption be documented?"

I confessed that this was more problematic, particularly with regard to the free-floating allegations against Mrs Sadat, Sadat's inner circle, fringe family and the ruling elite. People at the top tend to cover their tracks rather well, especially in a closed society.

Overall, though, I felt the corruption issue could be handled within the context of the story, which I felt was solid enough to stand on its own.

Westin, consummate television man that he is, was naturally looking for the sexiest exposé angle. Nonetheless he agreed that the situation in Egypt merited our attention and wholeheartedly supported the idea that I return to Cairo on a feasibility mission. Having understood why I could not stay in Cairo, he wisely dismissed the irony of my need to return on special assignment. If such a probing documentary should prove possible, Westin, aware of the risks involved in airing it – was prepared to jeopardize ABC's Cairo operation; if Sadat chose to shut down the bureau, so be it.

He wanted to discuss the story with the rest of the ABC brass and get back to me. I thanked him for his support and courage and while awaiting official approval, flew off to London to cover the Old Bailey trial of the Yorkshire Ripper. After two weeks of staring at a maniac and listening to the graphic details of how he mutilated and murdered thirteen women and how he failed to murder seven more – many of them prostitutes – New York pulled me off the story: lack of interest. America apparently had killers every bit as perverse and sensational as Peter Sutcliffe; "Good Morning America" managed to serve up the Ripper for breakfast one morning – hardly enough to justify the cost of a court artist and me.

Back in Paris, authorization finally came through to proceed to Cairo on my mission; a mission – finally – with a purpose, one to which I could give my undivided attention without the distractions of stake-outs and satellite transmissions. It was May 1981 by the time I arrived and there to greet me at the airport was a delighted Hassan. During the drive to the Nile Hilton I briefed him and we arranged to meet the following morning. I did not see Hassan again for ten days.

Five minutes after unpacking my bags – shortly after midnight – the foreign desk woke me up with the order to repack my bags for an early morning flight to Istanbul. The Pope had been shot and his alleged assailant was a young Turk by the name of Mehmat Ali Agça.

The next day with the help of a Turkish journalist who was also an ABC radio stringer, I pieced together a profile of Agça and waited for a camera crew, a producer and editor to arrive – each from a different point on the map. The crew arrived at 6:00 p.m., just in time to shoot a few pictures before dark, and the editor and producer made it in time to watch the crew and I finish transmitting our midnight report via satellite from Turkish television. The good news was that our competition had not yet shown up, which meant an ABC exclusive.

Several Mehmat Ali Agça stories and non-stories later I returned to Cairo to pick up where I left off. I now had two weeks in which to investigate and explore the Egypt story. In that period I was again side-tracked by hard news: Anwar Sadat and Menachem Begin were meeting for the first time in seventeen months – this time on the southern tip of the Sinai at Sharm el Sheik. Sadat had agreed to meet with Begin for only one reason: to ask him to de-escalate the missile crisis with Syria that had erupted in Lebanon and was threatening all-out war, not that an Israeli-Syrian war would threaten the peace treaty – it would not. Sadat simply wanted to warn Begin not to further destabilize the area, killing off whatever chance there was for a broader peace.

On the eve of the summit, "World News Tonight" and "Nightline" (the permanent sequel to the late-night "America Held Hostage" programme) each requested a report, the latter a lengthy (five-minute) background/situationer outlining Egypt and Sadat's problems. I did both and both were bumped off the air by more pressing news. The following day I reluctantly flew to Sharm el Sheik to cover the one-day summit where I was joined by Tel Aviv correspondent Bill Seamans and producer Pete Simmons. Having reported for the breakfast show we spent the rest of the day chasing the story through the hot sands before ending up on a dusty airport tarmac where we waited several hours for a flight out. Finally, an ABC charter plane rescued us and flew us to Israel. By the time we reached the Herzliya satellite point it was 10:00 p.m. New York had already decided the summit was worth one report, not two, and Seamans did the wrap-up. I returned to Tel Aviv, booked into a hotel and the next morning caught the forty-five minute El Al flight to Cairo.

During this entire period the Cairo bureau chief who had succeeded me was on assignment in Lebanon.

The thought that I could now tackle my special assignment without further interference was more wishful thinking. I had no sooner finished discussing the story in code over the telephone with the senior London producer when Hassan informed me that I was wasting my time talking in code; that Egyptian security had contacted him several weeks earlier – before I had even set a specific date for my arrival – informing him that I was returning to Egypt and inquiring as to the purpose of my mission.

Hassan and I agreed to proceed as normal. We had nothing to hide. If the Sadat regime wanted to censor my reports or curtail my freedom of expression or movement, or put me under surveillance, or threaten to take away my credentials or kick me out of the country, it would have proved my point: that Sadat and Egypt were in deep trouble.

It should be noted that Hassan did not admire Sadat. Thoroughly disillusioned with his leader's style of rule, he loathed everything Sadat had become. He had long felt that American television was guilty of transforming Sadat into an untouchable God with a mandate to ride roughshod over his people; that we were not nearly as critical and questioning in our over-all coverage as we might have been; that we were indeed responsible – along with the US, Israel and Sadat himself – for Egypt's dismal state of affairs – growing worse by the day. He was right on all counts. Hassan, at least, believed in the story I had come to investigate and would give me all the necessary co-operation and support. Just as he always had.

Another valuable ally and go-between, Gumbo, upon learning of the security check, went into a deep funk from which he would not emerge for three days. Already disillusioned and disgusted with what had become of Sadat and Egypt, the revelation that Egyptian security was stepping up its surveillance of the foreign media shattered him and put his own relationship with the government and contacts in even greater jeopardy. He recovered but decided to get out of Egypt and made plans for a sabbatical.

By now I was left with three days to investigate and explore the Egypt story before flying back to Paris with an assessment for Westin. I had just enough time to meet with some leading members of the political and Moslem fundamentalist opposition – all of whom agreed to express their views on-camera. It was enough to convince me we should proceed with the documentary or special report or exposé or whatever it developed into.

At a luncheon meeting in Paris on June 8, 1981, Westin and I were joined by a senior London producer, and ABC's London-based Iranian expert Chris Powell, a talented New Zealand-born journalist who had spent eight years in Iran reporting on both the Shah and Khomeini regimes for ABC Radio and the British and Australian media. She remarked on the striking parallels between the Shah's Iran and Sadat's Egypt – although it was agreed that Sadat was not a ruthless tyrant and Egypt did not yet have thousands of political prisoners or wide-scale torture. It was not a Nasser police state. There were no detention camps.

But the consensus was that we had a story to tell; that we dared not ignore or repeat the media's abysmal shortcomings in Iran during the Shah's era. The Paris bureau chief, who considered himself an expert on Iran on the strength of having produced a highly successful three-hour TV exposé on the secret year-long hostage negotiations, was also present, though somewhat less enthusiastic about my story. His part in what might have been a double-barrelled Iran-Egypt report was written out after his anticipated revelations fell through.

Westin endorsed the Egypt story, leaving me the freedom to pursue it as I saw fit. With Egypt now sweltering in the heat of high summer and

Ramadan approaching, I felt it best to wait until the country was mobile again. I took the risk of waiting until September when a camera crew would find shooting conditions more congenial and I would find my contacts and interviewees more accessible. I had only one immediate request of Westin: to notify the Cairo bureau chief about the secret project so as to prevent any ill feelings over an invasion of his territory. I would have appreciated the same small courtesy, which was not always forthcoming when I held the post.

That same day the world media was still reeling from Israel's latest bombshell. Three days after the Sadat-Begin summit – on June 7, 1981 – nine Israeli bombers flew to Baghdad, dropped their bombs on an Iraqi nuclear reactor on the outskirts, and fled. Sadat was looking more foolish than ever.

Having just completed an eleven-minute "Perspective" on the Summit for ABC Radio, I quickly rewrote it to include the devastating implications of this political debacle. That June 1981 radio commentary provided a perspective of what had gone before and what was to follow in the next four months. For that reason it bears reproducing here in full:

> It had been seventeen months since last they met. And there they were again: Anwar Sadat and Menachem Begin embracing in a warm Middle East bear hug. This time on a windy tarmac in Sharm el Sheik on the sun-scorched tip of southern Sinai. It is a piece of the Sinai still occupied by Israel which Egypt looks forward to having back next year. It was an appropriate meeting place for this tenth Sadat-Begin Summit; this one called by the Israeli Prime Minister and eagerly agreed to by the Egyptian President because of what were called "urgent concerns"; a euphemism for the Syrian missile crisis in Lebanon which had been threatening to erupt into all-out war between Israel and Syria.
>
> Sadat had claimed there would never be a summit during the Israeli election campaign. He did not want to appear to be interfering in Israel's internal politics. Yet, there he was, meeting with the man he had hoped he would not have to deal with after the June 30 election. But, President Sadat like everyone else had been watching the polls and Begin's spectacular resurgence in popularity. Better, he thought, to face reality and the leading candidate. The Egyptian leader after all is still waiting for that one-third of the Sinai to be handed back. And at all costs he wants nothing to jeopardize that. Until April 1982 then his top priority is not to upset the Israelis and not allow a further destabilization in the area. And so after that warm airport embrace, in the sizzling Sinai sun, Prime Minister

Begin took President Sadat on a helicopter tour of what he would have a year from now: Israeli airfields, tourist facilities in a scuba diver's paradise that contains some of the world's most spectacular coral reefs. And housing units.

In fact just to remind Sadat how much Begin was giving up, a group of local Israeli settlers demonstrated their anger at having to give up this idyllic life. Then, for ninety minutes the two men talked. And they totally agreed over the Syrian missile crisis in Lebanon: Syria was to blame, said Sadat and he backed Begin's demand that President Assad withdraw his troops from Lebanon. It was the Egyptian leader, in fact, not Prime Minister Begin who used the toughest language against Syria and Assad. He accused them of moving into Lebanon six years ago under the pretext of helping to keep the peace. But Assad, he said, was interested only in absorbing Lebanon into a Greater Syria. In provoking the conflict with Israel, Assad, he claimed, was trying to divert attention from a civil war raging at home. As far as war breaking out between Israel and Syria, Sadat said he doesn't believe that will happen because neither party wants it. And for Syria he believes it would mean the end of President Assad. In any event as far as the Egyptian President is concerned the Egyptian-Israeli peace treaty will survive. He and Begin reaffirmed that the October '73 war will be their last. And Sadat made it clear that, militarily at least, Egypt would remain neutral in any Israeli-Arab conflict, leading to charges from his Arab critics that Israel now had a green light to provoke war with Syria or any other Arab country. In return for Sadat's support and position of neutrality, Begin agreed to allow American peace envoy Philip Habib more time – with no deadline – to resolve the missile problem peacefully; a decision many officials and observers believe was already made, without urging from Sadat. But publicly, at least, Sadat took the credit. By appearing to help the cause of peace and possibly the prevention of war, the Egyptian leader had enhanced his own image and the credibility of the Camp David peace treaty. In the eyes of his Arab and Egyptian critics though he had given away far more than he got.

For them the summit was a painful joke: a blatant and successful exercise in electioneering tactics on the part of the Israeli Prime Minister. Many Egyptians were enraged. And I suspect Sadat was himself as he sat by while Prime Minister Begin reiterated his inflexible position on the status of Jerusalem, apparently for the benefit of the Israeli electorate because Jerusalem was not a subject that came up during their talks. It was during the news conference that followed that Begin spoke again of a Jerusalem that shall remain forever the undivided capital of Israel. He said this knowing full well that Sadat only a few days earlier spoke of the need for an undivided Jerusalem but one that would be jointly administered by the Arabs and Israelis. By raising the divisive issue of Jerusalem, Begin acted insensitively and provocatively. His behaviour, which does not enhance the cause of peace, was in poor taste. During this performance I glanced at President Sadat's face for any sign of the anger and exasperation he must be feeling. But his face was expressionless; betraying nothing. And I was reminded of the countless times and incidents since November 1977, that his dear friend Menachem Begin had slapped him in the face and made his life unnecessarily difficult. Sadat had obviously become immune to Begin's provocations and this latest one was simply more fuel for the fire of Sadat's Arab and Egyptian critics.

One other important disagreement surfaced during the official part of their talks. President Sadat asked Prime Minister Begin to stop Israeli ground and air strikes against Palestinian guerrilla positions in Lebanon. He was refused – on grounds that they were necessary for Israel's defence. Sadat fully expected to be rebuffed on this issue. Indeed, as his chief foreign policy advisor, Osama el-Baz, told me before the summit: "We do not expect the Israeli strikes against the Palestinians to stop. They will continue," he said, "as they always have."

Well, the Sinai Summit which the US encouraged, if not orchestrated, ended the way it began: with an embrace. But this time I felt I had witnessed not so much a summit as a public relations performance on Sadat's part and a campaign whistle stop for votes, on the part of Begin. Each leader did the other a favour. A political favour. And if war is averted between Israel and Syria, history, I suspect, will not credit this summit.

Little did any of us know that only three days later, Israel would lower the boom. Literally. And not on Syria but Iraq.

On Sunday, June 7, nine Israeli planes dropped their bombs on the Iraqi nuclear reactor outside Baghdad. With those bombs Begin all but emasculated Sadat. This latest blow has stripped him of whatever political and personal dignity he had left. None of us can know the real dimensions of Sadat's humiliation. We will have to await the history books and memoirs. All that's certain at the moment is that the Israeli Prime Minister has succeeded in making Sadat look like the fool his Arab and Egyptians critics have been saying he is, all along.

I must confess I find it rather obscene the way Begin has taken advantage of Sadat's weaknesses. Before he struck at Iraq he knew the Egyptian President would be in no position to retaliate with anything other than words. He knew Sadat – at any cost – wanted that one-third of the Sinai back and that until April next year, his peace partner was vulnerable. He knew Sadat was a generous, patient man; one who had built up impeccable credentials as a man of peace during the past difficult three and a half years. In short, he knew the man with whom he had signed a peace treaty. And he knew that peace treaty would not be a victim of his bombs over Baghdad. Begin knew the world would condemn him and Israel. He knew the Arabs would come down on him with the full force of their rhetoric; he knew the US would be offended, especially as American-made planes were involved in the attacks; he knew Sadat would be further cornered and isolated from his fellow Arabs; he knew the attack would finish off the stalled Camp David talks on Palestinian self-rule; and he knew it would set back the fragile hopes for real peace in the region. He knew all of this. And yet he ignored the long-term consequences of his act, in favour of the short-term benefits. The fact that he admits publicly he doesn't care what anyone thinks, especially the Arabs, proves his insensitivity not only to the agonizing struggle for peace, but to the man who more than anyone else has extended his hand – time and again – in the name of peace.

Anwar Sadat consistently has gone out on a limb for Menachem Begin. In return he gets kicked in the teeth and punched in the nose. Today he stands more ridiculed and battered than ever, where it matters most: in the Arab world and increasingly within Egypt. The internal voices of opposition are now screaming: "Enough, enough, we told you so," more loudly than ever. In fact the opposition forces have called for a halt to oil sales to Israel and an end to normal and diplomatic relations with a recall of the Egyptian ambassador from Tel Aviv.

The Egyptian leader has refused. Officially Egypt is restricting herself to a plea to the US and all peace-loving nations to force Israel to stop "its violence and aggression in the area and to respect international law and the UN Charter". The Israeli attack, says Egypt, was "irresponsible, unjustified and premeditated". Unofficially the mood in Egypt is one of shame, humiliation and frustration. In some quarters I'm told even tears were shed. As one Egyptian in Cairo put it to me: "This time it's more than we can take." But since President Sadat is still in charge, Egypt is taking it . . . one more time. The only question is: how many more times can he continue to turn the other cheek? How much further can he be pushed? And how much longer can he survive?

Six people, at least, got the message or rather what I could jam into eleven minutes: two *herograms* arrived from ABC Radio executives and another from ABC colleagues I had never met.

It was hardly "magnificent", as one of them put it, but I was deeply grateful for the ego massage, especially as it was clear Sadat's situation was growing worse not better. Indeed within a matter of days Egypt's worst sectarian clashes in years broke out in two of Cairo's poorest suburbs when mobs of Moslems and Coptic Christian extremists battled it out, leaving about sixty dead and several hundred wounded. While the violent outbursts signalled the simmering discontent that had been building amongst militants on both sides, the clashes did not in themselves constitute a serious threat to Sadat's regime: they were symptomatic of a broader, political, social and economic malaise exacerbated by Sadat's new links with Christian America and Jewish Israel. Nonetheless the Egyptian leader would file these incidents for future use. They would come in handy.

By mid-July Sadat's problems had expanded to cover the constituency that more than any other had given him the stature of international greatness: the foreign media, especially the American media. He should not have been so naïve; he should have known that those who build false gods tend to destroy them sooner or later. My successor in Cairo did a one and half-minute TV spot in which he hinted at possible similarities between Sadat and the Shah, and Egypt and Iran. The following day the government threatened to strip him of his presidential credentials with a warning to desist from such negative reportage. This was accompanied by an article in *Al Ahram* – the semi-official Cairo daily – stating that ABC News "Nightline" programme was planning an unflattering portrait of Sadat and Egypt to be aired on the eve of Sadat's Washington summit with President Reagan. Informally, ABC was charged with trying to sabotage Sadat's grass-roots support in America and taint his image with the new US administration. There were even suggestions of a conspiracy, an ABC News–State Department plot, to finish off Sadat in the same way Washington disposed of the Shah once he had become a liability. Sadat, after all, lived with that fear daily. And even though he abhorred the free-wheeling "American school of journalism", he and some of his officials still seemed to assume that the free press took its orders from Washington and – no doubt – that we were all CIA agents.

The honeymoon between Sadat and the American media was at long last officially over.

With his rule under increasing attack at home, Sadat finally resorted to his true instincts: he overreacted. By threatening to silence a powerful news organ; by trying to dictate what it could and could not report about him he helped create the very impression and image he sought to avoid: a man and his regime on the verge of collapse; at the very least a dictator whose paranoia now stretched to New York and Washington and back; the same paranoia he used to stifle his Egyptian critics so successfully for so long.

When ABC executives telephoned me in Paris with news of the Sadat threat we agreed that the Cairo bureau should neither lie low through intimidation nor launch a charge of the light brigade. Our reaction should be reflexive: business as usual. It might not, however, be business as usual for me and my September assignment. Clearly it was in jeopardy. With time and Sadat now working against it, I desperately suggested a preemptive measure to Westin: devote a portion of that week's "20/20" programme to a round-table discussion of Sadat, his troubles, his opposition and his fears – real and imagined. Westin rejected the proposal, preferring to take the risk and time of a studied documentary.

By now the Israeli electorate had renewed Menachem Begin's mandate once more to take international law into his own hands. With Anwar Sadat tucked safely in one pocket and his American allies secure in the other, Begin moved from Baghdad to Beirut, dropping his bombs with all the impunity of a Nobel Peace Prize winner. About three hundred people died and several hundred more were wounded (mostly civilians) in a blitz that left the PLO target intact and Anwar Sadat stumbling through the debris "feeling disappointed and betrayed". Since all he had to show for his November '77 gamble was the Sinai, and since he still had nine months to go before the Israelis delivered the last third of it, Sadat's hands would remain tied and his voice muted. That was the ransom price and Begin was determined to get his money's worth.

It was time to meet the new man in the White House. In early August, the Egyptian leader journeyed to Washington to charm and educate a new American president in desperate need of a few lessons. Sadat's lecture on Soviet adventurism (complete with map) was predictably better received than his briefing on the Arab-Israeli conflict and the "core of the Middle East problem": the fate of the Palestinians and the occupied West Bank and Gaza. Sadat suggested that it was time the United States seized the initiative – used the opportunity of an American-sponsored ceasefire in Lebanon between Israel and the PLO – to move the peace process forward. He asked President Reagan to change US policy and start dealing directly with the Palestine Liberation Organization. He was rebuffed. For one thing Reagan tended to agree with Begin that the PLO was nothing more than a terrorist organization and Sadat, presumably, did not think it kosher to bring up Begin's past terrorist credentials in the struggle for a Jewish homeland. Secondly, it was Sadat's dear friend Henry Kissinger who pledged in 1975 that the US would never negotiate with the PLO unless and until the PLO recognizes Israel's right to exist.

Sadat also felt the Americans were dragging their feet on delivery of promised military equipment such as F-16 jet fighters, M-60 tanks, Hawk anti-aircraft missiles and other weapons needed to bolster the sagging morale of his Egyptian forces. Overall, the Reagan administration seemed in no hurry to ease Sadat's problems. It still had not formulated a Middle

East peace policy and until it did Sadat would be left to dangle on his precipice.

The best that could be said about the Washington summit is that it gave the Egyptian leader an opportunity to fly to Plains, Georgia to see his old friend Jimmy Carter. Personally, it was my favourite summit. I did not have to cover it. Nor did I have to suffer through the Alexandrian duet that followed a few days later: the eleventh Sadat-Begin Summit the one in which Begin asked Sadat if he was prepared to resume the Palestinian autonomy talks which had broken down fifteen months earlier over Israel's de facto annexation of East Jerusalem.

"For sure," replied the compliant Sadat, "anytime you suggest, Mena- chem . . . why not immediately?" Whereupon they agreed to schedule ministerial-level talks for late September – after Begin wrapped up his own summit with President Reagan. Moving right along, Begin brought up another complaint: the abnormality of the normal relations called for by the peace treaty; too little was flowing from the Egyptian side of the border, like Egyptian tourists, joint business deals, cultural and sport exchanges. All the Israelis seemed to be getting were vitriolic barbs from the Egyptian press. Sadat reminded Begin that he had his domestic opposi- tion to consider; that his critics were unhappy over the lack of movement on the Palestinian issue and Israeli intransigence in general. An unsympa- thetic Begin made it clear that unless the bilateral climate improved – unless Sadat got his house in order – he might not be in a position, come April, to hand over the rest of the Sinai because the Israeli public would be too sceptical about Egypt's commitment to peace.

That was all Sadat needed to hear. The implied threat confirmed his suspicions that the Israelis were looking for the least excuse not to return the strategic last third of the Sinai. At that point Sadat assured Begin that Foreign Minister Kamal Hassan Ali would solve these "normalization" problems immediately. There was also the issue of the growing Islamic fundamentalist movement and its opposition to Sadat's policies. Better to have angry Egyptians he could subjugate than jittery Israelis he could not. For the sake of the Sinai and the future distinction of being the only Arab leader who could lay claim to having regained all of his occupied land from Israel, Sadat would have to improve normal relations and to do that he decided he would have to launch a pre-emptive strike – silence his internal opponents – Moslem fundamentalists and assorted political dissid- ents – if not once and for all at least for the next seven months. For a non-gambling man, Sadat seemed to thrive on betting the long shots.

One night early in September between midnight and 6:00 a.m. he embarked on the most sweeping crackdown in the history of his eleven- year rule. By the time it was over more than sixteen hundred dissidents had been rounded up – the vast majority of them Moslem fundamentalists plus a hundred and fifty Christian Coptic bishops, priests and their militant followers. But the dragnet swept up more than religious fanatics: virtually every prominent political and personal enemy of Sadat was detained, including a former deputy prime minister, eight former cabinet ministers and dozens of other left and right-wing politicians, professors, lawyers, journalists and broadcasters. The "Who's Who" list of Sadat critics included the confidante of the late Gamal Abdel Nasser, the author and journalist Mohamed Heikal; the popular blind preacher, Sheikh Abdul Hamid Kishk; the vice-chairman of Sadat's official opposition party – Dr Hilmy Murad; the septuagenarian head of the defunct New Wafd Party, Fuad Serrag-Din, and the zealous Pope Shenouda III, 117th Patriarch of the Coptic Church who was stripped of his powers and banished to a desert monastery. Only one of my dissidents was spared.

Seven publications, religious and political, including the weekly organ of his own official opposition party, were shut down; all political activity in mosques and churches was banned; forty thousand private mosques were nationalized and some of their preachers replaced by government moderates; all politics and religion were prohibited on university campuses along with the beards, *galabayias* and veils worn by fundamentalists; thirteen religious societies were disbanded and their funds confiscated; and one hundred and twenty-five journalists, broadcasters and university professors were reassigned to other jobs.

The cure seemed worse than the disease – officially diagnosed as "sectarian sedition". It was evident that Sadat was declaring all-out war not on the Moslem-Christian feud that had flared up three months earlier, but on the Islamic fundamentalist movement, *and* his political naysayers whom he feared might join forces in a conspiracy to unseat him. Admittedly these disparate voices of opposition shared some common complaints – the peace treaty, Israel, inflation, corruption, Sadat's general life-style and autocratic rule and not least his refuge to the Shah; they posed a potential threat but hardly an imminent one – they were still too unfocused to coalesce. The consensus, then, of Cairo's professional Sadat-watchers – Egyptian and Western – was that the Egyptian President had dangerously magnified the dual threat in order to snuff out the Ayatollah-like Moslem passions and in the process justify a purge of his personal enemies. A look at his political hit-list transparently exposed a personal vendetta against those who dared criticize him or his policies openly, and it was this aspect of his security clampdown that resulted in a barrage of criticism in the American, British and French media.

Predictably, the massive wave of arrests enraged the fundamentalists, several hundred of whom went out into the streets, only to be met by riot police and tear gas. As much as Sadat might have liked to use the same tactics on Western journalists, he chose instead to salvage his dented international image by summoning the foreign media to his Barrages villa north of Cairo for a lengthy and impassioned lecture on the "facts" which seemed once more to have eluded his powerful image-makers. Stunned by the negative reaction to his "political" detentions and anxious to control the damage done to his reputation as a world statesman "committed to peace, freedom and democracy", he admitted the crackdown was a "purge" but one aimed at nipping an elaborate politico-religious conspiracy in the bud; a well-coordinated plot to undermine the stability of his regime. Few were convinced. Insisting that his government was based on democratic principles he reminded the Western scribes that "democracy when it bites has fiercer claws than dictators" because "democracy defends the mass population of the country".

And the mass population – over 99 per cent of the voters (by his count) – would endorse the arrests and Sadat's call for national unity in the latest bogus referendum. When the Cairo-based NBC-TV correspondent asked the President whether he had consulted with President Reagan about the crackdown in advance, Sadat exploded at the impertinence of the question, confessing only half in jest that in other times (presumably less democratic) he would have had the correspondent shot. (Sadat mistook the NBC correspondent for the ABC correspondent who he was about to expel for graver sins.)

Then came the news conference blockbuster: proof (allegedly) that some members of the foreign media were out to do him in as well by "distorting Egypt's image abroad" through an interview he claimed was "full of lies". Fuming and perspiring excessively, he held aloft two video cassettes belonging to ABC News which his security men had confiscated at Cairo airport, replacing them with dummy tapes. The seized tapes, destined for ABC London, were obtained through a "friend" according to the head of the State Information Service and contained a raw, unedited interview conducted by my successor, Chris Harper, with British journalist David Hirst, *The Guardian*'s veteran Beirut-based correspondent who had just completed an unflattering biography of Sadat. He was expelled from Egypt after the January '77 food riots when he alleged corruption in high places including Sadat's family, and also predicted Sadat's downfall. Now he identified him as an "actor" (once for hire with a preference for comic roles), "opportunist", "anti-Semite" – one with an "inferiority complex" especially with regard to Nasser; charges not without some foundation. Hirst also felt Sadat's regime was as politically unviable as the Shah's and he questioned the US investment in Sadat, suggesting it would be every bit as catastrophic. He also thought that, while Sadat's opposition was strong, it was latent. Since the interview was taped in Beirut, confiscated on July 29 and never aired, Sadat merely hinted at one of its themes by alluding to the culprits, Hirst and Harper: "They are saying don't deal with Sadat. He is Shah number two." Apart from impugning his dear friend the late Shah, it did not occur to the affronted Sadat that his performance would be panned by the same news organs he was reprimanding for his bad press. The histrionics were just the latest example of Sadat-style overkill only this time it was not a threatened Sadat but a desperate Sadat, trying to save his well-cultivated foreign reputation. And this time it would backfire. Nor would his image be much enhanced by expelling the ABC bureau chief from Egypt.

Harper was given twenty-four hours to get out of the country.

And within twenty-four hours I was back in the country. My assignment: save the ABC News bureau.

The timing of the expulsion order could not have been worse: the eve of my previously scheduled departure for Cairo to begin work on the long-planned documentary on Sadat and Egypt, an assignment I now realized was doomed long before it was conceived and not entirely for political reasons. The new assignment bore a striking resemblance to the old, the one I had fled in such desperation seven months earlier: keep ABC alive, kicking and competitive. Since CBS and NBC News remained unscathed by Sadat's media attack, ABC could not afford to be inoperative. The name of the game was stay-on-the-air and, given our current predicament, that was a doubtful prospect.

Hassan met me at the airport where I was also welcomed in the usual manner by a press office official – a signal that I would not be shipped out on the next flight. Since the bureau was officially temporarily closed under government orders, ABC New York feared I might not be permitted into the country and alerted the local staff to stand by at the bureau until my entry or exit was assured. By the time I signed myself into the bureau, well past 1:00 a.m., a burst of relief greeted me but the atmosphere was as tense on the inside as it was on the outside; a tension so palpable and toxic I was urged to get a good night's sleep before choking on it.

Cairo for the next month would prove to be a nightmare; an orgy of frogs and scorpions. And worse, the bureau I used to know and love had become a microcosm of the political cancer bred by Sadat in my absence. The smell of fear, suspicion, betrayal, intrigue and despair promised to make the soap-operas on American, British and Egyptian television seem like Walt Disney cartoons.

All I knew was that something had gone awfully wrong in Sadat's Egypt *and* ABC's Cairo bureau between the months of February and September. I was determined to find out what and why. But first I would have to help rescue the Bureau from Sadat's excessive democracy. "Temporarily closed" meant we'd been stripped of our presidential credentials, which effectively meant we were prohibited from covering most stories or transmitting them. We were out of business. Dear old Dessouki though, was back on duty.

Several cordial meetings, three half-hearted lectures and dozens of cups of coffee later I was much enlightened: ABC's current *persona non grata* status was not necessarily directed at the Cairo bureau operation and its future depended on who would succeed Harper. A couple of officials suggested I return as bureau chief, which I accepted as both a compliment and an insult – a personal compliment and a professional insult. I reminded one that I didn't think Sadat would like what I would have to say any more than he could stomach what went before.

Despite the comforting clarifications I also reminded them that nothing justifies the expulsion of a correspondent and that Sadat's hysterical over-reaction had smeared his image far more than any "insulting" interview could. Most of them tended to agree, though only a couple dared admit it openly; all seemed embarrassed by their efforts to defend Sadat's action. One did not even try – one whom I had always highly respected because he levelled with me: Mansour Hassan. In addition to being the Minister of State for Information and Culture, he was also a close confidante and advisor to the President. He and I had established a good rapport about the time I discovered Sadat had discovered him, which was several months before he joined the elite inner-circle. It was during this period, when his star was rising rapidly, that he was regarded by some of us – Egyptian and foreign – as a knight in shining armour, a breath of fresh air whom we hoped Sadat would listen to because he had reasoned and enlightened things to say without benefit of rhetoric or polemics. Apart from the cosmetics – in his early forties and handsome – he was an ambitious, intelligent introspective idealist, yet realistic and honest enough to know the flaws of certain policies and style, and confident and forthright enough to hope he could influence change – however minimal. Before Hassan became a minister, I remember telling him rather unabashedly that his political ascendancy had been swift – perhaps too swift – and because he was a maverick, bent on speaking his mind, his descent from power could be just as swift mainly because sooner or later he would threaten his own sponsor. He laughed and said he would take his chances. Within months he was appointed to the cabinet and the Presidency directorate, and over the next two years he became an established power sitting at Sadat's right hand. I saw him only sporadically thereafter and assumed he was devoting his time to survival through compromise. Now as we talked of the expulsion, he seemed battle-weary and despondent, but there was still a trace of the old spark; the buoyant golden boy had not sold out.

A week later he was gone. In a cabinet re-shuffle, Mansour Hassan was the only one shuffled out. Sadat dismissed him from power for having counselled restraint. He disapproved of the President's crackdown on political opponents and the expulsion of foreign correspondents – by now, the veteran *Le Monde* correspondent, Jean-Pierre Peroncel-Hugoz, had also been ordered out of Egypt. As Minister of Information, Hassan was responsible for the foreign media and felt the expulsions were a grave mistake, and told Sadat so. In fact, had it not been for the temperate Mansour Hassan, ABC's Harper would have been expelled two months earlier when his credentials were first threatened.

The bureau at least survived the crisis: we were now re-credentialed and operational again. Instead of a high-powered ABC official flying to Cairo to apologize as requested by the government, a meeting in Washington between Ambassador Ashraf Ghorbal and a senior ABC News vice-president produced a *modus operandi*, although I'm not sure what it was precisely. Since I had little desire to see Anwar Sadat again – let alone stake him out – I was not entirely thrilled with the news that my presence in Cairo seemed to be as much a factor in the rescue mission as the government's desire to cut its losses.

ABC's survival, in fact, would claim another government official: the chairman of the State Information Service, Shafei Abdel Hamid. ABC's "Nightline" programme, which devotes its nightly half-hour to one story in the news, decided to take a look at sizzling Cairo and asked me to recruit a high-level Egyptian spokesman to defend Sadat's tough new measures, including the expulsions. Ambassador Abdel Hamid was given the unenviable task of defending his government. He agreed to be interviewed by the show's moderator in a live Cairo-Washington satellite hook-up at some ungodly hour like five in the morning. Clearly the government badly wanted to get its message across to America. Unfortunately – for technical reasons – the interview had to be cancelled at the last minute and rescheduled for the following night. Undaunted, the co-operative and charming career diplomat, who had been at his new post only a few months, agreed to try again and I accompanied him to the Egypt TV studio, mainly to hold his hand and serve as liaison. I knew nothing of the programme content or other possible participants and the only programme audio available to me was the voice of my guest as he sat in front of me and a camera answering his long-distance questioners. Lights. Action. Roll. Abdel Hamid was on. And within five minutes of his opening apologia it was evident from the expression on his face, the agitation of his body and the thrust of his defence that he was headed for a cataclysmic end. He found himself answering questions not just from the Washington host but also from an expelled Cairo bureau chief sitting in our London studio in the company of a prominent Egyptian leftist opponent of Sadat, Lofti El-Kholy, who had escaped the dragnet thanks to an overseas obligation. Whatever the interviewers were asking and whatever they were charging, the squirming apologist was disintegrating before my eyes. The pathetic government line he was obliged to push fell flat on its rhetorical face. Furthermore it was obvious he was not used to television or interrogation, which merely hastened his descent. Since he seemed not to believe that I had not set him up – that I was only a go-between – I tried assuaging him by telling him he was "terrific". Well, Sadat didn't think so. He was fired.

The Chairman of the State Information Service was re-assigned . . . back to the Foreign Ministry.

A couple of days later I bumped into *Al Akhbar*'s editor-in-chief Moussa Sabri. He chided me gently for killing off Abdel Hamid.

"No, Moussa. It was a suicide," I said. "A hopeless case. Pure and simple."

With ABC back in business it was impossible to avoid the bureau malaise. All I knew for certain was that the ABC bureau had lost its heart and soul in a nasty crisis of confidence that seemed to date back several months. The fact that the conscientious Hassan had chosen to take his three-week vacation the day after my arrival pointed me in the right direction. I soon learned that ABC suspected Hassan of complicity in the case of the confiscated tapes – that he must have been the mysterious government "friend"; the assumption being that since he was responsible for airport shipments and the infamous tapes had been seized and switched at Cairo International Airport en route to London, he was in a position to tip off Egyptian security. The lack of evidence or accusation did not dilute the ramifications: a demoralized Egyptian staff already estranged from its American bureau chief, producer and cameraman; a bureau split down the middle in which the foreign masters mistrusted the local help and the locals in turn mistrusted the foreigners – an environment hardly conducive to high-level performance and team effort. Worse, the Egyptian staff was now suffering regular harassment from the Security Police in the wake of the general political and religious crackdown and the expulsion of the bureau chief. It was an untenable situation and I was determined to get to the bottom of it if only out of sheer self-interest.

The hapless Hassan, now under attack from both sides, ABC News *and* the Egyptian government, was understandably enraged.

Was the erosion of confidence in the bureau deep enough for Hassan to have deliberately sabotaged his own bureau chief by alerting Security of the anti-Sadat tapes even though Hassan – the anti-Sadater – would have applauded the broadcast of such tapes? Or was he intimidated and coerced into collaborating with the security forces? Or was he simply a victim of an efficient state apparatus and a paranoid and/or misinformed ABC News?

My initial instinct that the latter was more likely the case would be borne out by the facts – facts easily accessible to anyone interested enough in digging them out. Cairo bureau chief Harper was in London. His tapes with the controversial anti-Sadat Hirst interview were in Cairo. Also in Cairo that day: a massive rather ugly protest demonstration staged by Moslem fundamentalists which Hassan and the camera crew covered – at Hassan's journalistic initiative. As the ABC team was departing the scene with video cassettes of same in hand, security police attempted to detain them and confiscate the tapes. A military officer – a general, in fact, seeing the commotion, interjected, ordering the security men to let the ABC team and the tapes go, "For now," he shouted.

Later that day, Hassan notified the ABC London bureau that he was shipping the "protest demonstration" tapes. Bureau chief Harper also requested that his "Hirst interview" tapes be shipped as well. Apparently he had neglected to hand-carry them with him to London. Hassan's assistant – as was normal – delivered both sets of tapes to the airport that night. And as normal – was greeted by a security man. What was abnormal was the presence of a censor who refused to allow shipment of the tapes. At midnight the ABC shipper called Hassan from the airport requesting that he come sort out the censor problem. It is now clear what the General had in mind earlier in the day.

Hassan arrived at the airport adamantly refusing to co-operate until the Minister of State for Information Mansour Hassan was consulted. Hassan and Mansour Hassan consulted via telephone, following which the Minister gave the order to the censor to permit the tapes to be shipped to London. The censor complied. Hassan left the airport. Between his departure and the morning flight to London the security official decided to take matters into his own hands. He confiscated and switched the tapes. While screening the incriminating tapes, i.e. the "protest demonstration" tapes, he inadvertently discovered the Harper-Hirst anti-Sadat interview.

And on that note I stopped playing private eye. The damage had already been done. And it was irreparable.

Outside the bureau there was an equally eerie emptiness. The only sounds to be heard above the Cairo din were the voices of the muezzin calling the faithful to prayer and Anwar Sadat declaring war on another front in another effort to justify his original call to arms which, much to his annoyance, continued to receive a bad foreign press. He hoped to subdue us by pulling out the Soviet card. The Soviets, he announced, were plotting to overthrow him, were actively involved in the sectarian troubles; and to prove it he went on Egyptian television armed with another three-hour speech and Egyptian security film clips of alleged secret meetings between Soviet embassy spooks and their Egyptian friends. To punish the meddlers he expelled the Soviet ambassador, six other Soviet diplomats, the *Tass* correspondent, another journalist and more than a thousand Soviet technical advisors and their families.

Then he set about travelling the country, drowning himself in the canned applause of the masses, attending popular rallies, opening new plants, desert towns and other pilot projects. Sadat's "desert is blooming" PR swing through the Delta was meant to show a strong, secure President in total command; one ready to crush fanatics and other troublemakers; one able to boast that "discipline has been restored to Egypt". But that nagging question still dominated private conversations: was there a real threat to the Sadat regime? Most Egyptians didn't think so and funnily enough neither did Sadat – to believe his speeches.

In yet another attempt to justify his crackdown on religious and political opponents he announced in a speech to his National Democratic Party's congress – live on TV – that he did it to avert another Iranian or Lebanese –style "bloodbath". Furthermore, he said, he had a list of more than seven thousand Islamic fundamentalists who would be rounded up if trouble broke out again. He even singled out one un-named extremist who had eluded the police dragnet first time around, confessing that: "One of you is going to betray me and I know who you are," said Sadat. "You got away this time but I will get you." "Bloodbaths" notwithstanding, in the next breath he claimed he was in no danger of being toppled nor was Egypt falling apart at the seams. The religious fanatics, he explained, were simply getting out of hand and had to be crushed to protect future generations. As for silencing his political opponents – they were "not opponents" he assured one and all but "enemies of Egypt" who abused their democratic freedom – simply "haters". So if his regime was not in danger why the wholesale clean-up? Some knowledgeable Egyptians felt it could only be the Israelis; that they were getting nervous about what they perceived as the fundamentalist threat to Sadat and the peace treaty. Whatever and whoever, Sadat's war on the fundamentalists now included daily potshots of ridicule. For example, in the speech to the Party Congress, he poked fun at them by saying: "They quote the Koran as saying God created man to worship him only, so they argue they do not have to learn anything, or even work, just pray all day and night . . . they say women should stay at home and if they go out should wear a veil with slits for eyes and a robe that makes them look like a tent. These are ways strange to us, strange to our teachings and our beliefs," said Sadat. Given the various strains and interpretations of Islamic teachings and given the fresh passions aroused by the arrests of hundreds of fundamentalists, Sadat's visceral contempt for this growing constituency was guaranteed to unleash a fundamentalist rage the dimensions of which we could not assess because he had by now dangerously suppressed the movement, driven it underground.

Those of us who heard or saw Sadat's Party Congress speech – in fact the last of his life – would never forget it. We were struck by the image of a desperate man, a leader flailing in panic, an Anwar Sadat out of control.

Egypt's summer of discontent then had turned into an autumn of disquiet:

"The political atmosphere is charged with silence. A deafening, penetrating silence," I began, in a radio "Perspective" dated October 6, 1981.

I left it unrecorded to go out and cover another story.

I had covered this story before and the thought of covering it again did not excite me. Apart from the forty-five minute journey through Cairo traffic I would have to stand on a parade ground trying to pretend I knew the difference between a MiG, a Mirage and a Phantom. But it was Sadat's favourite day of the year and he would be there and I could no longer avoid him. By the time the camera crew and I arrived at the checkpoint about one quarter of a mile from the parade stand in the north east Cairo suburb of Nasr City, the ritual row was underway between the media and military security, and after fifteen minutes of mutual verbal abuse, our cars were cleared to enter the parade route, but only to deposit us. Unlike previous years, non-official vehicles were prohibited from parking in the area. As planned, the media were in place and free to roam about, a good hour before the scheduled start and, while the atmosphere seemed more relaxed than I had remembered in the past, the security men seemed abnormally conscientious in their checks. In four years my bag had never been so thoroughly searched; cosmetics and other unmentionables were inspected piece by piece with a request to explain the purpose of each. Only when I assured the slightly embarrassed officer that each served no purpose other than to clutter my bag and complicate his job, did he proceed to dissect my ballpoint pens and other menacing objects. My lunch, a pear, was left intact. We parted with a smile secure in the knowledge that the media posed no physical threat.

Having made it this far I was determined to enjoy the October 6 celebration. In fact it was shaping up into Old Home Week: it had been a year since I'd last seen many colleagues – foreign and Egyptian – and it was good to see some familiar faces again and catch up on the local gossip. One of my favourite Sadat bodyguards wanted to know why I was dressed in black trousers and T-shirt?:

"I'm in mourning", I joked.

"Then why are you wearing those red shoes and that belt?" he laughed.

"So no one will notice." I jested.

By now the grandstand had filled up with hundreds of Egyptian officials, military and civilian; foreign diplomats, military attachés, visiting VIPs from various countries, foreign journalists and privileged family members of officials including dozens of children. Shortly before 11:00 a.m. the President and Vice President swept into sight aboard an open-air limousine complete with eight bodyguards astride running boards and others running on foot – front and back and both sides – in American presidential style. It was traditional for Sadat and his party to assemble at the Defence Ministry in nearby Heliopolis for the fifteen to thirty minute ride to the parade ground, so he could feed off the applause of crowds clumped along part of the route and hanging from balconies in the modern high-rise apartments built for the military in a district newly carved out of the desert. The route along which the military display would move was always off-bounds to the masses, who would have to watch the festivities on television.

When Sadat stepped out of his car and saluted his officers, he looked absolutely stunning. Had I not grown so weary of his imperial majesty I could have fallen in love with him; the *image* of him as symbolized by his impeccable costume: blue-grey jacket flashing with ceremonial medals, wide green sash and Star of Sinai; jodhpurs, the glistening knee-high black boots, the gold-braided cap – the field marshal's uniform of Egypt's Supreme Commander of the Armed Forces. Although it did not seem to be an exact replica of his 1978 and 1979 uniforms, it had the same Savile Row tailoring, and his larger companions – Vice President Hosni Mubarak and Defence Minister General Abdel Halim Abu Ghazala – decked out in similar matching outfits, were dwarfed by the shorter, trimmer Sadat.

As a martial band played in the background the trio walked across the traffic-free six-lane parade route where Sadat laid a wreath at the foot of the modernistic pyramidal arch that is Egypt's Tomb of the Unknown Soldier. The camera crews and photographers scrambled back to their parade positions and ten minutes later, after the customary footage of Sadat sitting front-row centre in the reviewing stand, the pomp and ceremony he so loved got underway in earnest with the traditional opening prayer from the Koran. The Defence Minister then moved to a podium to recount in glowing terms the glory that was Egypt's that October day in 1973 when Egyptian forces stormed across the Suez Canal and smashed the Israeli Bar-Lev line. Although the Israelis would turn the war in their favour, the "Yom Kippur War" was Egypt's "War of Liberation", its greatest military triumph; a moral victory that wiped out the shame and humiliation of the Arab debacle that was the June '67 war.

October 6, 1973 was perhaps Sadat's finest hour. Hailed as the "hero of the crossing" he now had the ammunition he wanted to wage his long-calculated peace campaign. In the eight years since, he had moved from local to international hero; a force no one could ignore, no one would ignore.

Now, from a distance of about fifty feet, as the speeches droned on, I watched him intently – this beleaguered, besieged, larger-than-life figure, and wondered if he was any longer in a position to know why he was so beleaguered and besieged; he looked so detached, so haughty, so lonely.

Here at least, I thought, he must feel secure, in the company of his loyal troops whom he always so fondly referred to as "my sons". Indeed he was one of them, had come from their ranks, knew their potential for trouble and tried accordingly to attend to their moods and military needs. Some were unhappy with the slow pace of modernization and delivery of American arms to replace the obsolete Soviet-supplied arsenal, but there was no doubting the loyalty of his generals and colonels, and his Defence Minister was popular with the men in the barracks. The air force, thanks to its former popular commander, Vice President Mubarak, was equally loyal. There was no fear of a military coup.

Trying to read Sadat's face during times when he was neither publicly enraged nor exuberantly on show was a little like a non-Egyptologist trying to decipher a hieroglyphic code. I turned away to scan the reviewing stand: no security net between the President and his "sons"; those who had been milling about in front of the five-foot high wall that stood between Sadat and the parade route had by now been dismissed and the hundreds of military police and republican guards either stood at attention, at ease, or milled about on the grounds and in the stands – a colourful assortment of red berets, orange berets, blue berets, green berets, pistols and bayonets. The dozen or so members of his security detail – the American-trained plainclothes bodyguards – tended to take a back seat to the military in accordance with the occasion and Sadat's wishes. They were scattered throughout the stand and on the ground and one, his oldest and most trusted who also acted as his personal secretary, Fawzi Abdul Hafez, was seated as usual directly behind the President. Although he was younger than Sadat he gave the impression of being much older and considerably less fit. All were equipped with pistols and all seemed proficient at protecting Sadat in small-crowd encounters, ever alert for the single assassin lying in wait to destroy the hero who inspired such passions of love and hate. High above the crowd in a glass-enclosed box sat Mrs Sadat and her grandchildren; not far below US Ambassador Alfred Atherton, British Ambassador Sir Michael Weir, Israeli Ambassador Moshe Sasson (who had succeeded Eliahu Ben-Elissar) and other identifiable notables packed into the roughly fifteen hundred wooden chairs set up on the presidential dias – all seemingly seated in alphabetical order of countries represented. A fairly predictable lot of diplomatic and military VIPs.

I was far more fascinated by the presence of one Egyptian official; one who made a habit of never attending public events, especially military parades. On spotting him I almost fell off my concrete perch and had to steady myself for a concentrated double-take. Desperately trying to appear inconspicuous in the middle of the crowd, sat Sadat's chief foreign policy advisor and had it not been for his rather unorthodox dress I'd have missed him: a white, open-neck shirt dominating a dark jacket, giving him the appearance of an Oxford doctoral candidate out slumming. In spite of my more conspicuously casual demeanour – rolled-up black trousers, red shoes, green pear and reporter's stare – he pretended not to notice me. I knew it was not the sunny, balmy dry October day that had prompted Osama el-Baz to desert the inner sanctum of the Foreign Ministry. The reason would have to wait: the two-hour display of men and machines was starting to roll. Everyone now seemed more relaxed and even Sadat was fiddling with his pipe in preparation for a good show on the ground and in the air. The camera crew – set up on the shoulder of the six-lane parade route – was already taping random shots of the first units passing by and a glance in the direction of the assembly point revealed one long, unbroken human wave of young conscripts high-stepping their way in formation past their President – or rather the man they assumed was their President, since they knew him only by pictures and television. Even though I'd seen it all before, the colourful Camel Corps got me into the spirit of things and before I knew it I was tapping my feet to the band music, oohing and ahing at the fireworks, clapping at the parachutists who managed to hit their targets smack on, a few yards in front of Sadat whom they saluted before jogging off. The armoured personnel carriers all looked like they came from the same country and I decided they did, but when a particular tank tracked by I knew it was the prized American M-60 because Defence Minister Abu Ghazala, who was sitting at Sadat's left, was chatting away with the nodding President, perhaps assuring him that there was something at least to show for all those ballyhooed billions in promised American hardware. Apart from the occasional engine failure – a couple of stalled trucks and motorcycles – it was shaping up into a better-than-average October 6 parade. Nonetheless my CBS competitor and I agreed it was hardly sexy enough to stir the imaginations and line-ups of our evening news producers back in New York. We also remarked on our NBC competitors being conspicuous by their absence, joking about the scoop they were probably working on while we were shooting hundreds of feet of file footage.

Slightly more than an hour into the show the Egyptian Air Force finally started showing off, especially the Mirage pilots who came equipped with glamorous trails of red, blue, green, yellow and grey smoke so they could play aerobatic games in the brilliant blue heavens. Just in case some of us missed their exciting stunts they kept coming back for more – six French-made jet fighters sneaking up on us from behind, seemingly out of nowhere – barely clearing the slanted semi-open concrete roof and spectators underneath, their thunderous roar swooshing us instinctively into crouch positions, hands over heads, ears and eyes in anticipation of the bombs that never fell and the crashes that never materialized.

"They didn't have kamikaze performances last year, did they?" I asked an Egyptian photographer looking for shelter. The look on his face matched my suspicions, which I tried hiding by glibly allowing that, if this were peace, I didn't think I'd much like war.

At least they were more entertaining than the drab green remnants of antiquated Soviet vehicles passing by virtually unnoticed on the ground; crawling along as though they were ashamed to be seen in public; a sign that the parade was winding up; another half hour at most and it would be over.

By now Françoise Demulder, a Beirut-based photographer who had covered more than her share of war had joined me, but whatever she was saying was soon drowned out by the continuing spectacle overhead. From our standing positions midway between the parade route and the reviewing stand all eyes, including ours, were involuntarily lifted skywards as the Mirages swooped up out of their low dives to link up in a rainbow embrace. Thrills galore. And more:

Gunfire. Shots. From that bland Russian lorry. The one over there. A few yards away. In front of us. Soldiers standing up in the back. One with a rifle. Gunfire crackling. Soldiers jumping out. How many? Two. Three. Four. Six. Eight. More? Soldiers running. Carrying rifles. Submachine guns. Weapons. Live ammunition. Listen. Running towards us. Towards the reviewing stand. Two soldiers. Shouting. What are they shouting? Why are they shouting? Paralysis. Silence. Deadly. Only gunfire. Shots. Whistling past me.

No. Not real. Can't be. Part of the show. Yes. A demonstration. For Sadat. For *el Raïs*. Yes. Yes. That's it. That explains it. No. Yes. No.

No.

No.

Real.

Move.

I move. Slow motion. Towards the stand. Towards Sadat. Parallel with the soldiers I move. The shooting soldiers. Soldiers in faded green battle fatigues. Moving towards the stand. It is a blur. Gone. Erased. Where is Sadat? No Sadat. No front row. Only chairs. Flying. People. Screaming. Guns. Firing. Piercing screams. Panic in the grandstand. Panic everywhere. Pandemonium. Bullets.

Where is the cameraman. Is he safe? Is he taping? Is his camera rolling? Is he recording this story? Real. Unreal. Story. "Doreen. Get down!"

Who said that? Who's shouting at me?

"Doreen. Don't stand there. Out in the open like that."

He grabs me. Hossaim, the ABC chauffeur who came to help out the crew because Hassan was just returning from vacation that morning. Hossaim yanks me with him, several yards further to the right of the grandstand. Away from the battle. Behind an army truck. We crouch. I don't like it here. Who is this soldier staring me in the face? Bent down. Holding a rifle. Pointing it at me. Young boy; sixteen, seventeen, eighteen years-old? Is this a terrorist attack or a military coup? He's scared. Poor boy. Stunned. Like the rest of us.

"Hossaim. Let me go. I must go. I have to see. See Sadat. Where is he? Is he hurt? Is he wounded?"

Silence. Time. What time is it?

No more shots. No more gunfire. Over. It's over. All over.

Forty-five seconds? Sixty seconds? Ninety seconds? Three minutes? Five minutes? Ten minutes? An eternity.

I leave my refuge, walk the few yards to the grandstand. People are shouting, screaming, running, walking, wandering, bleeding. Some pass me – dazed, uncomprehending, blank stares for faces. I move freely through the flailing mêlée of military police officials and security men shouting frantically at each other in a futile effort to construct order out of the chaos. No one is free to block my passage up the few steps into the presidential front row. No Sadat. No Mubarak. They are long gone. Where? How? In what condition? Alive? Dead?

Only a jumble of chairs. Blood. Contortions. The debris of a cyclone or whatever it was that unleashed its fury only moments ago. A few feet away, the cameraman is busily focusing his lens on the oriental carpeting; picking up blood, a mangled arm, a body nearby. There is no time to lose. He hands me a video cassette, takes another out of the recorder, hands that to me and inserts a fresh one, ready to resume the ritual of shooting everything in sight: the dead, the wounded, whoever and wherever. I have no way of knowing. No time. Clearly most people have left the stand or been taken out of it; ambulances and private cars continue to arrive and depart. None of it concerns me. Only Sadat. And he's gone. Somewhere. Somehow.

My only mission remains to get back to the bureau as quickly as is humanly possible, with the tapes and an eyewitness account. All I know is that the cameraman managed to record some of the action. I stuff both tapes in my bag, which I clutch in my arms like a dying baby. I cannot afford to be stopped, questioned, harassed. I must get out of the parade ground unimpeded. As I set off I pass a cabinet minister – a former prime minister – alone and aimless, in a state of shock. I want to ask him "What happened?" No time. If security should get its act together I am finished. Perhaps. I run, run the half mile over pavement and sand to where I hope Dessouki and the car might be waiting for me. Crowds of puzzled bystanders and police block an intersection. They seem to be calmly waiting, as though for President Sadat to drive by. Hossaim and Françoise catch up with me and together we negotiate our way through knots of traffic towards an improvised car park. Frenzied minutes later, Dessouki is located. He needs no instructions. He at least has heard the news. Françoise and I jump into the back of the car, hide the tapes under a front seat and Dessouki speeds off faster than anything on wheels has a right to move. If we reach the bureau it will be in record time. We do and it is: twenty minutes flat – forty minutes after the first bursts of gunfire. It is roughly 1:45 p.m. My competitive mind wonders what has become of my CBS colleagues. I don't have to worry about NBC. I tear up three flights of stairs, burst through the door shouting for someone to get me Radio News on the line pronto, forgetting it is 7:45 a.m. in New York and the breakfast TV show is on the air. Radio will have to feed off its more powerful sister. The bureau staff who had been watching the parade on Egypt TV saw the screen suddenly go blank after an abrupt pan shot of the wide blue yonder, and came to the right conclusion with no help from Egypt Radio and TV commentators, who simply announced the parade had ended, the President had left the parade ground and left it at that.

A phone is thrust at me; one equipped with a plug-in amplifier to enhance line quality; the Washington and New York TV studios are already patched into the audio line and within seconds I am reporting live to millions of Americans and Canadians; breathlessly trying to recreate a nightmare that could not have lasted more than sixty seconds; just long enough to throw history into a tailspin. That one nightmarish moment would prove to be only slightly less unpleasant than the eight hours of straight, uninterrupted, unadulterated media madness that followed in living colour on American television.

The three networks embark on a marathon orgy to outperform each other with speed and accuracy of information. We are reporting an assassination attempt that may or may not have succeeded. I was there – barely fifty feet away – when it happened. Yet, like hundreds of others present, I don't know if President Sadat is alive or dead. Our tapes reveal a spectacular made-for-TV-sequence with all the drama and suspense of as-it-happens news; news that played itself out with such blurring swiftness that only a handful of Egyptian officials were in any position to know what may have transpired and they're not about to tell us. Sadat was nowhere to be seen on the tapes.

Because the attack may be part of a coup d'état, all vital state installations are being secured, particularly communications. The Egypt Radio and TV centre across the street from the bureau is ringed with troops and tanks; satellite transmissions are banned; dubs are made of our tapes for shipment to the nearest satellite points, Amman and Athens, but Cairo International Airport is shut down as well. In the event commercial air traffic resumes, arrangements are made for private charter planes to carry the tapes out of Egypt for transmission to the States.

We are on our own: logistically, technically, editorially. The international wire agencies have started filing "urgents" and "bulletins" with dribs and drabs of information, misinformation and eyewitness accounts of the attack; I am glued to the telephone feeding radio and TV what I know and don't know; Hassan is on another telephone contacting sources and officials, feeding me valuable titbits as they become available; Hanzada is running between the wires, me and another telephone; the junior fill-in producer seems to be on a job-training programme in the editing room; the telex is burning up with messages and conversations with London and New York.

I soon learn from reliable sources that a colonel from an intelligence unit has been missing for two weeks – with copies of the parade plans; and that at least two other fundamentalist-inspired plots to assassinate Sadat have been foiled in the same period. I pass this on.

We still don't know Sadat's status. Only that he was taken to Maadi Military Hospital. We are in contact with hospital officials. The US embassy informs Washington that Sadat has indeed been injured, but only slightly.

When I am not actually reporting via telephone into our live programming, I am listening to a cast of thousands at the other end of the phone – correspondents, commentators, pundits, politicians, government officials, notables such as Henry Kissinger and Jimmy Carter; in short everybody and anybody who has anything to say – and several with nothing to say – seem to be saying it on ABC News. Good for the ratings. Given the interest in Sadat, none of it is considered banal. It is clear that Washington is even less informed than Cairo. No one can answer the only question that matters.

At precisely 2:50 p.m. Gumbo strolls into the bureau, turns to me and in typically dispassionate manner informs me: "He is dead."

"WHO is dead, Gumbo?"

"Sadat is dead."

"Says who?" I roar.

"The Presidency. Unofficially. Of course. They won't announce it. Not yet. For obvious reasons."

"Quick, get Hassan."

"Hassan, get on the phone immediately, to the presidential press secretary to confirm or deny that Sadat is dead."

The two charge off and within ninety seconds Hassan rushes over to declare: "Confirmed. Sadat is dead. He is dead."

For the next fifteen minutes I engage in a battle with my colleagues in New York – the producers, executives and anchor-men handling the live coverage; they are nervous about going with the news. In spite of the fact that they concede our sources have proved unimpeachable in the past (i.e. that we are wired into the information network, above and below ground) they are hesitant, given the magnitude and implications of the death, but more importantly because of the bitter memories of the American network fiasco over the assassination attempt on President Reagan earlier in the year, when all three networks pronounced Reagan's press secretary, Jim Brady, dead, when in fact he was alive. Caution then was the order of the day, at least at ABC.

To my mind this is not a case of caution but insanity and I am angry. We have the lead on Sadat's death – there is no doubt in my mind that the confirmation, however unofficial, is accurate, and we are frittering it away by dithering and dickering over the reliability of the press secretary. At this point I am so exasperated I want to scream. And do. That must have been enough to convince someone. I go on the air with news of Sadat's death, attributing it to Presidential Press Secretary Sharif Atiya. (Ironically Atiya's brother later served as defence counsel for Khaled el-Islambouley, one of Sadat's four assassins.) I breathe easier. Not only am I certain we are *right* but I sense we are *first* with the news, and if not, should be. Officially, the US administration still has Sadat suffering a slight arm injury. The Egyptian government remains mum.

In addition, the world has still not seen a foot of film or tape of the attack. By late afternoon the airport re-opens and Egypt Radio and TV lifts the ban on satellite transmissions. An alert ABC London bureau informs the Cairo producer that BBC TV has a line booked to feed Visnews film, and we join the BBC satellite to London. Shortly after, ABC New York is receiving our dramatic, unedited pictures. Unfortunately so are CBS and NBC who transmit them to their viewers, simultaneously, erroneously crediting the visuals to Egypt TV. Once that mess is resolved, it is clear the ABC footage – attacking soldiers, mayhem and bloody aftermath – is the best available anywhere; award-winning "bang-bang", in the crude parlance of showbiz journalism. Within hours the ABC pictures would be broadcast throughout the world and replayed ad nauseam with electrifying freeze-frame emphasis.

An hour or so after the pictures are televised for the first time, the still-silent Egypt TV finally interrupts regular programming with readings from the Koran – a sign that Sadat is indeed dead. New York is anxiously standing by to record the expected official announcement and I have moved to another telephone and another room, one with a television monitor, to be in position to supply voice-over simultaneous translation of the Arabic, with the able assistance of Hanzada Fikry. I am ensconced in the editing room when Khaled, the young Egyptian trainee editor, requests permission to turn off the lights for a couple of minutes, the better to fix a piece of equipment. In the dark he trips over the phone wire, pulling the plug and the connection out of the wall.

I do not believe this is happening. After six hours of non-stop communication with New York, I am now without my only link to ABC and our live coverage. At this point there is but one thing to do: commit suicide. While I contemplate the best means available, Hassan contacts our faithful telephone repair man who arrives within ten minutes. But not all the skill and *baksheesh* in the world seem able to produce a quick fix. The clock ticks away.

The Egyptian Cabinet is in session. Vice President Hosni Mubarak could appear on television any moment. An hour passes. The Cairo correspondent might as well be in China. A preoccupied Allah has deserted us. Seven hours after the assassination, shortly after 8:00 p.m., a grieving Mubarak appears on the screen to inform Egypt and the world of the death of the President: Mohammed Anwar el-Sadat is dead. Assassinated at the age of sixty-two. Five minutes into his address – as he is assuring America (and Israel) of Egypt's continuing commitment to Sadat's peace policies, the treaty, Camp David and all international obligations, just what America needs to hear – my umbilical cord is re-connected.

I manage to provide an English translation of the Vice-President's remarks, but by now he is midway through his address. It no longer matters. We have lost our competitive edge. As our marathon live coverage ends, I imagine the scene at ABC News New York: Roone Arledge ABC News President is watching his three monitors – as he has all day – clocking the performances of CBS, NBC and ABC. When Mubarak finally pops up on all three screens, he hears voice-over simultaneous translation from NBC's Cairo correspondent and CBS's Cairo bureau chief. He hears nothing from ABC Cairo. He flies into a rage demanding to know what the hell is going on. He is not interested in dead telephones. He cannot afford to be.

Since my day is only half over, I cannot afford to indulge further in mind readings and scenarios of what the brass may or may not be doing, or who won the day's battle of the ratings. I still have the "Evening News", the "Late Night News" and "Nightline" to think about, not to mention radio. More importantly, I have to come up with a few more facts and details than have become available thus far. I have work to do.

By the time the flying media circus and superstars arrive from London and New York I have managed to put together a respectable first-hand account of the assassination of Anwar Sadat.

By 4:00 a.m. the final story is good-nighted and I have to get some sleep before "Good Morning America" goes on the air. As I leave the bureau I think of my competitors for the first time: NBC missed the entire assassination scene, and the CBS correspondent, assuming Egypt TV would be shut down, flew to Rome with his tapes – about the same time

Egypt TV re-opened for business. ABC had nothing to be ashamed of. Except, of course, that dead telephone. Or so I thought.

I return to my hotel suite, I step out on the balcony. I need the peace of the Nile. A moment's reflection.

All that comes to mind is a night eight months earlier: a farewell party on the eve of my permanent departure from Cairo. I remember asking the hostess, a dear friend and journalist, Nabila Megalli, if she would read my coffee cup. Her track record was too good not to exploit.

"Please, Nabila, I pleaded. I can't go to Paris without a final reading."

"You have altogether too much faith in me, Doreen," she laughed. "You mustn't believe everything I see."

"I wish I didn't have to, Nabila."

Jenny Jobbins, wife of BBC correspondent Bob Jobbins, agreed, reminding Nabila of her uncanny ability to foresee the future.

She relented. In the course of her thirty-minute reading she kept returning to one theme, one dominant image: "You are going to be involved in some major drama . . . event . . . story perhaps. I can't say what it is really, or where . . . or when. But there's a man involved . . . he has a pointed head. A man wearing a peaked hat of some kind."

"Must be the Ayatollah Khomeini, or the Pope," I declared confidently. "Civil war in Iran or another attempt on the Pope's life."

Sadat had been wearing a peaked cap.

A week later, recuperating from laryngitis, I discovered – in *Time* magazine – that CBS News was being hailed as first in reporting the news of Sadat's death.

Anwar Sadat seemed to court death with all the serene abandonment of the fatalist. But the man who would say "no one will deprive me of one hour of my life before my time," seemed in the end to go out of his way to hasten its arrival. He teased it, played with it, dared it, defied it and finally the moment it came he mistook it for something else.

If his assassination was long expected and inevitable, the ugliness of it was not. Seven others were killed and many more wounded. The day after he succumbed to the bullets of his four assassins – Islamic fundamentalists – I reported in a television exclusive some rather bizarre revelations indicating that the Egyptian President's confidence and defiant arrogance had reached omnipotent proportions. Three weeks earlier, Egyptian intelligence, with the knowledge of the American CIA, foiled a plot by fundamentalists to kill Sadat. The culprits were supposedly apprehended. At the same time a military officer was on the loose and in possession of the October 6 parade plans; the same man Sadat so elliptically referred to in his September speech; the one he said would betray him; one Aboud el-Zomar. Within days at least one other fundamentalist assassination plot was foiled during Sadat's trip to Mansoura. Thought is given to cancelling the October 6 celebration. The morning of October 6, Sadat is advised not to attend the parade, for security reasons. Even though he is tired and does not feel up to attending, he rejects the advice on grounds that he must fulfil his duty. He is given a medical check-up by his physician who pronounces him in good health. When Mrs Sadat asks her husband if he is going to wear his bullet-proof vest, he replies: "Why? Where am I going? I am going to see my 'sons'." (There is no evidence Sadat ever wore the vest; he considered it unmanly.) At the parade, either out of the same pride or a desire to project a secure image, Sadat does not permit a sharpshooter in the reviewing stand tower; he does not permit military guards in the stands (only his pistol-carrying bodyguards) and he does not permit security directly in front of the five-foot high concrete wall of the dais. At the sight of the first attacking soldier, Sadat rises out of his seat.

His last word: an incredulous "*Mish mahoul*!" (Not possible).

Sadat lived with the daily threat of assassination. Indeed between 1977 and 1981 no fewer than a dozen plots were uncovered. Most were never publicly confirmed; all involved non-Egyptians. But the threat became acute with the rash of home-grown fundamentalist plots in the wake of the September crackdown on dissidents. He was aware of all of them. So was Osama el-Baz who later admitted to me that his unusual presence at the parade was prompted by suspicions that something *might* happen to Sadat, that indeed, anything was now possible. His personal bodyguards, who seemed every bit as shocked as the rest of us at the nature of the attack when it came, would come under fire in the Western media for failing to counter-attack promptly and adequately. But whether they were stunned by concussion grenades, hopelessly outgunned by the assassins' rifles and submachine guns or just plain negligent and incompetent – indeed whether there was a general intelligence and security failure – obscured the central and more historic issue: Sadat's recklessness; a seeming lack of concern about his own personal safety and security. Was he in fact a megalomaniac? Or, in the last month of his life, did the fatalist combine with the realist – who saw the assassins out there, dozens of them, knew they would get him if not today, tomorrow, and simply chose not to fight destiny. The assassins, in fact, succeeded on their third of five planned attempts to kill Sadat. Plan four was scheduled for later in the day during Sadat's traditional journey to his home village of Mit Abul Kum to pray at the tomb of his brother who had died in the October war. Had that failed, a fifth attempt was to have been made within days during another scheduled public event. Heroes, after all, do not die in their sleep, certainly not flamboyant controversial ones. Heroes inspire romantic notions. The speculation would go on endlessly. None of it really mattered any more. Only facts mattered and there was but one incontrovertible fact: Anwar Sadat was dead. Assassinated. And he would have to be buried.

On Saturday, October 10, 1981, Cairo is calm. There is none of the hysteria with which Egypt mourned the death of Gamal Abdel Nasser eleven years earlier. A state of emergency is in effect throughout the country. In the wake of the assassination, there is more death and destruction inspired by the religious fanatics but the uprisings have been quelled. Hundreds more dissidents have been detained. The streets of Cairo are all but deserted. Egyptians are at home celebrating the two-day Moslem feast of sacrifice *Eid al-Adha*. The man who considered himself the head of the "Egyptian family" is dead. The western world has come to bury him. His friends have come in sorrow to pay their last respects. They will give him a hero's farewell.

As the funeral procession moves heavily along the same route travelled by President Sadat and his assassins . . . all one can see are shoulder-to-shoulder men in dark suits; mostly foreigners; mostly Westerners. Men like former American presidents Jimmy Carter, Gerald Ford, Richard Nixon; German Chancellor Helmut Schmidt; French President Valéry Giscard d'Estaing; British Foreign Secretary Lord Carrington; the Prince of Wales; royalty, heads of state, statesmen and ambassadors from seventy-five countries; and Israeli Prime Minister Menachem Begin. He has come to say goodbye to his "dear friend Anwar" – the only Arab leader who dared make peace with him. Because of that, the Arab world has stayed home today; only Sudan, Oman and Somalia are represented at this funeral. Egypt is represented by Sadat's heir-apparent, Vice President Hosni Mubarak, and Sadat's government.

The television cameras close in on the sombre faces: the late President's son, Gamal; the late deposed Shah's son, Prince Reza; Jihan Sadat and her three daughters; the Shah's widow, Farah Diba; Mrs Gaafar Numeiri, wife of the Sudanese President – all sitting in the reviewing stand on the same dais where Sadat was killed.

As the horse-drawn caisson moves slowly towards the Tomb of the Unknown Soldier, followed by soldiers bearing medals and the same Star of Sinai Sadat was wearing when he was struck down a few yards away, the dimensions of the tragedy can no longer be ignored. Egypt TV, whose pictures are being transmitted live to hundreds of millions of viewers around the world, tries valiantly to hide the reality: this is a Western funeral for a Western hero.

Their cameras scrupulously avoid close-ups of the foreign mourners. But those of us sitting in our Cairo bureaux, in front of the TV monitors, are reporting live, one final time, to tens of millions of Americans. And for the first time in four years we are attempting to tell it like it is; to inject an element of reality and perspective into our reportage. Anwar Sadat's brutal death has finally brought US Television face to face with Anwar Sadat's life.

It is noon (dawn in New York) and I am sitting in front of a microphone with my two celebrity colleagues Barbara Walters and Peter Jennings both of whom have followed the drama of Anwar Sadat's life, both of whom have played a large part – as I have – in producing the hero the world had come to know and love. Now that he is dead and about to be buried, Walters wonders aloud on television. She is saddened, perplexed:

"Where are the Egyptians, Doreen? Where is the grief?" she asks. "Why don't we see Sadat's own people mourning his loss? Is it the security, the state of emergency in effect, the feast that is keeping Egyptians from mourning him publicly, openly?"

"Only partially." I try to explain the lack of mass mourning.

"Many *are* sad, of course, and the tight security deprives them of expressing their grief."

"But just as many are indifferent."

"And some are relieved."

"In short, the love Sadat so inspired in the West was never duplicated in Egypt."

If Walters was shocked so were millions of others for whom Sadat was a genuine, unblemished hero; a symbol of courage and peace; "one of the greatest leaders of our time".

A Western hero, a foreign hero, dead and buried.

Epilogue

PRESIDENT MOHAMMED ANWAR EL-SADAT
A HERO OF WAR AND PEACE.
HE LIVED FOR PEACE AND HE WAS MARTYRED
FOR HIS PRINCIPLES.

He would have liked his epitaph: hero and martyr. A fine Hollywood ending, sanitized for Western consumption. Unfortunately, our hero was not martyred for his principles. Peace did not kill Anwar Sadat. Anwar Sadat killed himself. And to have watched him die – slowly – of self-inflicted wounds was – in the end – to have witnessed the assassination of a corpse. Perhaps that is why I felt nothing that day. Except relief. A quiet overwhelming relief at death's rescue of Sadat from himself, and me from Sadat.

There are those who argue that the four Islamic fundamentalists who actually pulled the trigger were no more extreme or excessive than the man they felt compelled to silence. In their world, surely no more myopic than ours, the assassins and their accomplices are seen to be the real hero-martyrs. In the realm of the fanatical then – be it political or religious – there are no heroes or villains, only the hero-villain.

In the last two and a half years of his life, the Egyptian ruler had himself become a fanatic: a zealous, excessive, obsessive dictator, thanks in large measure to America and the West's approbation of him and his peace, and to the media's hysterical groupies worshipping at his feet; a combination he came to interpret as a passport to eternity as though it were a natural progression of his solo flight into history. Therein lies the tragedy of Anwar Sadat: a "hero" who got carried away with his own image of greatness; a megalomaniac with whom Egypt could no longer cope; an omniscient being who became a stranger in his own land; a personality cult who won the West and lost Egypt; a hero-villain.

Peace did not kill the visionary peacemaker. On the contrary, peace – or more accurately the Peace Initiative – braked his downfall which was inevitable given the debilitating cycle of costly, unwinnable wars, Egypt's entrenched socio-economic and political inequities, and Sadat's own inherently flawed character and personality. Peace bought him time. That is not to say that peace when it finally came in the form of a separate treaty with Israel did not paradoxically accelerate his fall. It did, unquestionably. But more because of style than substance: Sadat's repugnant obsequiousness in his courtship of America and Israel contrasted by the omnipotent disdain with which he came to treat his own seemingly less worthy subjects, grated on the Egyptian sensibility far more than the strategic shortcomings of his Camp David peace or even Egypt's pariah status in the Arab world.

To believe that the peace process – however flawed itself – killed Sadat is to deny or diminish his greatness which in its early pure stage consisted of a perspicacious judgement of Egypt's needs and national mood and the courage to act on it; to break what he called the "vicious circle of war and hatred"; to tear down the "psychological barriers" that divided Israel from her Arab neighbours. His "sacred mission" to Jerusalem in which he cracked that barrier by recognizing the reality and existence of the Jewish state had the overwhelming support of the Egyptian people for the simple reason that it offered hope; hope of a more peaceful, prosperous Egypt. Sadat had something else going for him: as a leader of the most powerful Arab country with its homogeneous population and traditional leadership role in the Arab nation, he was in a position to do what less viable, less influential Arab leaders could not: he could afford to play the maverick, lead the way, break out of the Arab fold if that was the eventual price to be paid for peace – for Egypt. Indeed one can't help but think that some of his more strident Arab critics must secretly have envied him his "electric-shock" diplomacy if only because theatrical action was a refreshing departure from the theatrical rhetoric Arab leaders, including Sadat, had practised so numbingly for so long.

One should also bear in mind that neither Sadat nor his visions of peace were born in November 1977. He'd been in power for at least seven years before the Western media propelled him into world orbit, as a reward for his peaceful plunge into enemy territory.

The man Egyptians disparagingly called "Nasser's poodle" when he inherited the presidency in 1970; the man American and other Western leaders didn't think would last beyond a few weeks or months, was the same man who in 1971 made his first peace offering to Israel by approving the US Rogers Plan. That it failed did not deter Sadat from pursuing his twin objective: peace with Israel and the American connection he saw as vital for the future of Egypt and the Middle East. In 1972 he then pushed forward and kicked the Soviets out of Egypt.

In 1973 he launched what can only be called the "peace war". Egypt's military success in the early days of the October War was all he needed to restore Arab and Egyptian honour so bloodied and battered from the '67 debacle. With head held high and olive branch in hand he moved another step closer to America and peace with Israel.

In 1974 his "friend Henry" Kissinger negotiated the first Sinai Disengagement Agreement. In 1975 came the Second Sinai Disengagement

Agreement. And that same year Sadat wooed the Americans by re-opening the Suez Canal to international traffic. In 1977 – after two years of no war – no peace and with little prospect of winning either, given Arab fractiousness and Israeli political and military supremacy, he bolted. He met the Israelis face to face – on their own turf. Egypt he decided could not wait forever.

In 1978 – to prove his point – he signed the American sponsored and negotiated Camp David Peace Accords: one outlined peace between Egypt and Israel, complete with Egyptian sovereignty over all Sinai; the other called for negotiations on autonomy for the Palestinians living in the Israeli-occupied West Bank of the Jordan and the Gaza Strip.

In 1979 he signed – finally – his peace treaty with Israel. His seven-year warm-up indicated he had been willing to go it alone, to cut a separate deal if necessary. Clearly in the end he had wanted a peace treaty and the Sinai, at any cost. That is all he got, largely because Israel was able to exploit Sadat's weak bargaining position. Camp David and the Treaty, then, made a mockery of Sadat's own passionate and sincere plea for "peace with justice". To his credit he had succeeded single-handedly in winning American support away from Israel and in pricking the Western conscience on the moral and political imperatives of five million stateless Palestinians which is more than any other Arab leader had done, but there was no disguising the final analysis: Sadat had sold out the Palestinians, with a little help from the Americans and the Israelis. And Israel, by neutralizing its most formidable Arab enemy had made a resolution of the "core and crux of the problem" more remote than ever, its intention all along being to bury the Palestinians along with their aspirations of a national homeland. Begin's strategy was divide and rule. He won the day. It is just as well that Anwar Sadat never lived to see subsequent manifestations of the Begin peace strategy. As it was, the Egyptian President would spend the rest of his days arguing that he had not done what he did. Stubbornly he kept hoping against hope that Egypt's treaty with Israel was but the "first step towards a comprehensive peace", insisting that once the benefits and realities of the Treaty started filtering through to the Israelis, the remaining barriers including Menachem Begin himself would melt like chocolate in the desert sun, no matter that the evidence littering the road to Camp David and back indicated otherwise.

In spite of it all, the majority of Egyptians supported the Peace Treaty just as they had supported Sadat's journey to Israel in search of peace. Like Sadat they cared about the Palestinians but like Sadat they cared about themselves and poor Egypt more. One can hardly fault them for that. They were fed up with war and poverty. A weary nation. Enough was enough. Egypt could not wait forever, especially not Sadat.

Those riots that struck the country ten months earlier were not simply riots over food price increases that were about to hit the consumer with the government's announcement that it was pulling subsidies out from under daily staples. Nor, as Sadat claimed, were the riots communist-inspired. Egyptians claim Egypt was in no need of "outside agitation". The riots, in fact, were a popular uprising; a warning from the have-nots to the haves that they wanted more; the message being that if they couldn't have their share, the greedy ten per cent should be deprived of theirs. The majority of Egyptians had come to feel like second-class citizens in a new consumer society spawned by Sadat's 1974 *Infitah* (Open Door) economic liberalization policy through which the nouveaux riches passed on their way to join the established rich, flaunting their foreign luxury wares as they went – everything from German cars, French perfume, Japanese video recorders, American jeans and British bon-bons to the hard currencies and cultural cornucopia that come with privilege and exposure to other worlds. The haves lived in nice apartments with telephones. The have-nots, including millions of university graduates, lived in cramped quarters with little or no bribe money to help them communicate via phone, so they took to the streets. The rioters who burned and looted in explosive frustration, and more significantly the silent majority who looked on sympathetically, chose as their main target Cairo's gaudy nightclub strip along Pyramid Road; a fitting symbol of the playgrounds of the wealthy who in addition to earning more in one week than the majority could earn in a lifetime, seemed exempt from the moral restrictions inhibiting the society.

The riots struck Sadat like an earthquake. Jerusalem and peace followed, not that peace would significantly improve life in Egypt. Peace, however, successfully distracted the masses. It put them on hold – a bit longer.

There is little doubt that Sadat gambled from the start on peace with Israel in the hope that an end to no wars–no peace, the return of the Sinai to Egyptian sovereignty and American largesse to help revive Egypt, would keep him in power, stave off the domestic hostilities to policies that seemed only to reinforce the status quo and feed the endemic corruption of a society whose legendary patience and passivity could not always be taken for granted. It was a politically astute move.

Jerusalem. Camp David. The Peace Treaty. And all the cliff-hanging dramas in-between. He mesmerized us – you and me – with his vision, his courage, his charm, his derring-do, his defiance; this charismatic hero of singular purpose; this Noble Peace Prize winner; this Arab anomaly who left the Israelis at the backstage door; this super-star of TV screen and glossy magazines; this political giant who inspired normally sober-minded journalists, writers, politicians and statesmen into an ecstasy of poetic paens and superlatives. Hardly a day passed when I or my media colleagues did not remind you of the greatness of Anwar Sadat, all the more so because of the smallness of the insufferable Menachem Begin, his so-called "partner in peace".

In those halycon days of peace I confess that I for one soon came to loathe Menachem Begin and all he stood for and against; a pygmy, ill-equipped to stand beside a giant. If my reports revealed any underlying pro-Egyptian or Arab bias, it was nicely offset by the pro-Israeli position emanating from my Jewish (ABC) colleagues in Tel Aviv and Jerusalem. In any case, ABC News gained a reputation for balanced coverage during the peace era, thus meeting the objective of fairness. Swept along then, by a phenomenon called peace and desperately wanting to believe in it, my Cairo media colleagues and I felt obliged to give peace and the peacemaker a chance. We were loathe to criticize the shortcomings and dangers of either in our dispatches and transmissions – we trusted the pundits would do their job but by and large they were more overwhelmed by Sadat than we were. The result was that we gave the audience – the expectant like-minded Western audience – what it couldn't seem to get enough of and we nurtured and coddled Anwar Sadat, this precious commodity so fragile he could not be left out of sight, not one public moment if only because some nasty Arab might kill him before our very cameras. (And God forbid that we should miss *that*.)

All in all, Sadat was the "good" guy and Begin the "bad" guy and as one who helped transmit that good-guy image it is not surprising that Sadat came to be pleased with my performance. I was too preoccupied with the job at the time to notice, but much later I would learn – from officials, journalists and diplomats – that Sadat "liked" me, found me a "challenge" so they say. Being female and of Arab abstraction, I was reminded, did not hurt my favoured status. Although in time I would come to dislike, even disown Sadat out of sheer frustration at his behaviour, mistakes and miscalculations, I too liked and admired him enormously in those early days and indeed fed off his power and success. Had we ever reached a first-name basis I would have thanked him for sweeping me into the pages of *Who's Who in America* – that annual listing of supposed VIPs. (Now that I am a nobody again I trust I've been struck off the list.)

Daily pampered then by American television at home and abroad and regularly reminded of his virtues during forays into the power palaces of Washington and the West, it is little wonder that Anwar Sadat believed he might be God. There were days in fact when I thought I was halluci-nating so palpable was the halo circling somewhere between Sadat's brow and crown. Those first sixteen months of media and public adoration literally went to the man's head. That was the beginning of the end.

From then on – from the signing of the Peace Treaty in Washington on March 26, 1979 – to the horrific end – it was hard to believe Sadat was not working from a master plan for self-destruction. The majority of Egyptians had stuck with him along the rocky road to peace. They were still with him. So were the political and religious dissidents – a minority albeit an irritating one – with legitimate and persuasive arguments against what clearly appeared to be a separate peace with Israel negotiated against a backdrop of Israeli intractability and American impotence. Shackled by a pseudo-democracy which Sadat had instituted as a good-will gesture to America during his seven-year prelude to peace, the opposition nonetheless was making itself heard and felt. Yet, the troublemakers in and out of government – the squawking intelligentsia that in most countries attempts to play the role of a nation's intellectual, moral and social conscience – hardly constituted a unified or viable opposition in Egypt, let alone a threat to the regime. Furthermore there was no broad-based grass-roots anti-Sadat movement, no anti-peace demonstrations, the media was controlled by Sadat, the Parliament stacked with his party supporters. Where was the threat? Those thirteen misguided missiles in Parliament who voted "no" to the Treaty? Those powerless Egyptian scribes like the Nasserist, Mohamed Heikal voicing doubts and attacking Sadat's domestic and foreign policies in *The Sunday Times* and other Western publications? Those ex-foreign ministers living out their memoirs on the cocktail circuit? Hardly – Sadat's critics were simply an embarrassment, an affront to his glorified sense of self. Who were these mere Egyptians to criticize him when all the world sanctified him and his peace?

Interpreting criticism as threat, the egocentric Sadat set about dissolving the very Parliament that had overwhelmingly endorsed his peace treaty; rigging the national referendum on the treaty when it was in no need of his ritual tampering; banning all public debate on the treaty during the campaign to elect a new Parliament; rigging those elections to ensure that the thirteen MPs who voted "no" would never sit in his Parliament again (twelve never did); preventing other candidates opposed to him or his policies from running for office, and eliminating the small official opposition parties of the left and right, replacing them with his own official opposition party of which he was also nominal head. In his little experiment with democracy what he gave with one hand he took away with both.

Whatever political freedom of expression existed before the peace treaty was further curtailed. With one swift blow Sadat emasculated Parliament – a move that amounted to a vote of no confidence in the Egyptian people. And the people didn't like it. The Pharoah, it seemed, could not be criticized. Nor his family, his peace, his economy, nor the corruption and vested interests that made it run in circles. If you were not with the Pharoah, you were agin him. No ifs, ands or buts. His worst enemies could not have done a better job of eroding Sadat's popular support.

His new friends didn't help. The Israelis no longer bothered camouflaging their nefarious intentions concerning the Camp David Accord dealing with the Palestinians. The negotiations for "autonomy" – the only thing that might have allowed Sadat a modicum of face-saving with his Egyptian and Arab critics – were conducted against a background of regularly proscribed "facts on the ground" in the occupied West Bank: Jewish settlements built as fast as public land could be cleared and Arab land confiscated. That the minister responsible for planning and implementing these bouts of provocation – Ariel Sharon – was dubbed the "Bulldozer" by some of his own people was of little comfort to a cornered Sadat and Egypt. That the United States seemed neither willing nor able to force Israel to halt the *fait accompli*; that the de facto annexation of the West

Bank and East (Arab) Jerusalem, and Israel's first invasion of Lebanon were carried out while autonomy talks were underway, not only humiliated Sadat but made him look the fool and traitor his detractors were convinced he was. Yet he took it, took the humiliation lying down which in turn rankled and humiliated the Egyptian people. It was one thing to have signed a treaty with Israel, quite another to have one's nose daily rubbed with what was not signed. Each time Sadat was reminded of Menachem Begin's fanatic ideology – a combination of bible and bomb – he turned the other cheek (for the sake of Sinai) or worse, responded with a double-dose of Egyptian goodwill, like his offer to give away the precious waters of the Nile. Sadat's every ingratiating gesture infuriated many Egyptians leading some to wonder, if only facetiously, whether their leader was prepared to go so far as to give away Egypt in return for the Sinai.

Summits such as the one in Haifa in the summer of 1979 exacerbated Sadat's image of over-kill amongst his people. In short, more and more Egyptians came to perceive their President as a hostage of the Americans and the Israelis which might have been tolerable were they themselves not being held hostage by his imperial presidency whose democratic pretensions had them playing a child's game of hide-and-seek. There was no escape for the escapist's subjects.

Another facet of Anwar Sadat's excessiveness which contributed to his waning popularity at home was his bear-hug embrace of America, Americana and the West in general; his cultural as well as political pretensions. Here Sadat became a caricature of himself: the Abe Lincoln of the Nile on a binge in Disneyland. Ironically, I don't think he ever made it to California or Florida. He didn't have to. With his daily diet of American movies he could indulge in the American dream factory in his own living room. Mit Abul Kum never had a chance.

Of all Arab countries, Egypt, for reasons of history and geography, seems forever destined to juggle her cultural duality; her oriental and occidental souls. The brilliant American-Lebanese Arabist, Fouad Ajami, sees this historic dilemma as a cultural tug-of-war, what he calls "the push of the desert, the pull of the Mediterranean". Abdel Nasser pushed towards the Arab-Muslim desert; Anwar Sadat pulled back towards the cosmopolitan West. In the 19th century Mohammed Ali (1805–42) and Ismael (1863–79) also pulled Egypt westwards. Although he is compared to both rulers, Sadat most resembled Ismael in that his vision rather exceeded his grasp. Poor Ismael tried turning Cairo into a Paris and might have succeeded had not Egypt gone bankrupt in the process. His Paris-on-the-Nile, alas, became Egypt under British occupation. Sadat's pull – no less spectacular – helped push *him* over the brink.

In his eloquent book, *The Arab Predicament*, published before Sadat's death, Ajami writes of our hero's love affair with America and the West:

... It is a supreme irony of recent Egyptian history that Anwar el-Sadat, who was part of traditional Egypt's revolt against the heritage of Ismael and the pretensions of the polished layers of Egyptian society, would live to be equated with Ismael, to reenact Ismael's wish (and fate?). Sadat's conversion is a riddle: Was his Westernism there all along? Had he acquired it through his second marriage to the urbane Jihan el-Sadat? Was it part of his own psychological settling of the score with Nasser, a search for a theatre wherein he could outdo and go beyond Abdul Nasser, whom he came to recall as a traditional man? Was it the despair of a leader anxious for help – any help – to keep a crowded, poor society afloat? Or was he stuck with the United States and the West when he found himself cut off from other Arabs?

There is no doubt that Sadat underwent an immense psychological transformation: The man who in the early 1950's had complained to an American journalist that "the West hates Arabs because they think we are negroes" became one of America's most popular figures; the man who once hated the West moved all the way to full partnership with the United States, offering his society as sentry to a barbarian region in turmoil. Anwar el-Sadat, a self-defined peasant from the dusty small village Mit Abu al-Qom, had exceeded his own expectations and travelled far beyond the bounds of the world; he had become more comfortable with American television reporters and French visitors than with former colleagues and friends. . . ."
(Fouad Ajami *The Arab Predicament – Arab Political Thought and Practice Since 1967*, Cambridge University Press, 1981)

Indeed. More comfortable with Henry, Jimmy, Cy, Bob, Sol, Ezer, Frank, Elizabeth ... and yes, Barbara, Walter, Doreen et al. than with Mohammed, Mustapha, Ibrahim, Leila, Mansour, Hilmy, Shenouda et al.

In exploiting Egypt's occidental soul, Sadat unfortunately turned a dialogue into an orgy; his orgy with the West. Worse, he forgot to invite the folks back home.

As one of those American television reporters who daily encouraged his Western ego trip, his pilgrimage in search of identity, his escape from reality, I watched oriental Egypt sitting on the sidelines wondering what in the name of Ismael was going on? Where would it all end? This eternally servile dependence, this blind faith, in foreigners? Yesterday the Russians. Today the Americans. Tomorrow. . . . Whoa! Hold it! Not so much so fast, Egyptians seemed to be saying. But Sadat was too far gone, too distant to hear or listen or care. He talked, behaved and dressed as though his wretched country were beneath him and the new company he kept; as though it were an embarrassment to his new, superior identity. Sadat's mistake was not in exploiting Egypt's western soul but in exceeding it, abusing it. Poor Sadat. Lost in a fantasy. Poor Egypt. Shoved aside. In the end, victim once more to a leader's delusions of grandeur.

The West was "in", the Arab "out". Such was the message Sadat came to preach day in and day out; the repetitively endless speeches celebrating the West, denigrating the East; the bile and spleen attacks on the Arabs whom he portrayed as little more than duplicitous prostitutes selling their souls for petrodollars; the thundering proclamations on "good Islam" versus "bad Islam" which comforted the West and raised the decibel of disaffection and dissension at home amongst the one constituency already alienated by his separate peace with "infidel" Israel; by his increasingly autocratic and corrupt rule and by his flamboyant western pretensions. Sadat's venomous ultimatums, loaded with contempt and ridicule for the fundamentalists, backfired.

The Islamic fundamentalist movement which is as old as modern Egypt and which Sadat cultivated as a tactical counterweight to the more dreaded "leftist and communist threat", grew phenomenally under his rule. Politically castrated by his "democracy" – the devout, the frustrated, the young and the disillusioned thronged to the mosque for comfort, guidance and political ventilation. Their one escape from Sadat was God. Their numbers swelled on university campuses and city streets. They took refuge from the vicissitudes of Sadat and his Egypt, covering their bodies and faces in flowing robes, veils and beards as though somehow this might immunize them to both. As a Western woman I'm not sure which disturbed me more: the proliferation of young intelligent women and men from the cities and villages retreating behind their veils and beards or the conditions that widened the gap between Egypt's two traditional solitudes, forcing the Islamic revivalists to seek out a secure, non-threatening hiding place. With or without the ballot box Sadat would get their message – albeit far too late.

Towards the end the rising expectations of a better life left fourteen million Cairenes staring up at luxury skyscrapers and hotels to accommodate the foreigners – tourists, businessmen and investors – who presumably would bring the prosperity with them. One day. Maybe. True, the Americans, British, French, Germans and Japanese were beavering away somewhere repairing and constructing an infrastructure for the commercial and industrial boom Sadat daily promised was just around the corner. That was about as credible as his prognostications on the "blooming desert". No one was fooled. The economy was rotten – however it was painted on paper and so was the corruption – the one issue around which all his diverse critics coalesced including the long-suffering silent majority.

Again he had miscalculated. And again, he underestimated or ignored the population's disenchantment with Mrs Sadat who no less than her husband personified the Western ideal as model/threat. Indeed, Western audiences saw her as a political asset: the beautiful, charming, fair-haired, half-Maltese First Lady as modern Arab woman; an outspoken advocate of women's rights and birth control in a country in dire need of both; a university graduate with liberal views who didn't hesitate to speak out on peace, politics and husband. The Egyptian audience on the other hand saw Jihan Sadat as a political liability: Sadat's co-star and leading lady as the Imelda Marcos of the Middle East; a power behind the throne; too ambitious, too vocal, too active and too shrewd a businesswoman for Egypt's own good. This negative image fleshed out with rumours, gossip and innuendos surrounding her public and private life, further damaged the President's image.

The Egyptian ruler's final miscalculation came that September day in 1981 when he arrested those hundreds of religious and political foes. That was his death warrant. He realized it too late. That was part of his tragedy.

That ultimately he was guilty of his own death hardly exonerates those of us who served as his unwitting accomplices; those of us who were his partners in peace, notably the United States, Israel, Menachem Begin and American television news. We all blew it. We failed. We missed our cues. We helped kill the "hero of peace".

Only time and history can judge the strengths and weaknesses of this modern Arab leader who shook the world by 'flying to the ends of the earth'. Since I do not expect to live to see peace in the Middle East, all I am certain of – finally – is that Mohammed Anwar el-Sadat served his country both with his life and with his death.

Covering the peace story was an immensely intense, rich experience. Indeed it was great fun for a while – full of novelty, excitement, anticipation, hope and history – and for that I am grateful to both Anwar Sadat and ABC News. My one personal regret perhaps is in having performed my job too well: life in the Middle East is dramatic and perilous enough without the super-imposed theatrics of a Sadat or TV's showbusiness-journalism. But since the Middle East story has become a permanent part of our satellite-age lives, war and peace will be decided in America's daily battle of the ratings.

By the time my episode ended, my feelings towards Sadat had gone all the way from admiration and respect through disappointment, frustration, anger, relief and, finally, sadness. That is what I feel today when I think of the man who in the words of one Egyptian writer, "lived like an American president and, sadly, he died like one". On American television. Anwar Sadat's drama ended as it began.

This made-for-TV tragedy did not end, at least, without a touch of poetic justice: as an accessory to the crime, I was not to be spared the bloody end; having fled Sadat, Egypt and the "mission" once, circumstances would force me back to witness the brutal last act; as an accomplice, I would be positioned in the direct line of the assassins' fire.

Spared the bullets, my fate, nonetheless, seemed inextricably tied to Anwar Sadat's. In the end, the story I had once "owned" came to own me: two months after Sadat and the story were dead and buried, ABC

News informed me that my usefulness had expired; that my contract would be legally terminated after six months.

So, I packed my bags – one final time – and left Cairo and the debris behind me. I took Anwar Sadat with me. I had no choice.

Those familiar with the ancient Middle East allegory see it as something more than a simple tale of trusting frogs and treacherous scorpions perishing in the insanity of the Middle East. Most interpret it as a tale of "frogs will be frogs and scorpions will be scorpions". As one Arab writer reminded me recently, "a scorpion must do what he must do; sooner or later he must do what comes naturally. The scorpion, you see, stung the frog midway across the river simply because he could not hold out any longer. The frog's folly was to ignore reality."

None of us then who lived this drama intimately could have survived intact. None of us did: some of us lived, some of us died, many of us lost our innocence, all of us lost our way.

Index

DOREEN KAYS was born in Prince Edward
Island, Canada in 1941, the daughter of
Lebanese immigrants. She graduated from the
University of King's College, Halifax, Nova
Scotia in 1963 and has spent twenty years in
journalism with newspapers, radio and
television. In 1981, she shared the Overseas
Press Club Award for a radio perspective
analysis on Egypt after Sadat's assassination.
Doreen Kays now lives in Paris.